THE REAL WORLD OF THE
BAYEUX TAPESTRY

MICHAEL J. LEWIS

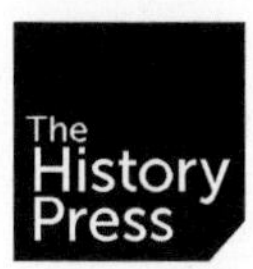

The History Press

For Emily and Sophie

First published 2008
Reprinted 2026

The History Press Ltd
97 St George's Place,
Cheltenham, Gloucestershire, GL50 3QB
www.thehistorypress.co.uk

British Library Cataloguing in Publication Data.
A catalogue record for this book is available from the British Library.

ISBN 978 0 7524 3446 9

Printed by TJ Books, Padstow, Cornwall

EU Authorised Representative: Easy Access System Europe
Mustamäe tee 50, 10621 Tallinn, Estonia
gpst.request@easproject.com

CONTENTS

ACKNOWLEDGEMENTS

This book was conceived several years ago, before I embarked on studying for a PhD in history, which examined the archaeological authority of the Bayeux Tapestry. At that time Peter Kemmis Betty of Tempus kindly offered me the opportunity to publish a general introduction to the Bayeux Tapestry, which I accepted. However, my study for the PhD and the publication of my thesis as a British Archaeological Report meant the publication of this book was delayed, and delayed, and delayed! Peter, quite rightly, was beginning to lose patience and thought that the project was never going to come to fruition, but I am thankful he stuck with me and finally the book has been published. To this end I am also grateful to Wendy Logue, Archaeology Publisher at The History Press, who has guided me in the final stages of this project.

My studies of the Bayeux Tapestry have benefited from the experience of many people, especially Richard Gameson and Gale Owen-Crocker. I am also grateful to Gale for commenting on earlier drafts on this book, as well as Emma Lewis and Andrew Shore, who have been a great help. This said, I entirely accept responsibility for any errors that this book contains and offer apologies to the many scholars to whose work I am indebted, and to whom I am unable to properly give credit in a book such as this. I am also extremely grateful to the town of Bayeux who have allowed me to reproduce images of the Tapestry itself, and I am particularly indebted in this respect to Sylvette Lemagnen and Isabelle Attard-Robert.

Eleventh-century images of the Bayeux Tapestry are featured here by special permission of the City of Bayeux.

CHAPTER 1

INTRODUCTION

The Bayeux Tapestry is one of the most celebrated surviving works of medieval art. The story it recounts - the events leading to the Norman Conquest of England – is one of the best known in English history. Also famous is the Tapestry's imagery, which is commonly used to illustrate anything from textbooks to tourist souvenirs, and may arguably also offer an insight into life and warfare on the eve of the Conquest. Even so, much of what is known about the Tapestry remains a mystery. Ever since this stunning textile was rediscovered in the seventeenth century, scholars have endlessly discussed who might have been its patron, and where, when and why it was created. Although there is general agreement on these aspects, there has been no full consensus, and it is fair to say we are far from a comprehensive understanding of the Tapestry. Of course this is good news for the historians and archaeologists who make it their lives' work studying this 1000-year-old relic!

The purpose of this book is to offer a general introduction to the Bayeux Tapestry, and, in particular, to examine some of its main aspects that I think are most important or interesting. As such, this study draws upon the research and thoughts of many before me. The format of this publication excludes footnotes and so does not allow me to properly acknowledge all of those scholars who have influenced the thoughts and ideas presented here, but I have included a bibliography for those interested in learning more and gaining at least an impression of the wealth of scholarship there is on the Bayeux Tapestry. The reader should also be forewarned that this book is neither intended to be a comprehensive study of the Tapestry nor a summary of the scholarly debate that has taken place since it began about 300 years ago.

This book begins by recounting the story told by the Tapestry of the events leading to the Norman Conquest of England. Intriguingly it ignores some of the most important episodes in that tale, such as King Harold's victory over the Norwegians at Stamford Bridge less than a month before the Battle of Hastings, whilst embellishing aspects seemingly of less significance, like Duke William's campaign against the Bretons. Furthermore it names characters, such as Ælfgyva and Turold, whose identities mystify us today. Next, the historical background of the Tapestry will be explored. The most important events of the eleventh century will be recounted and, it is hoped, put the Tapestry's story (and other accounts of the Norman Conquest) into context. Thereafter, the history of the Tapestry, from the earliest indications of its existence to the modern day, will be examined. It will be demonstrated that it is by more luck than judgement that this magnificent textile still survives – and in such relatively good condition.

The latter chapters will look more closely at the artefact itself. First, the real world of the Bayeux Tapestry will be examined, assessing the extent to which the Tapestry provides a reliable insight into the material culture (architecture, arms and armour, ships and clothing) and natural world (animals and plants) of the eleventh century. Understanding that the Tapestry is a product of an art historical tradition where artists borrow from one another, rather than attempt to accurately recreate the real world around them, also provides a context for exploring the design and production of the Tapestry, examining who made it, where, when and why, as well as looking at the technical aspects of producing such a work. Finally, a general summary of work on the Bayeux Tapestry will be offered, as well as what might be expected from scholars in the future.

DESCRIPTION

The Bayeux Tapestry is embroidery work, not a tapestry at all. However, as Shirley Ann Brown (1988) once said, 'to call it by any other name now – given its fame and reputation – would seem pedantic'. An analysis of the Tapestry fabric by Isabelle Bédat, Béatrice Girault-Kurtzeman, Marie-Madeleine Massé and Véronique Monnier in November 1982 (published in 2004) has done much to advance our technical understanding of the embroidery. The Bayeux Tapestry is now about 68.5m long; its height varies between 45.7 and 53.6cm. It comprises nine (until recently, previously thought to be eight) conjoined strips or sections of embroidered linen of different lengths; the individual strips vary in length between 2.43 and 13.9m. The joins between lengths are barely visible, with the exception of that between Sections 1 and 2. The work has been damaged in a number of places, particularly at the end, which is incomplete; much of the Tapestry was extensively restored in the nineteenth century.

The Tapestry was embroidered onto a bleached linen base cloth in coloured wools using a type of embroidery generally known as laid and couched work, defined by a stem stitch. Essentially the Tapestry's characters, artefacts and inscriptions are outlined in a single stitch of wool (the type of stitches being used, which vary, include stem, chain and split stitching), with 'blocks' of colour being in-filled (using a couched stitch).

The colours used are pinkish or orange-red, brownish-violet red, mustard yellow, beige, blue-black, dark blue, mid-blue, dark green, mid-green, light green and white, and were created by mixing various dyes, including indigotin (used in the blues and greens), madder (used in reds) and woad (used in mustard yellow, beige and the greens). These colours are not applied naturalistically, so horses have limbs of different colours and human hair can be blue or green. Instead they are used to provide a dimension of space, to add clarity to the design, and, of course, for decorative effect.

There is little attempt at visual perspective. The Tapestry's style is bold, colourful and lively, reminiscent of contemporary manuscript illuminations. It also demonstrates great attention to detail, within the limitations of the medium.

The events shown in the main frieze unfold, for the most part, chronologically, though a few scenes are reversed for particular effect or as a result of conflicting pressures on the designer. The Tapestry's characters appear to wear contemporary clothing, mostly comprising tunics and tight-fitting trousers. Most, especially the leading characters, gesticulate enthusiastically, thereby indicating both movement and emotion. The ground upon which they stand is sometimes shown as small bumps, but more generally it is the edge of the lower border. Where water is illustrated, it appears as wavy parallel lines; hillocks are embellished with scrolls. Buildings are stylised so as to frame the characters that act within them, whilst being decorated and adorned with other features for effect. Scenes are generally divided by highly stylised trees or sub-classical architecture, interpreted by some scholars, such as Francis Wormald (1957) and Lucien Musset (2002), as punctuation marks. Otherwise, however, there is little extraneous detail in the main frieze.

The main narrative is surrounded by a border decorated with various anthropomorphic, zoomorphic and vegetal embellishments. These are not generally related to the content of the main frieze, though some, such as James Bard McNulty (1989), have suggested otherwise. Occasionally, however, these details spill into the borders.

Throughout the Tapestry there are Latin inscriptions, which are often abbreviated. Moreover, separate words are sometimes joined together, while individual words may be split apart, reflecting contemporary conventions for display scripts in the context of art works, a fact recognised by Richard Gameson (1997). Sometimes words seem to be squeezed into the available space between the pictorial subject matter, though this need not imply that they were an afterthought, as Jan Messent (1999) has suggested.

PATRON

Originally, it was widely believed that William the Conqueror's wife, Matilda (who died in 1083), and her ladies had embroidered the Bayeux Tapestry, a tradition recounted by Bernard de Montfaucon (1730). This was later questioned by Lord Lyttelton (1769), and by the Abbé Gervais de La Rue (1811), who both suggested that Matilda (1102-67), daughter of Henry I and wife of Geoffrey Plantagenet, was a more likely candidate. In 1824, Honoré François Delauney first presented the hypothesis that Bishop Odo of Bayeux – William the Conqueror's maternal half-brother – was the Tapestry's patron. It is this view which remains current.

Odo was born in about 1032/3 to Herluin de Conteville and Herleva (Arlette), former mistress of Duke Robert I of Normandy (r.1028-35); William himself was the illegitimate son of Duke Robert. When aged about 18, Duke William bestowed upon him the bishopric of Bayeux (in 1049/50) and, shortly after the Norman Conquest (in about 1067), the earldom of Kent, often leaving him de facto ruler of England in his absence. It was a position which afforded Odo great wealth; Domesday Book records that he was one of England's largest landowners, second only to the king. However, in

1082, in circumstances which remain obscure, Odo fell from grace and was imprisoned in Rouen until the Conqueror's death in 1087. William of Malmesbury, in his *Gesta Regum Anglorum* (of which the first edition was written in about 1125), suggests that Odo was 'trying to bribe his way to the Papacy and was mustering a private army in England'. Upon his release from prison in 1087, Odo conspired with his brother, Robert of Mortain, and others against King William (Rufus) II (1087-1100) and consequently was expelled from England in 1088 with the loss of all his English possessions. In 1097 Odo died at Palermo en route to the First Crusade.

The case for Odo's patronage of the Tapestry is substantial. Most significantly, the work highlights Odo's role in events to an extent which greatly exceeds that in any other account of the Conquest. Odo advises William to build his fleet (Scene 35), says grace at the banquet after the landing (Scene 43), dominates the subsequent council of war (Scene 44), and in a critical moment of battle rallies the 'young men' (Scene 54). Indeed, James Bard McNulty (1989) described the Tapestry as having 'an Odonian view of the Conquest'.

Besides the major historical characters, only four others are mentioned by name, of which three – Turold, Wadard and Vital – were identified by Bolton Corney (1838) as retainers of Odo, a theory developed by Hirokazu Tsurushima (1985). These men held lands in Kent, the centre of Odo's lordship in England, but are not referred to in any other account of the Norman Conquest. More importantly their presence does not significantly add to the narrative, so far as can now be judged. Odo's association with the Tapestry is further strengthened by the fact that his bishopric is the setting for a central point in the narrative. In contrast to the accounts of contemporary and near contemporary chroniclers (such as William of Poitiers' *Gesta Guillelmi Ducis Normannorum et Regis Anglorum*, probably written between 1071 and 1077, which places the oath at Bonneville-sur-Touques, and Orderic Vitalis in his *Historia Ecclesiastica*, written between *c.*1123 and *c.*1137, which places it at Rouen), it is at Bayeux, and upon its holy relics, that Harold swears a sacred oath; however it is intriguing that Odo himself does not appear in this scene. Furthermore, Odo undoubtedly possessed the financial resources and political power to commission such a work.

PROVENANCE

Early commentators assumed the Tapestry was produced in Normandy, which is unsurprising given that Queen Matilda was believed to have been its patron and that it has resided in France for all of its known history. In the modern period this view has been maintained by Wolfgang Grape (1994) who believed that the Tapestry was a clever piece of propaganda produced in Normandy for a Norman patron. Certainly, its narrative has much in common with early Norman accounts of the Conquest, such as those offered by the chroniclers William of Jumièges (in his *Gesta Normannorum Ducum* of about 1070) and William of Poitiers.

Nonetheless, on certain issues crucial to the interpretation of the years 1064 to 1066, the Tapestry abandons the Norman version and appears to be following traditions that are found in some of the English sources, highlighted by Nicholas Brooks and H.E. Walker (1978). For example, Eadmer in his *Historia Novorum* (compiled in 1093-1100 and written after 1109) takes the view that Harold persuaded a reluctant Edward to allow him to go to Normandy to recover his brother Wulfnoth and his nephew Hakon, who were being held as hostages by William, and that upon his return Edward reprimanded Harold with the words 'did I not tell you that I knew William, and that your going [to Normandy] might bring untold calamity upon this kingdom?'. This version seems to be recounted in the Tapestry (Scene 25).

Similarly, whereas Norman chroniclers refer to the indecent haste of the proceedings in which Harold procured the throne, the Tapestry highlights Edward's role in Harold's nomination. Here there are parallels in the account given in the *Vita Eadwardi* (*c.*1067) where it is recounted that when Edward 'addressed his last words to the queen' he stretched 'forth his hand to his governor, her brother, Harold, he said, I commend this woman and all the kingdom to your protection'. Nicholas Brooks and H.E. Walker (1978) noted that 'the parallel between the Life [*Vita*] and the Tapestry – in the position of the queen at the king's feet, and in Edward's gesture of designation by stretching out and touching Harold with his finger tips – cannot be a coincidence'. Also significant is that the Norman chroniclers do not dispute the fact that Edward made such a bequest to Harold. It is also the case that the Tapestry's account of Harold's death, which shows the English king being hit by an arrow (possibly in the eye) and then being cut down by a Norman knight, seems closer to the later English accounts of the battle offered by William of Malmesbury and in Henry of Huntington's *Historia Anglorum* (written between 1129 and 1154).

Mistakes in the depiction of individual events have also led some to believe that the Tapestry was manufactured in England. Examples include the Tapestry's incorrect account of the Brittany campaign, which also contrasts with the account offered by William of Poitiers, cavalry techniques and mailed hauberks – both discussed by Nicholas Brooks and H.E. Walker (1978). On the other hand some scholars, such as Wolfgang Grape (1994), have suggested that the Tapestry's depiction of Mont-Saint-Michel reveals that it was produced in Normandy.

It may be the case that such a mix of both English and Norman influences reflects the political situation in England immediately following the Norman Conquest. It is not inconceivable that the Tapestry could have been interpreted in one way by its Norman audience and another by Anglo-Saxons.

INSCRIPTIONS

The Tapestry's inscriptions (see Appendix A) seem to add credibility to the view that it was produced in England. Old English letter forms, such as '-' in 'GYR-', 'Æ' in Ælfgyva, and the less diagnostic single example of a Tironian 'et' ('7'), seem to indicate English work. It is also generally agreed that English personal names, such as 'ÆLFGYVA' and 'EADWARDVS' are mostly spelt in an English way. Although a study of the language of the inscription has identified certain French elements, there seem to be more English ones. For example, David Bernstein (1986) noted that William's name appears in a variety of forms, but only three times is the Norman form of *Wilgelm* used, compared with 15 instances of the form found in Anglo-Saxon texts (*Willelm*). The modest coexistence of English and French forms evident in the inscriptions is indicative of what we may expect in the post-Conquest period; this was highlighted by Nicholas Brooks and H.E. Walker (1978). Likewise, Richard Gameson (1997) believed that, in general terms, the letter forms used in the Tapestry were fairly widely used in England, France and Normandy and can be paralleled in examples of manuscripts from St Augustine's, Mont-Saint-Michel, Jumièges and Christ Church. He also suggested that, whilst multi-coloured script, such as that found in the Tapestry, is more pronounced in Normandy than England, the use of inscriptions with pictorial matter is better represented in English material.

ENGLISH TEXTILE TRADITION

In the early nineteenth century 'S.L.' (1803) suggested in a 'letter' to the *Gentleman's Magazine* that the Bayeux Tapestry may have been manufactured by English women, on account of the fame of Anglo-Saxon embroidery. Goscelin, a Fleming resident in England in the second half of the eleventh century, noted in his *Vita Sancti Augustini* that English women were skilled in embroidery work and commented 'on how they embellish garments of the princes of the church and the princes of the realm with gold-work and gems and with English pearls that shone like stars against the gold' – not that the Bayeux Tapestry was ever this opulent! Likewise, William of Poitiers wrote that 'the women of the English people are very skilled in needlework and weaving gold thread'.

It is known that works similar to the Bayeux Tapestry were being produced. Ælfflæd, widow of Bryhtnoth, ealdorman of Essex, presented the church of Ely with a woven hanging representing the deeds of her husband (recounted in the Anglo-Saxon poem *The Battle of Maldon*) as a memorial to him. Extant examples of such work are rare, but include the stole, girdle and maniple worked on the order of Queen Ælfflæd, wife of Edward the Elder (r.899-924), for Bishop Frithestan of Winchester, between about 909 and 916. Another example noted by David Wilson (1985) is a rarely discussed tenth-century English textile fragment in the Museo di Sant'Ambrogio in Milan (thought by Mildred Budny (1991) to be Italian), which favourably compares with the Bayeux Tapestry in terms of medium, style and to some extent subject matter.

Examples of narrative needlework surviving from the early Middle Ages are rare, but include the Gerberga embroidery of about 960 in the Treasury of Cologne Cathedral in Germany, which commemorates Gerberga's victory over Reginar III.

There are a number of Scandinavian textiles, such as the Norwegian tenth-century Oseberg fragment and another of the ninth or tenth century from Rolvsøy, which George Wingfield Digby (1957) and Lucien Musset (2002) credibly compared with the Bayeux Tapestry in terms of subject matter. The Oseberg fragment, like the Tapestry, depicts soldiers and horses, is narrow and has decorative borders. However, it differs from the Tapestry in terms of style and by the fact that it is a true tapestry – a textile worked on a loom, not by a needle. The Rolvsøy example is also similar to the Tapestry in as much as it shows a ship's stem and soldiers and has a lower border, but like the Oseberg fragment, the Rolvsøy textile is a true tapestry. Another case worthy of some consideration, though much later in date, is a late twelfth- to early thirteenth-century textile fragment from Røn in Norway, which David Wilson (1985) thought was similar to the Bayeux Tapestry in technique (it is worked in wool on a linen background) and subject matter (it illustrates a horse, dead soldiers, trees with acanthus leaves and has a lower border). Also noteworthy are three minute textile fragments from Urnes, Norway, and a group of Icelandic examples (though probably late in date); an embroidery of the late twelfth century from Høyland in Norway, showing the Adoration of the Magi; and a twelfth-century textile from Balishol in Norway that shows April (a man with birds), a knight on horseback, architectural elements and ornate borders. All of these examples come from a tradition which produced the Bayeux Tapestry, and as such have similar aspects, but as George Wingfield Digby (1957) noted, all are comparatively late in date or too fragmentary for an opinion to be formed of in terms of style and form.

There are also continental European works which have points of comparison with the Bayeux Tapestry. Of particular interest is a hanging said to be woven of gold, silver and silk thread, encrusted with pearls and jewels, and bearing inscriptions. This was described in a poem by Baudri, Abbot of Bourgueil, and like the Bayeux Tapestry was said to represent the Conquest of England, though it is not certain that it existed. Extant materials include the mid eleventh-century Bamberg textiles (deposited in the tomb of Pope Clement II, r.1046-47), which have arrangements of birds and beasts alternating with leaf-work in their woven borders – aspects common with the Bayeux Tapestry. Francis Wormald (1957) suggested that the pairs of birds and beasts found in the Tapestry's borders may be traditional motifs for decorating textiles, and noted that similar creatures are found on textiles that came to Western Europe from Byzantium and the East. Also of note is a woollen embroidery of the second half of the eleventh century in Gerona Cathedral in Italy, depicting the Creation; the eleventh- or twelfth-century tapestry from St Gereon, Köln in Germany, which has a border that is entirely Romanesque in character; and the three twelfth- or early thirteenth-century tapestries from Halberstadt Cathedral, Westphalia in Germany.

The fables in the Bayeux Tapestry's borders seem to be purely ornamental and do not relate to the main frieze, though some scholars, such as James Bard McNulty (1989) have argued otherwise. Francis Wormald (1957) highlighted the use of such fables in art of the ninth century, such as the Canon Tables of the ninth-century Gospels from Morienval, now in Noyon Cathedral in France. He also noted that the borders contain a number of 'genre scenes', including agricultural tableaux of harrowing, sowing and scaring birds. In the Tapestry a man is shown attacking a chained bear. This is a strong parallel with the depiction of a man with a club fighting a bear that has broken his chain, in Arundel 91 (folio 47b). Likewise, Francis Wormald (1957) likened the Tapestry's images of fish, animals, a centaur and a figure with a knife to constellation pictures found in Cotton Tiberius B.v. These theories have been advanced by Cyril Hart (2000) who identified numerous parallels between the motifs in the Tapestry's borders and contemporary manuscript illuminations.

ILLUMINATED MANUSCRIPTS

Since there are few surviving eleventh-century textiles, illuminated manuscripts, which are rather more plentiful, offer a useful tool for evaluating the art and style of the Tapestry. Most agree that the best general parallels are provided by English manuscripts of the first half of the eleventh century, such as the Old English Hexateuch (produced at St Augustine's Abbey in Canterbury in the second quarter of the eleventh century), the poetry codex Junius II (probably produced at Christ Church, Canterbury, in the second half of the tenth century, but traditionally thought to be late tenth or early eleventh century), and the Harley 603 Psalter (illustrated, in the most part, at Christ Church, Canterbury, in the late tenth or early eleventh century). These will be examined in more detail below.

Francis Wormald (1957) fairly said that in comparing the style of the Tapestry with contemporary illuminations, the identification of its place of origin is handicapped by the fact that both English and Norman manuscripts of the second half of the eleventh century were deeply indebted to the great Anglo-Saxon school of illumination which had flourished in the second half of the tenth and first half of the eleventh centuries. Richard Gameson (1997) thought this to be particularly evident in illuminations produced at Jumièges and Mont-Saint-Michel, which imitate both Anglo-Saxon ornament and figure styles. Nevertheless, the examples noted above, and others that will be discussed in due course, show that it is in Anglo-Saxon manuscript art that the best parallels are found. Significantly, there are also some stylistic parallels in post-Conquest illuminations, which reflect the intertwining traditions of Normandy and England in English manuscripts of the first generation after the Norman Conquest.

CANTERBURY

It is Canterbury illuminations, in particular, that seem to have had a profound impact on the design of the Bayeux Tapestry. The drawing of both faces and figures in Canterbury illuminations of the second half of the eleventh century show a number of stylistic similarities to the Tapestry. Specific mannerisms noted by Francis Wormald (1957) include distinctive rounded shoulders, large open hands, large heads and square jaws, which Richard Gameson (1997) described as 'the hallmarks of the Utrecht Psalter-derived style that was prominent in late Anglo-Saxon art, especially at Canterbury'. Besides the Harley 603 Psalter, parallels in illuminated manuscripts include drawings in Egerton 3314 and Cotton Caligula A.xv.

However, it is the striking parallels between the imagery, rather than the style, of the Tapestry and some Canterbury produced illuminations which are particularly revealing. The most convincing parallels, many of which were first discussed by Francis Wormald (1957), are found in the Old English Hexateuch. Examples include a figure (number 97) in the Tapestry shown casting sling-stones at birds, which is matched by the depiction of Abraham in the Hexateuch (folio 26v) (1). In particular Wormald highlighted 'the gesture of the hands and the shape of the sling with a small tassel on the end'. Likewise, in the Hexateuch (folios 14r, 14v & 15r), as well as in Junius II (pages 66 & 68), we find parallels for

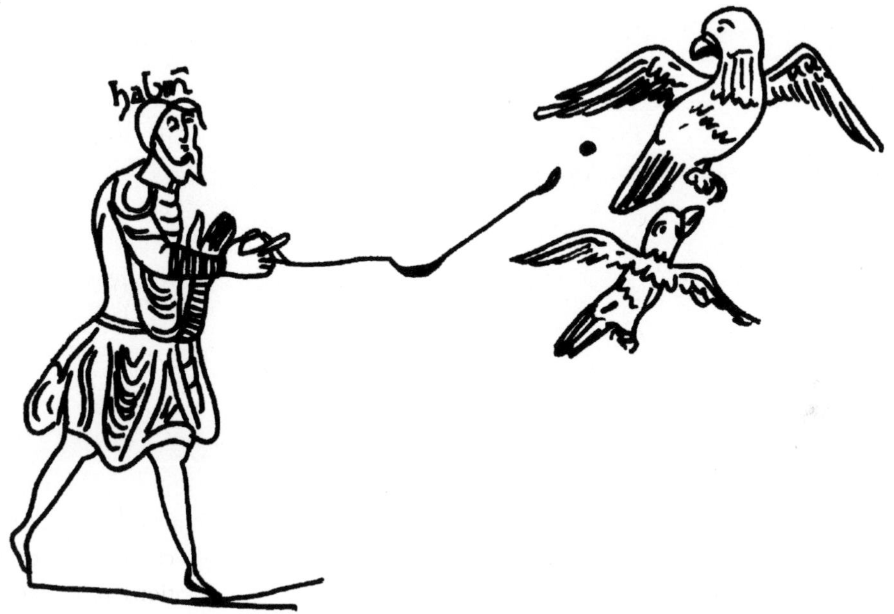

1 Abraham casting sling-stones at birds in the Old English Hexateuch (folio 26v)

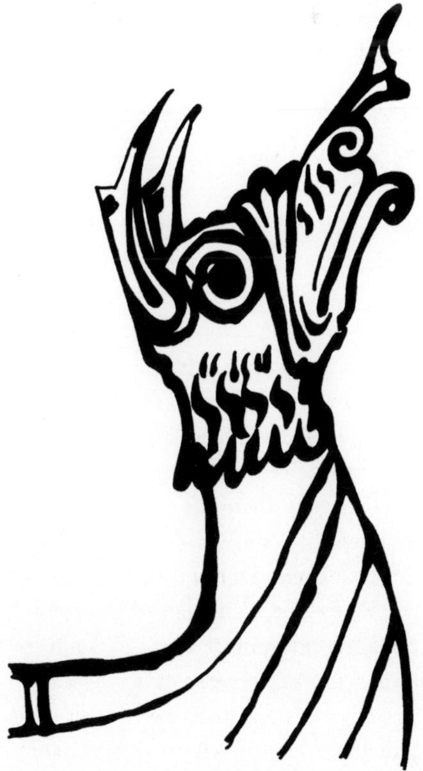

2 Zoomorphic figurehead in Junius 11 (page 68)

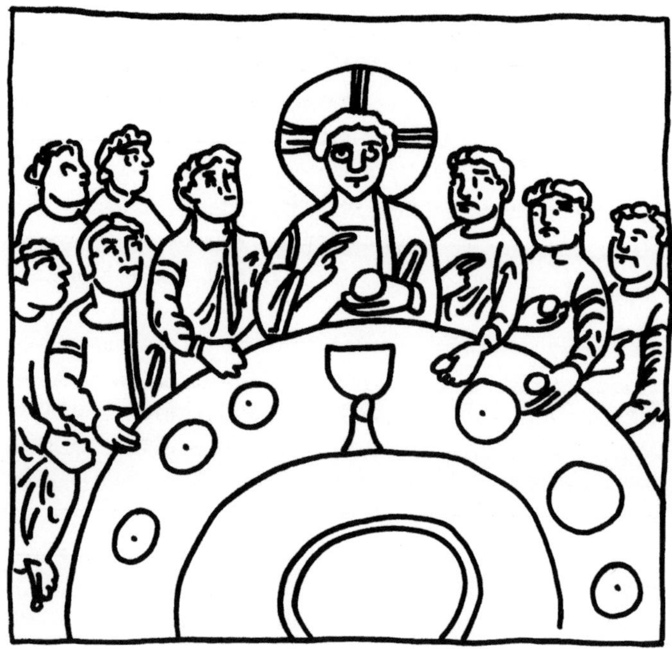

3 The Last Supper scene in the St Augustine's Gospels (folio 125r)

the Tapestry's ornamental ship figureheads (*2*); these are shown in a style reminiscent of Viking Age 'Ringerike' art. Similarly, Conan's escape from Dol (Scene 18) is extraordinarily similar to a scene in the Hexateuch (folio 141v), where Rahab lowers an Israelite spy from Jericho. David Bernstein (1986) noted that both Conan and the Israelite wear a short tunic, are mid-way down the rope and cross their legs in the 'same balletic manner'. Cyril Hart (2000) noted the close comparisons between two individuals (Figures 625-6) escaping from Hastings in the Tapestry, shown 'urging their horses on with scourges' and a similar scene in the Hexateuch (folio 126r). Further, he paralleled aspects of the death of Edward the Confessor in the Tapestry (Scene 27-28) with motifs found in the Hexateuch. These included the shrouding of Edward (Figure 235), which is likened to that of Jared and Malaleel (folio 11r), Methusaleh and Lamech (folio 12v) and Pharoah (folio 59r) in the Hexateuch, and the weeping Edith (Figure 228) in the Tapestry with Enoch's wife (folio 11v) in the Hexateuch. It is also the case that in the Tapestry, Edward (Figure 207) sits enthroned in a posture apparent in the Old English Hexateuch (folio 60r), though this is a motif also found in other late Anglo-Saxon illuminations.

Moreover, there are similarities between the feast in the Bayeux Tapestry (Scene 43), where Odo is shown blessing the food, and scenes of the Last Supper in the St Augustine Gospels (folio 125r) (*3*), a late sixth-century Italian Gospel book, which was certainly owned by St Augustine's Abbey in the eleventh century. Of particular note is the position of Odo (in the place of Christ) and the semi-circular shape of the table, which Wolfgang Grape (1994) believed was uncommon in 'Western iconography of the Last Supper', though common in Byzantine art. Another example is the parallel of the figure carrying a coil or rope (or winnowing sieve) and a labourer illustrated in Cotton Cleopatra C.viii (folio 27), which was produced at Christ Church, Canterbury, in the late tenth century. Francis Wormald (1957) noted that in other manuscripts of the Psychomachia this figure is holding a boulder on his back, which seems to have been misunderstood by the artist of the Canterbury illumination and was then fossilised in the Tapestry.

The case for the English origin of the Tapestry therefore rests in part upon specific parallels with illuminations produced or owned in Canterbury, including both St Augustine's and Christ Church, though there are echoes of the Tapestry in illuminations produced elsewhere. It is also known that Odo was patron of St Augustine's Abbey, Canterbury. He is believed to have enjoyed a good reputation there, even after his imprisonment between 1082 and 1087, his subsequent banishment and the confiscation of his estates in 1088. The community at St Augustine's sought Odo's advice on the translation of Abbot Hadrian's relics and, even after his death, remembered and recorded his benefactions to the abbey. In recent times scholars such as Nicholas Brooks and H.E. Walker (1978) have questioned whether Odo would have turned to the community of Christ Church, the nearby cathedral in Canterbury, for artists and inspiration, as he was in litigation with them over land. However, it would seem unlikely that a man as powerful as Odo, who was Earl of Kent and Bishop of Bayeux, could not have assured access for his designer to the libraries of both St Augustine's and Christ Church. Further, Cyril Hart (2000) noted that 'there was much coming and going between the members of the two communities' at this time – 'in spite of squabbles over property rights and ecclesiastical privileges, the monks of St Augustine's and Christ Church appear to have worked together over a wide range of artistic activity for nearly two centuries, from [c.] 985 to [c.] 1150'.

DATE

Since most commentators have attributed the Tapestry to either Queen Matilda or Odo, an eleventh-century date for its construction is imbedded in our understanding of its history. Whilst a later date for its production has been suggested by some, such as Lord Lyttleton (1769) and the Abbé Gervais de la Rue (1811), albeit not in recent times, the current widely held belief is that the Tapestry was produced quite soon after the events it depicts. Richard Gameson (1997) suggested there is also 'circumstantial evidence' to support this view. For example, there are events shown in the Tapestry, such as the (to us) enigmatic Ælfgyva incident (Scene 15) and the burning of domestic houses, which must have had a resonance in the years immediately after the Conquest, but the significance of which will have faded thereafter. Likewise, as we have seen, the Tapestry's style ties in well with that of Anglo-Saxon manuscripts produced in the eleventh century. Further, if, as seems likely, Odo was the patron, then the date of production is intimately associated with his career. We can be reasonably certain that the Tapestry was commissioned before his death in 1097, and it is likely to have been completed prior to his imprisonment in 1082. If the Tapestry was produced in England, there would have been little time for Odo to commission such a work between 1082 and 1097, for his release from prison in Rouen upon William's death in 1087 was quickly followed by his exile to Normandy in the following year for partaking in the rebellion against King William II. Banishment from England would have left Odo without

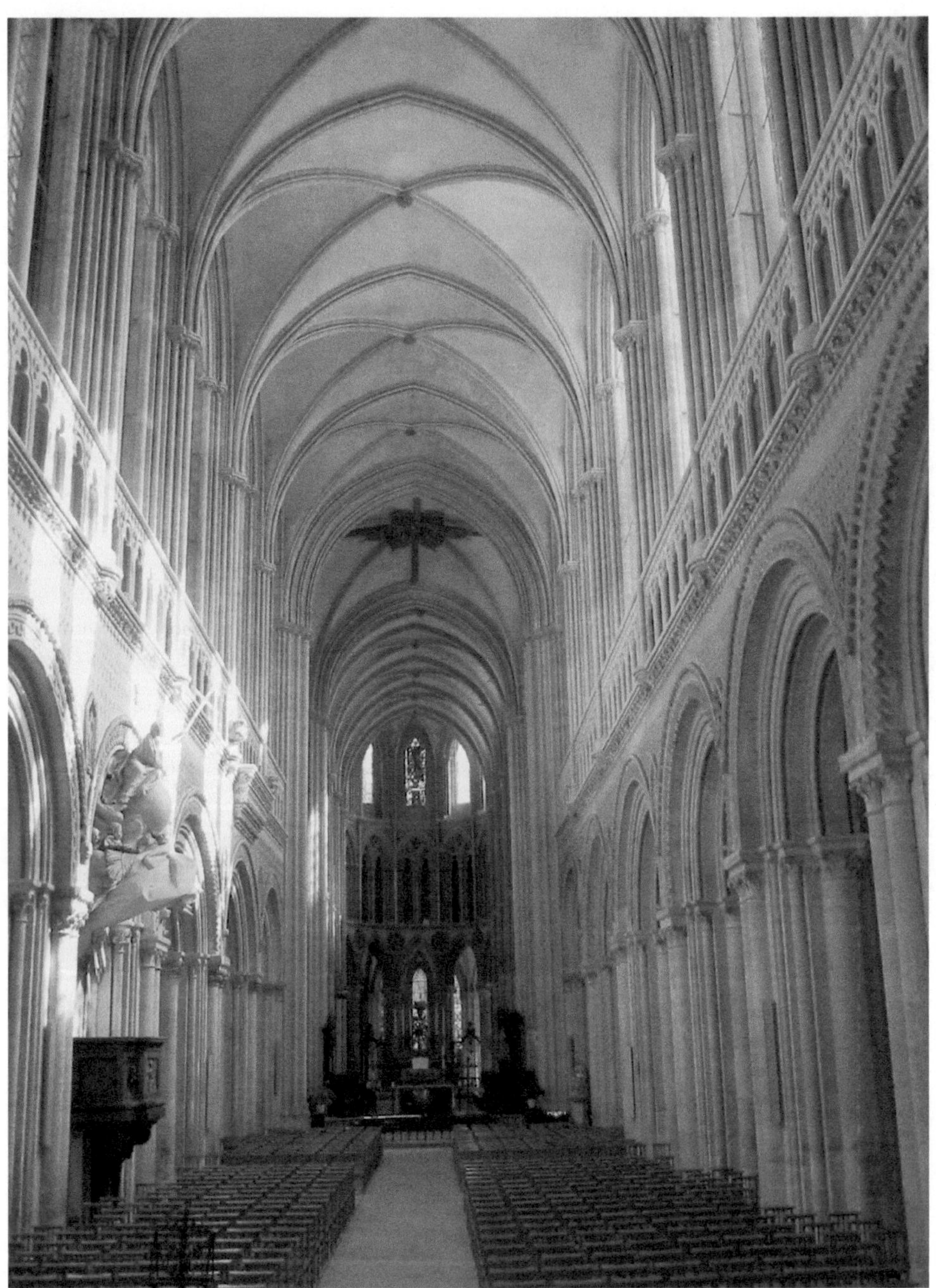

4 The nave of Bayeux Cathedral today

appropriate possessions, the use of local resources, and the impetus to manufacture the Tapestry.

Since 1732 it has been intermittently proposed that that the Tapestry was produced for the consecration of Odo's cathedral at Bayeux in 1077 (4), a theory first proposed by Antoine Lancelot. In recent times this theory has lost favour, and instead it has become fashionable to imagine the Tapestry was produced for a secular residence, such as a great hall, because of its 'secular content', 'lewd imagery' and 'unusual shape'. However, these theories, advocated by Charles Dodwell (1966) and David Bernstein (1986) amongst others, ignore the fact that by (at least) 1476 there was a custom that 'a very long and very narrow hanging of linen, embroidered with figures and inscriptions representing the Conquest of England', believed to be the Bayeux Tapestry, was 'hung round the nave of the church [of Bayeux] on the Feast of Relics and throughout the Octave', and this could also have been the case in the last quarter of the eleventh century. This said, it is possible to concede that the Tapestry was not produced specifically for the cathedral's consecration.

If we assume that an artist familiar with the resources of St Augustine's Abbey was involved with the Tapestry's production, then it might be possible to narrow the date range further. Richard Gameson (1997) hypothesised that since Abbot Scotland (who was consecrated Abbot of St Augustine's Abbey in 1072) came from Mont-Saint-Michel, it is perhaps no coincidence that this famous abbey is also illustrated in the Tapestry (Scene 16). Gameson also noted that Abbott Scotland worked at Mont-Saint-Michel, and therefore suggested 'it seems likely that the presence of an abbot from the most decoratively active Norman scriptorium contributed to the continuing tradition of fine book production and decoration at St Augustine's during this period'. If Abbot Scotland was the impetus for this element of the design, then this might date the Tapestry between 1072 and 1077. It would certainly seem to be the case that St Augustine's Norman abbot would have been approachable, as well as geographically convenient for Bishop Odo. It is also known that this was a calm period for the abbey, unlike that of his successor, Abbot Guy (r.1087-93), when, according to Richard Gem (1997), 'tension between the Archbishop and Abbey erupted into open rebellion'.

THE TAPESTRY AS A HISTORICAL SOURCE

The Bayeux Tapestry is one of the earliest surviving accounts of the events leading up to the Norman Conquest of England. The others are versions C (compiled at Abingdon in the mid eleventh century), D (perhaps of Worcester, Evesham or York and written in the twelfth century) and E (Peterborough, also written in the twelfth century) of the *Anglo-Saxon Chronicle*, the *Carmen de Hastingae Proelio* ascribed to Bishop Guy of Ameins (written in about 1070), William of Jumièges' *Gesta Normannorum Ducum* and William of Poitiers' *Gesta Guillelmi ducis Normannorum et Regis Anglorum*. The Bayeux Tapestry is therefore a very important primary source for the events of 1064-66, as well as a source for the real word of the eleventh century.

A number of later sources are also of value, including Gilbert Crispin's *Vita domini Herluini abbatis Beccensis* (written after 1093), John (Florence) of Worcester's *Chronicon ex Chronicis* (written between about 1095-1106 and about 1140-3), Orderic Vitalis' *Historia*

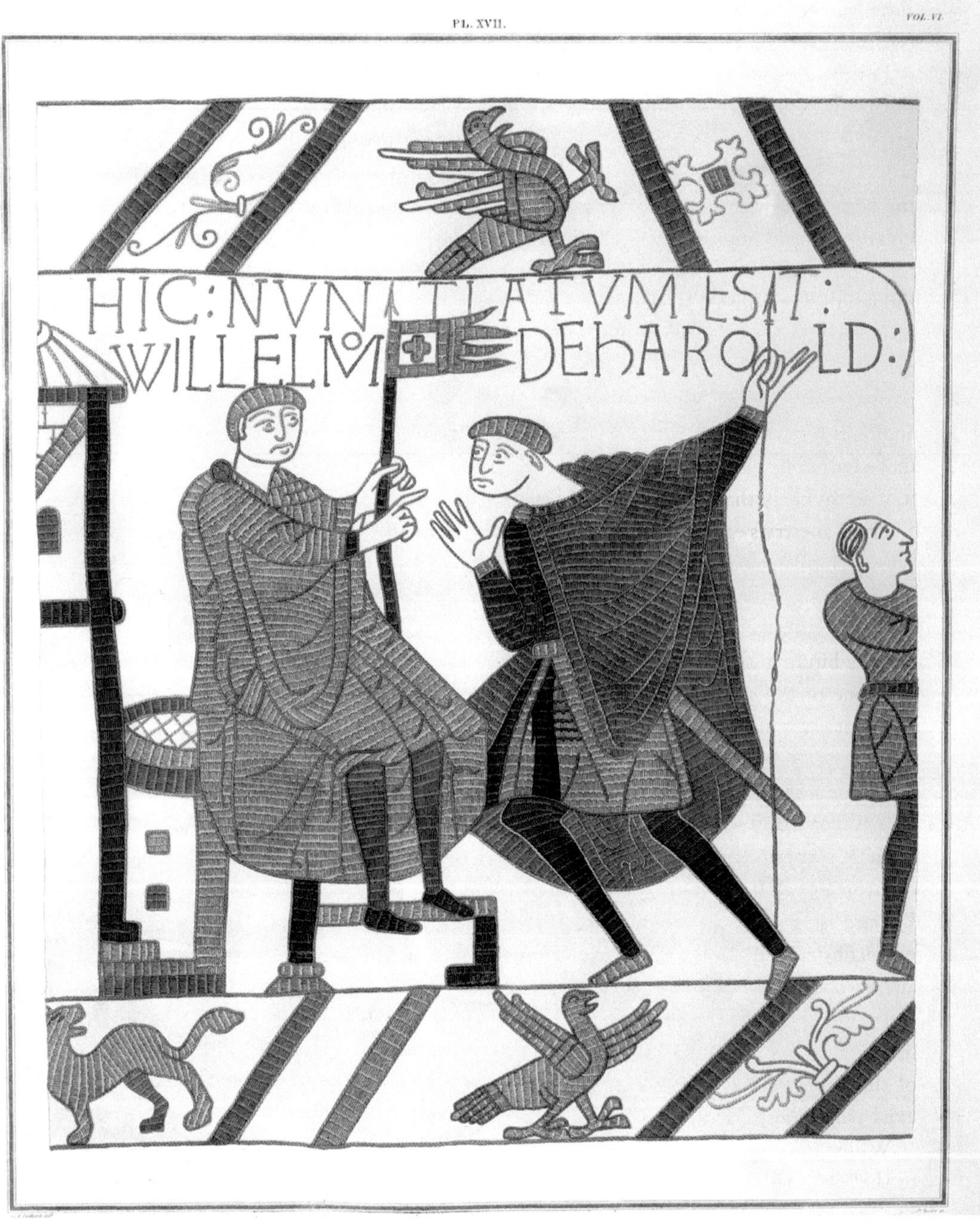

5 Plate of the Bayeux Tapestry engraved by James Basire from the drawings of Charles Stothard.
© *Society of Antiquaries of London*

Ecclesiastica, William of Malmesbury's *Gesta Regum Anglorum* and the *Chronicle of Battle Abbey* (written from about 1094 to about the 1180s).

For the most part, the version of events shown in the Tapestry appears to be fairly reliable; the major exception seems to be its account of the Breton campaign, which contrasts with that given by William of Poitiers. Whilst some elements broadly follow contemporary English accounts (briefly discussed above), it is nonetheless of interest that certain key episodes from the English perspective are missing (such as the rebellion against Earl Tostig; the Norwegian invasion – including the Battles of Fulford Gate on 20 September 1066 and Stamford Bridge on 25 September 1066 – and the deployment and withdrawal of Harold's southern naval fleet; though the latter might be depicted in the lower border of Scene 33). Conversely, some aspects of its account are uncertain or obscure. Since Odo is believed to be the Tapestry's patron it is generally thought that he would commission a reliable account, but this is perhaps over-simplistic. Unlike other contemporary accounts, the Bayeux Tapestry is neither an obvious apologist for the Anglo-Saxon nor Norman perspective. However, assuming the Tapestry was made for public display, and contemporaries familiar with the events depicted would have seen it, it seems likely that its account is broadly reliable.

The Tapestry's exact purpose or function is unknown. The significance of the oath scene, where Harold swears on sacred relics, has been much discussed, and has traditionally been interpreted as the moment when Harold promised he would champion William as King Edward's successor. Reginald Allen Brown (1984) believed it was the Tapestry's 'artistic theme, binding the whole together'. Likewise, David Wilson (1985) thought this scene was 'one of the cruces of the Tapestry'. Frank Stenton (1957) thought it was 'the supreme moment'. It is unclear whether this, though clearly important, was the main message of the Tapestry. This said, the oath scene certainly highlights the role of Bayeux and its relics in William's victory at Hastings and the subsequent conquest of the English.

The Bayeux Tapestry is definitely incomplete, but how much more once existed and what it showed is uncertain. Some scholars, including Eric Maclagen (1945) and Frank Stenton (1957), have guessed that it ended with a depiction of William enthroned, just as Edward is shown at the beginning. The extent to which the Tapestry has been repaired or reconstructed over time, notably during the nineteenth century, is fundamental to any discussion of it, and has been recently studied by David Hill and John McSween (forthcoming, 2008). Indeed, it seems that elements of the Tapestry design may have been misconstrued by modern restorers. It is also the case that the inscriptions in the later part of the Tapestry were not included in the earliest illustrations of it, so presumably did not exist when these copies were made.

Whilst some of these repairs may be clearly distinguished as such, others are much closer to the 'original' and hence more difficult to identify. It is therefore imperative to refer to the pre-reconstruction illustrations and etchings of Bernard de Mountfaucon (produced in 1729-30) and Charles Stothard (1817-19), as well as modern photographic facsimiles and the surface of the Tapestry itself (5).

However, before such technical aspects of the Tapestry are examined in the hope of understanding the real world of the Bayeux Tapestry it is useful to first explore the tale told in the Tapestry – the Tapestry's story.

CHAPTER 2

THE BAYEUX TAPESTRY'S STORY

The Bayeux Tapestry recounts the story of the events leading to the Norman Conquest of England in 1066. In the nineteenth century numbers were added to the linen backing cloth upon which the Tapestry was hung, and serve as a useful index to the 58 main scenes (shown on pages 64 to 100 of this book). Following these scene numbers the Tapestry's story can be re-told.

Scene 1: The year is about 1064. King Edward the Confessor, now an elderly man, has ruled England in relative peace for 22 years. As he nears the end of his life (though at this time he seems to have been in relatively good health) the kingdom faces an uncertain future, as Edward remains childless. The situation is of grave concern for England's elite – especially Harold Godwinson (Figure 2), the Earl of Wessex and the most powerful man in England – who all worry about the stability of the kingdom, their own fate and what will happen to Edward's wealth once he dies. Edward probably envisages that Edgar Ætheling, grandson of Edmund Ironside, but still a young man without experience or stature to run a kingdom, will succeed him. It is perhaps the succession that Edward (Figure 3) and Harold (Figure 2) discuss when they meet in the royal palace (probably Westminster). Whilst the Tapestry tells us nothing about the detail of this conversation, the following scenes offer some clues.

Scene 2: From London, Harold and his men ride to Bosham in Sussex, his ancestral home; his father, Godwin, was Earl of Wessex before him. Although Harold was almost certainly born in England, he was half Danish – his mother, Gyrtha, King Cnut's sister-in-law, was born in Denmark. The Tapestry shows Harold (Figure 9) leading his men on a hunting expedition; these men are all moustached, denoting them as English. Harold carries a hawk and is accompanied by hounds; these devices help identify him, and show he is a man of rank and status.

Scene 3: At Bosham, Harold (Figure 11) and a companion take time to pray at a small church, perhaps the one which survives today, although it is largely rebuilt. Only the small crosses on its roof and the inscription – ECCLESIA – identify the building's function. It is not certain what message (if any) the Tapestry designer intended to make by illustrating this scene, though it may be inferred that Harold was a religious man, like most in his age, and that he wished for God's protection during his onward journey.

Scene 4: With suitably rejuvenated souls, Harold and his companions take food and drink in the upper level of a grand, if somewhat peculiar, structure, perhaps intended to be Harold's manor at Bosham. The Anglo-Saxons talk amongst themselves, drink from horns and a bowl and eat as they wait for favourable winds before embarking on a seaward journey. Soon it is time to board a ship (or ships) waiting offshore; it is not clear whether one ship or multiple vessels are shown. Harold's men hoist up their tunics, to protect them from getting wet, and wade out to sea. Apart from Harold's hawk and dogs, few provisions are taken aboard. The anchor is raised and the oarsmen make off.

Scene 5: 'With the wind full in his sails', Harold sets off 'to the country of Count Guy' of Ponthieu; the Tapestry seems to show Harold twice (Figures 29 & 44), though he is not named, steering the ship himself. Though much discussed, it is doubtful if Harold intended to land at Ponthieu. Instead he might have been making for Normandy to discuss with Duke William the English succession, a marriage alliance or to negotiate the return of hostages of his family given in 1051. Alternatively, though unlikely, William of Malmesbury suggested he was blown off course while on a fishing expedition. Unfortunately the Tapestry does not say one way or the other.

Scene 6: It may have been that several ships took Harold and his companions across the Channel, though the Tapestry appears to depict the same ship several times, as Harold (Figures 29, 44 & 56) seems to be shown aboard at least three of them. Eventually, land is spotted by a man in the mast (Figure 50), and the ship, with Harold (Figure 56) at the prow, is landed. Throughout this expedition across the Channel, the lower borders show animals interacting and chasing one another, perhaps scenes from Aesop's fables. As such, James Bard McNulty (1989) and others have interpreted these as relating to the scenes in the main frieze, though it is equally possible, perhaps likely, that they are purely decorative.

Scene 7: No sooner than Harold (Figure 59) is ashore he is apprehended by Count Guy of Ponthieu (Figure 63). Harold defends himself by drawing his knife, but he is no match for Count Guy's men, who are on horseback and heavily armed.

Scene 8: Guy (presumably Figure 73) then leads Harold (Figure 74) to his palace at Beaurain 'and kept him there'. Both men are mounted and carry hawks, but interestingly it is Harold, not Guy, that leads the party. Guy's men are shown with a distinctive hairstyle, shaved at the back in the Norman style. At this point the Tapestry's lower border reverts to facing (or opposing) animal motives, and occasional vegetal element, the 'pattern' found earlier on in the Tapestry's borders.

Scene 9: At Beaurain, Guy (Figure 85) and Harold (Figure 84) talk. The Tapestry does not show the two men as equals; Guy is seated, with sword raised upwards (adopting a pose suggestive of his rank), whilst Harold stands with his sword sheathed and unbelted. We know nothing of the conversation the two men have, but we might guess Harold is giving an account of how he arrived in Ponthieu and the purpose of his journey across the Channel. Seemingly unknown to the two men, another (Figure 87), perhaps a spy, wearing what appears to be tattered clothing, listens in. Soon word of Harold's predicament gets back to Duke William.

Scene 10: The next three scenes show events in reverse chronologically, with the narrative now running from right to left. The word is out that Guy has a high profile prisoner, and Duke William's messengers arrive at Guy's palace. Guy (Figure 91) is shown in an impressive scaled coat and carrying a broad-axe, highlighting his status. Also shown is a dwarf named 'Turold' (Figure 95), who steadies the horses of William's messengers, though H.E.J. Cowdrey (1988) believed Turold is the man shown standing beside the dwarf. It is not known for certain who this man is, but he must have been of some significance to the Tapestry story, else he would not have been named. Here the lower borders show scenes of agricultural life, evoking calendar illustrations of the time.

Scene 11: Further back in time, William's messengers are shown riding out to Beaurain; the wind blows their hair straight. A man (Figure 101) in a tree watches the men as they lead out from Rouen.

Scene 12: It now becomes clear that William (Figure 106) had received word of Harold's capture from an Anglo-Saxon (Figure 105); perhaps this man, identified as an Anglo-Saxon by his moustache, had been with Harold when he arrived in Ponthieu, but escaped and somehow made his way to William's court. Whatever the case, the Tapestry shows the Norman duke, seated and in a pose clearly emphasising his authority, setting forth his messengers to Guy. The Tapestry also seems to depict the outside of William's palace at Rouen, which is shown as a walled structure, with towers and domed roof, and suitably guarded.

Scene 13: The Tapestry narrative then returns to its usual orientation of left to right. Here we see that William is quick to exercise his authority over Guy, and orders that Harold is handed over. Interestingly, instead of asking Guy to bring Harold to his palace, Guy (Figure 117) and William (Figure 118), accompanied by armed men, meet at an undisclosed location, perhaps Eu. The Tapestry shows Harold (Figure 116), Guy and William all on horseback, but only Harold and Guy carry hunting hawks. Instead William is shown wearing an embroidered cloak that has ribbons on it. Gale Owen-Crocker (1998) has made comment of the fact that Guy's mount has the ears of a mule, which might be intended to demean the rider. In the lower Tapestry borders naked individuals (Figures 114 & 115) interact, but their meaning or significance, supposing there is one, is unclear. Here ends the first Tapestry length. The join between Sections 1 and 2 is poorly executed, with the upper border clearly shown not to join properly; whilst the seam is very neat, it is the embroidery which is out of alignment.

Scene 14: Next 'William [Figure 124] came with Harold [Figure 125] to his palace', probably at Rouen. As in Scene 8 it is the man we presume to be Harold (Figure 125) who leads the party; this figure even points to 'HAROLDO' above him, which Gale Owen-Crocker (2007) suggests helps identify him. The Tapestry now shows William, rather than Harold, with a hawk, and it has been suggested by David Bernstein (1986) that this is symbolic of William gaining the advantage over Harold in the quest to succeed Edward, though it is uncertain at this time whether Harold in particular considered himself a possible successor to the English king. At the palace the ducal party is welcome by a man (Figure 126) beside a tower, perhaps intended to represent the town of Rouen. Beneath a long structure with arcading in the roof space, intended to be William's palace, Duke

William (Figure 128) and Harold (Figure 129) talk. William is shown seated, whilst Harold stands. Beside Harold is a man (Figure 130), who some, including David Wilson (1985), have suggested is one of Harold's relatives – perhaps Wulfnoth or Hakon – offered to William as a hostage in about 1051. This seems unlikely as the man is armed, like the Normans beside him. The Tapestry does not tell us what Harold and William talk about, but a clue is offered by the fact that Harold seems to gesticulate towards the next scene.

Scene 15: This meeting between Ælfgyva (Figure 135) and a priest (Figure 136) is one of the most mysterious and intriguing scenes in the Tapestry and has long been discussed by scholars, with no firm conclusions about who Ælfgyva was, the meaning of the scene and its relevance in the context of the Norman invasion of England. The inscription – 'where a clerk and Ælfgyva' – is also unhelpful. Ælfgyva is shown beneath an arch or doorway. From outside this structure, which frames her, a priest (Figure 136) – almost certainly inappropriately – touches her on the face. The suggestive nature of this scene is inferred by the posture of the naked man (Figure 137) in the Tapestry's lower border, which mimics that of the priest. There were two famous women called Ælfgyva. The first was also known as Emma; Edward's mother and William's great aunt. Ælfgyva was also the name of Cnut's common-law wife. Some, such as Denis Butler (1966) have also suggested that Ælfgyva may have been a daughter of William, who was betrothed, or offered, to Harold to cement an alliance or agreement between the two men. However, whilst Ælfgyva was a common aristocratic name, it is not known that any of William's daughters had this name, though the betrothal of William's daughter Agatha to Harold is mentioned by Orderic Vitalis. A tower provides a break between this scene and the next.

Scene 16: In about 1064 William invaded Brittany to suppress its duke, Conan. William had come to the aid of Breton rebels, notably Rhiwallon of Dol. Of particular interest is the fact that the Tapestry recounts a different (and more favourable for William) version of events than given by the only other chronicler of the campaign – William of Poitiers. The Tapestry shows William (probably Figure 143), dressed in elaborate armour or a padded coat (a similar garment is also worn by Odo during the Battle of Hastings), and his men embarking on the expedition into Brittany. His contingent is well armed, some wearing mail and carrying pennant banners.

Scene 17: 'William and his army came to Mont-Saint-Michel', Normandy's most famous shrine and pilgrimage site, 'and here they crossed the river Couesnon', which marked the border between Normandy and Brittany. Interestingly, David Hill and John McSween (forthcoming, 2008) believe that the Tapestry shows Mont-Saint-Michel on the wrong side of the river! Here some of William's men fall into the nearby quick-sands, but 'Duke Harold pulled them out...'. The Tapestry clearly shows Harold (Figure 153), distinguished by his moustache, carrying one Norman on his back whilst dragging another (by his hand) to safety. The upper border shows a man (Figure 146) seated on a chair by Mont-Saint-Michel. The identity and significance of this man is not clear, though Simone Bertrand (1966) has suggested it might be Abbot Ranulphe of Mont-Saint-Michel. Alternatively, this could be Abbot Scotland. Here the lower border of the Tapestry shows sea creatures, such as fish and eels, evoking the environment above.

Scene 18: William's knights, though not in full armour, attack the Breton stronghold of Dol, shown in the Tapestry as a rectangular fortress upon a mound. Conan (Figure 159) is shown escaping from the fortress by means of a rope (a scene, as already mentioned, seemingly inspired by the Old English Hexateuch). William's army, now in full armour, then rides past Rennes, which is shown as a palisade on top of a mound; sheep seem to graze on its slopes and the castle appears empty.

Scene 19: William's knights then ride on to Dinan and attack a heavily defended castle; two men (Figures 174-5) are shown trying to set fire to the stronghold, whilst those defending the structure throw spears at William's cavalry. It is interesting that the Tapestry does not distinguish between the arms or armour of the opposing armies; even their shields have the same quasi-heraldic devices.

Scene 20: Finally Conan surrenders. The Tapestry shows him (Figure 173) handing over the keys of Dinan to Duke William (Figure 176). According to William of Poitiers, Conan escaped. He describes how in fact the Normans rode to Dol to raise Conan's siege of Rhiwallon's castle there. Conan managed to retreat to Rennes, but instead of following him deep into Breton territory, William returned home. The Tapestry then offers William a more complete victory than does William of Poitiers.

Scene 21: After the campaign 'William [Figure 179] gave arms to Harold' (Figure 180). Both William and Harold wear the same armour, though William is distinguished by ribbons on the back of his helmet and shoulders; Harold holds a pennant banner. For many scholars, including Charles Gibbs-Smith (1973), the giving of arms by William to Harold implies that Harold became William's vassal. If this is the case it is unclear what obligations Harold may have relinquished, though we can assume his authority and position were almost certainly compromised.

Scene 22: Next William (perhaps Figure 183) took Harold to Bayeux, which is shown as an elaborate structure, with a domed roof, upon a hill or mound. Interestingly the Tapestry does not clearly show either William or Harold.

Scene 23: At Bayeux, 'Harold [Figure 187] swore a sacred oath to Duke William [Figure 186]'. William is shown seated, with sword raised – a pose of authority, shown elsewhere in the Tapestry. Harold stands before him between two reliquaries, of which one – closest to William – seems to be portable, and the other seems to be an altar. The Tapestry gives little indication of the purpose of the oath, though William of Poitiers makes it clear that by swearing this sacred oath (which he places at Bonneville-sur-Touques) Harold agreed to help William secure the English throne: 'he [Harold] pronounced, clearly and of his own free will, … that he would be the agent of Duke William at the court of King Edward for as long as the king lived; that he would try with all his authority and power to ensure for him the possessions of the kingdom of England on Edward's death…'. Next, 'Duke Harold returned to English soil'. His ship is shown crossing the Channel.

Scene 24: In England a lookout spots the returning earl, as do the inhabitants of a house on the coast. Harold (perhaps Figure 203, though lacking a moustache) and a companion (Figures 204) ride on horseback towards London, or possibly Winchester, 'and came to King Edward'.

Scene 25: At Westminster, Harold (Figure 206) and a companion who holds an axe are met by the king (Figure 207). Edward is shown seated and robed in his palace. He wears his crown and carries a staff, possibly a walking stick which Gale Owen-Crocker (personal correspondence, 2007) has suggested shows he was infirm. The building is shown with towers and pediments and a curtain hangs from the arched roof of the palace. Harold seems to stoop before the king, and it has been suggested by Nicholas Brooks and H.E. Walker (1978) that Edward is shown reprimanding the earl. This reflects the account by Eadmer in his *Historia Novorum*, where Edward says to Harold 'did I not tell you that I knew William, and that your going [to Normandy] might bring untold calamity upon this kingdom?'

Scene 26: Once again the Tapestry's narrative runs from right to left, and the chronology is reversed. Edward's funeral (*c*.6 January 1066) is depicted. His corpse is shown being carried on a bier, covered by a richly embroidered pall, to his cathedral of St Peter the Apostle at Westminster (Westminster Abbey), which was consecrated on 28 December 1065. Priests follow the procession, singing hymns, and bells are rung. The cathedral is shown in some detail: an ornate structure with central domed roof flanked by towers, and an arcaded nave. God's hand is shown blessing the church, and a workman (Figure 209) erects a weathervane, showing the cathedral has only recently been completed. Here ends the second Tapestry length.

Scene 27: Edward (Figure 231) is now shown dying 'in his bed', in the upper story of an elaborate building, and 'addresses his faithful followers': the Archbishop of Canterbury (Figure 230), Harold (Figure 229), Queen Edith (Figure 228) and another (Figure 232), perhaps Robert fitz Wimarch. Edward is shown touching the hand of Harold, and Edith weeps at the bottom of his bed. This scene seems to reflect the *Vita Eadwardi*, where Edward 'addressed his last words to the queen… and stretching forth his hand to his governor, her brother, Harold, he said, "I commend this woman and all the kingdom to your protection"'.

Scene 28: In the lower storey of the same building Edward 'has died'. A cleric (Figure 234), perhaps Archbishop Stigand, is shown administering the last rites, whilst two men lay out Edward's body.

Scene 29: Once again the Tapestry returns to its usual reading of left to right. Shortly after Edward's death, the Witan, the king's council, 'gave Harold the King's crown'. Two men are shown before Harold (Figure 239); one offers him a crown (Figure 237) whilst the other (Figure 238) offers him an axe.

Scene 30: On the very day of Edward's funeral, Harold is crowned king. Both William of Poitiers and William of Jumièges protest at the indecent haste with which Harold assumed the crown, but current research, undertaken by Stephen Church (2007), shows that it was not particularly unusual for a new king to be crowned quickly. Indeed, it was traditional for a new king to be crowned at the time of an important Christian feast – Christmas was ideal. The Tapestry shows Harold (Figure 242) enthroned 'King of the English' underneath an arched building with towers, presumably Westminster Abbey. He wears a crown and holds an orb and sceptre, the regalia of state. Two men (Figures 240-1) present the king with the sword of state. The Tapestry shows that Archbishop Stigand (Figure 243) officiated at the coronation, though John (Florence) of Worcester suggests it was Archbishop Ealdred of York who crowned Harold king; instead it seems likely that both men were present.

Scene 31: Crowds rejoice at the crowning of Harold – but these celebrations were short-lived...

Scene 32: A 'star', purportedly a bad omen, is spotted in the sky; in 1066 it was visible from February 1066 onwards. The Tapestry shows men wondering at the star, now known as Halley's Comet.

Scene 33: Harold (Figure 256) is told of the star's appearance. Harold, unusually clean-shaven, is shown seated on a high back throne, carefully listening (his head to one side) to a messenger (Figure 256). The building within which he sits, perhaps the palace at Westminster, is ornate, with towers, pillars and an elaborate roof. A ghostly fleet of ships is shown in the lower border, probably representing the forthcoming Norman invasion fleet, although David Hill (1998) has instead suggested these are Harold's ships at harbour in London. A single tree represents the end of this phase of the Tapestry.

Scene 34: 'An English ship came to the country of Duke William'; the Tapestry implies it is this ship that brings William news that Harold had been crowned king of England.

Scene 35: Upon learning this news 'Duke William [Figure 263] ordered ships to be built'. William is shown seated discussing his plans with an individual we believe is his half-brother, Odo, Bishop of Bayeux (Figure 264). The Tapestry implies the immediacy of this decision; William and Odo are flanked on one side by the messenger (Figure 262) who brings news of Harold's coronation, and on the other by a shipwright (Figure 265) who is to oversee the construction of William's naval fleet. Men are shown chopping down trees, working trunks into planks and building ships.

Scene 36: The finished 'ships are hauled to the sea'. Unsurprisingly the Tapestry gives little indication of the time it took William to gain support for his mission or the logistics involved in taking an army across the Channel to invade England. Likewise, the Tapestry is silent on English preparations to defend the English south coast from a Norman attack or Harald Hardrada's invasion of the North.

Scene 37: The success of the Norman invasion was by no means certain in late summer 1066. The planning and resources involved were tremendous. Not only were provisions needed for the voyage, but William had to be sure he could establish his army once in England, as well as set up a base from which to mount an invasion. The Tapestry shows men carrying arms and armour and boarding food and wine on the Norman ships. It is possible the small building at the start of this scene is a storehouse. Here ends the third Tapestry length.

Scene 38: On the evening of 27 September 1066 William's invasion fleet left St Valéry-sur-Somme for the Channel crossing to England. The Tapestry shows William (perhaps Figure 296) and some of his knights boarding ships and sailing across the sea; at this point the upper border of the Tapestry gives way to allow more room for illustrating the Norman fleet. Many of the ships are shown with horses and men aboard. Ship 22 is probably William's flagship, the *Mora*, which was given to him by his wife, Matilda. There is some speculation about the device shown at the masthead. Tradition has it that this was the papal banner, signifying papal approval for the mission. Alternatively, Charles Gibbs-Smith (1957) thought it might be the lantern described by William of Poitiers. This possibility is supported by the fact that a man blowing a horn appears in the Tapestry (Figure 334) and is also mentioned by Poitiers:

Fearing lest they reach the opposite shore before daybreak and so incur danger in a hostile and unknown anchorage, the duke issued verbal orders that as soon as they gained the high sea the ships were to lie at anchor close to him for part of the night, until they should see a lantern lit at his masthead, and then at the sound of a trumpet at once set course.

Scene 39: On 28 September William's fleet arrived near Pevensey, 'and here the horses leave the boats'; the ships themselves are shown beached on the shore.

Scene 40: Upon arrival in England the Normans soldiers hurry 'to Hastings to seize food'. Although William had brought some provisions with him for the campaign, it would have been vital, given the size of the invading army, that food be sought once in England; inevitably this would have been seized from the local community against their will. Given that William's men were raiding Harold's ancestral lands this would have also enticed the English king to engage with the Norman duke as soon as possible. The Tapestry shows the Normans stealing food from local people; it is perhaps an Anglo-Saxon (Figure 362) who wields an axe in a vain attempt to protect his livestock.

Scene 41: Small houses identify the place being pillaged as a small town or village. One of the Normans overseeing the looting is named as Wadard (Figure 366); little is known about this man, but he is believed to be a vassal of Odo, Bishop of Bayeux – the Tapestry's patron.

Scene 42: The Normans next prepare a feast in the open air. The Tapestry shows both the cooking and the serving of the food. Here ends the Tapestry's fourth length.

Scene 43: Servants serve William's army. The Normans eat from skewers and drink from cups. A man with a horn (Figure 375) perhaps announces the commencement of the feast. The Tapestry shows that kite-shields were used as makeshift tables. Next, Odo (Figure 380), is shown blessing the food and drink; William (Figure 379) is probably shown to his right. In front of the table a servant attends those who are seated. We have already seen that this scene is important in terms of the design and production of the Tapestry as it seems probable that the designer based it on an illustration of the Last Supper in the St Augustine Gospels (traditionally believed to have been brought to England by St Augustine in 597 or by the following mission a few years later). The fact that Odo takes Christ's place at the head of the table would have been immediately obvious to contemporaries, and highlights the importance of Odo's role, according to the Tapestry, in the Norman Conquest of England.

Scene 44: William (Figure 385) holds council with his half-brothers, Odo (Figure 384) and Robert of Mortain (Figure 386). The three men sit on a bench under a structure with a triangular pediment. Again, Odo's role seems to be emphasised; it is he who is shown telling William what to do, whilst the Duke and Robert carefully listen. The fact that this is a war council is implied by the fact that William points to his sword, while Robert draws his from its sheath; the Tapestry's inscription merely gives the first names of the characters shown, rather than any detail on what they are discussing.

Scene 45: An anonymous man (Figure 387) 'ordered a fortification to be dug at Hastings'; the location of this early castle has not been established for certain. At this point the Tapestry shows some banter; two men (Figures 390-1) hit each other with s pades. In the same scene men are shown building a castle, which seems to be a wooden fortification on a motte. Following the Conquest such fortifications were rapidly built across the country; they played an important role in suppressing rebellion and providing protection for the Norman garrisons that inhabited them.

Scene 46: 'William [Figure 398] receives news of Harold' from a messenger (Figure 399). The duke is shown seated carrying a pennant banner in one hand. By this time William had probably learned that Harold had destroyed the forces of King Harald Hardrada of Norway.

Scene 47: The Tapestry next shows a house being burned and the occupants, a woman and a child (Figures 401-2), fleeing. It was vital for William that his army met Harold in battle at the earliest opportunity. The Norman duke would have difficulty sustaining his army in south-east England for any considerable time, and therefore it was vital a decisive battle gave him a powerbase from which to conquer the English kingdom. In order to entice Harold into battle William laid waste to Sussex, the heart of Harold's ancestral homelands. Harold indeed acted, and moved south to defend his kingdom. Next, William (Figure 404) is shown dressed in full armour and is identified by ribbons hanging from his helm and shoulders; he has brought his horse for the forthcoming battle. The scene ends with a copse of three trees.

Scene 48: On 14 October 1066, William's troops 'set out from Hastings and advanced' about 8 miles north of Hastings 'to do Battle against King Harold'. The Tapestry shows the Normans, fully armed, riding out to battle on horseback. In the upper border there are two pairs of naked people; like the others in Scene 13, their significance is unclear. Shortly after ends the fifth section of the Tapestry.

Scene 49: The Tapestry shows Duke William (probably Figure 424) leading out his men to meet a man named Vital, thought to be another of Bishop Odo's vassals. The Tapestry tells us that 'Duke William asks Vital whether he has seen Harold's army'. In the same scene Norman scouts on horseback spot Harold's army ahead.

Scene 50: Behind trees, Harold's own scouts look out for the invading Normans. The Tapestry shows Harold (Figure 430), mounted on horseback, receiving news of William's movements from one of his scouts (Figure 429). A tree divides one scene from the next.

Scene 51: The Battle of Hastings commenced at about 9am. Harold had grouped his men on higher ground, where they used their shields to form a wall. The Normans, mostly on horseback, arranged themselves in three main divisions on the lower ground below the shield wall: Normans in the middle, Bretons on the left, and French on the right. 'William [Figure 431] exhorts his troops to prepare themselves manfully and wisely for battle against the army of the English'. The Normans are shown charging forward on horseback, with spears aloft; these men are supported by archers. Here (in the second cohort of charging Normans) ends the sixth section of the Tapestry.

Scene 52: The Normans charge the English, both from left to right and right to left. Steadfast, the English stand, like a wall, from behind the protection of their shields, throwing missiles such as spears and axes at the attacking Normans. A lone English archer operates from deep within the English position. From this scene onwards, the animals that fill the lower borders are replaced by the dead of battle. Soon after, early in the battle, 'Leofwine [Figure 494] and Gyrth [Figure 498], King Harold's brothers are killed. Leofwine is shown bravely fighting off the Norman cavalry with a broad-axe, whilst Gyrth is impaled by a spear.

Scene 53: The battle becomes more confused with 'both English and French' being killed. The Tapestry shows horses being felled from beneath their riders, in quite dramatic fashion. Weapons are broken and the borders fill with body parts and weaponry. Here the ground is shown as marshland, which perhaps explains why so many horses are lost. Nearer the end of the scene, lightly armed Englishmen, distinguished by their moustaches, defend some higher land, perhaps a strategic hillock. Normans charge at them from both left to right and right to left.

Scene 54: At a crucial point in the battle 'Bishop Odo [Figure 534], holding his baton, cheers on the boys'. Odo is shown wearing an elaborate coat of armour or padded coat. There has been a rumour that William is dead and the left (Breton) flank of the Norman army break rank and start to flee. The Tapestry seems to show Odo staving off this retreat.

Scene 55: William (Figure 542) then raises the nasal of his helmet to show that he is still alive, and the Norman troops charge forward again. This is clearly illustrated in the Tapestry; the figure generally thought to be Eustace of Boulogne (only part of his name preserved) identifies the Norman duke, though David Spear (2007) thinks this is Robert of Mortain. Once again, the Normans charge forward, but this time the cavalry is supported by Norman archers, shown in the Tapestry's lower border. These had a major impact on the English line, weakening its shield wall. Shortly after the depiction of Eustace, the seventh length of the Tapestry ends.

Scene 56: The Normans renew their charge, and have success breaking down the English. The Tapestry describes that 'the French do battle, and those who were with Harold fell', perhaps a reference to his housecarls – Harold's elite troops. Norman horsemen are shown cutting down the English, who, peppered with arrows, battle in vain, with sword, spear and axe, to save their lives. Gruesomely, another man (Figure 583) is shown with his head being split open. The Norman archers in the lower border are now interspersed with the dead and dying.

Scene 57: The Normans charge again, and finally 'King Harold was slain'; the Tapestry shows Harold, perhaps twice according to Nicholas Brooks and H.E.Walker (1978), once (Figure 591) with an arrow in his eye or forehead, and then (Figure 593) hacked down by a Norman knight. Before him, Harold's standard-bearer (Figure 587) is shown with the dragon standard of Wessex, before being struck down (Figure 585). From behind Harold, troops put up a brave fight, but the battle is already lost. The Tapestry's lower border shows the dead being looted for their arms and armour.

Scene 58: In the final scene of the Tapestry, Norman horsemen chase the English from the battlefield. The Tapestry shows Englishmen, holding an unusual type of mace (perhaps stones tied to sticks), fleeing in the upper half of the main frieze. In the lower part of the main frieze, Norman horsemen whip an Anglo-Saxon tied to a tree. At this point the extant, though heavily restored, remains of the Tapestry end.

While we do not know how the Bayeux Tapestry ended in its original form (assuming it was ever finished) we might imagine that it once showed Duke William crowned king of the English, just as it begins with Edward enthroned.

CHAPTER 3

HISTORICAL BACKGROUND

Shortly before Edward 'the Confessor' was crowned king, Bishop Beorhtweald of Ramsbury had a vision, at Glastonbury, in which St Peter came to Edward and told him 'the kingdom of the English is the kingdom of God' and 'after you he has already provided a king according to his will'. However, upon Edward's death on 5 January 1066, no man knew with certainty what God's will was.

THE EARLY YEARS

Edward was born in about 1005, the eldest son of King Æthelred (the Unready) II (r.978-1016) (6) and his second wife Emma, daughter of Duke Richard I of Normandy (r.944-96). In 1013, Edward, along with his father, mother and younger brother Alfred, sought exile in Normandy (his wife's homeland), following the conquest of northern England by King Svein (Forkbeard) of Denmark (r.987-1014) and his son Cnut. On 3 February 1014, Svein died and the Danes elected Cnut to succeed him.

In spring that year, Æthelred sent a delegation to England, including Edward, to negotiate his return. This was successful, and in March 1014 Æthelred reassumed power and Cnut withdrew to Denmark, only to return the following year to resume his struggle against an ailing King Æthelred. On 23 April 1016, Æthelred died and was succeeded by Edmund 'Ironside' (r.1016), his son by his first marriage to Ælfgyfu of Northampton. Edmund fought valiantly to preserve his kingdom against the Danes, but suffered a major defeat in battle at Ashingdon in Essex on 18 October 1016. At Alney in Gloucestershire it was agreed that the country should be divided between the two men, with each to be the other's heir – Edmund retained Wessex, while Cnut took control of Northumbria, Mercia and London. Fate favoured Cnut; on 30 November 1016, Edmund died and Cnut succeeded the whole kingdom (7). Subsequently Edmund's wife and infant children fled into exile, as did Æthelred's children (Edward and Alfred) by Emma. Emma herself stayed in England and married Cnut!

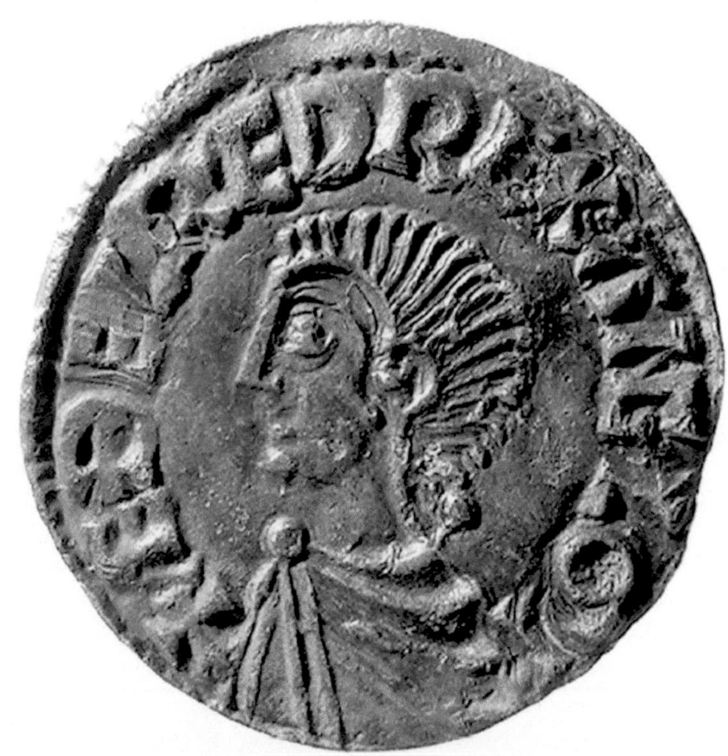

6 Silver penny of King Æthelred II 'the Unready'. *Courtesy of the Portable Antiquities Scheme*

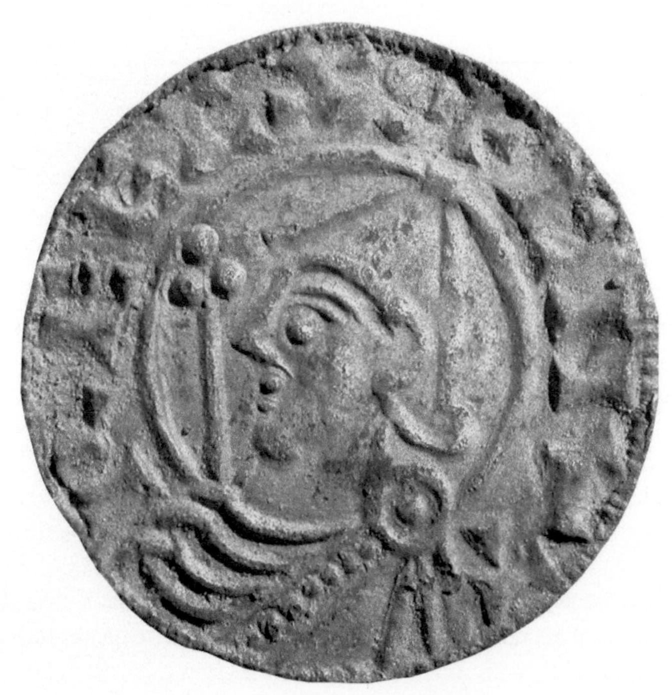

7 Silver penny of King Cnut. *Courtesy of the Portable Antiquities Scheme*

Amongst Cnut's most loyal earls was Godwin, son of Wulfnoth Cild, a Sussex thegn who had also served under Æthelred II, but had been exiled in about 1009. Though Wulfnoth seems to disappear from history, and was almost certainly dead by 1014, Godwin remained in England, serving both of Æthelred's sons; first Athelstan, until his death in 1014, and then Edmund Ironside. Upon Edmund's defeat at Ashingdon, Godwin, like the rest of the English nobility, submitted to Cnut. Whilst many of these were either killed or exiled, Godwin survived and excelled; by 1018 he was Earl of Wessex, which by 1023 incorporated all lands south of the Thames. In about 1020 he was married to Cnut's sister-in-law, Gyrtha, with whom he had at least six sons (Svein, Harold, Tostig, Gyrth, Leofwine and Wulfnoth) and three daughters (Edith, Ælfgyva and Gunnhild).

At this time it would have seemed extremely unlikely that Edward would one day be crowned king of England. Little is known about Edward's life in exile, though it seems that he and his brother were educated as nobles and well looked after. Edward certainly travelled elsewhere in France and perhaps visited the French royal court.

On 12 November 1035, Cnut suddenly died at Shaftesbury. At once, Emma claimed the kingdom for Harthacnut, her son by Cnut, who was ruling Denmark at the time, and Harold 'Harefoot', Cnut's son by Ælfgifu, also declared himself king. The Witan met at Oxford to discuss the succession. Earl Leofric and the Mercians, and Cnut's Danish mercenary fleet (stationed in London) favoured Harold as king, whilst Earl Godwin, the men of Wessex and Archbishop Æthelnoth of Canterbury, supported Harthacnut. Harold Harefoot's position was clearly strengthened by the fact that he was in England, while Harthacnut was not. In order to avert civil war the Witan made Harold protector of the kingdom for himself and his half-brother. As part of the deal, Queen Emma and Godwin held Wessex for Harthacnut, whilst Earls Leofric and Siward held Mercia and Northumbria for Harold Harefoot. Under this arrangement Emma and Godwin must have anticipated that Harthacnut would arrive in England to claim his part of the kingdom, but war with King Magnus of Norway (r.1035-47, and King of Denmark – r.1042-7) detained him, and consequently Harold Harefoot was able to consolidate his power; he seized the royal treasure from Emma at Winchester and took control of the southern coin mints.

In 1036, presumably at Emma's instigation, Edward came to England with a force of '40 ships filled with armed men' and landed at Southampton. His aim, presumably, was to meet with his mother at Winchester, but he was forced to flee and returned to Normandy. Meanwhile, Edward's brother, Alfred, sailed from Wissant in Flanders and landed at Dover with 'a few armed Frenchmen'. He was intercepted by Earl Godwin's men and taken to Guildford, perhaps with good intentions. Here he was captured by Harold Harefoot's men, taken to Ely, and cruelly blinded, dying of his wounds. His companions were executed. Contemporary sources lack consensus on the extent of Godwin's involvement in Alfred's murder, but it was only a matter of time before the repercussions were to fully manifest themselves.

By 1037, Harold Harefoot was 'chosen as king everywhere' (*8*) and Emma fled to Bruges. Here she was joined by Edward, where mother and son plotted how to take England by force. This opportunity came in 1039 when Harthacnut made peace with King Magnus of Norway (r.1035-47) and came to his mother (and Edward) in Bruges. In the event, force was not needed; on 17 March 1040 Harold Harefoot died at Oxford, and the following June,

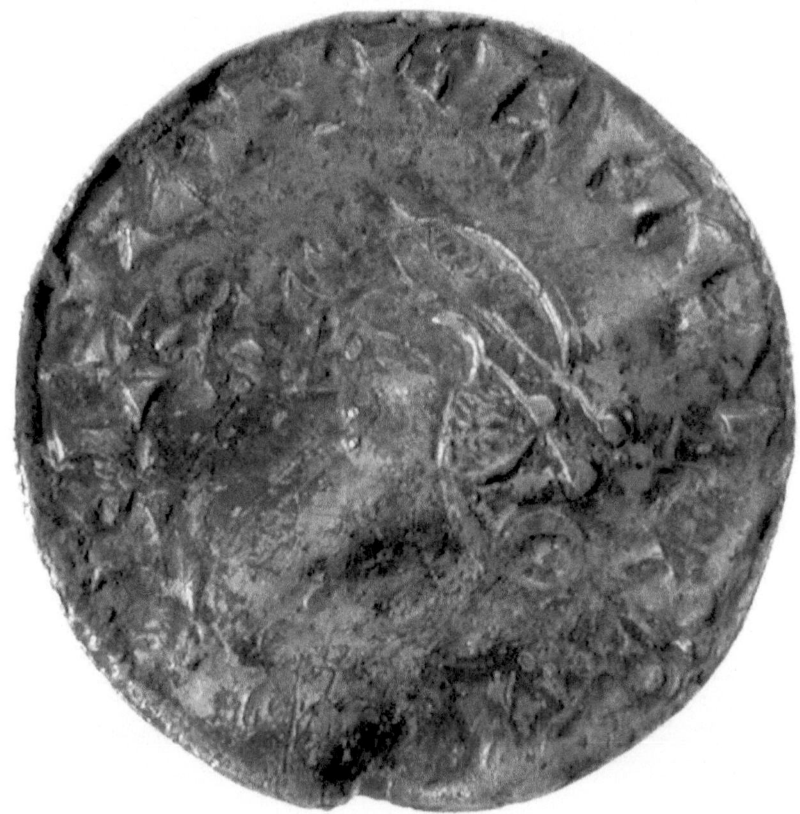

8 Silver penny of King Harold I. *Courtesy of the Portable Antiquities Scheme*

Harthacnut crossed to Sandwich to claim the crown (*9*). One of his first acts as king was to have Harold Harefoot's body exhumed and cast into a marsh. Godwin and Archbishop Ælfric Puttoc of York, perhaps as punishment for their support for the former king, were ordered to take part in this desecration. At about this time, Archbishop Ælfric and others accused Godwin and Bishop Lyfing of complicity in the murder of Alfred. Consequently, Godwin was forced to clear himself of the charge by swearing an oath that Harold, not he, ordered the blinding of the English prince. He also presented Harthacnut with a magnificent ship.

In 1041, Harthacnut ordered Godwin and other earls to ravage Worcester and its shire in punishment for the killing of two royal housecarls by the townsfolk. Such actions, and huge tax demands, seemed to have weakened Harthacnut's support amongst the English nobility. Consequently, Harthacnut invited Edward to England to share the rule of the kingdom, which was a practice common in Scandinavia.

Little about Edward's life is known during the rest of Harthacnut's reign, which was surprisingly short. On 8 June 1042, Harthacnut died suddenly, intoxicated at a wedding feast in Lambeth. Edward, almost certainly a guest at the wedding, was in an ideal position to take advantage and ensure his succession to the English crown.

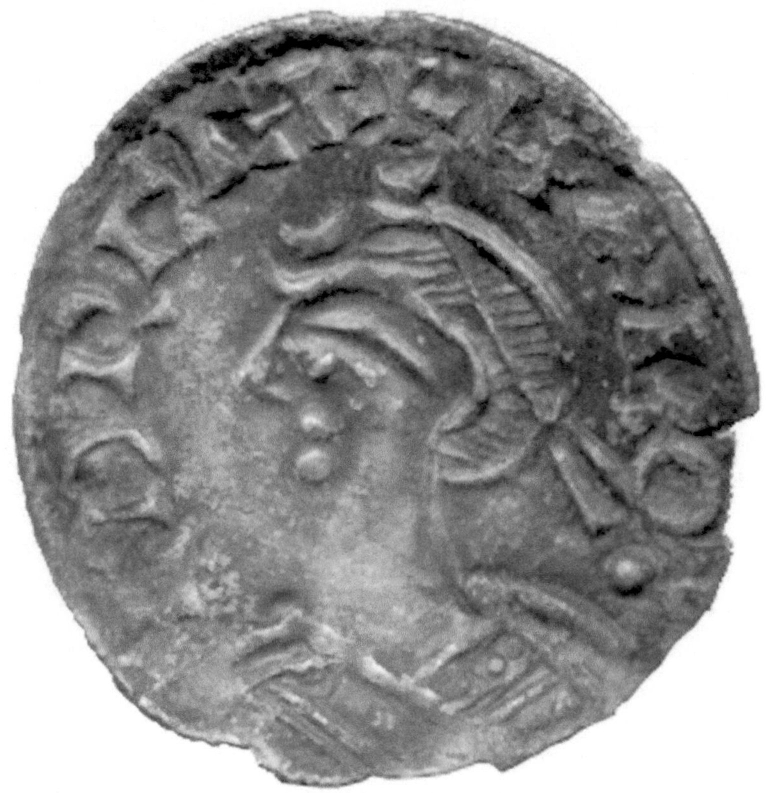

9 Silver penny of King Harthacnut. *Courtesy of the Portable Antiquities Scheme*

EDWARD THE KING

Whilst Edward was the obvious choice, it was not immediately certain he would have the backing of the English nobility. He enjoyed his strongest support from the southern English aristocracy, including Earl Godwin. Both Earl Leofric of Mercia and Earl Siward of Northumbria eventually followed suit, but only after they sought the opinions of the northern nobles. Edward then punished those who displeased him most, including his mother Emma, who on 16 November 1043 was accused of treason and deprived of all her lands and treasures; however, these were restored soon after. On Easter Day (3 April) that year, Edward was crowned king at Winchester by Archbishops Eadsige of Canterbury and Ælfric Puttoc of York.

Edward rewarded Godwin for his support giving the earl's sons (Svein and Harold) and nephew (Beorn) land and authority. Further cementing the alliance between king and earl was the marriage of Godwin's eldest daughter, Edith, to Edward on 23 January 1045; at least 15 years divided the royal couple. Although it would have been desirable for England and its aristocracy, Edward and Edith were not blessed with children. It was even suggested, after Edward's death, that the marriage had not been consummated, owing to the king's piety. More likely is that Edward was sterile or impotent, or that Edith was barren, but none of this would have been known in 1045 – an heir would have been expected.

By exercising his ecclesiastical patronage Edward increased his influence in the shires and strengthened his position at court. Often such appointments lacked local support and it has been suggested (perhaps unfairly) that Edward was forwarding the interests of foreigners, particularly Normans; these included Robert of Jumièges (Bishop of London from 1044), Hereman (Bishop of Ramsbury from 1045), Ulf (Bishop of Dorchester from 1049), Earl Ralph and Robert Fitzwilliam. Edward seemed to have less power over his leading earls, such as Leofric of Mercia and Siward of Northumbria, and especially those of his wife's family, led by Godwin of Wessex; in 1045 Godwin and his family held four of England's earldoms.

Following Edward's death it was, of course, Godwin's second eldest son, Harold, who became king, but in 1045 Harold Godwinson's meteoric rise to power could not have been imagined; he was only a junior earl (of East Anglia) aged about 25. It was about this time Harold took Edith 'Swan-neck', a woman of some status, an heiress to extensive lands and influence in Cambridgeshire, Suffolk and Essex, as his concubine.

Edward and Godwin had an uneasy relationship and things came to head in 1046 following the outrageous behaviour of Godwin's eldest son, Svein, whose earldom included Somerset, Herefordshire, Gloucestershire, Oxfordshire and Berkshire. On return from an expedition into South Wales, in alliance with Gruffydd ap Llywelyn of Gwynedd and Powys (r.1039-63) and Deheubarth (r.1055-63), perhaps in order to prevent Welsh attacks on this earldom, 'he ordered the Abbess of Leominster [Eadgifu] to be brought to him and kept her as long as it suited him'. A year later he was persuaded to release the abbess and, in late 1047, fled to Bruges, Flanders. Here he stayed over winter before going on to Denmark the following summer (1048). Edward promoted his nephew, Ralph of Mantes, as Earl of Hereford (part of Svein's earldom); Harold and Beorn also seemed to have benefited from Svein's downfall.

Edward increasingly felt threatened by King Magnus of Norway, and began to oust influential Danes from the country. Initially war between Magnus and Svein Estrithson (Ulfson) of Denmark (r.1047-76) had thwarted any plans the Norwegian king might have had to invade England, but things changed when Magnus drove Svein from Denmark in 1046, following the Battle of Helganes. The following year the Dane asked for Edward's help, sending ambassadors to England. Earl Godwin was in favour of supporting Svein, his wife's nephew, and urged Edward to provide 50 ships, but this was opposed by Earl Leofric of Mercia and others. Edward heeded Leofric's advice and consequently Svein capitulated and was driven from Denmark. However, Svein's exile was short-lived. On 25 October 1047, Magnus died and Svein was able to return to Denmark and assume the throne. In Norway, Harald Hardrada (r.1047-66), Magnus's uncle, succeeded as king, and soon the two northern kingdoms were again at war. Whilst Earl Godwin still favoured an alliance with Denmark against Norway, Edward favoured a policy of non-intervention. This proved successful, though Edward had to deal with pirates, harboured by Count Baldwin V of Flanders (r.1035-67), who raided the English coast.

THE FALL OF THE HOUSE OF GODWIN

In the summer of 1049, Svein Godwinson returned from exile in Denmark with a fleet of eight ships, having 'ruined himself with the Danes'. He slipped through an English naval blockade (which had been assembled at Sandwich in support of the Emperor Henry III – r.1039-56 – against Baldwin V of Flanders) and landed at Bosham. He then travelled overland to Sandwich, in the hope of making peace with the king and regaining his lands and earldom. Svein anticipated that his brother Harold and cousin Beorn would lobby Edward on his behalf, but they did not; in fact they refused to surrender anything the king had granted them. Edward gave Svein four days in which to leave the country.

At about the same time, Irish 'Vikings', in alliance with King Gruffydd ap Rhydderch of Deheubarth (r.1045-55), of South Wales, raided England. They sailed up the River Severn, over the Wyre, and into the Forest of Dean, where they surprised and defeated an army led by Bishop Ealdred of Worcester. Edward acted decisively to intercept the invading army, and dispatched a naval fleet of 42 ships led by Earl Godwin, which included vessels commanded by Earls Harold, Beorn and Tostig. The tactic left England vulnerable from attack in the east, of which Osgot Clapa (exiled by Edward in 1046) sought to take advantage. Mustering a fleet said to have been 29 or 39 vessels, Osgot waited at Wulpe, Flanders, with six ships, while the rest raided Essex. Fortunately for Edward this fleet was decimated by bad weather.

Inclement conditions were also proving to be a problem for Earl Godwin, whose fleet was weather-bound at Pevensey. Here Svein met with Beorn and appealed to him to intercede with the king on his behalf, to which he agreed. It was an ill-fated judgement. Svein took Beorn to Bosham (presumably to travel by sea to Sandwich to meet King Edward) where he was taken aboard Svein's ship. At Dartmouth Beorn was murdered, and then buried on the shore in an unmarked grave. Consequently, Edward declared Svein *nithing* (someone utterly and irreparably disgraced) and the earl fled to Bruges; many of his men also deserted him. Beorn's body was later recovered and buried at Winchester beside his uncle, Cnut.

Godwin did not give up on Svein and even persuaded Edward to pardon him. This was achieved by summer 1050 when Bishop Ealdred of Worcester and Bishop Herman of Ramsbury brought Svein back to court. Redistribution of Beorn's earldom probably ensured Harold and Ralph did not lose out from Svein's return.

In the end it was ecclesiastical appointments, not Godwin's wayward son, which were to lead to a political crisis between the great earl and King Edward. On 29 October 1050, Archbishop Eadsige of Canterbury died, and the monks of Christ Church sought to elect Æthelric, a kinsman of Godwin, as their new archbishop; it was a choice Godwin supported and he lobbied Edward accordingly. However, on 1 March 1051, the king chose to appoint Robert of Jumièges, Bishop of London, to Canterbury, and Abbot Spearhafoc of Abingdon to replace him in London. Another vacancy was caused by the death of Archbishop Ælfric Puttoc of York on 22 January 1051, who was replaced by Cynsige, a royal clerk. These appointments (and others) caused resentment and tension, most significantly between Earl Godwin and Archbishop Robert.

During Lent, Archbishop Robert left for Rome to collect his pallium from Pope Leo IX (r.1049-55) and was installed on 29 June 1051. Perhaps impressed by the power of the Church in Rome, Robert returned to England with reforming zeal. First, he refused to consecrate Spearhafoc to the bishopric of London, because 'the Pope had forbidden him', in direct defiance of the king. He also seems to have had a hand in furthering the ambitions of the papacy over appointments in the English Church. Next, Robert accused Godwin of usurping lands of the archbishopric and monastic estates, and attempted – unsuccessfully – to recover these through the shire courts. Further, Robert reminded the king of Godwin's involvement in the death of his brother, Alfred, also implying that Godwin was plotting to kill Edward himself.

In summer 1051, Edward's former brother-in-law, Eustace of Boulogne, came to England to visit the king (in 1036 Eustace had married Edward's sister Godgifu, but she died in 1047). Nothing is known of the purpose of the visit, though Eustace may have come to discuss his concerns regarding a closer alliance between Normandy and Flanders. On his way home (although the *Anglo-Saxon Chronicle* (D) says it was on his inward journey), Eustace and his men were involved in an incident with the men of Dover whilst searching for accommodation. One of Eustace's men killed a townsman, and one of Eustace's men was killed in revenge. Thereafter, Eustace's men retaliated and killed a number of men and women, trampling children and babies with their horses. More townsmen joined the fight and Eustace's party was forced to flee, whereupon they reported the incident to Edward. Edward sided with Eustace and ordered Godwin to ravage the town, since it was within his earldom, but the earl refused. Edward summoned his council and army to Gloucester on 8 September 1051 to discuss the crisis. Godwin demanded the surrender of Eustace and summoned the forces of his earldom, and those of his sons Svein and Harold, to Beverstone, near Gloucester. Edward rallied his own supporters, including Archbishop Robert, Eustace, and Earls Ralph, Leofric and Siward. Godwin demanded the opportunity to refute the charges that had been made against him, including complicity in Alfred's murder, but Edward was unimpressed by Godwin's show of force and refused. The northern earls then called out the full armed forces of their earldoms and prepared to oppose Godwin by force. Civil war looked inevitable, though neither side must have wished it.

Eventually, Edward negotiated with Godwin and it was agreed to exchange hostages and to reconvene at London on 21 September 1051; Godwin's hostages were his youngest son, Wulfnoth, and Svein's son, Hakon. On 21 September the two armies met on opposite sides of the Thames; Bishop Stigand of Winchester mediated between them. By this time, Edward's force had increased in size and Godwin's had begun to dwindle. The king then declared Svein an outlaw and commanded Godwin and Harold to appear before the council to answer the charges brought against them. Godwin asked for additional guarantees of safe conduct with hostages before agreeing to this request, but the king refused, so Godwin and his family fled.

Around the beginning of October, Edward proclaimed Godwin and his sons outlaws. Godwin, his wife Gyrtha, Svein, Tostig and Gyrth all boarded a ship at Bosham for Flanders, taking with them a great hoard of treasure. They stayed at Bruges under the protection of Count Baldwin V; Tostig had recently been married to Baldwin's sister, Judith. From here, Svein travelled on a pilgrimage to Jerusalem, but never returned; he died on 29 September 1052 at Lycia, near Constantinople, on his return home. Meanwhile, Harold and Leofwine made for Bristol, avoiding forces of Bishop Ealdred of Worcester, and sailed for Ireland. Here they were received by King Diarmait mac Mail-na-mBo of Leinster (r.1042-72), who also controlled much of Dublin. It was a potential turning point in English history. The country's most powerful earl and his whole family had been exiled; the defeat seemed comprehensive and permanent. The *Anglo-Saxon Chronicle* (D) recalls 'it would have seemed remarkable to everyone in England if anybody had told them that it could happen, because he [Godwin] had been exalted so high, even to the point of ruling the king and all England, and his sons were earls and the king's favourites, and his daughter was married to the king'.

Edward himself held most of the land previously owned by the Godwin family, but he granted Odda of Deerhurst an earldom including Cornwall, Devon, Dorset and Somerset, and he granted Ælfgar, son of Earl Leofric, most of Harold's earldom of East Anglia. Earl Siward seems to have received Huntingdonshire and Cambridgeshire. Ralph was re-established in his possession of Herefordshire, and the Frenchmen of Herefordshire were given the manors of Burghill and Brinsop. Archbishop Robert was rewarded with land in Kent. Edward finally expelled Bishop Spearhafoc, appointing William, a Norman clerk, in his place. Edith, Edward's queen and Godwin's daughter, was deprived of her lands and possessions and sent to the nunnery at Wilton. Archbishop Robert probably advised the king to divorce her, though he did not.

It was during the exile of the Godwin's family, in late 1051, that according to the *Anglo-Saxon Chronicle* (D), William, Duke of Normandy (r.1035-87) came to England. The purpose of the visit is not recorded, though it has been suggested that this is the likely occasion that Edward promised William the English throne. Most scholars are now unconvinced that this visit actually took place, as William was preoccupied in Normandy at the time and later Norman sources fail to mention it.

William was born in Falaise, Normandy, in autumn 1027 or early 1028, to Duke Robert of Normandy (r.1028-35) and his mistress, Herleva. In about 1035, Herleva had married Herluin de Conteville, having two sons by him, Odo (later Bishop of Bayeux) and Robert (later Count of Mortain). In 1035, Duke Robert died on pilgrimage to Jerusalem, upon which William succeeded as duke, aged about eight years old. Following the death of William's guardian, Archbishop Robert of Rouen (brother of Duke Richard II) in 1037, the duchy descended into chaos, feuding and civil conflict; a murder even took place in William's bedchamber. Gradually, William's fortunes changed. In 1047, with the support of King Henry I of France (r.1031-60), he defeated Count Guy of Brionne at Val-ès-Dunes. From this time on, William began to establish his authority, achieving dominance over the Norman aristocracy and the dukedom's northern neighbours. In late 1049, he led a Norman force in support of King Henry I of France against Count Geoffrey Martel of Anjou (r.1040-60), and in 1051-2 he attacked and captured Alençon and Domfront. Following an alliance between Henry and Geoffrey in early 1052, William was forced to defend his dukedom from invasion on three occasions, each time successfully. From this position he consolidated his power even recovering land lost during his minority.

Whilst it is unlikely that William visited Edward in England during 1051, it is possible that the two men agreed a treaty. Such an alliance may have been useful to Edward. He would have hoped that it would lessen the threat of Baldwin V of Flanders; in 1050 or 1051 William married Matilda, Count Baldwin's daughter. Such an agreement between Edward and William, real or not, was used by Norman writers (most notably William of Jumièges and William of Poitiers) to justify the invasion of England in 1066. William of Jumièges states that Edward sent Archbishop Robert to William to nominate him as his heir to the kingdom. This is expanded upon by William of Poitiers, who states that this offer was made to William in gratitude for the refuge given to Edward in his early years and came with the assent of the English nobility, including Earls Godwin, Leofric and Siward, and Archbishop Stigand. It is possible that Godwin's kin, Wulfnoth and Hakon, were given as hostages to guarantee the agreement.

The Norman claim that William was made Edward's heir is difficult to accept. At this time, Edward was unlikely to have been contemplating death, though the succession must have played on his mind, and the English earls would never have welcomed a Norman duke as their king; they might still have hoped for Edward to produce an heir of English stock. Besides this there were other possibilities, perhaps more palatable to the English nobility, including Earl Ralph, Edward's nephew by his sister Godgifu, and Ralph's elder brother, Walter, Count of the Vexin.

In March 1052, Edward's mother Emma died and was buried with her second husband, Cnut, and son, Harthacnut, at Winchester. Though very much in power, Edward was very much alone.

GODWIN FIGHTS BACK

It seems likely that the Godwin family selected Bruges and Dublin as their places of exile as both were suitable springboards for a return to England; both were geographically close and ideal for recruiting mercenaries. By 1052, Godwin was using his wealth to recruit Flemish mercenaries, and Harold obtained King Diarmait's influence to do likewise in Dublin; it seems that Godwin was able to communicate with his sons in Ireland. Edward was also aware of these preparations and organised a defensive force of 40 ships at Sandwich, commanded by Earls Ralph and Odda. On about 24 June 1052, Godwin crossed the Channel and landed at Dungeness, thereafter recruiting seamen from Hastings and Kent ports. When Ralph and Odda moved to oppose him, Godwin retreated to Pevensey. A storm forced Ralph and Odda to return to Sandwich and Godwin escaped to Bruges. Edward ordered his fleet back to London and dismissed the two earls and their crews.

Soon after, Godwin sailed again from Bruges, but this time with an enlarged fleet. He proceeded to ravage the Isle of Wight and then sailed on to Portland, which he also attacked. Edward, lacking a fleet, was unable to respond. At about the same time, Harold and Leofwine sailed from Ireland with nine ships, entered the Severn, and landed at Porlock, Somerset, ravaging the area. Here Harold defeated a local force, before sailing to join his father at Portland. The combined fleet then made for the south-east coast, gathering support in Sussex and Kent. Next, it made its way up the Channel, enlisting volunteers and ships, and taking hostages, from Pevensey to Sandwich, before mustering at North

Foreland. In the Thames, part of the fleet went to Sheppey and burnt the royal manor of Milton.

Edward made plans to hold London and sent for reinforcements, though it seems Earls Leofric and Siward did not respond to this call. Nevertheless, by mid-September Edward had amassed a large land army and some 50 ships. This did not deter Godwin who sailed up the Thames, arriving at Southwark on 14 September 1052. Here he negotiated safe passage with the citizens of London and moved his fleet on past London Bridge. Godwin then came face to face with Edward's forces, separated only by the Thames. Once again, the two armies had no appetite for war, preferring to negotiate; Bishop Stigand was again the intermediary. Negotiations resulted in a truce, and a meeting of the council was called for the next day. Archbishop Robert fled, in fear of vengeance, as did Bishops Ulf of Dorchester, William of London and the Frenchmen of Herefordshire.

On 15 September 1052, Godwin and Harold met with the king's council (probably at Westminster), and on oath declared themselves innocent of the charges brought against them. Edward reinstated Godwin and his sons with everything they had lost, and Queen Edith was restored to the royal household. The council also made judgements of outlawry on all those deemed responsible for the crisis. Unfortunately for Earl Ælfgar, he was forced to resign his earldom to Harold. Earls Ralph and Odda kept their lands, as did those who had not promoted injustices, such as Robert the Deacon, Richard fitz Scrob, Alfred the king's equerry, Anfrid Cocksfoot and Bishop William of London. Stigand replaced Robert as Archbishop of Canterbury (though he continued to hold Winchester in plurality) and Wulfwig replaced Ulf as Bishop of Dorchester. Robert travelled to the continent. Upon hearing of his banishment he protested to the Pope and asked him to condemn Stigand; it was later argued by Norman chroniclers that Stigand had not been properly consecrated. Soon after, Robert died at Jumièges.

The strengthening of Godwin's hand also seems to have strengthened that of England. Instead of looking to resolve internal differences, the great earls of England looked to deal with external threats, in particular the Welsh and Scots. In 1052 during Godwin's exile Herefordshire was ravaged and the local castellans defeated, perhaps by King Gruffydd ap Llywelyn. At Christmas 1052, Edward ordered the assassination of Rhys, the brother of Gryffydd ap Rhydderch because 'he was causing injuries' and his head was brought to the king at Gloucester on 5 January 1053. In 1054 Edward ordered Earl Siward to invade Scotland in support of Malcolm Canmore (later Malcolm III of Scotland – r.1058-93) against King Macbeth (r.1040-57), and on 27 July the Scottish king was defeated in battle in Perthshire. Consequently, Malcolm was able to gradually take control of Scotland, which was achieved by 1058. The following year he became king and came to Edward, probably to pay homage.

For Easter 1053, the royal court sat in Winchester. On 12 April 1053, whilst dining with the king, Godwin suffered a stroke. He was taken to the king's bed-chamber by his sons, Harold, Tostig and Gyrth, where he lay speechless for three days until he died. He was buried in the Old Minster in Winchester. Harold succeeded his father as Earl of Wessex, allowing Ælfgar, Earl Leofric's son, to be restored to East Anglia.

SEARCH FOR AN HEIR

By 1054, King Edward realised his marriage to Edith was not going to produce an heir, so sought to bring Edmund Ironside's son, Edward, known to be alive in Hungary, back to England. In 1016, Cnut had planned to kill Prince Edward and his elder brother, Edmund, and sent them to Sweden to be murdered there. Fortunately for the young princes, King Olaf Skötkonung of Sweden (r.995-1022) ensured they were sent to safety, and they ended up at the Hungarian royal court. Edmund died there in 1054. Prince Edward fared much better, and was married to Agatha, a daughter of Emperor Henry II's brother (probably Bruno, later Bishop of Augsburg) by whom he had three children: Margaret, Christina and Edgar (Margaret was later married to King Malcolm of Scotland in about 1070). In 1054, Edward 'the Exile' was about 36 years old. Though a direct descendant of King Æthelred the Unready, and therefore of good English stock, he could not speak much English.

Bishop Ealdred of Worcester was charged with the search for Prince Edward. Sometime after 17 July 1054, Ealdred, perhaps with Abbot Ælfwine of Ramsey, travelled to Cologne, where he was received by the Emperor Henry III and Archbishop Herman. Here Ealdred conveyed Edward's request that messengers should be sent to Hungary, but the request was impossible due to a dispute between the Emperor and the Hungarian king.

On 5 October 1056, the Emperor Henry III died, and was succeeded by Henry IV as king of Germany (r.1056-1106; Holy Roman Emperor from 1084) who sought peace with King Andrew I of Hungary (r.1046-60). This provided the opportunity to seek the return of Prince Edward. It is unlikely King Edward declared the prince his heir (Ætheling) without first meeting him, but the intention was clear.

On 13 November 1056, Earl Harold was at St Omer, probably on a journey to Rome. Perhaps Harold used this opportunity to meet with Baldwin V of Flanders and join him in Cologne, where on 5 December 1056, Baldwin and Agnes of Poitiers (regent on behalf of her son Henry IV) agreed peace terms. Here Harold may have gained local support for the mission to bring Prince Edward back to England. The imperial party then travelled to Regensburg on the Danube for Christmas. It was here that Harold probably began negotiations with King Andrew I of Hungary and Prince Edward. It seems Edward was reluctant to leave Hungary at first, but a worsening political situation in his adopted country probably persuaded him to leave. Harold then seems to have travelled with Pope Victor II (r.1055-7) to Rome, returning, via Bavaria, to collect Prince Edward and his family and escort them to England.

In spring 1057, Prince Edward and his family arrived in England, but on 19 April, before he met the king, he died in London and was buried in St Paul's. It is suggested that Prince Edward may have been prevented from meeting the king, though it is not stated why, nor is foul play hinted at. Prince Edward's only son, Edgar (r.1066), was probably aged about five at the time of his father's death. King Edward seems to have brought Edgar and his sisters up at court as if they were his own. Whilst Edgar was still a minor, it seems likely Edward considered him to be his eventual successor.

THE STRENGTHENING OF THE HOUSE OF GODWIN

In early 1055, Earl Siward of Northumbria died. On 17 March that year, the king's council met in London and it was agreed that Earl Tostig, at the expense of Siward's son, Waltheof, should succeed Northumbria. Waltheof probably felt deprived, but Northumbria was lawless and it seems Edward was keen to assert his influence, through Tostig, in the north. In the past, Edward had used the Earls of Mercia and Northumbria to check the power of the House of Godwin, but this policy had now been abandoned.

Ælfgar of East Anglia protested to the king about Tostig's appointment, and as a consequence was outlawed. This was to the benefit of Gyrth Godwinson, who succeeded at least part of Ælfgar's earldom. Ælfgar fled to Ireland and thereafter to Wales. Here he made an alliance with Gruffydd ap Llywelyn. With Ælfgar, Gruffydd made a raid into South Wales to depose of Gruffydd ap Rhydderch. Then Gruffydd ap Llywelyn led their combined forces against Hereford, defeated a cavalry force of Earl Ralph on 24 October 1055 and sacked Hereford; four or five hundred of its inhabitants were killed, including the clergy who defended the cathedral. Edward summoned Harold to help defend the border with Wales. This army, with men from across the country, mustered at Gloucester. Harold first advanced into Wales, causing Gruffydd ap Llywelyn to retreat. Then Harold went to Hereford to fortify the city, and to open negotiation with the invaders. At Billingsley, Ælfgar met with Harold, made peace with the king and recovered his earldom. Gruffydd, it seems, remained in control of some of his conquests along the border. It was not an ideal conclusion for Edward, but at least the threat from Gruffydd was tempered – for now!

On 10 February 1056, Æthelstan, Bishop of Hereford, died. Edward, in his attempt to subdue the Welsh, appointed Leofgar, a warrior cleric of Earl Harold, to Hereford. In June 1056, Leofgar led an army against Gruffydd ap Llywelyn, only to be defeated and killed at Glasbury-on-Wye. Earls Harold and Leofric and Bishop Ealdred gathered to protect the border in the wake of the defeat, but did not attempt to venture into Wales. Instead, the Englishmen again negotiated peace with Gruffydd. He was acknowledged as king of all Wales, in return for recognising Edward as his overlord. It was agreed Bishop Ealdred of Worcester should also administer the see of Hereford.

On 30 September 1057, Earl Leofric of Mercia died and was succeeded by his son Ælfgar. Soon after, on 21 December 1057, Earl Ralph also died, leaving only an infant son, Harold, who passed into the guardianship of Queen Edith. Perhaps at this time Gyrth succeeded all of East Anglia, and Leofwine the eastern part of Ralph's earldom. By 1057, Earl Ælfgar was the only earl not of Godwin stock.

Ælfgar was evidently still on good terms with Gruffydd ap Llywelyn, as he permitted Gruffydd to marry his daughter, Ealdgyth. In 1058, Ælfgar was again outlawed on the charge of treason, though the reasons for this are not altogether clear. Ælfgar fled to Gruffydd and sought to reclaim his earldom by force; this was supported by a Norwegian fleet led by Magnus, son of King Harald of Norway, that was in the vicinity by chance. The Norwegians raided the English coast, whilst Gryffydd raided by land. At Easter 1058, the royal court met at Gloucester to discuss the crisis and agreed to restore Ælfgar to his earldom (he possibly also gained Oxfordshire), and perhaps made further concessions to

Gruffydd (at this time he may have acquired lands beyond the Dee). An uneasy peace ensued for a number of years.

In about 1062, Ælfgar died and was succeeded by his young son Edwin. Gruffydd ap Llywelyn took this opportunity to strike at the young earl. At Christmas 1062, Edward's court met at Gloucester where it was agreed to destroy Gruffydd once and for all. Harold was dispatched with cavalry to surprise Gruffydd at Rhuddlan (more than 100 miles away from Gloucester) in his palace in North Wales on the Clwyd, but the Welsh prince received word of the planned attack and fled by sea. Harold, nonetheless, burnt Gruffydd's palace and ships.

In spring 1063, Harold and Tostig undertook a joint expedition to deal with Gruffydd ap Llywelyn. On 26 May, Harold sailed with a fleet from Bristol to ravage the Welsh coastline and take hostages (and to deter Gruffydd's escape), while Tostig invaded North Wales with a cavalry force, probably via Chester. The English employed swift-moving small units to ravage and defeat any opposition. Gruffydd was forced to retreat into the mountains of Snowdonia, from where he was able to resist the English forces. Although Gruffydd had escaped again, most of the Welsh nobles submitted to Harold, renounced Gruffydd, gave hostages and paid tribute. Harold and Tostig chose not to follow Gruffydd into the mountains, but instead left the Welsh to deal with him. On 5 August 1063, Cynan, son of Iago, killed Gruffydd and brought his head to Harold, who in turn delivered it to Edward. It was decided that North Wales should be divided between Gruffydd's two half-brothers, Bleddyn and Rhiwallon; both men swore oaths to Edward and Harold, gave hostages and agreed to pay tribute. A number of English border territories were now recovered and some Welsh lands were reclaimed. In Deheubarth (South Wales), Maredudd and Rhys ab Owain emerged as leaders, and in Morgannwg (South Wales), Cadwgan ap Meurig claimed power. Wales was now fractured and threats of attacks into England were suppressed.

HAROLD'S TRAVELS TO NORMANDY

In about 1064, Earl Harold visited Normandy. William of Jumièges says that Edward had sent Harold to Normandy to swear fealty concerning the crown and confirm the succession by oaths. This seems unlikely as Edward clearly envisaged that Prince Edgar Ætheling would eventually succeed him. There is also little suggestion that Edward's death was imminent.

Alternatively, Harold may have journeyed to Normandy to cement a marriage alliance, perhaps that of Harold's sister, Ælfgyva, to a Norman, possibly William's eldest son Robert, or even that of Harold himself to William's daughter Agatha. If this was the case, nothing came of it. According to Eadmer, Harold may have been hoping to secure the release of hostages given in 1051, and was subsequently tricked by William. Further, but less likely, Harold may have been on a fishing trip and thrown disastrously off course, as related by William of Malmesbury!

Whatever the reason for his voyage, Harold in fact landed in Ponthieu, seemingly wrecked by bad weather. Immediately, Harold and his companions were apprehended by Count Guy of Ponthieu and imprisoned at Beaurain, probably in hope that a ransom would be paid for the English earl. On hearing this, William sent messages to Guy and ordered his release; Guy handed over Harold to William at Eu. Harold was next taken to Rouen, as William's guest, and then on to Bonneville-sur-Touques, where, according to William of Poitiers, he swore an oath to assist William's succession to the English throne and promised to place Dover and other fortified places at William's disposal.

In 1064 or 1065, William took Harold on an expedition into Brittany; this took the form of a raid against Duke Conan II of Brittany (r.1056-66) in support of the rebel Rhiwallon of Dol. William's force crossed the Breton border at the estuary of the River Couesnon, where Harold rescued Normans caught in the quicksands. Thereafter the Normans rode to Dol to raise Conan's siege of Rhiwallon's castle there. However, Conan managed to retreat to Rennes. Instead of following Conan deep into Breton territory, William returned home. Interestingly, the Bayeux Tapestry seems to show that William passed Rennes and attacked Dinan, where Conan submitted, but none of this is supported by William of Poitiers. Following William's withdrawal, Conan joined forces with Count Geoffrey of Anjou and threatened Normandy itself, but this came to nothing.

Upon returning to Normandy, William seems to have revealed his aspirations concerning the English throne and may have promised to uphold Harold's position in England, were the Norman duke to become king. Harold seems to have accepted these terms under oath, which the Bayeux Tapestry places at Bayeux (though Orderic Vitalis suggested it happened at Rouen). William seems to have retained Harold's brother, Wulfnoth, as a hostage, who was never to be freed. Thereupon, Harold was released with elaborate gifts, accompanied by his nephew, Hakon.

It is inconceivable that Harold did not discuss the implications of his trip to Normandy with King Edward before he left England. However, had Edward intended to bequeath William the kingdom in 1064, it seems likely that he would have handed over more (and higher status) hostages. He also could have ensured key places in England were given over to William, and possibly crowned William his successor in some ceremony before his death. It is of course possible (though unlikely) that Harold's visit was entirely unconnected with the succession.

About this time, Edward began building Westminster Abbey, England's first Romanesque cathedral, which was dedicated on 28 December 1065. Edith began to rebuild the nunnery at Wilton, where wooden buildings were rebuilt in stone.

REBELLION IN NORTHUMBRIA

In autumn 1065, King Edward was hunting with Earl Tostig in Wiltshire when rebellion broke out in Northumbria. Tostig's rule in the northern earldom had started well. He made a wise choice appointing Copsi, who held lands in North Yorkshire and Lincolnshire, as his deputy and advisor. Tostig and his wife, Judith, also lavished veneration and gifts on St Cuthbert's Church in Durham, and in 1056, Tostig installed Æthelwine as Bishop of Durham. He also maintained a close relationship with King Malcolm of Scotland and, in 1059, escorted him to make formal submission to Edward.

Discontentment with Tostig's rule started in about 1063. About this time, Tostig had Gamel son of Orm and Ulf son of Dolfin, members of the highest Northumbrian aristocracy and descendants of Earl Waltheof, murdered in York whilst under safe conduct. Then on 28 December 1064, Gospatric, son of Uhtred, was slain on the order of Queen Edith while attending Edward's Christmas court, reportedly as a result of a dispute between Gospatric and Tostig. Hence, Tostig was accused of using the law and his power to remove local rivals. Tostig also seems to have furthered the ambitions of his favourites, including perhaps Gospatric, son of Maldred, a grandson of King Æthelred and a cousin of King Malcolm. However, besides these murders, the leaders of the rebellion (including Gamelbearn, Dunstan son of Æthelnoth and Gluniarn, son of Heardwulf) were concerned that Tostig had 'unjustly levied' taxes 'on the whole of Northumbria' and that he had 'repressed [the Northumbrians] with the heavy yolk of his rule'. Perhaps Tostig had attempted to impose the same tax levels on Northumbria that were levied in the rest of England. It is also possible that he was dispensing arbitrary justice, including killings and forfeitures, to enforce the collection of taxation.

On 3 October 1065, the rebels marched on York and occupied the city. They killed many of Tostig's officials and supporters, including his housecarls Amund and Ravenswart, and plundered his armoury and treasury. They then sent for Morcar and recognised him as their earl. Under Morcar's leadership they marched south via Lincoln and Nottingham (or Derby) killing Tostig's men and plundering his lands in Nottinghamshire, Lincolnshire and Northamptonshire. At Northampton, they were joined by a force led by Earl Edwin and Welsh allies.

On news of the rebellion, Edward summoned his council at Britford, near Wilton. It was agreed that Harold should meet the rebels at Northampton, which he did. The rebels made it clear that they would not accept Tostig as their earl. Harold left for Oxford, where the king's council was to meet on 28 October 1065. Here Harold advised Edward not to take up arms against the rebels but instead to meet their demands. The king refused and ordered that the rebellion be suppressed. Tostig accused Harold of instigating the rebellion, which Harold repudiated by swearing an oath. Finally, Edward reluctantly agreed to the terms of the rebels. Harold returned to Northampton to tell the rebels that Tostig was deposed and replaced by Morcar, that they were pardoned, and that the laws of Cnut (with more favourable taxes) were renewed. Tostig was outlawed shortly after and he left England with his family for St Omer to take refuge with his brother-in-law, Count Baldwin V of Flanders. Tostig never forgave his brother for what he saw as an act of treachery.

EDWARD'S DEATH

Soon after the Northumbrian rebellion, Edward suffered the first of a series of strokes, and was gravely ill for most of November and December. At this time, Harold probably took over more control governing the kingdom; Edgar Ætheling was probably too young and inexperienced to undertake this role. Harold might have also considered how he fitted into the future government of the country once Edward died. He may have lobbied support for his plans with the other major earls and the leading ecclesiastics; his marriage to Ealdgyth, the sister of Earls Edwin and Morcar, and the widow of Gruffydd ap Llywelyn, sometime between 5 August 1063 and 14 October 1066, may have been significant in this respect.

That Christmas, the royal court assembled at Westminster. On Christmas Eve, Edward suffered another stroke, but recovered sufficiently to attend the service in the church and the banquet that followed. However, on Boxing Day he had to retire to his chamber. On 28 December, the festival of Holy Innocents, the new abbey church at Westminster was consecrated, but the king was absent. Edward finally sank into a coma. Nearing the end of his life, he was so restless that his courtiers tried to rouse him, and were successful. At this time, Edward was joined by Queen Edith, Earl Harold, Robert fitz Wimarch and Archbishop Stigand. When Edward recovered consciousness, he ordered his household to assemble and recounted a vision which prophesised that England would fall into the hands of its enemies because the highest echelons were the servants of the Devil, not God. This concerned all those present, apart from Stigand who said the prophecy was no more than delirious raving. After this, Edward made his last will and testament. He told those gathered not to weep but pray for his soul. He asked God to repay Edith for her love and dutiful service, and then, offering his hand to Harold he said 'I commend this woman and all the kingdom to your protection'. Edward then asked that Harold should keep in service all his foreign vassals and servants, and offer safe protection for those that wished to return home. Finally, he gave instructions on his burial. The last rites were administered and the king passed away on 4 or 5 January. If there was a plan to make Harold king, it was a conspiracy in which all who witnessed Edward's death were complicit. Even William of Poitiers recognises that Edward bequeathed Harold the crown on his deathbed.

Edward was buried in Westminster Abbey on 6 January 1066. A month of prayers for the dead was ordered and large sums of money were given to the poor. On the same day, Harold was crowned king (*10*), probably also at Westminster. While Norman sources, and the Bayeux Tapestry, suggest Harold was consecrated by Archbishop Stigand of Canterbury, the English sources say this was done by Archbishop Ealdred of York.

It is possible that soon after becoming king, Harold received messengers from Duke William, demanding that the throne be surrendered to him and reminding him of the oath he had sworn. Harold may have also made plans to protect his kingdom from attack. It seems the northern earls expressed concerns upon Harold's coronation, so the new king journeyed north with a small party, including Bishop Wulfstan of Worcester, to reassure them and received their allegiance. At this time, Harold may have married Ealdgyth.

Harold made several appointments in his kingdom. On 22 January 1066, Abbot Ordric of Abingdon died and Ealdred the provost was appointed to replace him. Around 19 August 1066, Abbot Wulfric of Ely died and was succeeded by Thurstan, also upon Harold's nomination. Between October 1065 and spring 1067, Waltheof, son of Siward, was appointed to an earldom in part of the East Midlands, possibly by Harold.

Harold was in Westminster for Easter. Soon after, on 24 April 1066, a comet, known to us as Haley's Comet, was seen in the sky and was interpreted as an omen. It remained in the sky for a whole week.

In May 1066, Tostig returned to England with a large Flemish fleet provided by Baldwin V of Flanders. He landed on the Isle of Wight and extracted money and provisions from the local inhabitants. He then raided along the south coast until he reached Sandwich, where he recruited sailors. Harold ordered both naval and land forces to deal with the

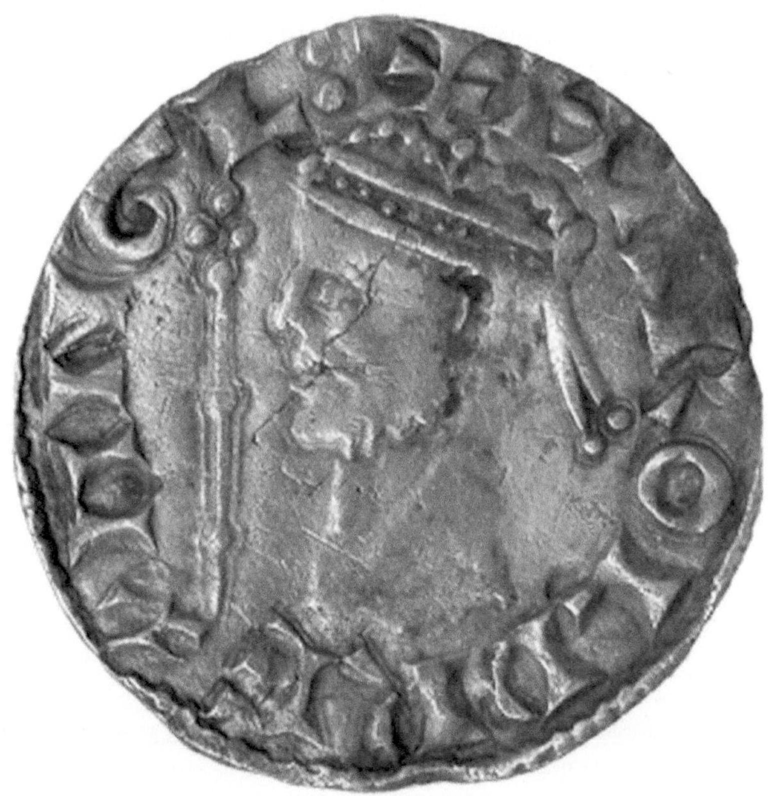

10 Silver penny of King Harold II. *Courtesy of the Portable Antiquities Scheme*

incursion, and Tostig swiftly retreated. Harold also mustered a large fleet to defend the south coast from attack or invasion from Duke William; this fleet was probably assembled in London before proceeding to Sandwich. He also put together a large land army which was stationed along the Channel coast.

Tostig, meanwhile, sailed north, attempting to entice his brother Gyrth to join him, which failed. Tostig then raided near the mouth of the River Burnham in Norfolk. Moving north, he entered the Humber estuary with 60 ships, ravaged Lincolnshire and killed many men. Consequently, Earls Edwin and Morcar led a land force into Lincolnshire and expelled Tostig. Facing mass desertion, Tostig fled to King Malcolm of Scotland with only 12 ships and stayed there all summer.

Harold had now based his fleet, probably commanded by Eadric the Steersman and organised by Abbot Ælfwold of St Benet of Holme, on the Isle of Wight to counter the threat of Duke William of Normandy. He appropriated the estate of Steyning in Sussex from Fecamp Abbey, fearing its possible strategic importance to the Normans. Harold also sent spies to Normandy to learn of William's preparations.

Initially, William had difficulties persuading his nobles to participate in an audacious plan to invade England. Nevertheless, William was able to allay these concerns, probably promising his nobles great wealth in England, and he started constructing a fleet and assembling an army. William held council with the Norman magnates throughout 1066 and entertained great lords from other parts of France whom he hoped would support his mission.

William was fortunate that the political situation at the time was in his favour. King Philip of France (r.1060-1108) was a minor under the tutelage of Baldwin V of Flanders. The other principalities of Northern France were either vassal states of William or too embroiled in their own internal troubles to jeopardise the security of Normandy. The duke also sought the blessing of Pope Alexander II (r.1061-73) for the invasion (though it seems not all in Rome supported this) and was presented with the papal banner; the Pope may have hoped that William would bring about a reform of the English Church. Furthermore, William also made treaties with Kings Henry IV of Germany and Svein Estrithson of Denmark. In addition, he prepared for the provision of government whilst he was away and in case the endeavour failed; Matilda was named as regent in Normandy and his son Robert was accepted as his father's heir in both Normandy and Maine.

Sometime after 18 June 1066 (following the dedication of Matilda's abbey of La Trinité, Caen), William's fleet was in the estuary of the River Dives and nearby harbours, and was probably ready to set sail in July, subject to favourable weather conditions. In the event the weather did not cooperate, and the fleet was forced to harbour for a month. Subsequently, the Norman fleet moved from Dives to St Valéry-sur-Somme in Ponthieu at some point between mid-July and 27 September 1066, most probably in late August or early September. During this short voyage, some of the fleet was lost; perhaps it was actually on its way across the Channel when it left Dives, but was forced into St Valéry by bad weather. William ordered news of these deaths to be kept secret so as not to lower morale.

Meanwhile, Harold maintained his watch on the other side of the Channel. All summer he waited, but the expected invasion never arrived. It seemed as though William's opportunity to invade had passed, as crossing the Channel later in the year would be dangerous. On 8 September, Harold disbanded his fleet, which returned to London; all their provisions had been spent and Harold could not keep the fleet any longer. By 20 September, Harold was back in London for the feast of the True Cross.

However, England was not safe, this time the threat came from the north, from King Harald Hardrada of Norway (r.1047-66). Harald, together with his uncle, Magnus Olafson, had sought exile at the court of Prince Iaroslav of Novgorod (r.1054-69), following the conquest of Norway by King Cnut, ruler of Denmark and England in 1030. Upon Cnut's death, and that of his son, King Svein of Norway (r.1030-35), in 1035, Magnus claimed Norway. Harald, for his part, went on to serve with the Varangian guards of the Byzantine Emperors (between 1034 and 1043), and campaign in Sicily and Bulgaria. He gained great wealth marrying Elizabeth, daughter of Prince Iaroslav, in about 1044. In 1047 he succeeded the kingdom of Norway upon the death of Magnus and also attempted to claim Denmark, which Magnus had ruled (r.1042-7), but which had been reoccupied by Svein Estrithson. Thus began a sixteen-year struggle between the two kings, which ended with a truce in 1064. This allowed Harald to focus his energies elsewhere.

In summer 1066, Tostig was still at the court of King Malcolm of Scotland. From here he seems to have contacted Harald Hardrada and the two men planned to invade England. In late autumn 1066, Harald summoned a large army and crossed the North Sea with 300 ships.

The Norwegian fleet sailed down the east coast of Scotland and was joined by Tostig en route south, perhaps at the mouth of the Tyne. The two allies sailed down the coast and then up the Rivers Humber and Ouse, before landing at Riccall in Yorkshire. Harald led his army towards York. Just south of the city, at Fulford, the Norwegians encountered opposition from Earls Edwin and Morcar, and perhaps also Earl Waltheof.

Battle was joined by the opposing forces on Wednesday 20 September 1066, and was a bloody affair. In the event, English losses were high, many were slain, or drowned in the nearby marshes, and Edwin and Morcar fled. As a result, the victorious Norwegians entered York, were given hostages and provided with provisions.

Upon hearing of the invasion in the north, Harold amassed a 'very great' army. Men from all over the kingdom agreed to fight for Harold, though it is most likely that the majority came from the *fyrd* (men of the local shires) supported by the housecarls, or *huscarls*, the king's professional army. Most of Harold's force, certainly the housecarls, were mounted and had reached Tadcaster, south of York, by 24 September. On the way, Harold would have received news of the defeat of the army of Earls Edwin and Morcar at Fulford and would have known that he had to deal with Harald of Norway himself. At Tadcaster, Harold learnt that the Norwegian army was 8 miles east of York at Stamford Bridge, some 13 miles from their ships at Riccall; the Norwegians probably gathered at Stamford Bridge to be able to collect hostages and live off Harold's estate at Catton.

Harold attempted to surprise the Norwegians and on Monday 25 September moved north to York. The Norwegian army was at least 4000 men strong; Harold probably had more or less the same number of men at his disposal. Encamped in a river valley, the Norwegians were not aware of Harold's army until it was upon them. Then they retreated across the River Derwent. Harald rallied his troops, to the east of the river, and opposed the English army in close combat. The ensuing battle seems to have been long and bloody, but late in the day King Harald of Norway and Tostig Godwinson were killed, causing the Norwegians to flee to their ships. The English army pursued them, reducing their number, so that in the end only 24 ships (carrying perhaps 500 to 1000 men) were needed to take the remnants of the army back to Norway. These men and their surviving leaders, Olaf son of Harald Hardrada and Earl Paul of Orkney, were saved by Harold upon an understanding that they would never again conspire against him or threaten the English kingdom. Harold's achievement was total victory over one of the most renowned and feared warriors of the day, and a strong deterrent to any other would-be invaders.

Duke William had not disbanded his fleet, now trapped at St Valéry by bad weather. However, on 27 September 1066, the winds changed direction and William crossed the Channel overnight, landing at Pevensey on 28 September, unopposed. A few of William's ships became detached from the main fleet and landed near Romney, Kent. At Pevensey, William constructed a castle, before consolidating his position at Hastings, where he built another castle. From here, his forces raided the countryside for provisions, which also enticed Harold south. Upon learning of Harold's victory over Harald Hardrada, William seems to have been cautious, preferring to consolidate a defensive position close to the sea and his ships rather than lay siege to a major town, such as Canterbury or London. No doubt William wanted to keep his options open and prevent his army from being separated.

Harold was possibly in York when he received news of the Norman invasion. Immediately, he started to assemble an army and marched south, probably drawing recruits as he journeyed; he reached London by about 8 October 1066. Here he rested his troops and allowed reinforcements to join him. He then ordered his army, which lacked Earls Edwin and Morcar, who may have been injured, south into Sussex.

Harold's army met at a local landmark known as the 'hoary apple tree'. Tradition has it that Harold may have intended to surprise the Norman army, although since he seems to have sent a messenger to William to advise him to retreat this may not have been the case. Harold interposed his army between the Normans and the open country beyond the peninsula on which Hastings stood; from here he could build his own army and watch the Normans.

At dawn on 14 October, the Normans advanced upon the English. Harold assembled his army, about 7000 men, on higher ground north of Hastings, at a place now known as Battle. Here, on foot, they formed a shield-wall. The Normans were disadvantaged by fighting uphill over heavy ground, facing an enemy force which could not be easily outflanked. This said, Harold's army was compacted and had little room to manoeuvre. The Norman army was of similar strength as Harold's, but consisted of infantry, cavalry and archers.

Battle began at about 9am. The Normans launched missiles at the English, followed by an infantry attack, which was repelled by English missiles. Next, the Norman cavalry advanced, but were again held off by the English. Soon, Breton troops on the left flank of the Norman army panicked and began to retreat. This became widespread upon news that Duke William may have been killed. The English began to move from their defensive position in the hope of routing the enemy. However, the Norman duke was not dead, and instead was able to rally his troops to attack the English and overwhelm those that pursued them.

By midday, both sides had re-formed. Again, the Normans attacked and the opposing forces fought at close quarters. William then seems to have ordered a series of feigned retreats in the hope of drawing the English from their positions. This had some success, but not enough for victory. As the sky darkened, it became vital for William that battle should be won; he, unlike Harold, could not hope for reinforcements. William now seems to have ordered his whole army to attack, infantry, cavalry and archers. Under this hail of arrows, Harold, by chance rather than judgement, was killed, perhaps being pierced though the eye or forehead. The news of Harold's death caused disarray amongst the English, opening opportunities for the Normans to break though their lines of defence. At this point, under the cover of dusk, many of the English fled the battlefield.

Harold lay dead, together with his brothers Leofwine and Gyrth and many of the English nobles. Harold's body was identified by his mistress, Edith Swan neck, by marks only known to her, and brought to William's camp. Gyrtha, Harold's mother, offered William the weight of his body in gold if she could have it to give her son a Christian burial, but he refused her request. Instead, Harold was buried in an unmarked grave on the Sussex coast, though later tradition says his body was removed and reburied at his foundation, Waltham Abbey. Other traditions say that Harold was buried at Bosham, or even he survived the battle with terrible injuries and lived as a hermit. What is certain is that William left the bodies of the fallen English unburied on the battlefield.

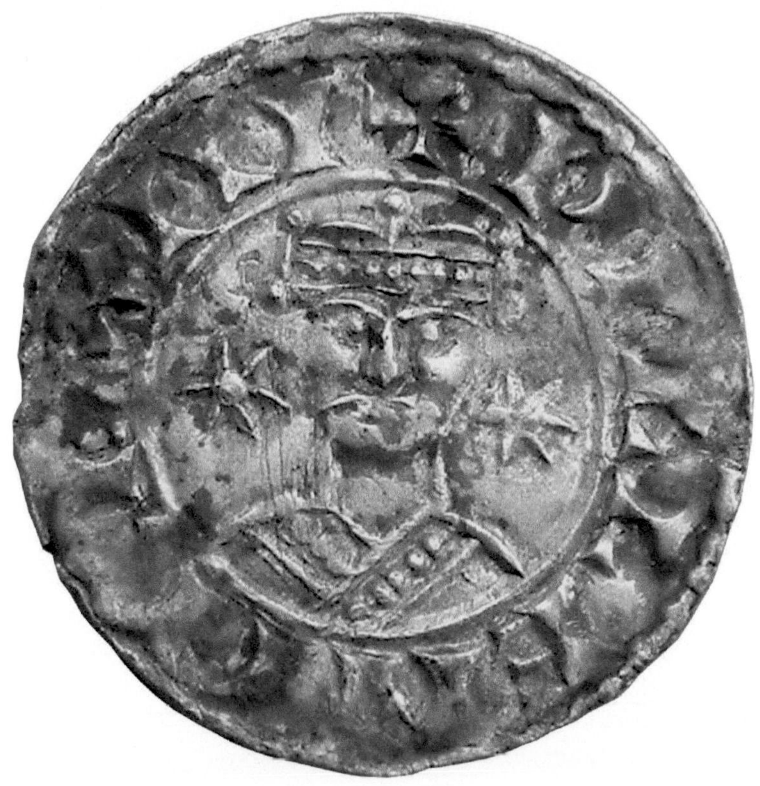

11 Silver penny of King William I 'the Conqueror'. *Courtesy of the Portable Antiquities Scheme*

Following the battle, the Norman army encamped at Hastings for about a week, after which it rampaged through Kent, via Romney, Dover and Canterbury. In London, Archbishops Stigand of Canterbury and Ealdred of York, Earls Edwin and Morcar, and the men of London proclaimed Edgar Ætheling, aged about 14, their king. As William moved towards Southwark, Edgar's men held the bridge across the Thames, so the Normans were forced to march west, through Surrey, Hampshire and Berkshire, before crossing the Thames at Wallingford. A detachment of William's army was sent to Winchester, where Queen Edith surrendered herself and the royal treasure. Soon after, Earls Edwin and Morcar returned to their earldoms, following their sister, Harold's queen, Ealdgyth. Archbishop Stigand surrendered to William at Wallingford, and subsequently the other English leaders did so at Berkhampstead. Finally, William entered London.

On Christmas Day 1066, William was crowned king by Archbishop Ealdred of York. During the ceremony, Bishop Geoffrey of Coutances sought the assent of the Normans present. Their loud shouts terrified the guards outside the church who, fearing an English uprising, set fire to houses in the vicinity. So began the reign of King William I of England (*11*).

CHAPTER 4

THE HISTORY OF THE TAPESTRY

Though incomplete, and in part restored, the Bayeux Tapestry is a remarkable survival of medieval art. Behind glass, in environmental conditions suited to its long-term preservation, it is easy to imagine that the Tapestry, impressive and precious, has always had its guardians. However, history is turbulent, and that of the Tapestry is no exception. Ideology and fortunes change, impacting not only on the lives of human beings, but also their material culture. In part, it is good fortune that the Tapestry survives, and in such good condition.

Our current understanding of the Tapestry's history is indebted to the research of Simone Bertrand (1957), Shirley Ann Brown (1988), Sylvette Lemagnen (2004) and Carola Hicks (2006).

EARLY YEARS

Nothing certain is known about the history of the Bayeux Tapestry until the late fifteenth century. However, if it was commissioned by Bishop of Odo of Bayeux, perhaps in about 1070, it is likely that it was brought to its current location at Bayeux sometime before the Bishop's death in 1097, and probably before he was imprisoned by King William I the Conqueror in 1082. Until recently, most scholars thought it likely that Odo commissioned the Tapestry for his cathedral, dedicated in 1077.

In a poem of 1100, Abbot Baudri of Bourgeuil refers to a wall hanging that decorated the bed chamber of Adela, Countess of Blois, youngest daughter of William I. Whilst this is not the Bayeux Tapestry, as the poem describes a hanging woven from silk and gold threads embellished with jewels and gems, it is possible that Baudri knew of the Bayeux Tapestry or had even seen it; indeed some scholars think that Baudri's poem was inspired after seeing the Tapestry.

Likewise, an inventory of the treasures held by the Dukes of Burgundy at Dijon, dated to 1420, mentions 'a large good quality tapestry, without gold, the history of Duke William of Normandy, how he conquered England'. If the Bayeux Tapestry had been in Bayeux in the early years, then it is plausible (though perhaps unlikely) that it may have been taken to Dijon by Duke Philip II the Bold of Burgundy (r.1363-1404). If this is believed, then the Tapestry was certainly back in Bayeux by the late fifteenth century.

FIFTEENTH CENTURY

The first clear reference to the Bayeux Tapestry is an inventory of the 'Treasures of the Church of Notre-Dame of Bayeux', dated 1476, which notes that among the textiles kept in the vestry of the church was 'a very long and very narrow strip of linen, embroidered with figures and inscriptions representing the Conquest of England, which is hung round the nave of the church on the Feast of Relics and throughout the Octave'. It seems likely that this tradition of displaying the Tapestry in the cathedral was an old one.

If the Tapestry had been in Bayeux since the eleventh century then it was fortunate to have survived. In 1106, King Henry I of England (r.1100-35) invaded Normandy, burning Bayeux to the ground. The cathedral also suffered damage in a fire of 1159. At this time, the Tapestry may have been stored in a blocked up crypt, opened in 1412. Here, it would also have been safe when Bayeux was (again) devastated by fire in 1335, upon the orders of King Edward III of England (r.1327-77).

SIXTEENTH CENTURY

On 10 May 1562, French Calvinists ransacked Catholic buildings, including the cathedral at Bayeux. Firing guns, they maimed and killed the clergy, smashed glass windows, stole relics and treasures, and desecrated ancient tombs. Amongst the items lost were gold and silver chalices and candelabras presented by Bishop Odo to the cathedral, reliquary caskets and embroidered garments. Yet the Tapestry, still presumably at Bayeux, survived.

SEVENTEENTH CENTURY

Sometime in the 1690s, Nicolas Joseph Foucault, regional governor of Normandy and an antiquarian, elected *savant* of the *Académie des inscriptions et belles-lettres* (by King Louis XIV of France, r.1643-1715), commissioned a drawing of part of the Bayeux Tapestry (Scenes 1 to 11) after viewing it first hand.

EIGHTEENTH CENTURY

Upon his death in 1721, Foucault's papers and various antiquities were left to the *Académie des inscriptions et belles-lettres*. Here they were sorted by Claude Gros de Boze, Secretary to the *Académie*, who discovered Foucault's coloured drawing. De Boze did not know what the illustration showed, but sought the expertise of Antoine Lancelot, another savant of the *Académie*, who recognised it as showing events leading up to the Norman Conquest of England.

On 21 July 1724, Lancelot delivered a paper (published in 1729) to the *Académie des inscriptions et belles-lettres* at which he also exhibited Foucault's drawing. At this time, he still did not know what artefact the illustration showed, stating that 'in spite of all my endeavours, I have, up to the present, been unable to discover whether this sketch represents a bas-relief or a sculpture round the choir of a church, or a tomb; whether it is a fresco, a painting on the glass of several windows, or possibly, a tapestry'. He thought the artefact had come from the Cathedral of St Étienne, Caen, and enquired with the authorities there, to no avail.

Bernard de Montfaucon, a Benedictine cleric and a well-known scholar of the time, was amongst those who heard Lancelot's lecture. He was researching the history of the medieval kings of France, and was keen to learn more about the artefact Foucault had drawn, as it seemed to be a potentially important source for the early history of the French monarchy. Through his contacts, he wrote to all the Benedictine houses in France, including (in September 1728) Romaine la Londe, Prior of St Étienne, Caen. La Londe had initially told Lancelot he knew nothing of the artefact illustrated in the drawing, but agreed to make further enquiries. He discussed Montfaucon's request with Nicolas Flays, who had been at St Étienne for nearly 30 years. Flays remembered seeing something similar in Bayeux Cathedral, so La Londe forwarded Montfaucon's letter to Mathurin Larcher, Prior of St Vigor, Bayeux. Larcher approached the Cathedral Chapter and one of the canons confirmed that they hung tapestries such as this around the nave 'from the feast of St Jean to the end of July... to air them in nice weather' (letter from the Cathedral Chapter to Larcher); local tradition attributed the work to Queen Matilda. Larcher reported what he had learnt to La Londe, who then realised he had once seen the Bayeux hanging himself, but had not associated it with Montfaucon's investigations! By October 1728, this news had reached Montfaucon, and in early 1729 Larcher agreed to copy the Tapestry's inscriptions on his behalf.

In July 1729, Montfaucon published the first part of the Tapestry, following Foucault's drawing, in his first volume of the *Monuments de la Monarchie Française*. In the meantime, Montfaucon commissioned Antoine Benoît to draw the remainder of the Tapestry, which appeared as engravings in the second volume of *Monuments de la Monarchie Française* in 1730; in 1750 *Monuments* was first published in English.

At about this time, a linen backing cloth was added to the Tapestry and, based on a list of inscriptions compiled by the bishop's secretary, its 58 scenes numbered in green ink; this lining was replaced in the nineteenth century.

William Stukeley, Secretary of the Society of Antiquaries of London, was the first Englishman known to have an interest in the Bayeux Tapestry, and published a note on it in *Palaeographia Britannica* (1743). Stukeley, though believing that the Tapestry dated to the late twelfth century, declared it 'indubitably the noblest monument of English antiquity abroad'. The first Englishman to actually see the Tapestry, however, was Andrew Ducarel, who in 1752 was studying historical records in Normandy.

During the French Revolution, the Bayeux Tapestry was almost destroyed. On 2 November 1789, the National Assembly nationalised all Church property, and from

20 March 1790 suppressed the abbeys. As a result, most ecclesiastical treasures became the responsibility of the new Monuments Commission and were taken to national or local depots. Many treasures, including those in Bayeux Cathedral, were lost or destroyed.

In 1792, the National Assembly issued a general call to arms to defend France from an anticipated British invasion. In Bayeux, volunteers of the sixth Calvados Battalion requisitioned wagons to carry equipment to their camp at Meaux, and the Municipal Council agreed they could use the Tapestry to cover the wagons. Thankfully, Lambert Léonard-Leforestier, a local administrator and lawyer, was able to convince the troops to use sacking instead and had the Tapestry moved to his office for safekeeping.

Again, the Bayeux Tapestry was almost destroyed. On 23 February 1794, plans were made to cut up the Tapestry to decorate a carnival float carrying the Genius of the Arts for a procession around Bayeux. This time, the Commission for the Arts, a new organisation set up by the National Convention in all regions of France to preserve of all works of art, intervened. On 27 April 1794, the Bayeux commissioners wrote to the Mayor informing him of their concerns regarding the safety of the Tapestry, that it was 'public property' and requesting that they should be informed 'of the place at which the Tapestry is stored so that we may effect its removal to one of the depots in this district'. Consequently, on 18 August 1794, the Tapestry was taken to 'Depot B'. Here it was spread out and dusted. Its condition was compared with the description and drawings published by Montfaucon and listed in an inventory of antiquities prepared for the Commission of the Arts in Paris.

NINETEENTH CENTURY

The start of the Napoleonic Wars saw the Tapestry leave Bayeux for the first time in its recorded history. In May 1803, Britain blockaded French ports and reoccupied ceded territories in the West Indies in response to French plans to reoccupy Egypt. At about this time, the Tapestry was transferred to 'Depot C'. By November, Napoleon Bonaparte (r.1799-15) had orchestrated a plan to invade England, and sought the help of the Bayeux Tapestry to enthuse the public. On 19 November 1803, Charles Caffarelli, Prefect of Calvados, wrote to the Commission for the Arts (Bayeux District), outlining plans for the Tapestry to be exhibited in the Musée Napoléon in Paris and requested that the hanging should be delivered to Dominique Vivant Denon, Director of the museum. The authorities in Bayeux were reluctant to see the Tapestry leave, but relented.

From 29 November, the Tapestry was displayed in the Galerie d'Apollon at the Musée Napoléon, where it captured the imagination of Parisians; it even inspired a play. On 5 December 1803, Napoleon himself visited the exhibition and was said to have been particularly interested in the scene where Harold is told of the comet (Scene 33). Following the exhibition, the Tapestry was returned to Bayeux on 18 February 1804.

At a meeting of Bayeux's Municipal Council, on 13 March 1804, it was agreed that the Tapestry should be consigned to the secondary school library in Bayeux, under the joint supervision of the Director of Education and the Mayor of Bayeux. It was also agreed that, in accordance with custom, the Tapestry should be exhibited in the nave of Bayeux Cathedral during the Octave of Relics, but neither resolution was put into effect. Instead, the Mayor ordered that the Tapestry should be taken to Bayeux Town Hall, where it was made available for public viewing in September and otherwise only by appointment.

By 1805, Noël Conseil, Mayor of Bayeux, had the Tapestry kept on two cylinders, so that each portion of it could be examined in turn. This failed to impress Hudson Gurney, Fellow of the Society of Antiquaries of London, who likened this contraption to something like 'which lets down buckets into a well'. On 2 July 1816, Gurney delivered a paper about the Tapestry to the Society of Antiquaries (published the following year in *Archaeologia*) which, four days later, inspired the Council of the Society to direct Charles Stothard, the Society's historical draughtsman, to 'make drawings of the Bayeux Tapestry during the summer… for the use of the Society'.

In autumn 1816, Stothard arrived in Bayeux to start work on drawing the Tapestry. It was clear to him that the Bayeux Tapestry had been greatly damaged since 1730, when it had been illustrated by Montfaucon. Montfaucon's drawings and the fabric of the Tapestry itself, especially the needle holes, helped Stothard create his colour facsimile. By February 1817, he had completed his first set of drawings, and in August returned to Bayeux to colour them. About this time, Stothard removed two small pieces of the Tapestry and also made several plaster casts; these casts he painted to mimic the actual colours of the Tapestry (*12*). After Stothard's death, the antiquarian Francis Douce acquired the casts (which are now in the collections of the British Museum and Society of Antiquaries of London) and one of the fragments of the Tapestry (*colour plate 27*). Upon Douce's death, these were left to Dr Samuel Meyrick, who exhibited them in his home at Goodrich Court in Hereford.

By February 1818, the first part of Stothard's facsimile of the Tapestry was on display at Somerset House, the headquarters of the Society of Antiquaries of London. On 1 July 1818, the Society of Antiquaries requested that Stothard return to Bayeux that summer to complete his drawings of the Tapestry, which he did, this time accompanied by his wife, Eliza; the couple were on honeymoon.

In March 1819, Stothard completed his drawings, and was subsequently asked by the Society of Antiquaries to oversee the engraving process by Thomas Cooper on behalf of James Basire; the facsimile was to be reduced by one third and hand-coloured by Mr Martin (*5*). Early in 1821, the first sets of hand-coloured engravings were ready, only a few months before Stothard was tragically killed (falling from a ladder) whilst drawing effigies at St Andrew's Church at Beer Ferrers in Devon, in April 1821.

By 1838, a new permanent exhibition gallery for the Bayeux Tapestry was under construction in the Municipal Library. Before the Tapestry was displayed, Edouard Lambert, Keeper of the Tapestry, organised some repairs to it, including a replacement of the old lining. In 1842, the new gallery opened and here the Tapestry was shown at eye level behind glass. However, not all visitors to the new exhibition were impressed; in summer 1867, Charles Dickens complained that the exhibition was poorly advertised.

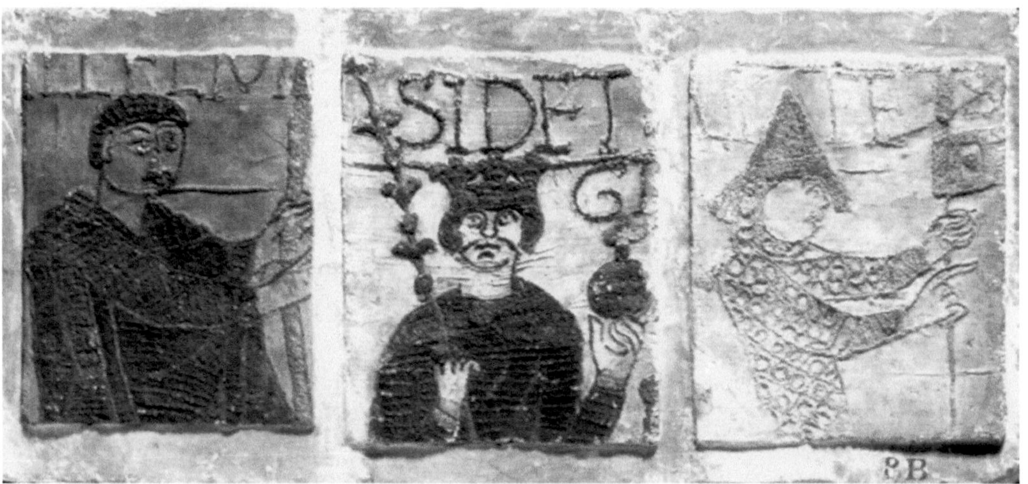

12 Charles Stothard's plaster casts from the Bayeux Tapestry. © *Trustees of the British Museum, London*

In 1853, the French Government awarded a conservation grant of 5000 francs. This resulted in further additions to the fabric and the use of chemically dyed machine-spun wools that, even to this day, are relatively easy to tell from the originals.

By the mid 1860s, the small fragment cut from the Tapestry by Charles Stothard in about 1817, as well as a plaster cast of part of the Tapestry showing Harold at his coronation, were on display in South Kensington Museum (later to become the Victoria and Albert Museum); the museum had acquired the fragment from the estate of John Bowyer Nicholls in 1864.

The Bayeux Tapestry was again removed from display during the Franco-Prussian war (1870-1), following the invasion of France by German troops on 4 August 1870. It seems the Bayeux authorities were so surprised by the invasion that the glass encasing the Tapestry was broken in the rush to remove the precious textile. The Tapestry was then tightly rolled up and packed into a cylindrical-shaped zinc case, with the lid soldered down, and housed in an unknown place of safety. A few weeks later, it was returned to the Municipal Library and put back on display.

Following advances in photography, the South Kensington Museum approached the municipal authorities in Bayeux to produce a photographic facsimile of the Tapestry. Initially, Bayeux refused, fearing the risk of damage to the embroidery. However, in August 1872, Henry Cole, Director of the South Kensington Museum, wrote to the Mayor of Bayeux offering the fragment of the Tapestry removed by Stothard in the hope they would reconsider the proposed photographic project. The bribe worked. In September 1872, the fragment was presented to the Tapestry's curator. It was never sewn back on to the Tapestry, as the section had been restored, but instead exhibited in a separate case. Between September and December 1872, the Tapestry was photographed in its case (though the glass was removed). Prints, hand-coloured by Walter Wilson, were produced, and mounted on linen for display in the museum.

TWENTIETH CENTURY

In 1913, the Bayeux Tapestry was transferred to the first floor of the Hôtel du Doyen, formerly the Old Episcopal Palace. It was here, in 1938, that Ernest Dodeman, Mayor of Bayeux, commissioned Monsieur Hallier, the municipal architect, to design a bombproof concrete shelter for the Tapestry in the corner of one of the vaulted cellars. In time of danger the Tapestry was to be wound around a wooden spool and then stored in a locked zinc-lined case padded with glass wool; another spool would be used to unwind the Tapestry onto a trestle table so that its condition could be regularly checked. It was not long before the shelter was needed. On 1 September 1939, following the German and Russian invasion of Poland, the Tapestry was taken off display, rolled onto its spool, sprinkled with moth-preventing naphthalene and crushed peppercorns, wrapped in two sheets and stored in its case in the shelter. Here, the Tapestry was cared for by René Falue, in accordance with guidance from Monsieur Sauvage, Head Archivist and Curator for Calvados. By June 1940, Normandy was under German occupation and administered under military command. Locally, Bayeux was run by Major Hoffmann, though Dodeman remained as mayor.

The first record of German interest in the Bayeux Tapestry was on 22 September 1940, when a member of the local *Nazi Propagandastaffel* (Propaganda Squadron) established by Joseph Goebbels, was granted permission to see it. Several more times the Tapestry was inspected and photographed by members of the occupying forces.

Before the war, Heinrich Himmler, the head of the SS and Gestapo, had established the *Ahnenerbe* (Ancestral Heritage), a research group dedicated to the study of German culture and the racial supremacy of Germans. Soon, the Tapestry became the subject of their work. The *Ahnenerbe* worked alongside (and cooperated with) both the *Deutsches Kunsthistorisches Forschungs Institut* (German Art Historical Research Institute) in Paris, which had an excellent reputation, and the *Einsatzstab Reichsleiter Rosenberg – ERR* (Misson-staff of Reich-leader Rosenberg) – run by Alfred Rosenberg, a proponent of Aryan superiority, that had powers to confiscate art that originated in, or had some connection with, Germany. However, the Tapestry was protected as a Historical Monument and came under the jurisdiction of the *Kunstschutz beim OKM* (the Military Commandant's Bureau for the Protection of the Fine Arts), headed by Count Franz Wolff-Metternich, whose responsibility (under the 1907 Hague Convention) was that in the event of war an invading force must protect culturally significant items in their own country. It was clear that the remit of this group conflicted with the plans of both the *Ahnenerbe* and *ERR*, but this relationship was fundamental to the complicated history of the Tapestry during the Second World War.

Amongst the first Germans to inspect the Bayeux Tapestry were members of the *Ahnenerbe*, who reported its interest to Wolfram Sievers, Head of the *Ahnenerbe*, and soon after plans were put in place to make a detailed examination and photographic record of the Tapestry. A research team, headed by Professor Herbert Jankuhn, an expert in medieval art and archaeology at Rostock University, was organised, as well as the infrastructure to support their project, including accommodation, transport and the services of a local photographer, Monsieur Le Prunier. On 4 June 1941, Jankuhn and his team left Berlin for Bayeux.

The *Kunstschutz* had been informed by the *Ahnenerbe* of their intentions to study the Tapestry, and were probably concerned about its eventual fate. As such, they colluded with Jean Virrier, Inspector-General of Historic Monuments for Calvados, to have the Tapestry moved to Château de Sourches, near Le Mans, which would function as a museum store. It was a plan that was supported by the French Ministry of Fine Arts, the Mayor, and other local experts. The *Ahnenerbe* received news of these plans and, via Major Hoffmann, informed the Mayor of Bayeux that the Tapestry was instead to be moved to the Château of Monceau in Bayeux on 10 June, so it could be studied and drawn.

The Mayor protested, saying he did not have the appropriate authority to allow the Tapestry's removal. On the evening of 9 June, German soldiers turned up at the home of René Falue, the Tapestry's custodian, informing his wife (for Monsieur Falue was out) that they were coming to remove the Tapestry at 9am the next morning. In the meantime, the Mayor attempted to frustrate plans to relocate the Tapestry without the necessary permissions.

By this time, the *Ahnenerbe* research team had arrived in Bayeux and were staying at the hotel Lion d'Or. At 11am on 10 June 1941, Jankuhn and his colleagues gathered in the basement of the Hôtel du Doyen to view the Tapestry.

Finally, on 13 June 1941, the Ministry of Fine Arts granted permission for Jankuhn's team to inspect and photograph the Tapestry immediately prior to its removal to Château Monceau, where it would be fully researched and recorded. On 17 June, a small team was dispatched to the Château Monceau to assess its suitability for the task in hand, but all agreed it would be best (and safest) to study the Tapestry at the abbey at Juaye-Mondaye; it was arranged that this would take place on 23 June.

On the eve of the Tapestry's removal to Juaye-Mondaye, the famous embroidery was displayed for elite *Wehrmacht* (army) and SS officers. The move itself was organised by the Mayor of Bayeux. The Tapestry was transported in a chest in the back of a covered truck loaned by Monsieur Mabire, a local building contractor, driven by his son Jean, and escorted by a German policeman on motorbike. The party arrived safely. At the abbey Juaye-Mondaye, the Tapestry was unfurled in the north gallery on the first floor. Here members of Jankuhn's research team worked on it every day between 23 June and 31 July from about 8.30am until 9pm.

The research team included Professor Herbert Jankuhn (Rostock University), the project director, who studied the archaeological aspects of the Tapestry; Dr Karl Schlabow (Neumunster Museum of German National Dress), who studied the Tapestry's fabric (until 18 June 1941); Herbert Jeschke, an artist from Berlin, who produced pen and watercolour illustrations of the Tapestry (until 28 July 1941); Professor Richard Hamann (History of Art Institute, Marburg) and assistants, who made a complete photographic copy of the Tapestry in colour and black and white; Rolf Alber, a photographer, who helped photograph the Tapestry (until 29 June 1941); Frau Uhland (History of Art Institute, Marburg), who helped photograph the Tapestry (between 24 and 31 July 1941); Professor Otto Vehse (Hamburg University), who studied the wider context and implications of the Tapestry; Professor Alfred Stange (Munich University), a medieval art historian, who studied the Tapestry's artistic style; Herr H. Loeb (SS military correspondent), who made two films about the Tapestry, and René Falue (custodian of the Tapestry), who also assisted the research team.

On 1 August 1941, Mabire's truck returned to collect the Bayeux Tapestry and take it back to the Hôtel du Doyen. From here, the Tapestry was to be transferred to the Château de Sourches, as originally intended by the *Kunstschutz* and the Ministry of Fine Arts. Due to petrol rationing, the Tapestry was transported in a 10cv van loaned by Monsieur Delahaye, a local tradesman, which ran on gas produced by burning wood. 18 August 1941 was scheduled as the date for the move but it was delayed until the following day due to administrative reasons. The vehicle proved unreliable; it started its journey at 7am, two hours late, and took until 5pm to reach Sourches. Here the Tapestry was stored in the basement for the next three years, though it was made available for experts to study. In place of the famous embroidery, the municipal authorities in Bayeux exhibited the full-size photographic facsimile of the Tapestry that had been presented by the South Kensington Museum in 1873.

By spring 1944, the Allies were heavily bombing northern France in advance of preparations to liberate Europe. At this time, Himmler made plans to seize the Tapestry in an operation coded as *Sonderauftag Bretagne* (Special Project Brittany). The plan was to transport the Tapestry to Paris, from where it would be easier to arrange export to Germany; but on 6 June the Allies invaded Normandy, liberating Bayeux itself on 8 June 1944.

By 14 June 1944, Himmler had contacted the German ambassador in Paris ordering that the Tapestry should be moved from Sourches to a safer location. Negotiations between the German Embassy and Ministry of Fine Arts reached agreement whereby the Tapestry would be moved to the Louvre on 27 June, but it seems Louvre staff at Sourches had not been notified of these plans. At about 5pm, a group of Gestapo officers carrying sub-machine guns, accompanied Jacques Dupont, Inspector of Historic Monuments, entered the office of Germain Bazin, Curator of the Château at Sourches, and demanded that the Tapestry be handed over. From here, the Tapestry was transported to the Louvre, where, in early July, it was examined and sprinkled with para-dichlorbenzine, a moth repellent.

By August 1944, Paris was close to being liberated. Even at this time of crisis, Himmler was still thinking about the Bayeux Tapestry. On 18 August 1944, he sent a radio message to Carl Oberg, Head of the Gestapo and SS in France, commanding him to 'bring the Tapestry to a place of safety'; a message intercepted by General Communications Headquarters at Bletchley Park. Four days later, on 22 August 1944, General Dietrich von Choltitz, the *Befehlshaber* (commander) in charge of Paris, was visited by two senior SS officers who had come on Himmler's orders 'to remove the Bayeux Tapestry to a place of safety'. However, by now the Louvre was occupied by Allied troops so it was impossible for the SS troops to get to it. On 25 August 1944, Paris was liberated.

Meanwhile, no one in Bayeux seems to have realised that the Tapestry had been removed from Sourches to Paris. A week after D-Day, Captain Bancel LaFarge of the Allies' Monuments, Fine Arts and Archives, an organisation established to ensure the protection of buildings and works of arts, set up his headquarters in Bayeux. Following a request from Mayor Dodeman, who thought the Tapestry was still at Sourches, LaFarge was able to discover that the Tapestry was in the Louvre. Dodeman hoped to send a van to collect the Tapestry, but was refused by the Ministry of Fine Arts on security grounds. Instead, the Bayeux Tapestry was displayed in the Louvre for five weeks; the opening of the Museum was timed to coincide with Winston Churchill's visit to Paris on 11 November 1944, but the Prime Minister did not visit the exhibition.

On 2 March 1945 the Tapestry returned to Bayeux, where the local authorities planned to create a new display for it in the Hôtel du Doyen. Whilst the new gallery was being prepared the Tapestry was temporarily stored in its old exhibition case, and thereafter, from 28 March to 31 May 1948, it was exhibited in the Chapel of the Municipal School.

By June 1948, a permanent exhibition gallery had been created in the first floor of the Hôtel du Doyen. Here, the Tapestry was exhibited in a single continuous strip (though in a zigzag formation) in a glass frame and lit in subdued lighting. The inauguration ceremony of the new exhibition space was presided over by President Vincent Auriol on 6 June 1948 in the presence of the Mayor of Bayeux and other dignitaries.

By 1980, it was agreed that the Bayeux Tapestry needed a more up-to-date exhibition space, and the Grand Seminary, built in 1653, was chosen. In 1981, the Ministry of Culture invited textile restoration specialists to inspect the hanging and advise on conservation prior to re-exhibition. At this time, the Tapestry was studied, cleaned and the backing linen was also removed, so the reverse of the Tapestry could be inspected and photographed. On 6 February 1983, the Tapestry was installed in its new display.

This, the current exhibition, arranges the Tapestry around a hairpin bend, so that it is only possible to see one side at a time. In an ideal world, the Bayeux Tapestry would be displayed as a single length, but this would need a specially built structure, no doubt at great public expense, to cater for such an incredibly long piece of work.

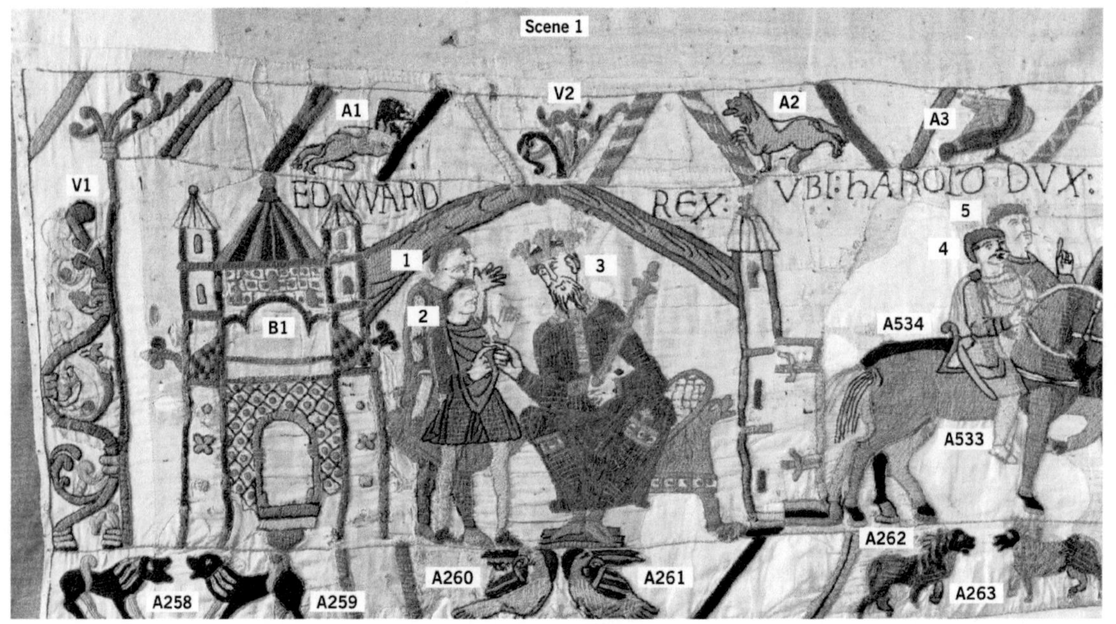

Scene 1
V2
A1
A2
A3
V1
ED·VVARD
REX·
VBI·hAROLD DVX·
5
4
1
3
A534
2
B1
A533
A262
A258
A259
A260
A261
A263

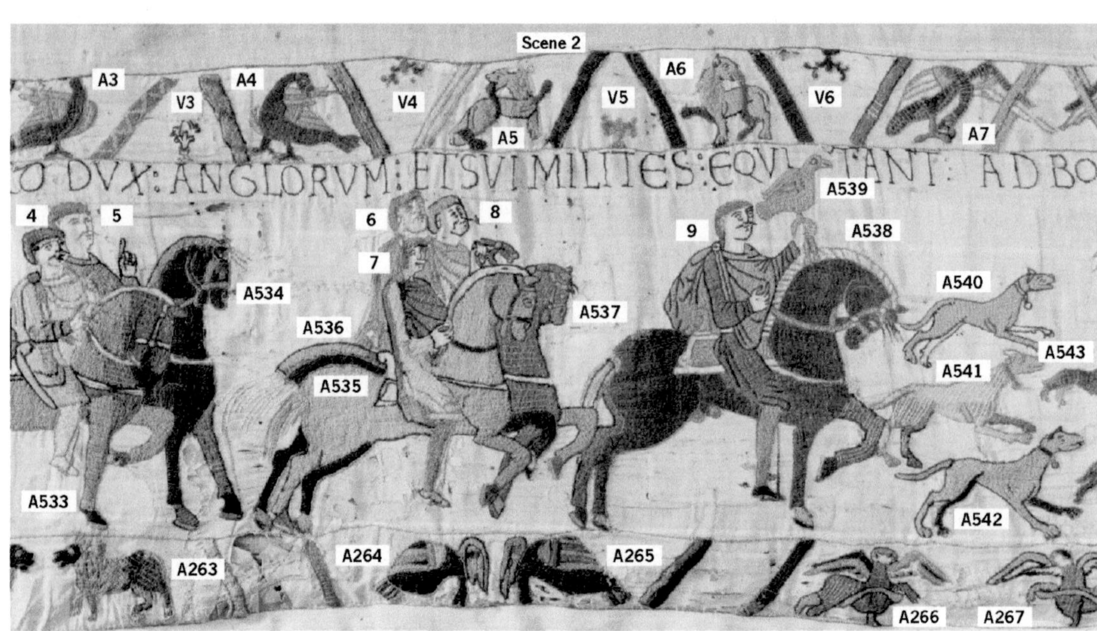

Scene 2
A3
A4
A6
V3
V4
V5
V6
A5
A7
:O DVX·ANGLORVM·ETSVIMILITES·EQVITANT· AD BO
A539
4
5
6
8
9
A538
7
A534
A540
A536
A537
A535
A541
A543
A533
A542
A263
A264
A265
A266
A267

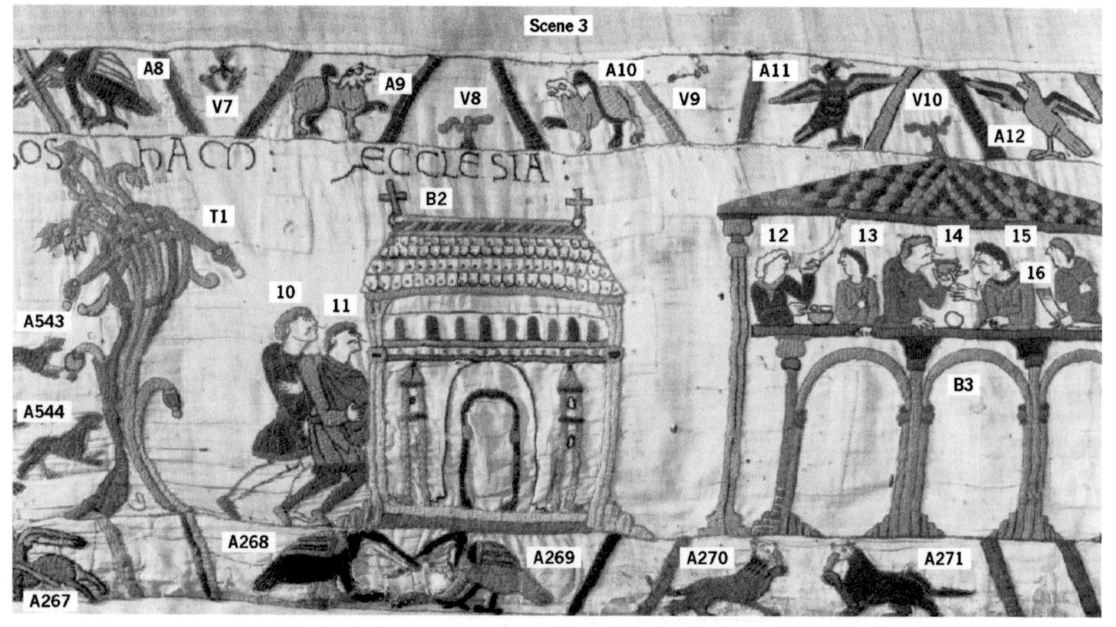

Scene 3

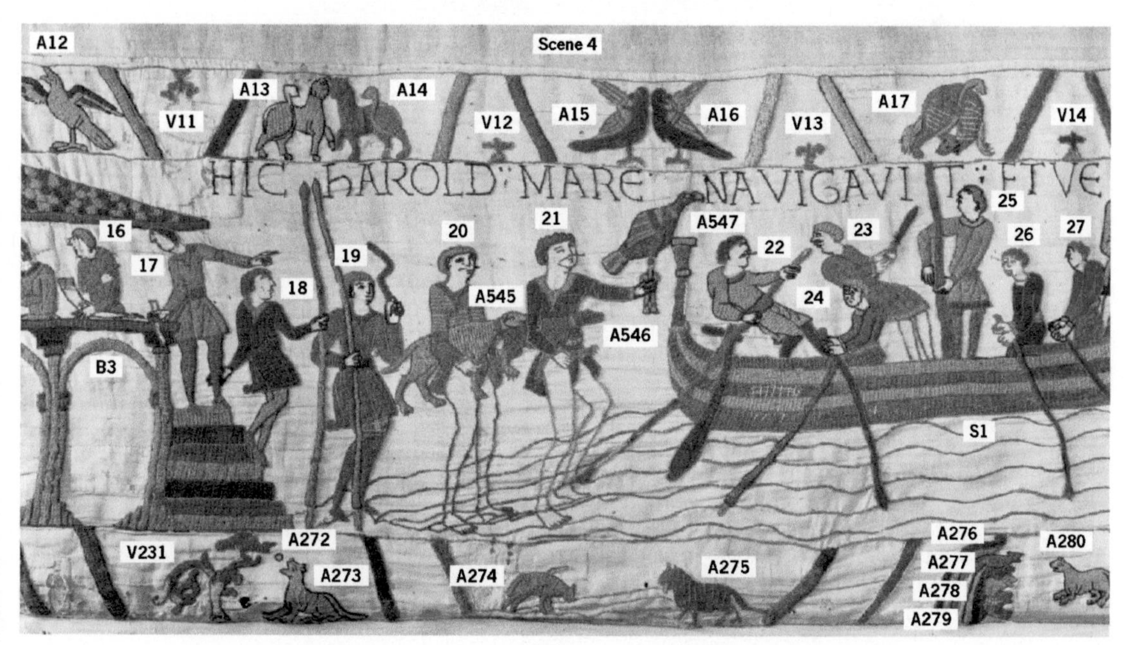

Scene 4

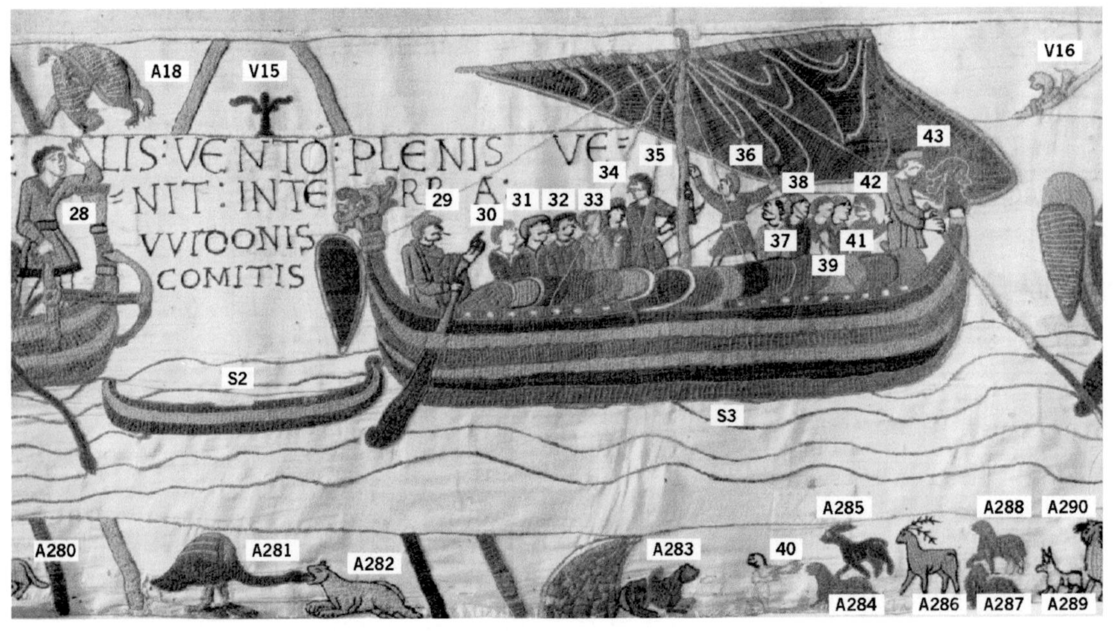

A18
V15
V16
28
LIS·VENTO·PLENIS VE=
=NIT·INTE RD A
VVIDONIS
COMITIS
29
30
31 32 33
34
35
36
37
38
39
41
42
43
S2
S3
A280
A281
A282
A283
40
A284
A285
A286
A287
A288
A289
A290

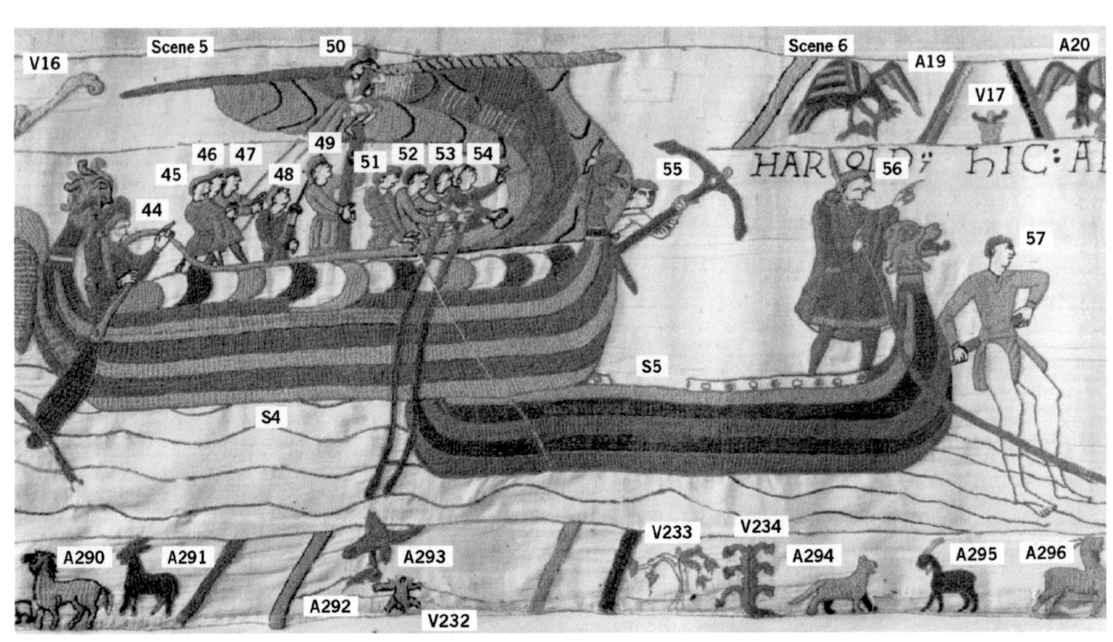

V16
Scene 5
50
Scene 6
A19
A20
V17
44
45
46 47
48
49
51
52 53 54
55
HAROLD HIC·A
56
57
S4
S5
A290
A291
A292
A293
V232
V233
V234
A294
A295
A296

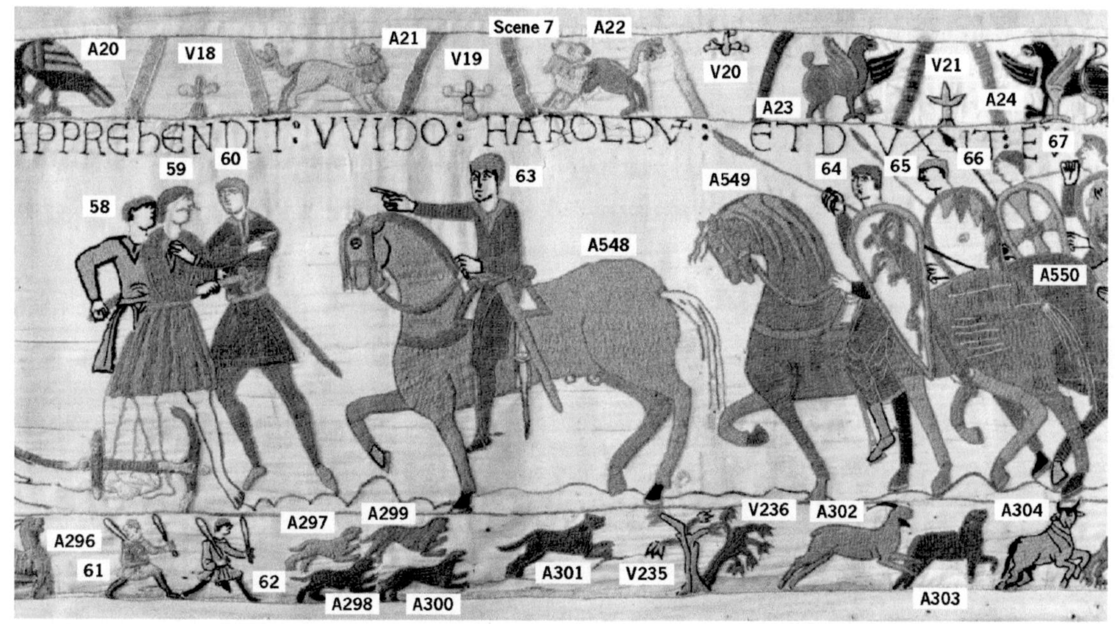

A20
V18
A21
Scene 7
A22
V19
V20
A23
V21
A24
APPREHENDIT: VVIDO: HAROLDV: ET DVX IT E
59
60
58
63
A549
64
65
66
67
A548
A550
A296
A297
A299
V236
A302
A304
61
62
A301
V235
A298
A300
A303

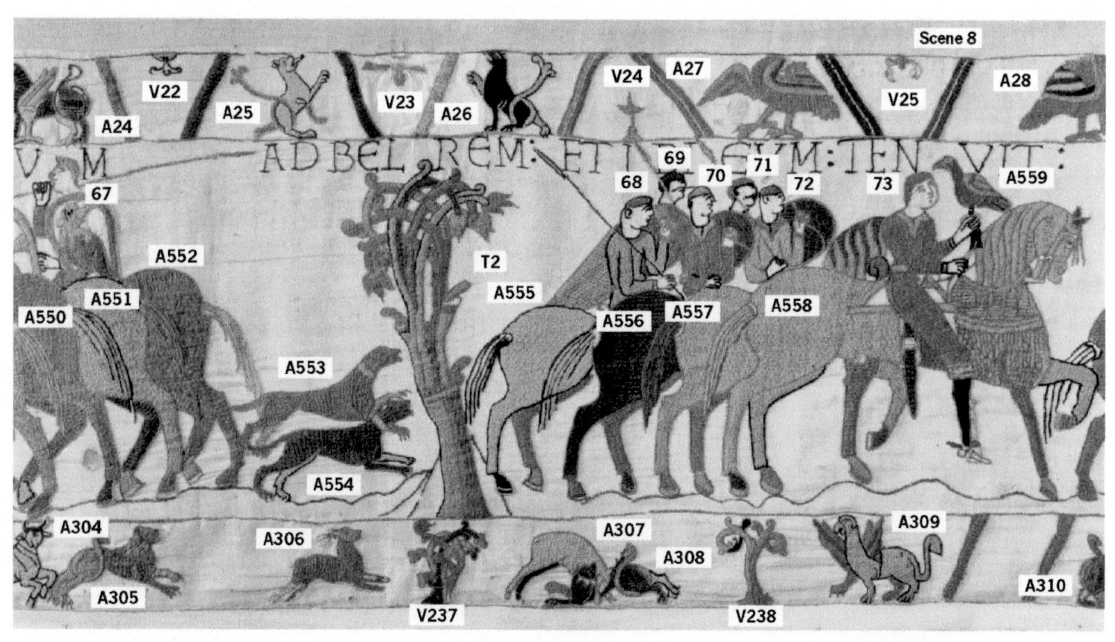

Scene 8
V22
A25
V23
A26
V24
A27
V25
A28
A24
U M AD BEL REM: ET I EVM: TEN VIT
69
70
71
67
68
72
73
A559
A552
T2
A555
A551
A550
A556
A557
A558
A553
A554
A304
A306
A307
A309
A308
A305
A310
V237
V238

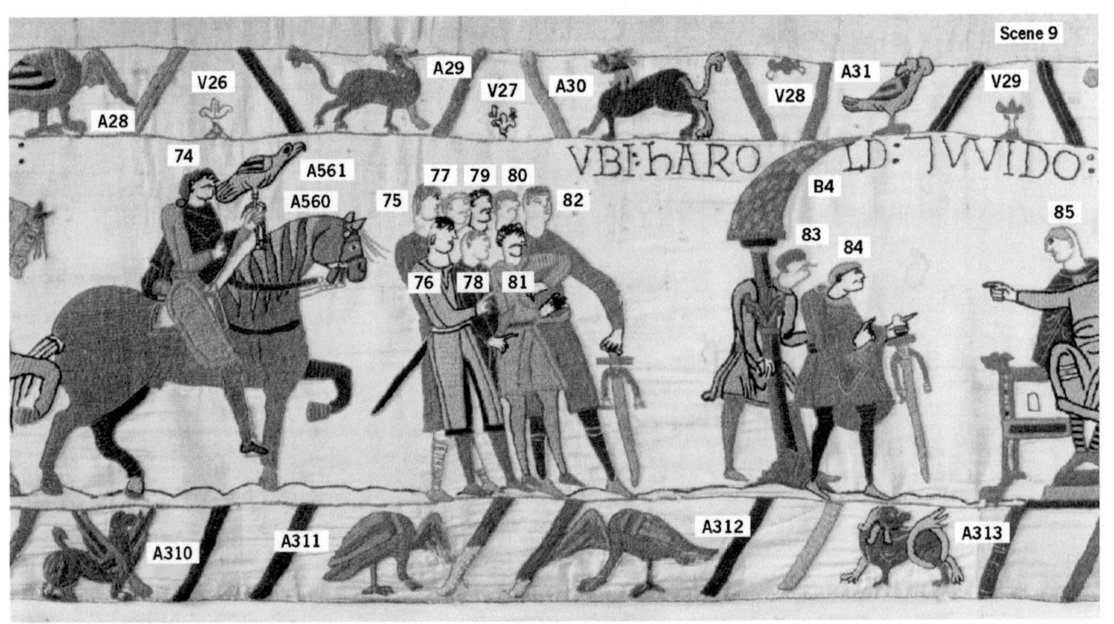

Scene 9
A28 V26 A29 V27 A30 V28 A31 V29
74 A561 77 79 80 VBI:HARO LD:⁊WIDO: B4 85
A560 75 82
76 78 81 83 84
A310 A311 A312 A313

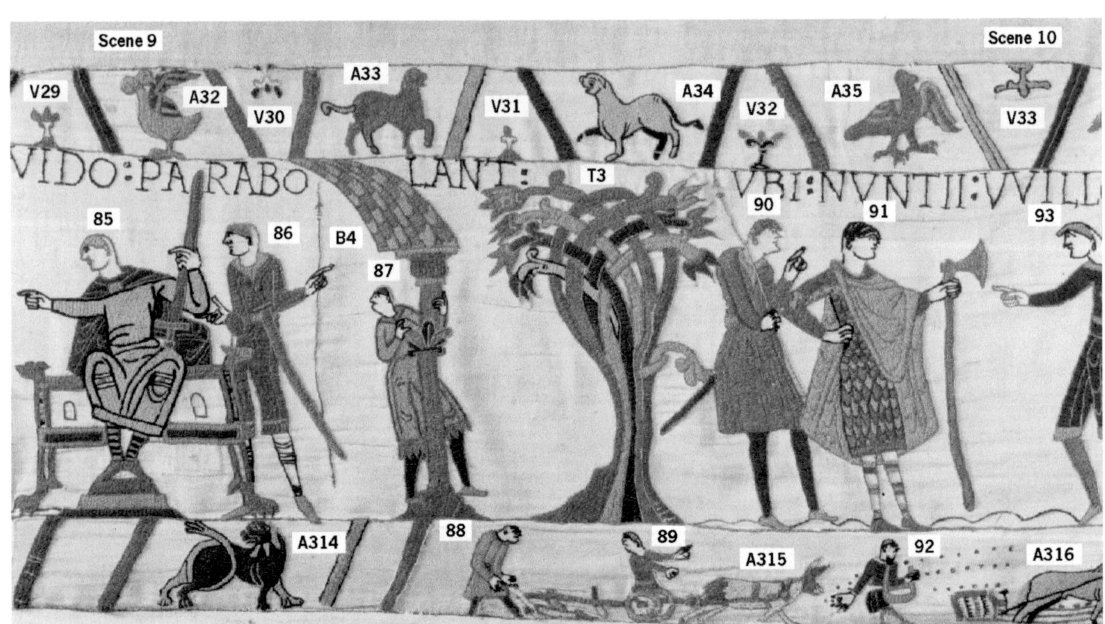

Scene 9 Scene 10
V29 A32 A33 A34 A35
V30 V31 V32 V33
VIDO:PA RABO LAN T: T3 VBI:NVNTII:VVILL
85 86 B4 90 91 93
87
A314 88 89 A315 92 A316

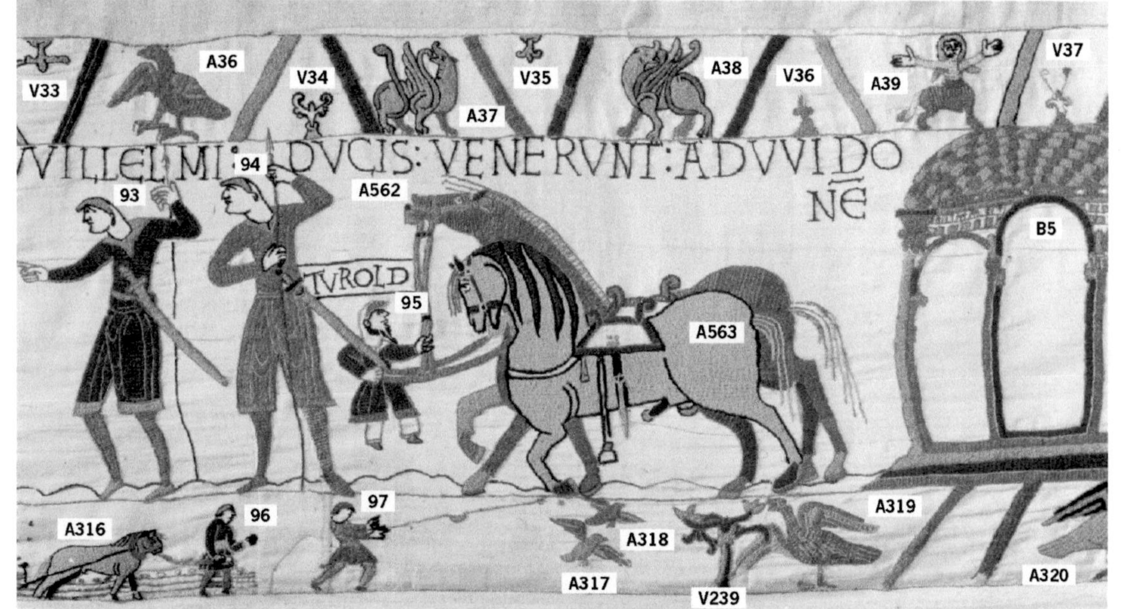

V33
A36
V34
V35
A38
V36
A39
V37
A37
VVILLELMI : DVCIS : VENERVNT : ADVVIDO
NE
94
93
A562
B5
TVROLD
95
A563
A316
96
97
A319
A318
A317
A320
V239

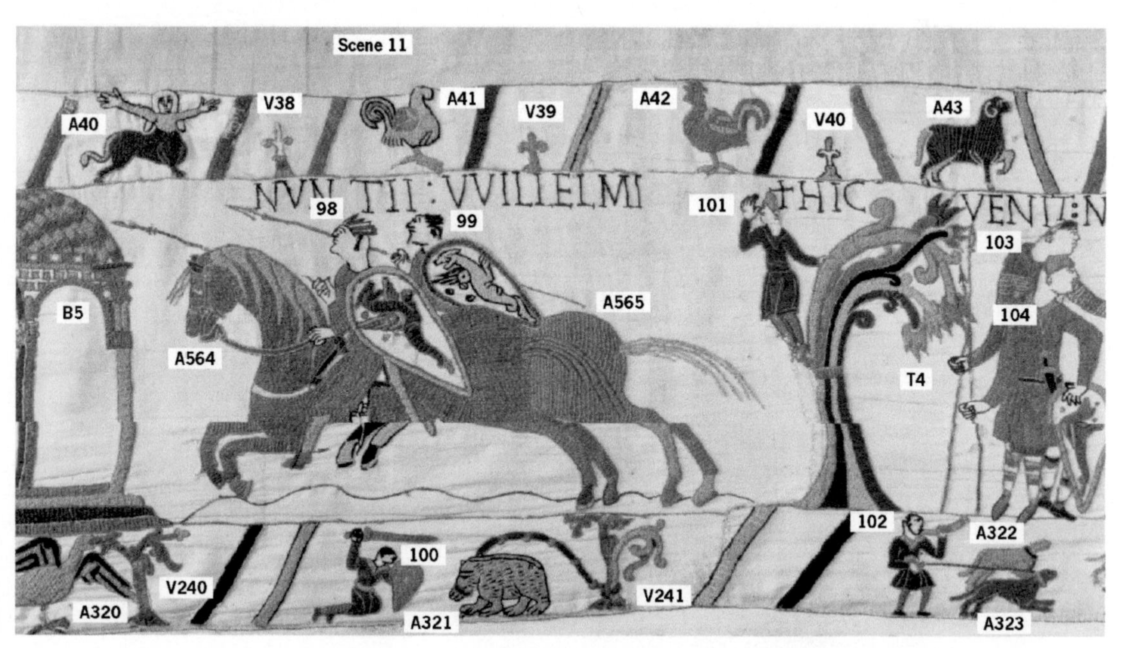

Scene 11
A40
V38
A41
V39
A42
V40
A43
NVN TII : VVILLELMI
98
99
101
THIC
VENIT : N
103
B5
A565
104
A564
T4
102
A322
V240
100
A320
A321
V241
A323

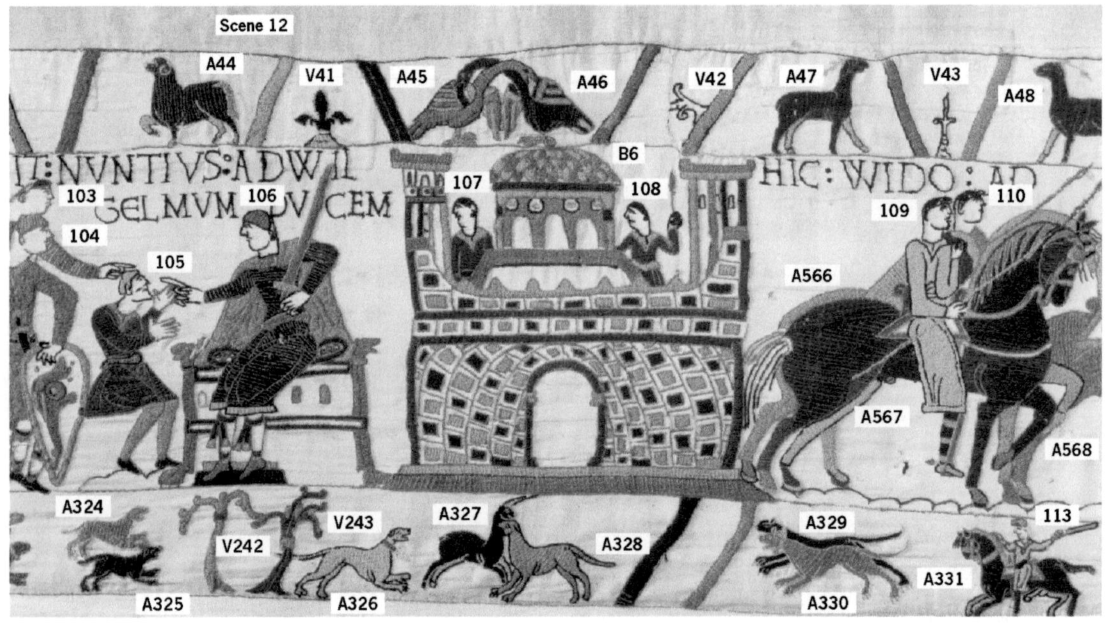

Scene 12

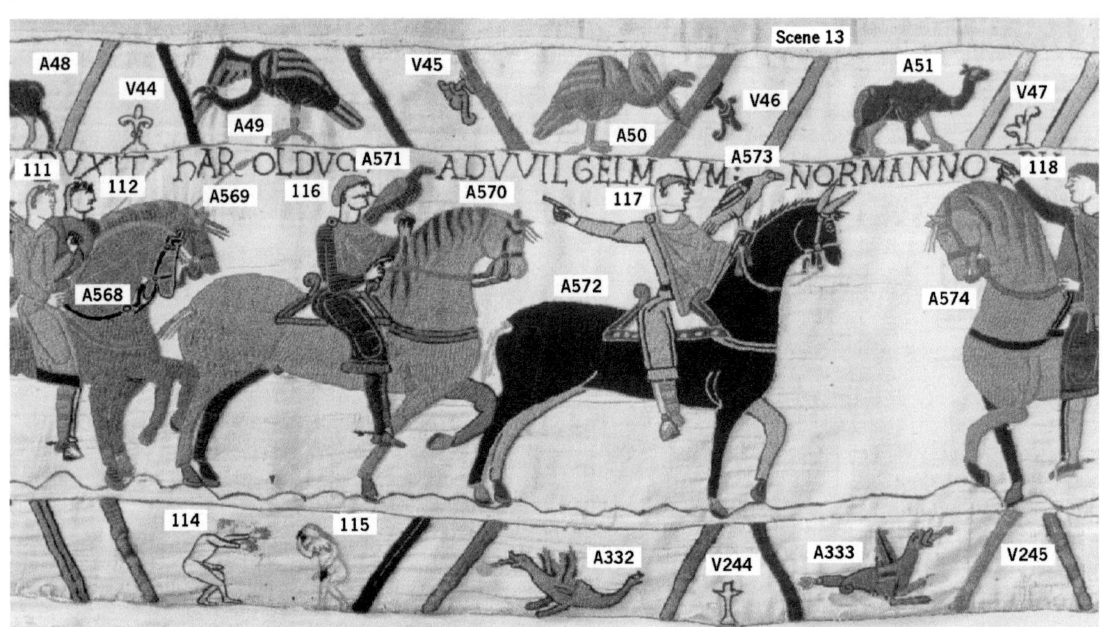

Scene 13

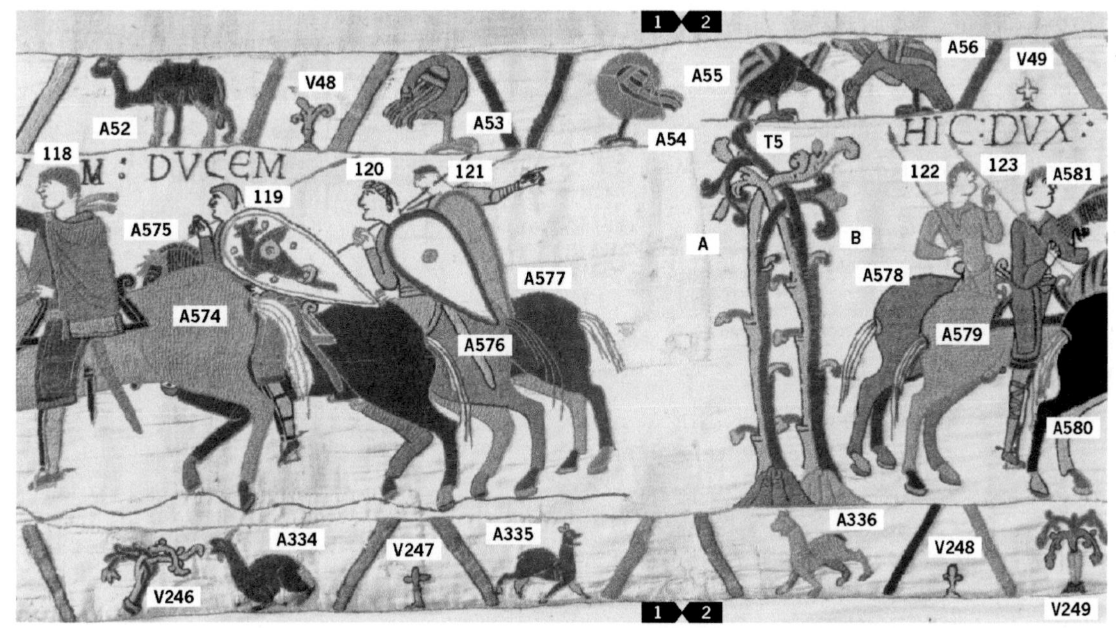

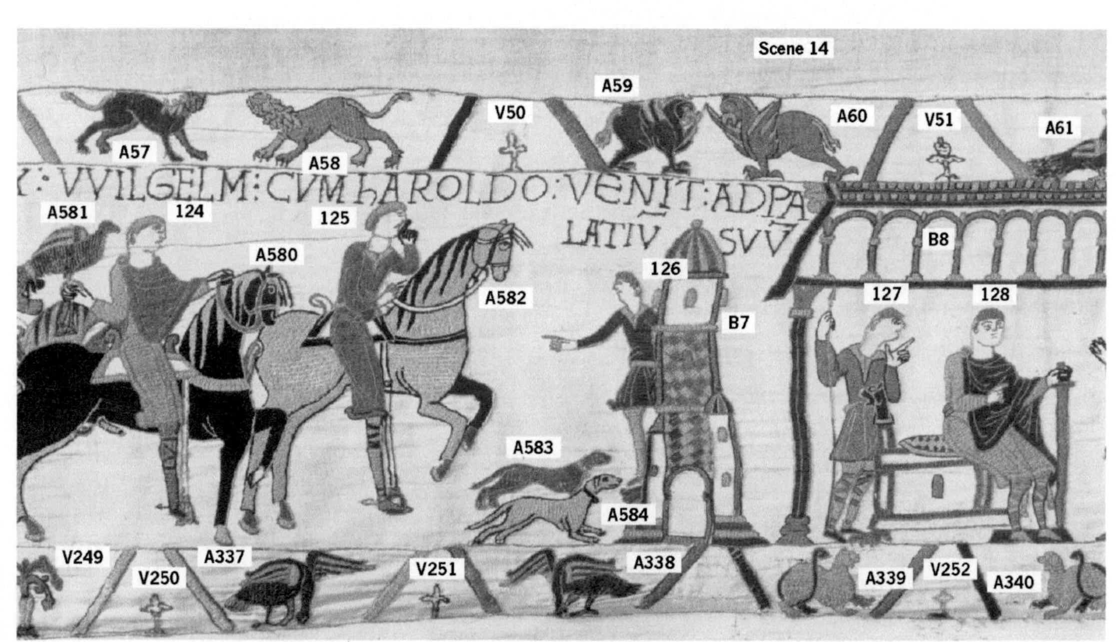

Scene 14

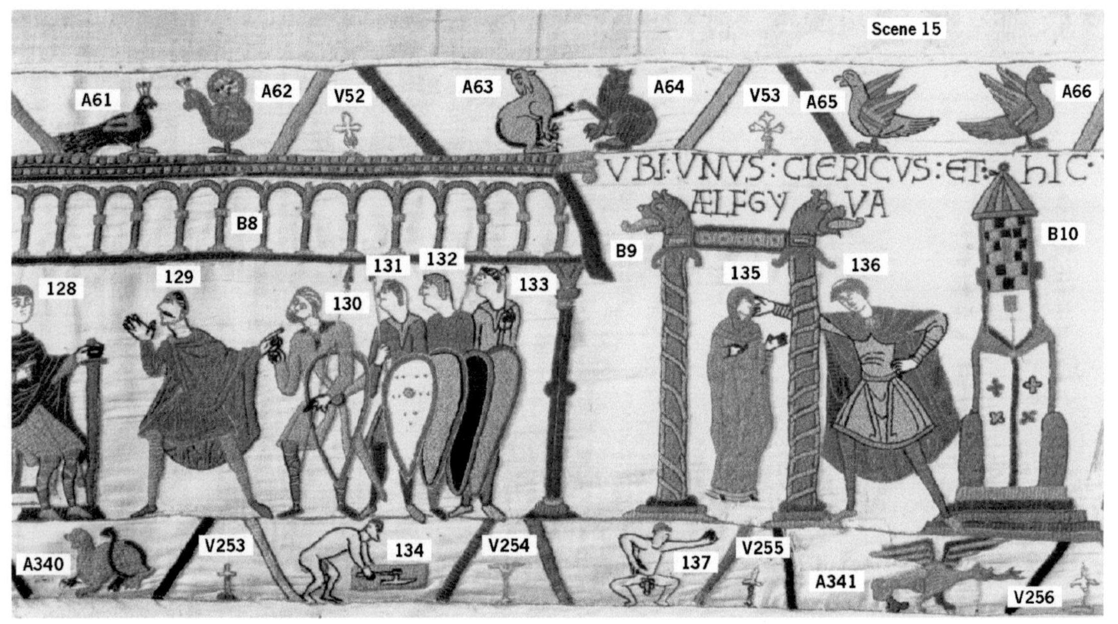
Scene 15
A61 A62 V52 A63 A64 V53 A65 A66
VBI · VNVS : CLERICVS : ET · HIC ·
ÆLFGY VA
B8 B9 B10
128 129 131 132 133 130 135 136
A340 V253 134 V254 137 V255 A341 V256

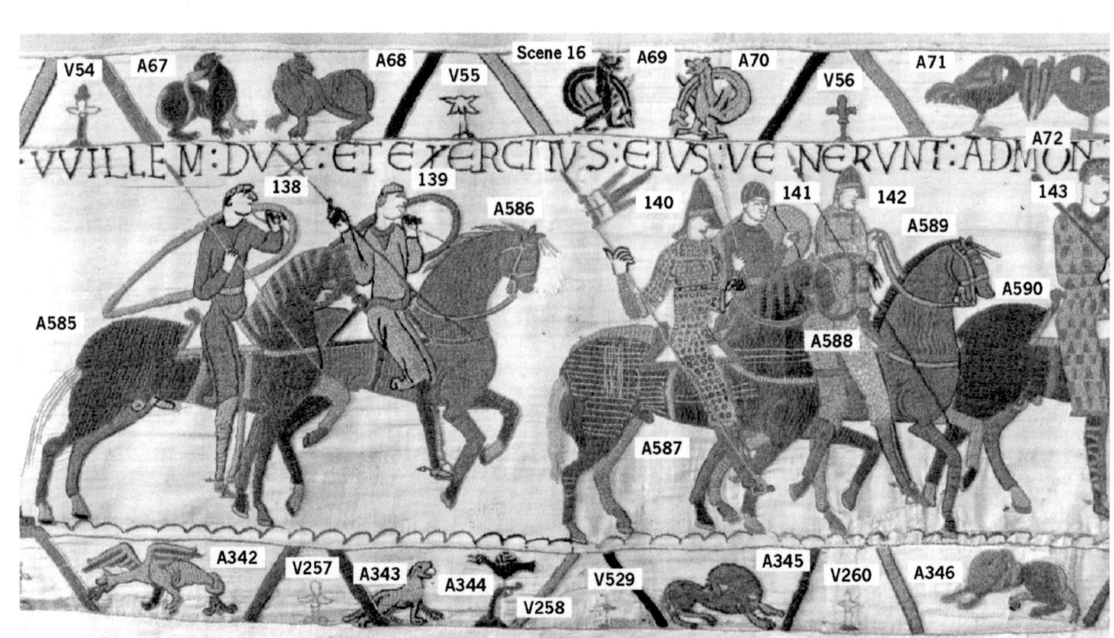
V54 A67 A68 V55 Scene 16 A69 A70 V56 A71
A72
· VVILLELM : DVX : ET EXERCITVS : EIVS : VE NERVNT : AD MON
138 139 A586 140 141 142 143
A585 A588 A589 A590
A587
A342 V257 A343 A344 V529 A345 V260 A346
V258

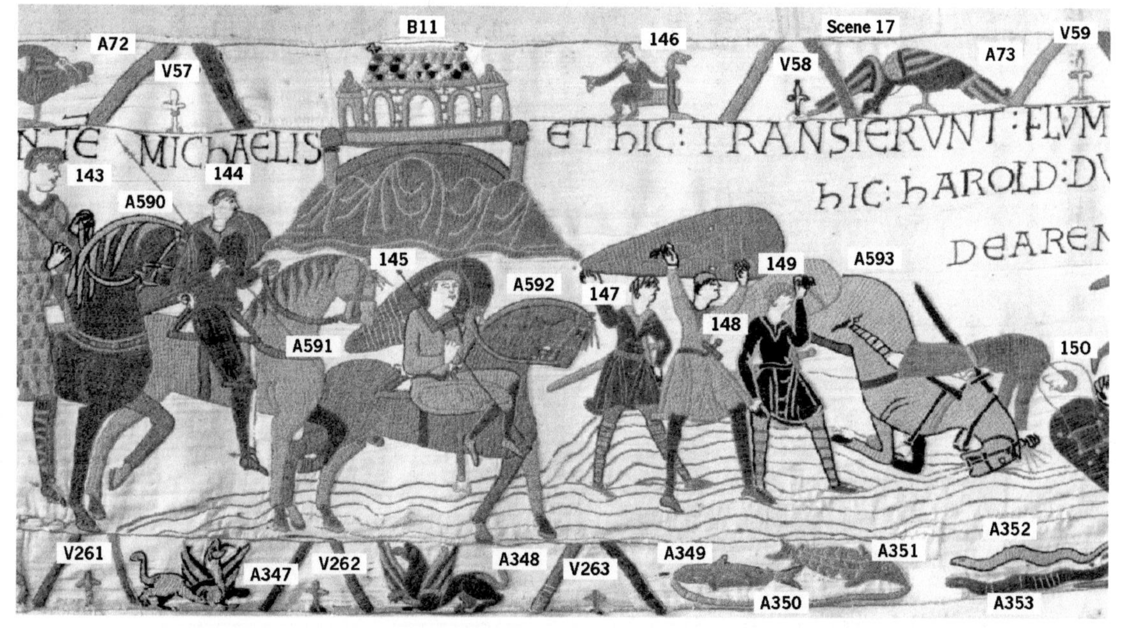
A72
V57
B11
146
Scene 17
V58
A73
V59
...TE MICHAELIS
ET HIC:TRANSIERVNT:FLVM
HIC:HAROLD:DV
DEAREN
143
144
A590
145
A591
A592
147
148
149
A593
150
A348
V261
A347
V262
V263
A349
A350
A351
A352
A353

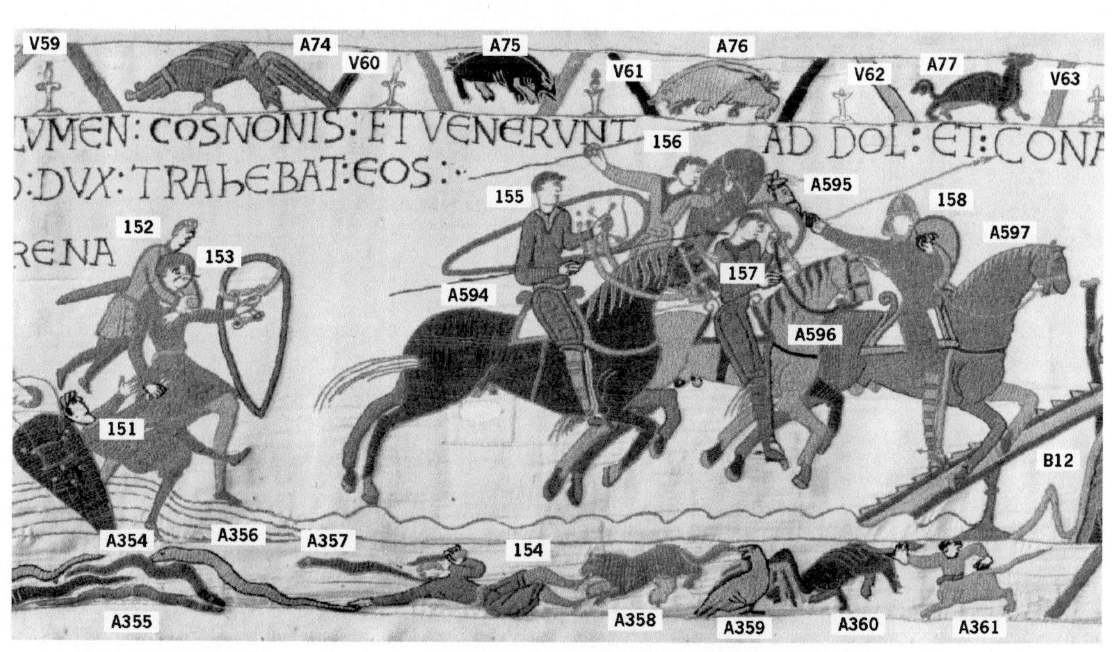
V59
A74
V60
A75
A76
V61
V62
A77
V63
LVMEN:COSNONIS:ETVENERVNT
AD DOL:ET:CONA
DVX:TRAHEBAT:EOS
RENA
152
153
155
156
A595
158
A594
157
A597
A596
151
B12
A354
A356
A357
154
A355
A358
A359
A360
A361

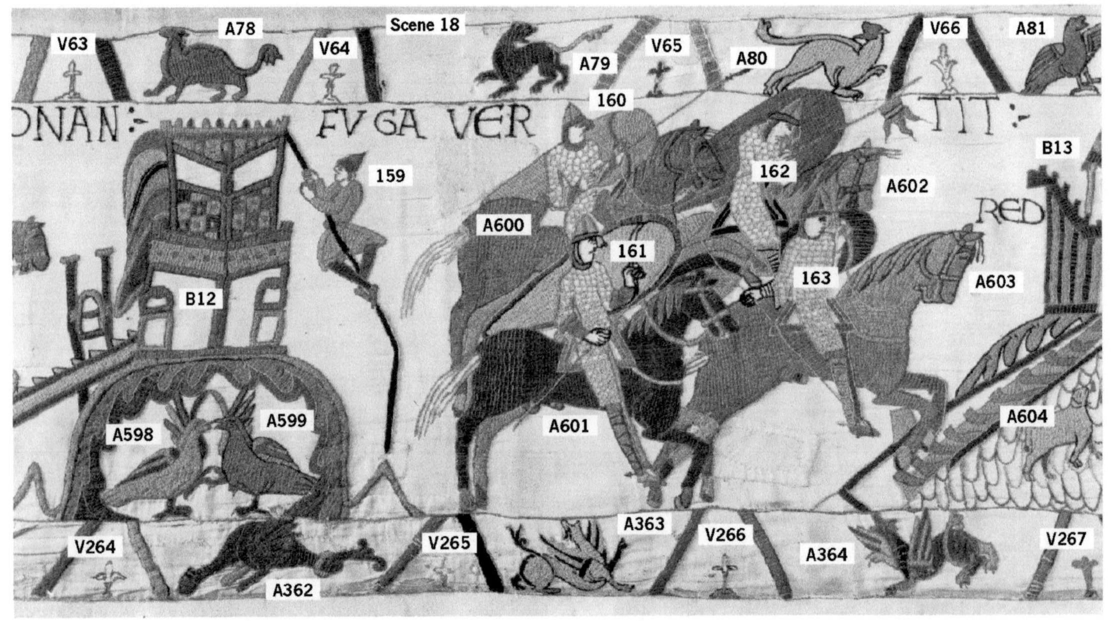

V63
A78
Scene 18
V64
V65
V66
A81
A79
A80
160
ONAN:
FV GA VER
TIT:
159
B13
162
A602
RED
A600
161
A603
163
B12
A601
A598
A599
A604
V264
V265
A363
V266
V267
A362
A364

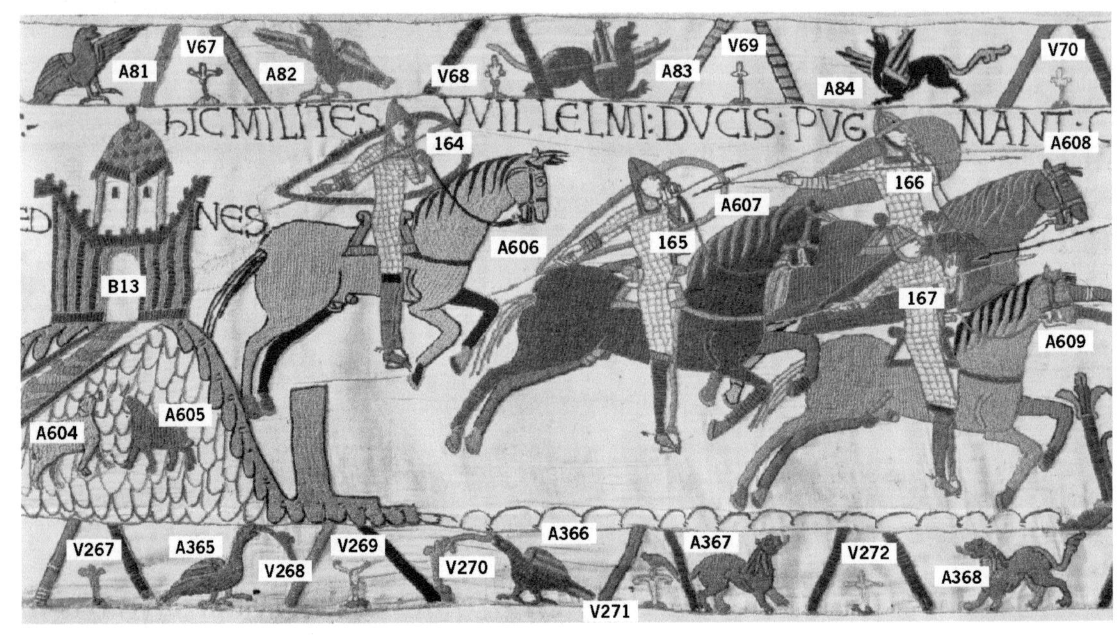

V67
V69
V70
A81
A82
V68
A83
A84
hIC MILITES
VVILLELMI:DVCIS:PVG
NANT:
A608
164
ED
NES
166
A607
B13
A606
165
167
A604
A605
A609
V267
A365
V269
A366
A367
V272
V268
V270
A368
V271

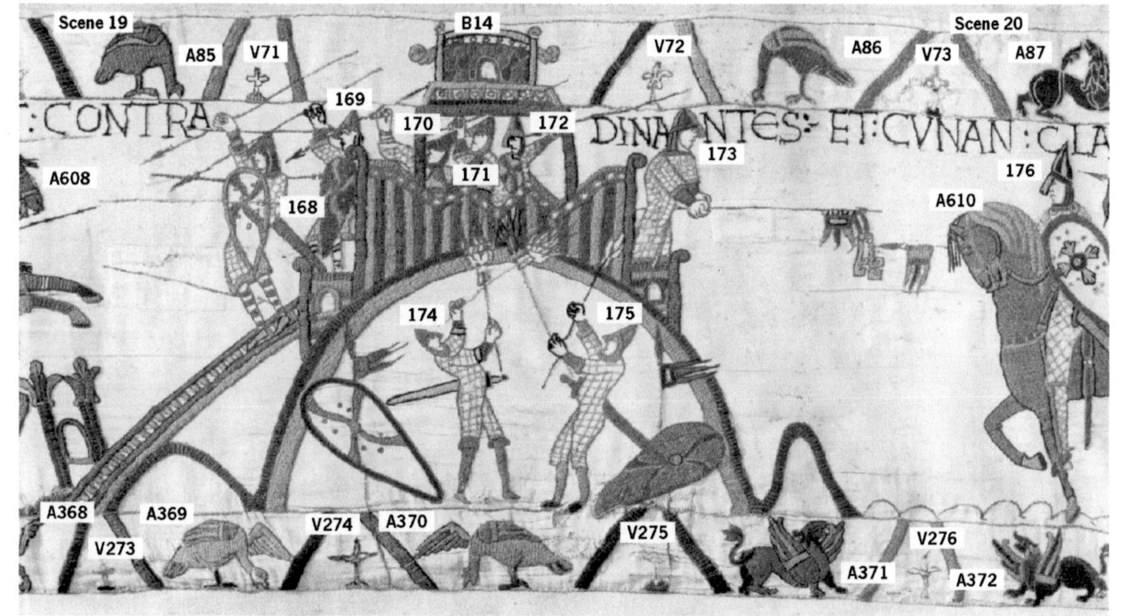

Scene 19
Scene 20
:CONTRA
DINA NTES: ET CVNAN: CIA

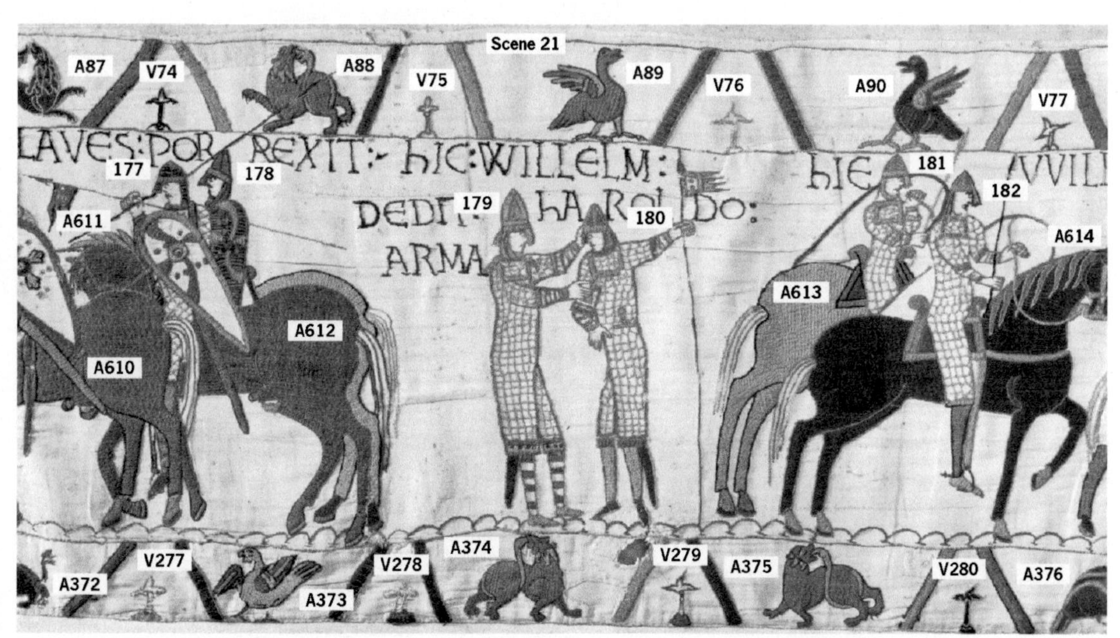

Scene 21
LAVES:POR REXIT:· HIC:WILLELM:
DEDIT HAROLDO:
ARMA
HIE WILL

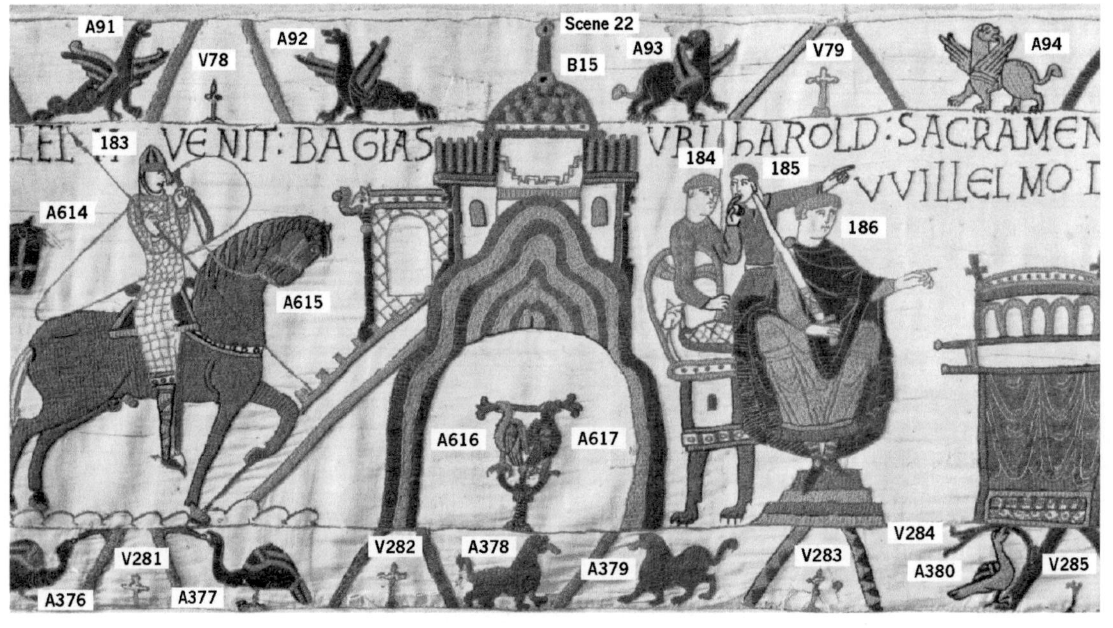

A91
V78
A92
Scene 22
B15
A93
V79
A94
LEL ... VENIT: BAGIAS VBI HAROLD: SACRAMEN
183 184 185 VVILLELMO I
A614 186
A615
A616 A617
V281
V282 A378 V283 V284
A376 A377 A379 A380 V285

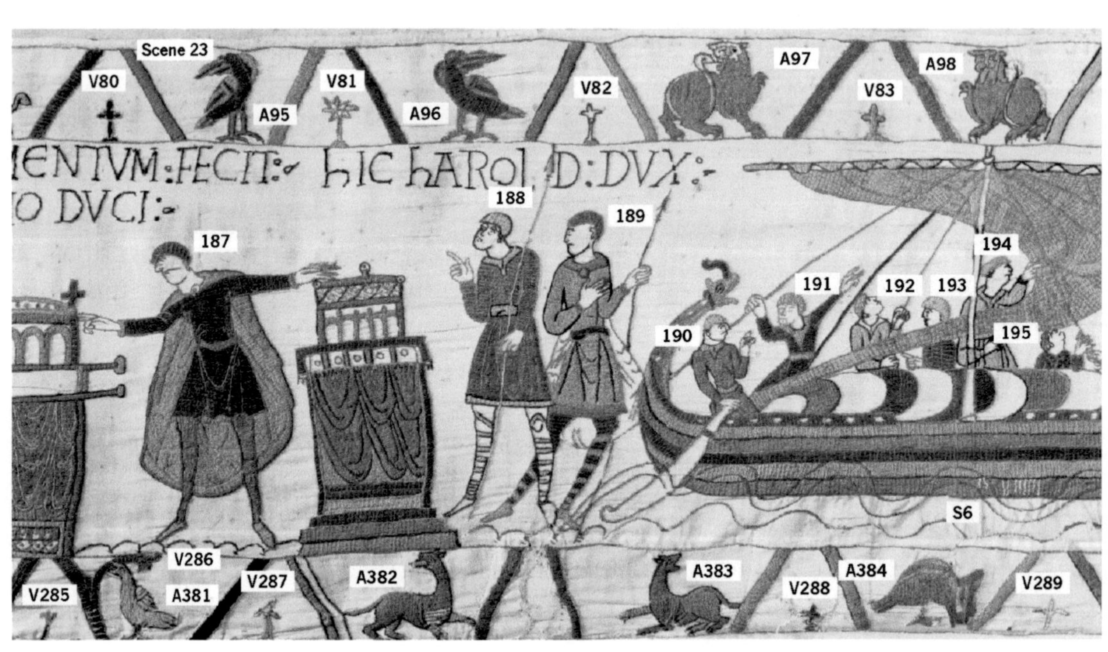

Scene 23
V80 A97 A98
V81 V82 V83
A95 A96
MENTVM:FECIT: HIC HAROLD:DVX:
O DVCI: 188 189
187
194
191 192 193
190 195
V286
V285 V287 A382 A383 A384
A381 V288 V289
S6

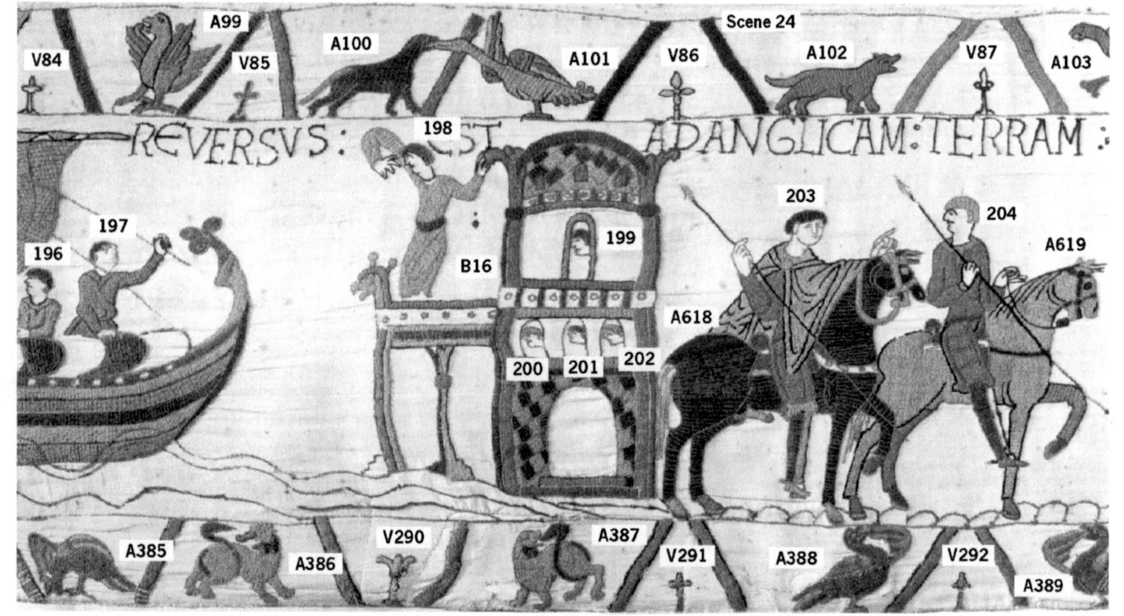

V84
A99
V85
A100
A101
Scene 24
V86
A102
V87
A103
REVERSVS : EST AD ANGLICAM : TERRAM :
198
197
196
199
B16
203
204
A619
A618
200 201 202
A385
A386
V290
A387
V291
A388
V292
A389

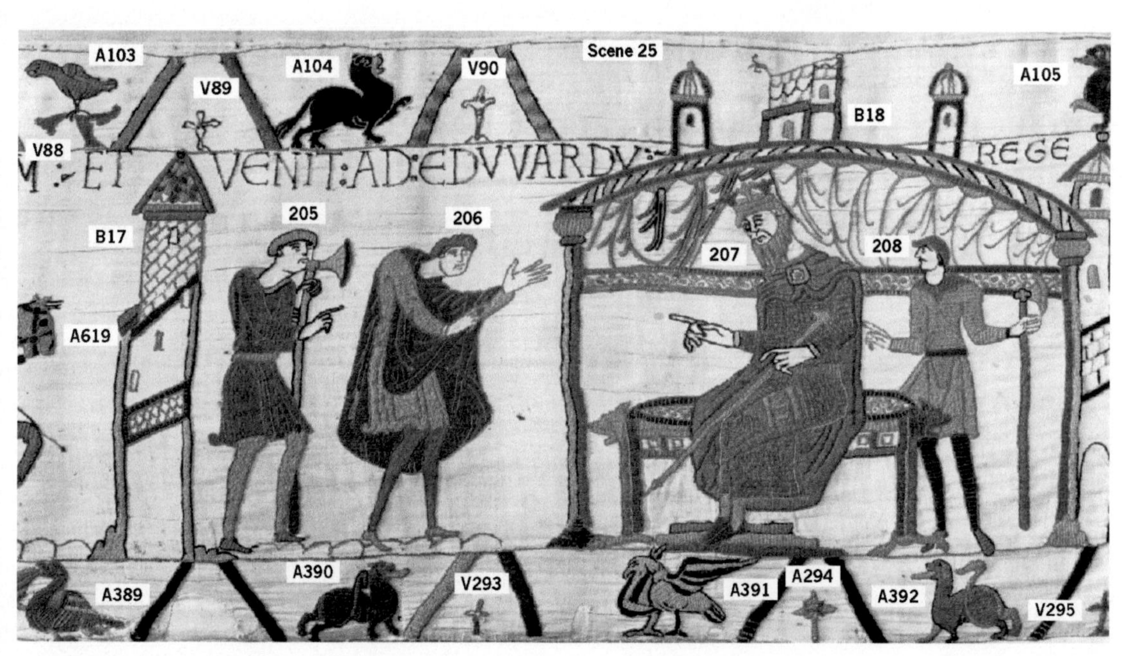

A103
A104
V90
Scene 25
A105
V89
B18
V88
ET VENIT : AD : EDVVARDV :
REGE
B17
205
206
207
208
A619
A389
A390
V293
A391
A294
A392
V295

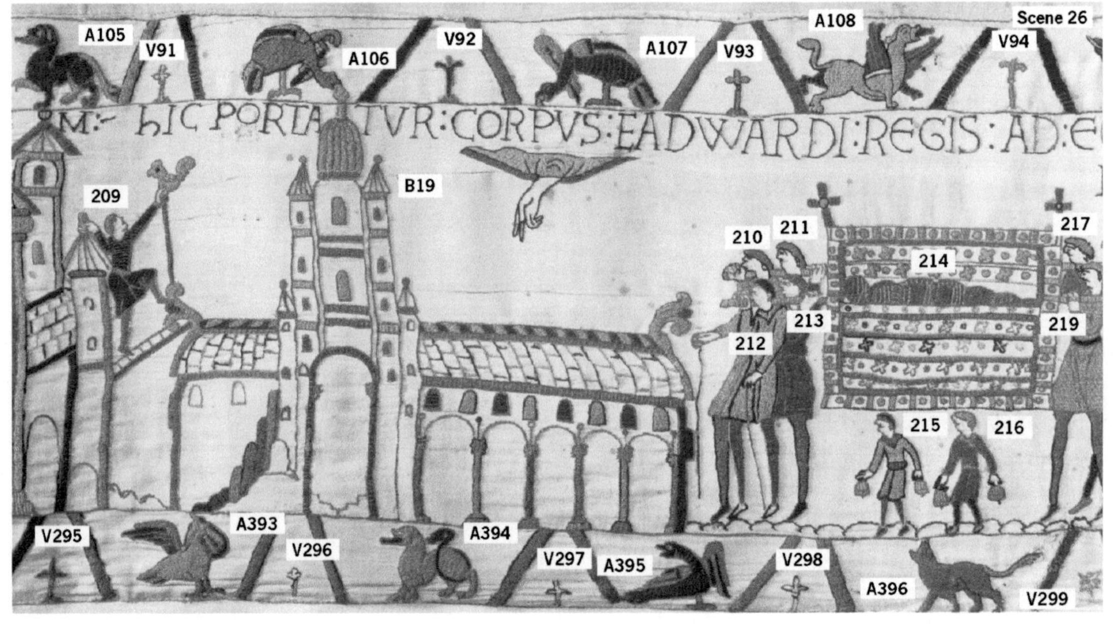
Scene 26
hIC PORTATVR : CORPVS : EADWARDI : REGIS : AD : E

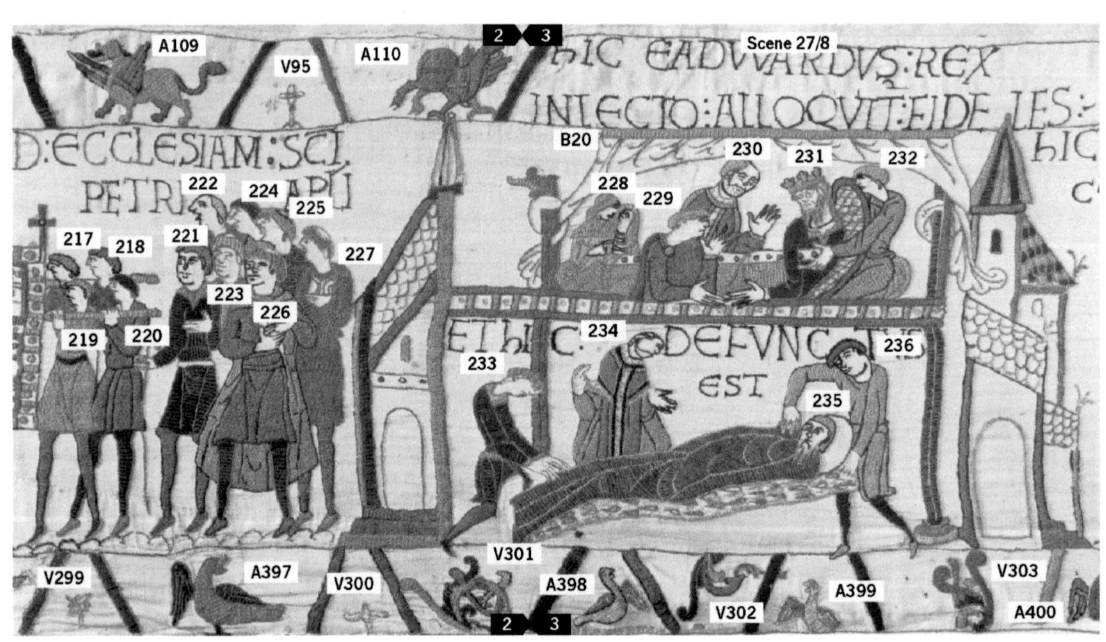
Scene 27/8
hIC EADVVARDVS : REX
INLECTO : ALLOQVIT : FIDE LES :
D : ECCLESIAM : SCI
PETRI APLI
ET hIC DEFVNCT
EST

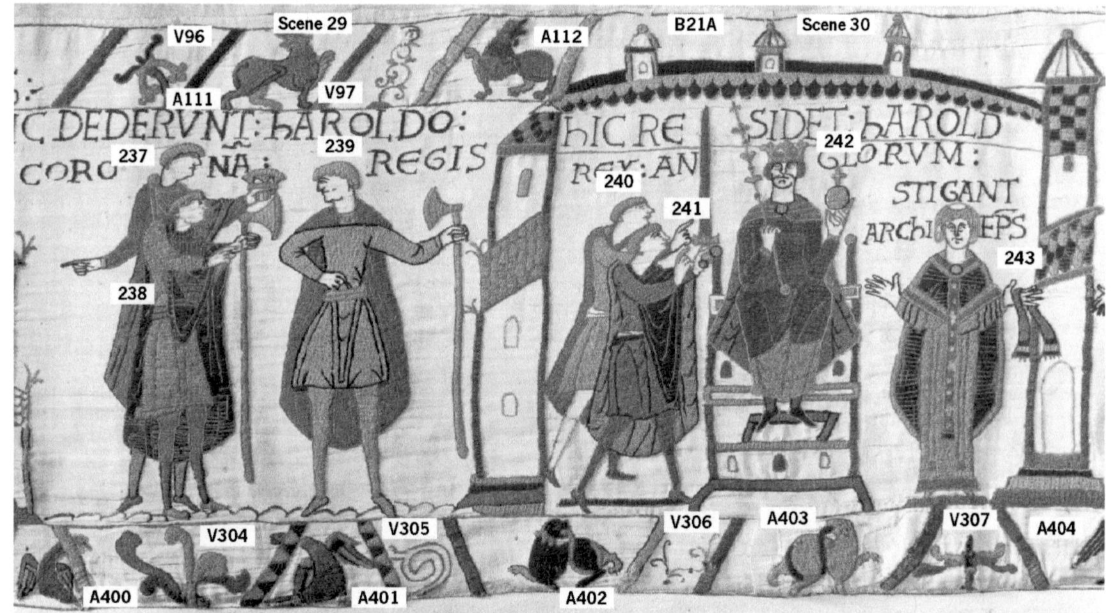

V96
Scene 29
A112
B21A
Scene 30
A111
V97
IC DEDERVNT:HAROLDO:
CORO NÃ: REGIS
237
239
hIC RE SIDET:HAROLD
REX:AN GLORVM:
240
241
242
STIGANT ARCHI EPS
238
243
V304
V305
V306
A403
V307
A404
A400
A401
A402

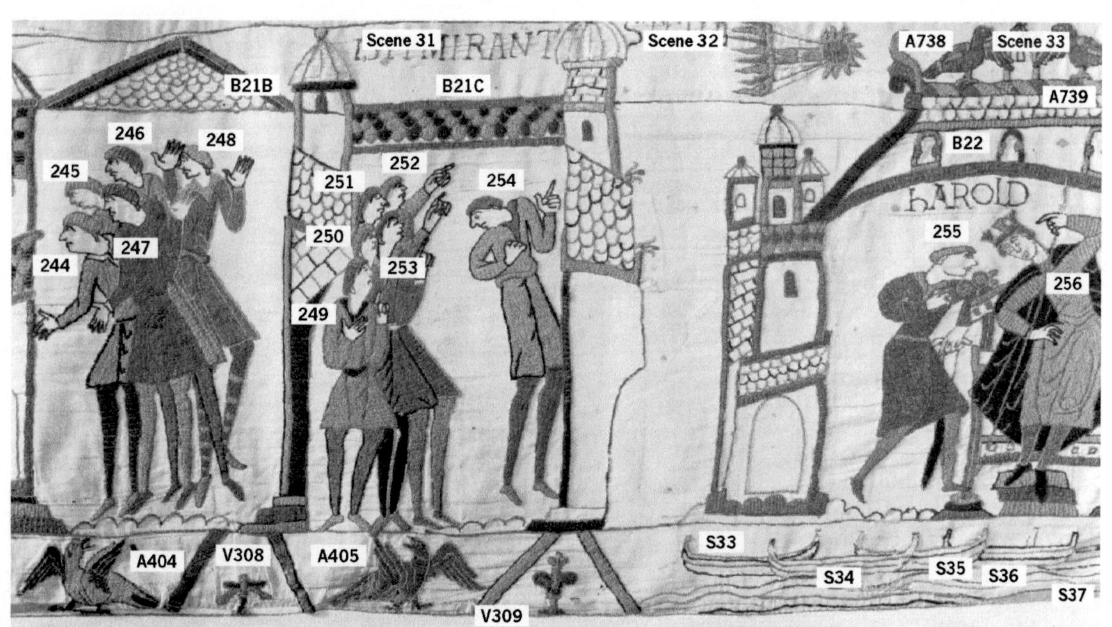

Scene 31
ISPTMIRANT
Scene 32
A738
Scene 33
B21B
B21C
A739
B22
HAROLD
245
246
248
251
252
254
250
255
244
247
253
256
249
A404
V308
A405
S33
S34
S35
S36
S37
V309

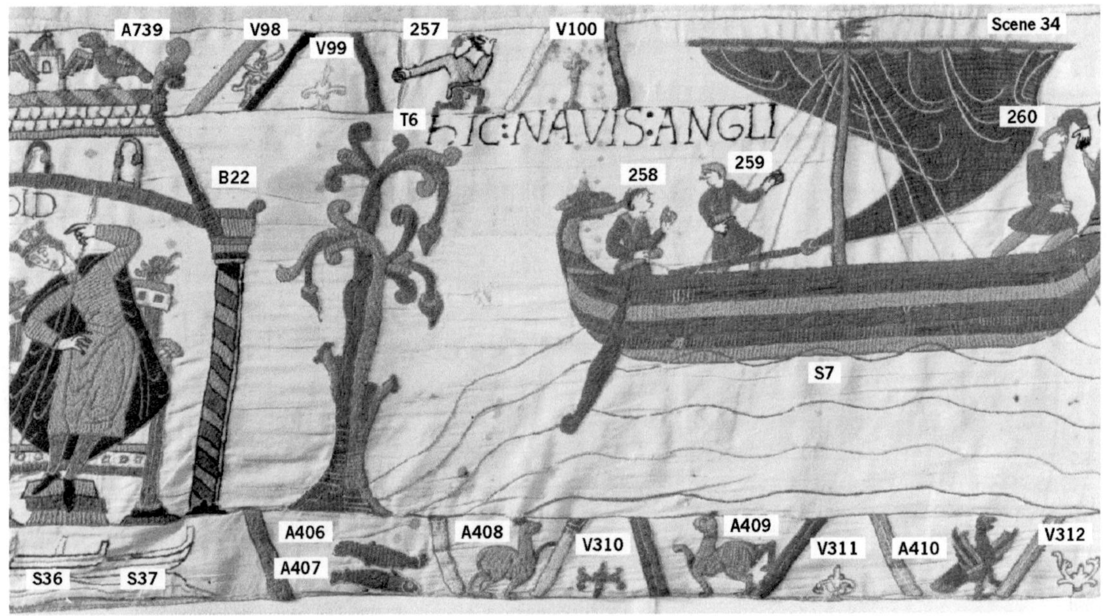

A739
V98
V99
257
V100
Scene 34
T6
HIC:NAVIS:ANGLI
260
B22
258
259
OLD
S7
S36
S37
A406
A407
A408
V310
A409
V311
A410
V312

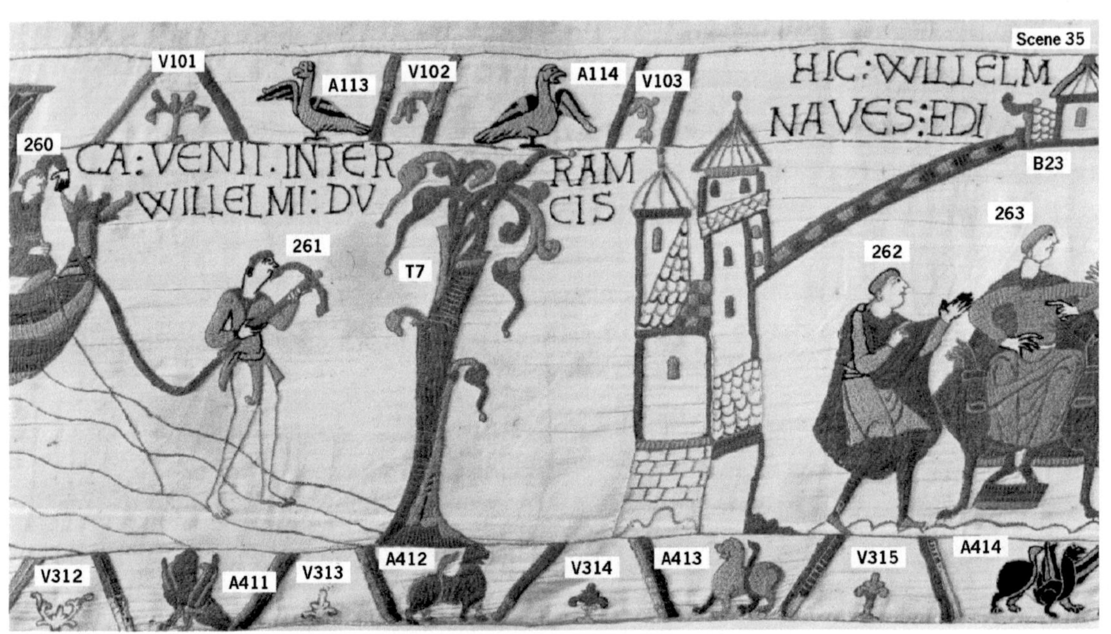

Scene 35
V101
A113
V102
A114
V103
HIC:WILLELM
NAVES:EDI
260
CA:VENIT.INTER
WILLELMI:DV
RAM
CIS
B23
261
263
T7
262
V312
A411
V313
A412
V314
A413
V315
A414

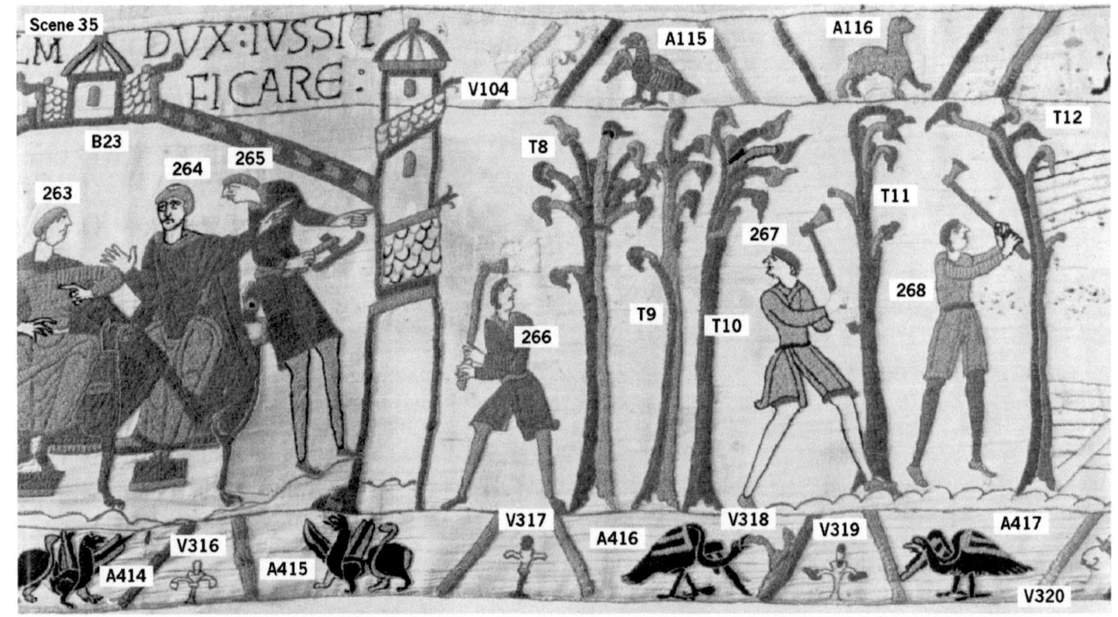

Scene 35
ƜM DVX:IVSSIT FICARE:
B23
263 264 265
V104
A115
A116
T12
T8
T11
267
268
T9
T10
266
V317
A416
V318
V319
A417
A414
V316
A415
A416
V320

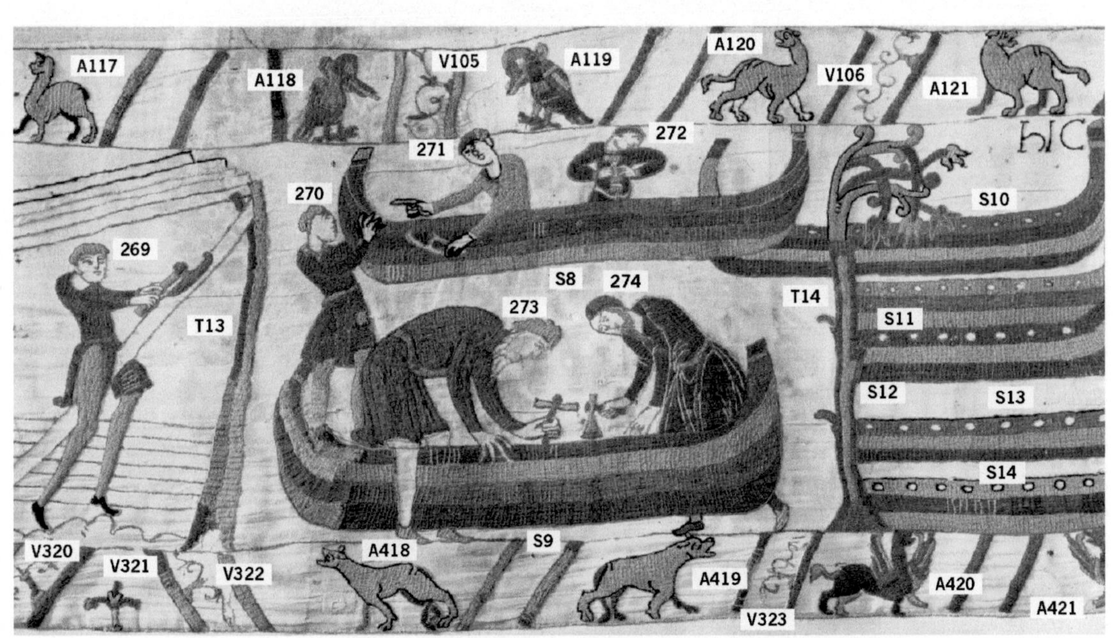

A117
A118
V105
A119
A120
V106
A121
HIC
S10
271
272
270
269
T13
S8 274
273
T14
S11
S12
S13
S14
V320
V321
V322
A418
S9
A419
V323
A420
A421

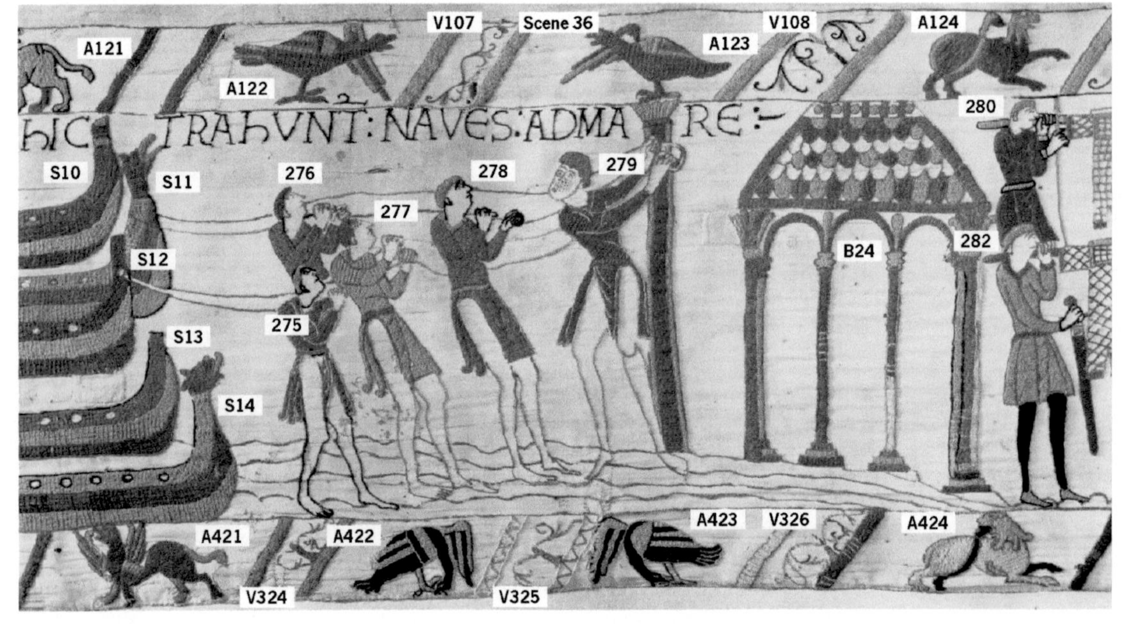

A121
V107
Scene 36
V108
A124
A122
A123
280
HIC TRAHVNT:NAVES:ADMA RE:-
S10
S11
276
278
279
277
S12
B24
282
275
S13
S14
A421
A422
A423
V326
A424
V324
V325

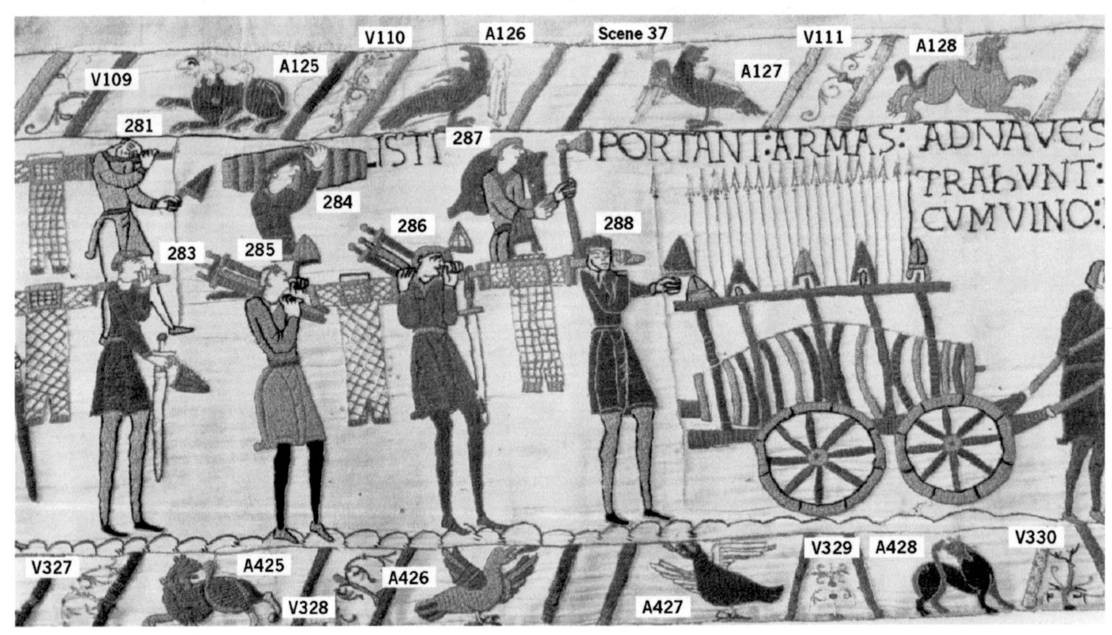

V110
A126
Scene 37
V111
A128
V109
A125
A127
281
ISTI
287
PORTANT:ARMAS:ADNAVES
284
TRAHVNT:
286
288
CVMVINO:
283
285
V327
A425
A426
V329
A428
V330
V328
A427

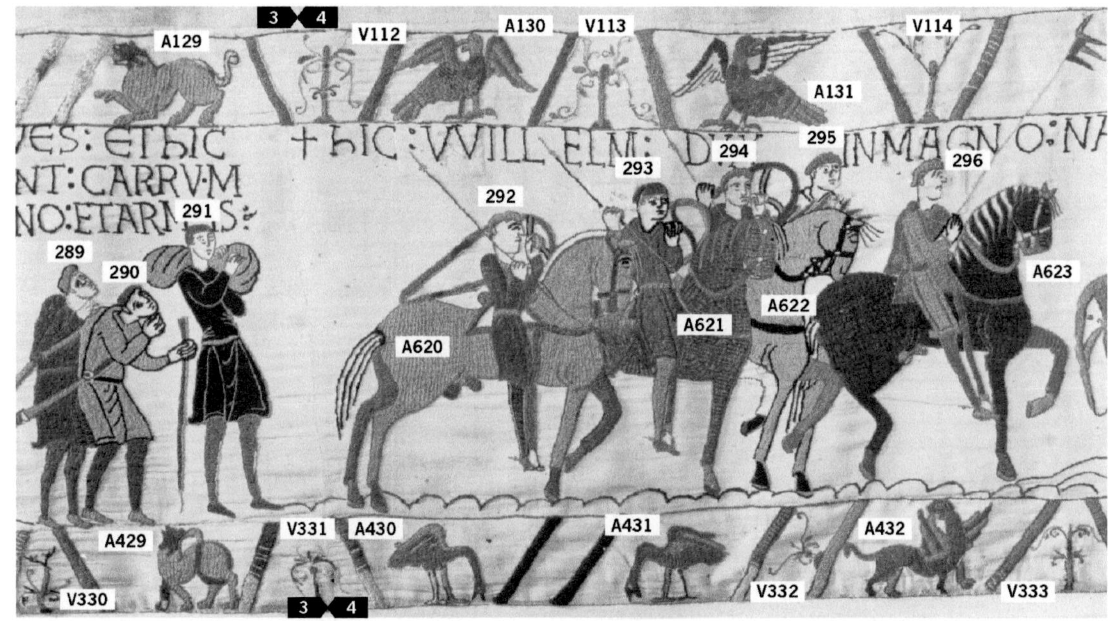

A129
3 4
V112
A130 V113
V114
A131
295
INMAGN O:N
296
VES: ET hIC
+ hIC: VVILL ELM: D
294
293
NT: CARRV·M
292
NO: ET ARM S:
289
290
291
A620
A621
A622
A623
A429
V331 A430
A431
A432
V330
V332
V333
3 4

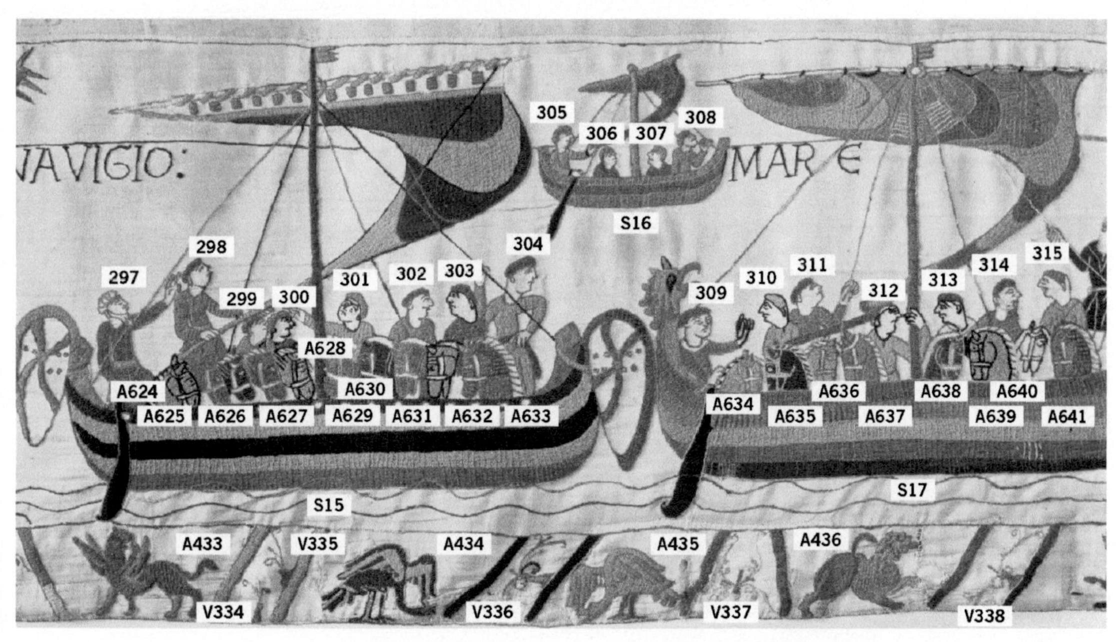

305
306 307 308
NAVIGIO:
MAR E
S16
304
298
297
301 302 303
299 300
A628
311
314 315
309 310
312 313
A624
A630
A634
A636
A638
A640
A625 A626 A627 A629 A631 A632 A633
A635 A637 A639 A641
S15
S17
A433
V335
A434
A435
A436
V334
V336
V337
V338

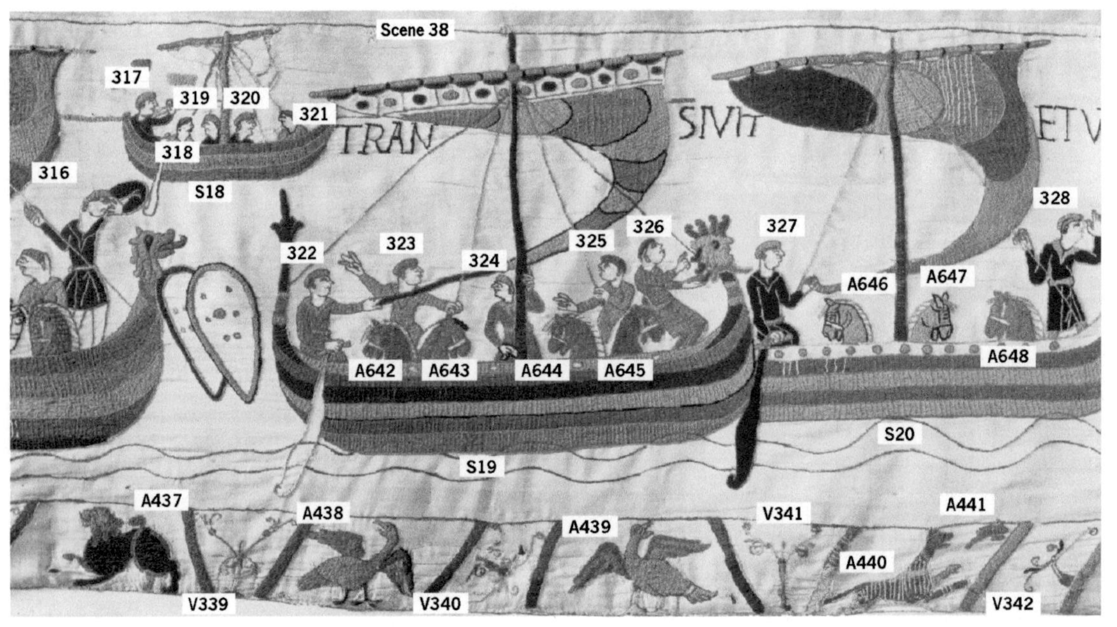

Scene 38
TRAN SIVIT ET V

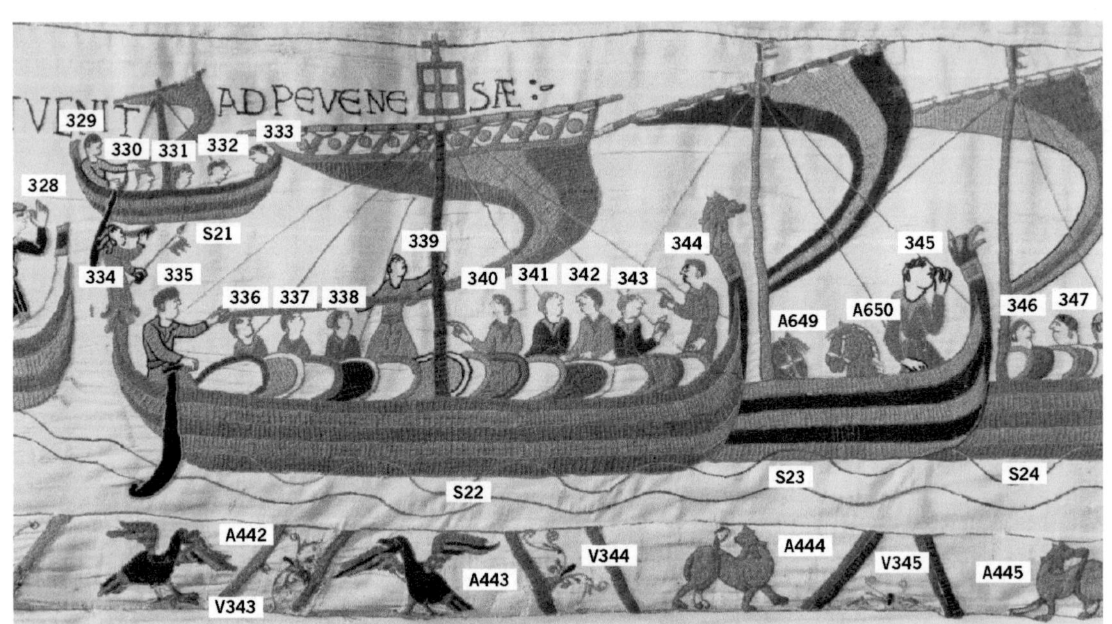

VENIT AD PEVENE SÆ :-

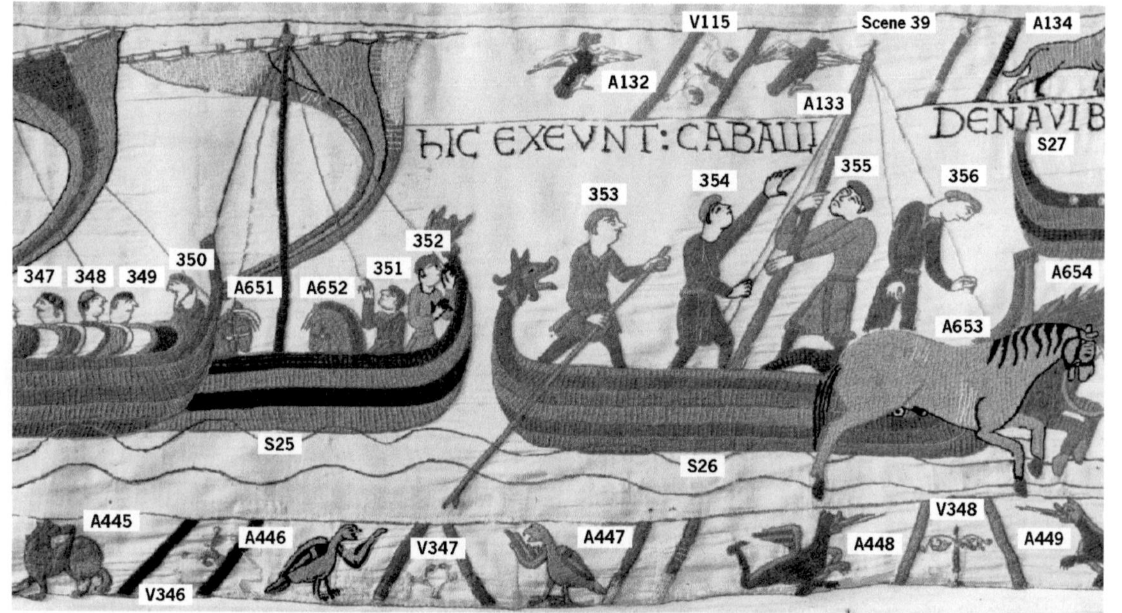

V115
Scene 39
A134
A132
A133
HIC EXEVNT:CABALLI
DE NAVI B
S27
353
354
355
356
352
350
351
347 348 349
A651
A652
A654
A653
S25
S26
V348
A445
A446
V347
A447
A448
A449
V346

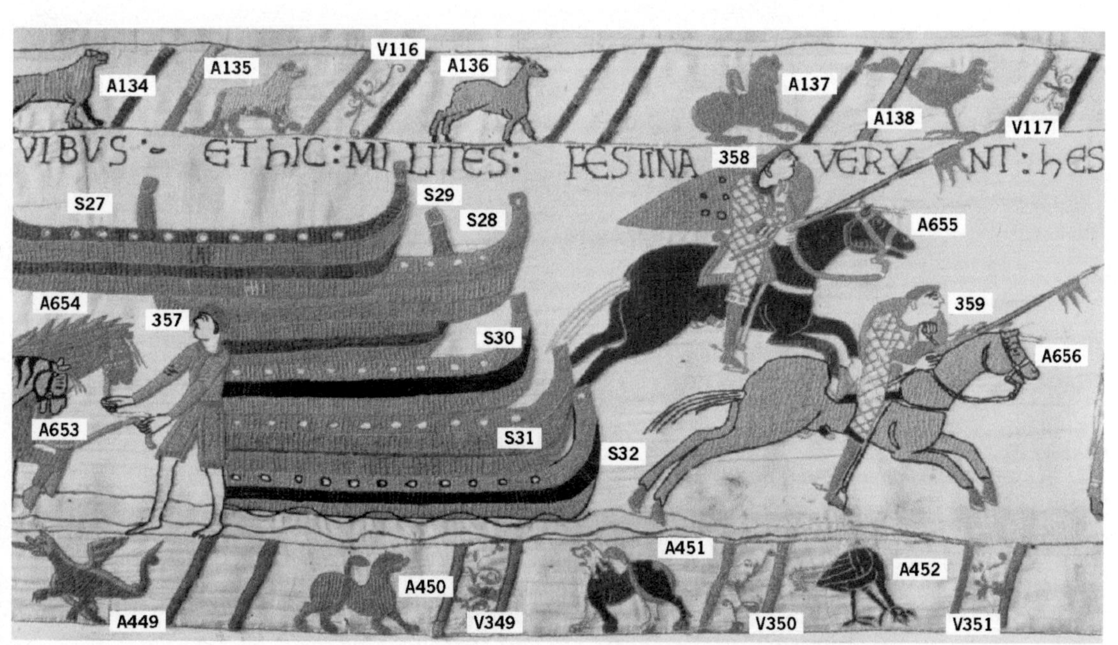

V116
A136
A134
A135
A137
A138
V117
VIBVS:- ET HIC:MILITES: FESTINA VERV NT:HES
358
S27
S29
S28
A655
A654
357
359
S30
A656
A653
S31
S32
A451
A452
A450
A449
V349
V350
V351

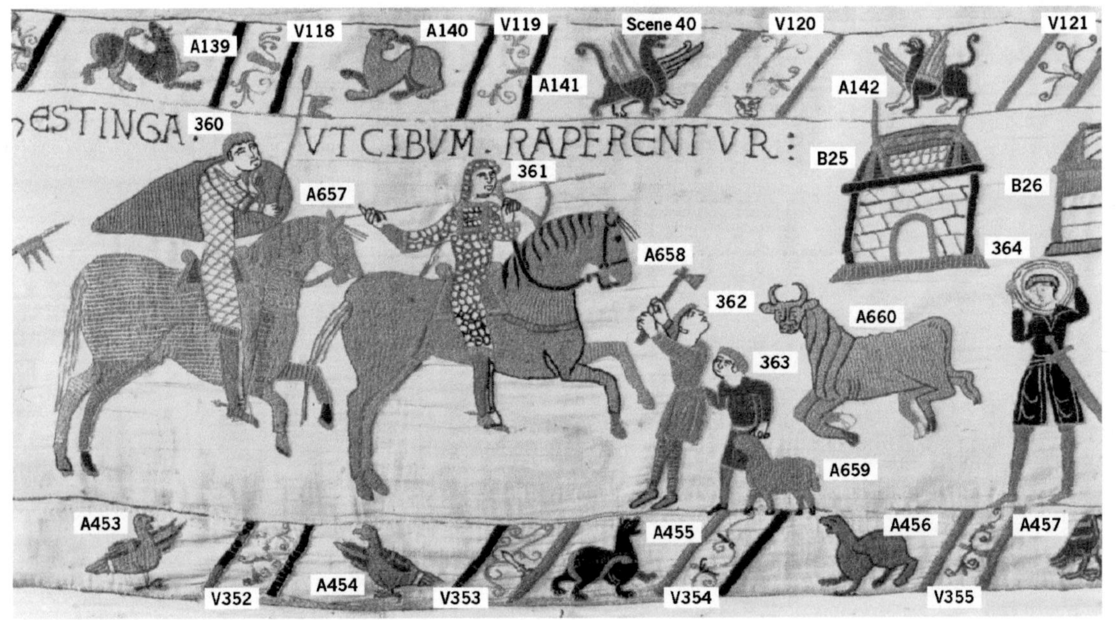
ESTINGA.
VT CIBVM . RAPERENTVR :

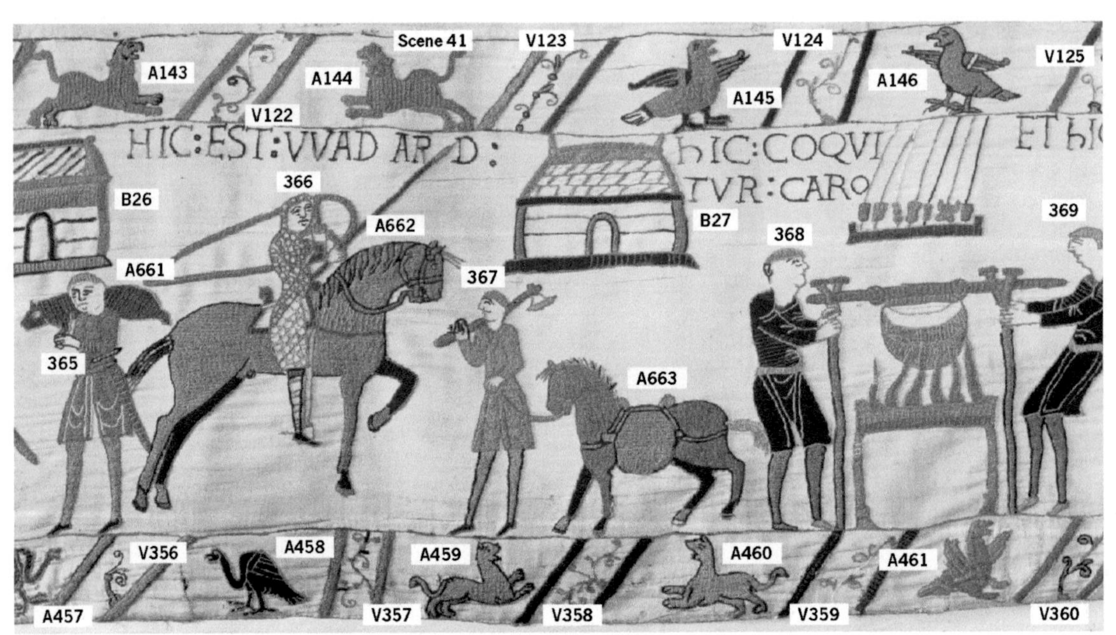
HIC : EST : VVADARD :
hIC : COQVI
TVR : CARO
ET hI

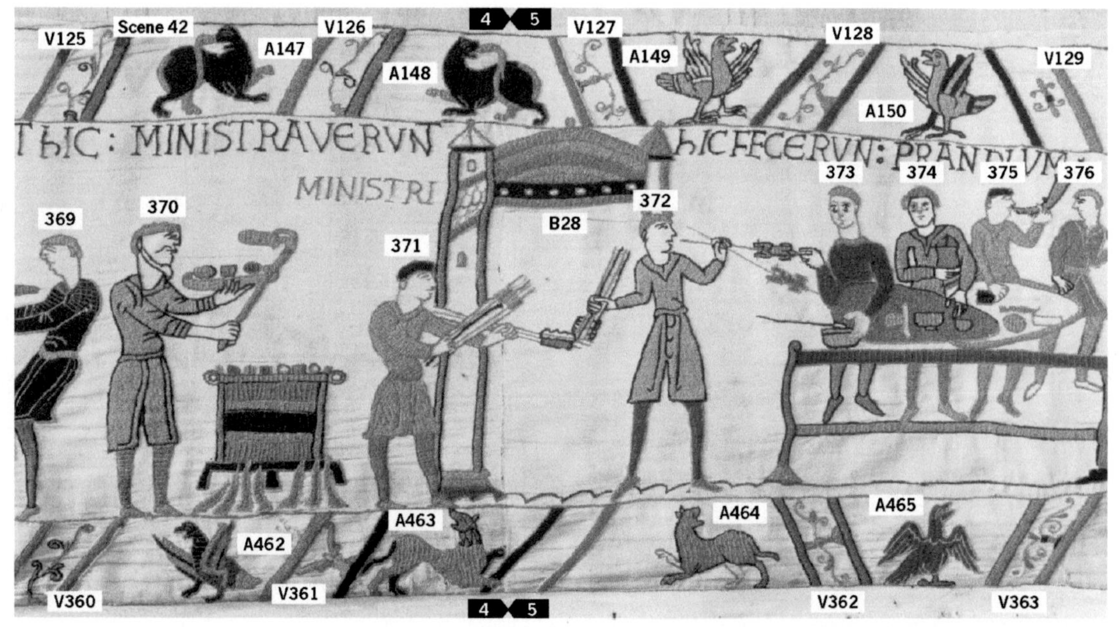

ET HIC: MINISTRAVERUNT
MINISTRI
HIC FECERUN: PRANDIUM

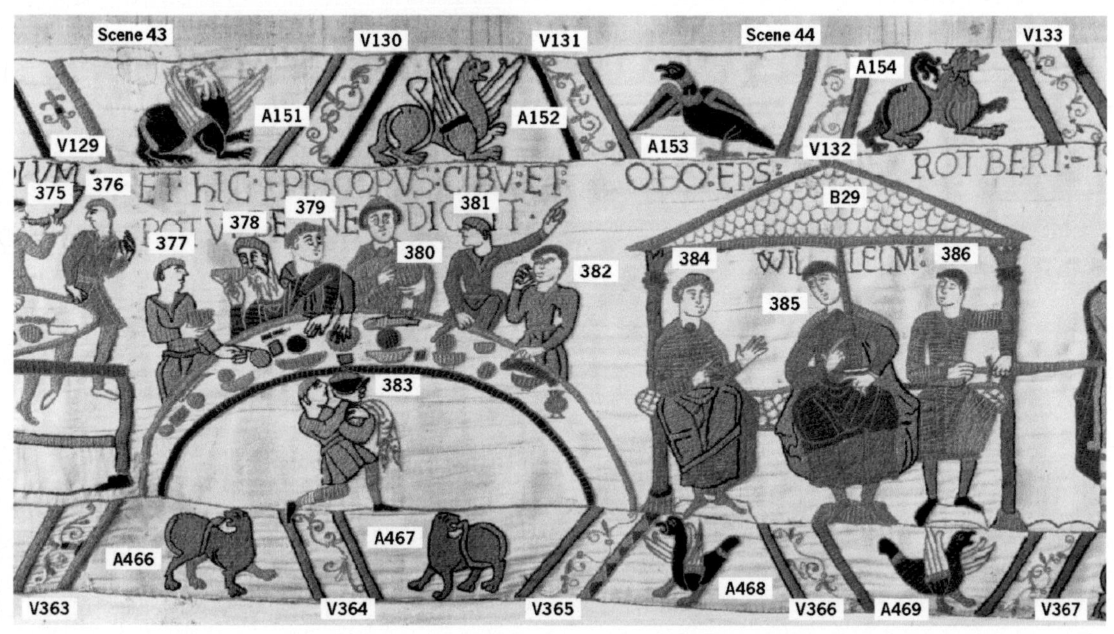

ET HIC EPISCOPVS: CIBV: ET
POTV: BENEDICIT
ODO: EPS
ROTBERT:
WILLELM:

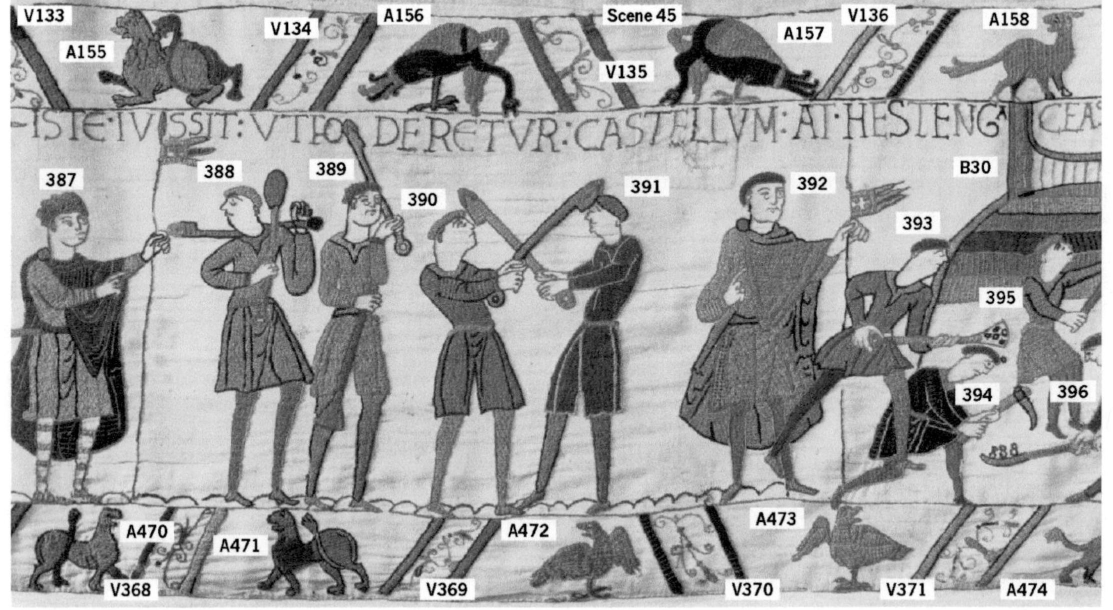

V133
A155
V134
A156
Scene 45
A157
V136
V135
A158
:ISTE:IVSSIT:VT FODERETVR:CASTELLVM:AT·HESTENG̅ CEA
387
388
389
390
391
392
B30
393
395
394
396
A470
A471
A472
A473
V368
V369
V370
V371
A474

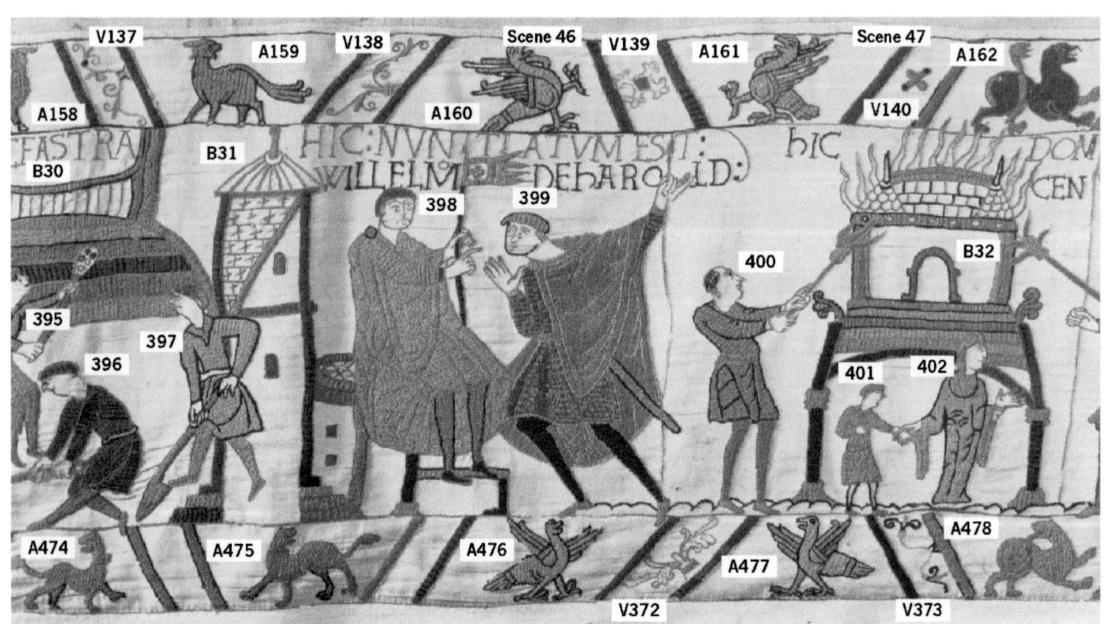

V137
A159
V138
Scene 46
V139
A161
Scene 47
A162
A158
A160
V140
FASTRA
B30
B31
HIC:NVNTIATVM EST:
WILLELM DE HAROLD:
hIC
DOM
CEN
395
397
398
399
400
B32
396
401
402
A474
A475
A476
A477
A478
V372
V373

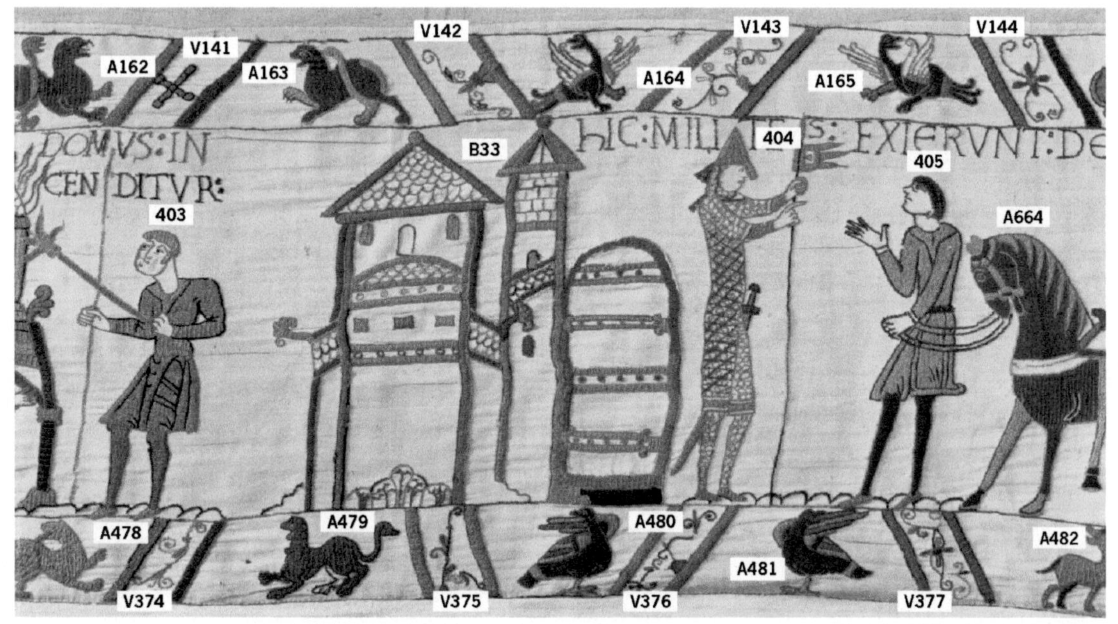

V141
A162
A163
V142
V143
V144
A164
A165
DOMVS:IN CENDITVR:
B33
HIC:MILITES:EXIERVNT:DE
404
405
403
A664
A478
A479
A480
A481
A482
V374
V375
V376
V377

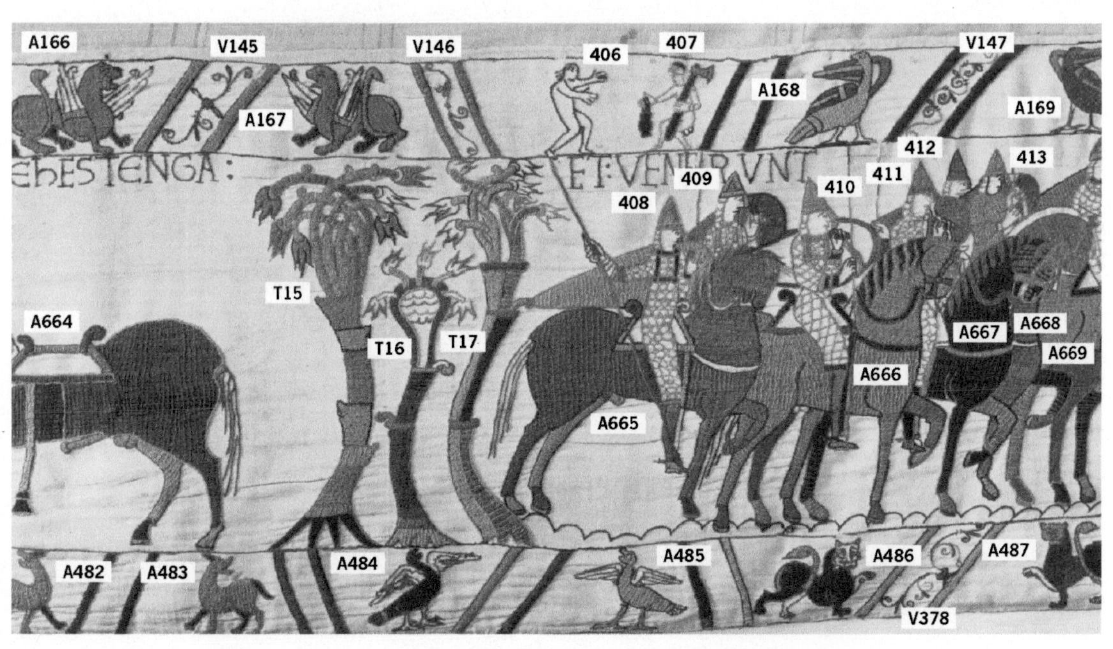

A166
V145
V146
406
407
V147
A167
A168
A169
412
413
EhESTENGA:
ET:VENERVNT
408
409
410
411
T15
T16
T17
A664
A665
A666
A667
A668
A669
A482
A483
A484
A485
A486
A487
V378

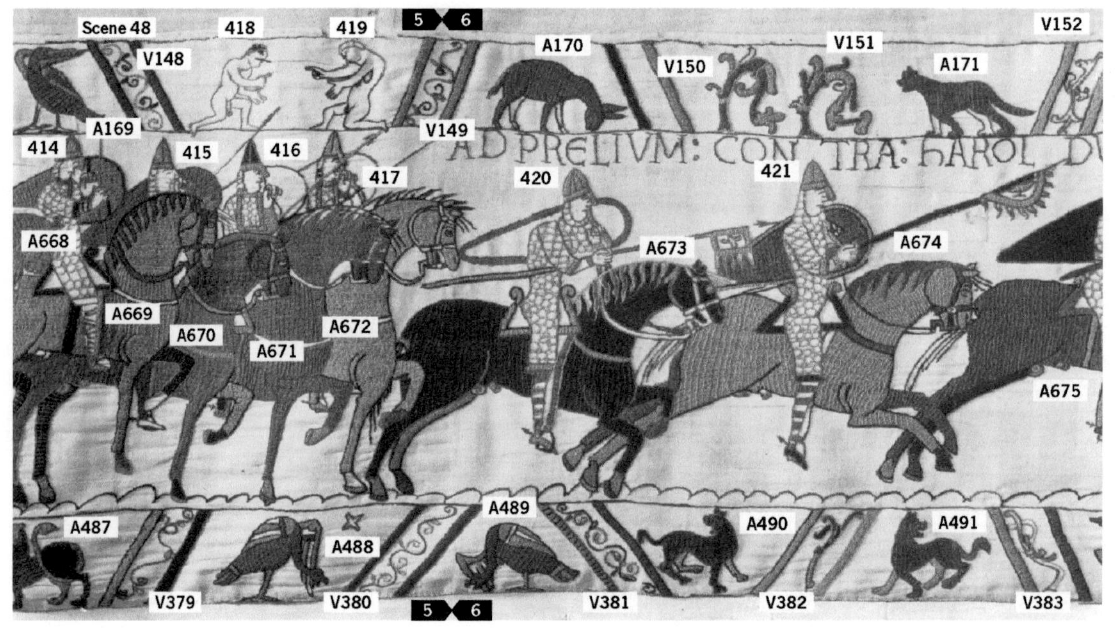

Scene 48
418
419
V148
V150
A170
V151
V152
A169
A171
414
415
416
417
420
421
A668
A673
A674
A669
A670
A671
A672
A675
AD PRELIVM: CON TRA: HAROL DV
A487
A489
A490
A491
A488
V379
V380
V381
V382
V383

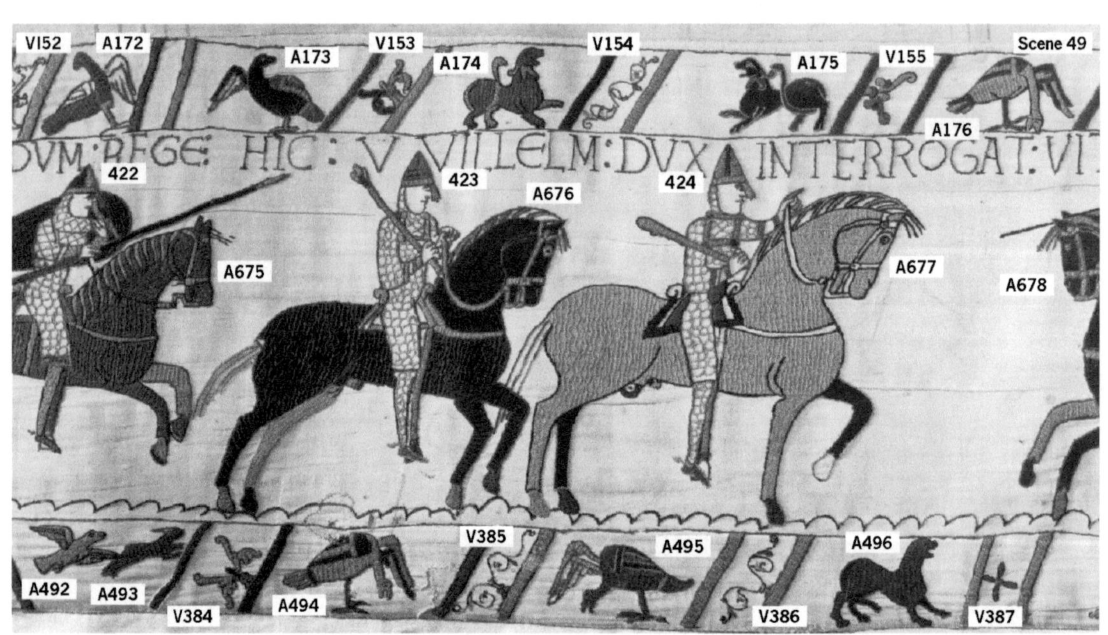

VI52
A172
V153
V154
V155
Scene 49
A173
A174
A175
A176
DVM: REGE: HIC: V VILLELM: DVX INTERROGAT: VI
422
423
A676
424
A675
A677
A678
A492
A493
V385
A495
A496
V384
A494
V386
V387

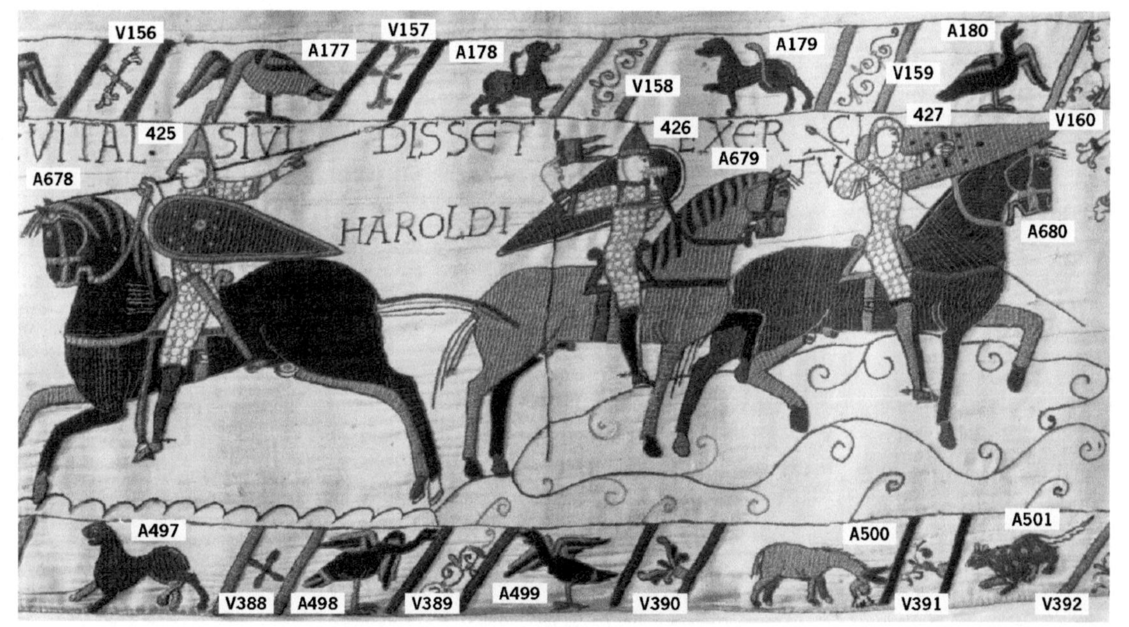

VITAL: ASIV DISSET
HAROLDI
EXERCITV

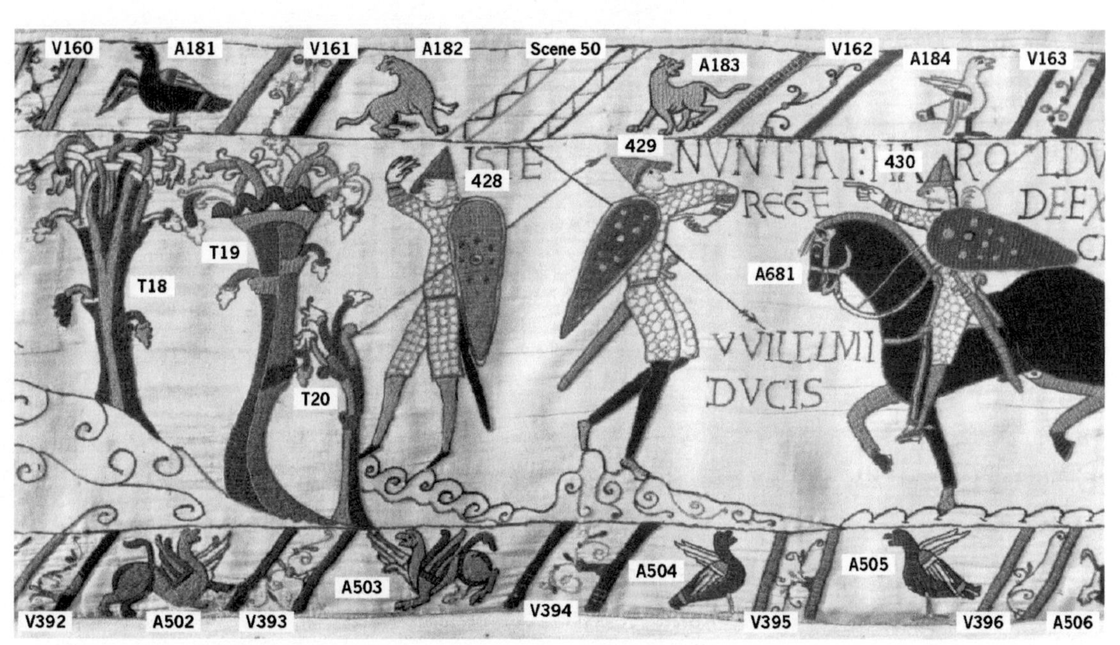

ISTE NVNTIAT:
REGE
ROLDV
DEEX
CI
VVILELMI
DVCIS

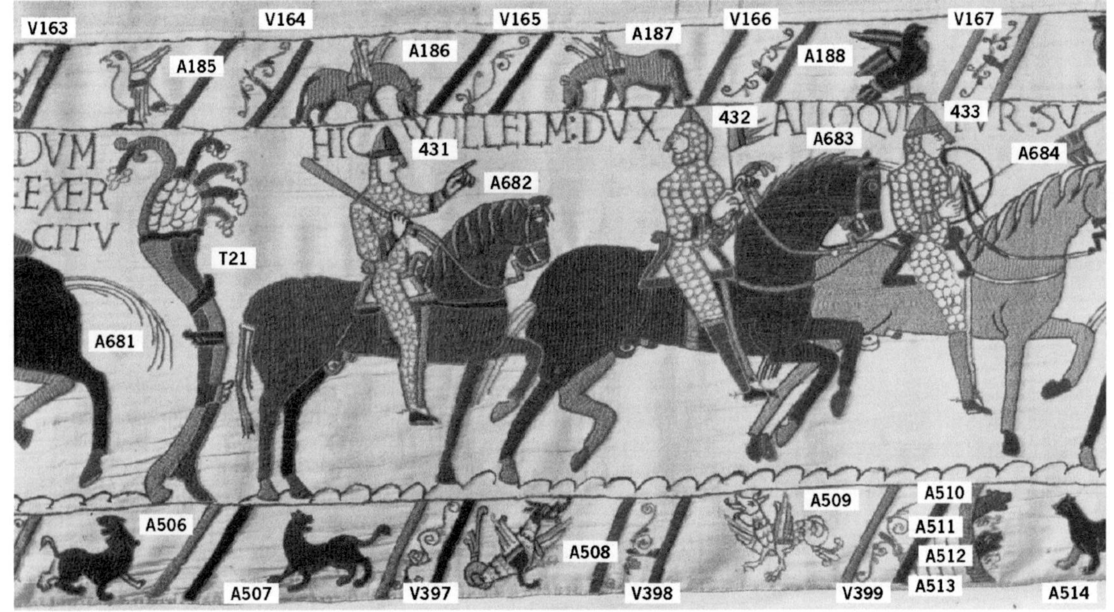

DVM
EXER
CITV
HIC WILLELM DVX
ALLOQVITVR SV

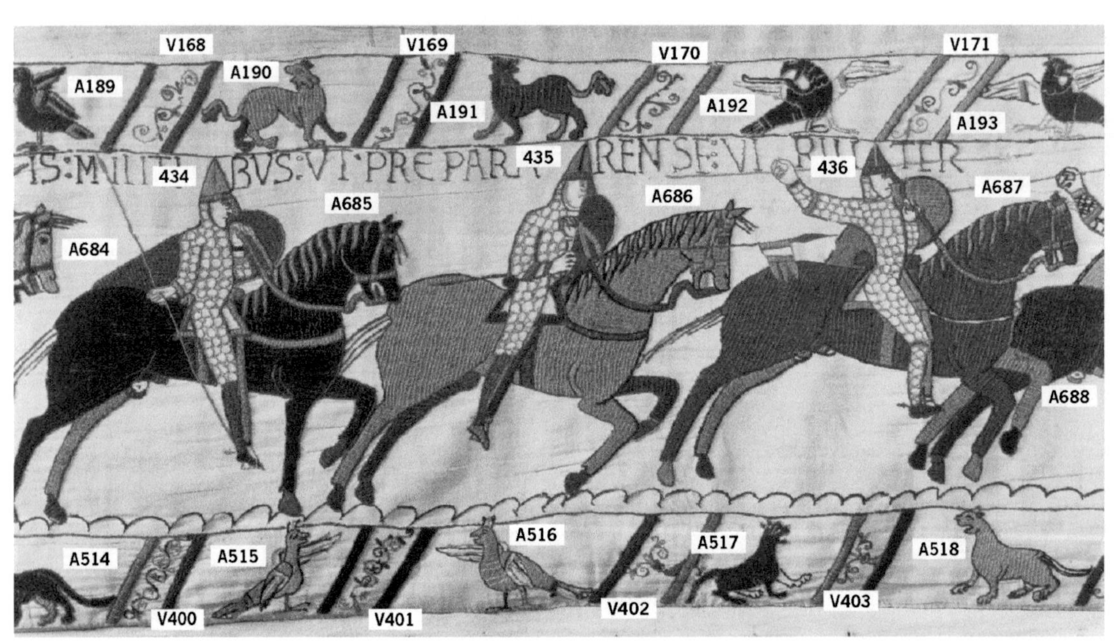

IS MILITIBVS VT PREPARA RENSE VI RVITER

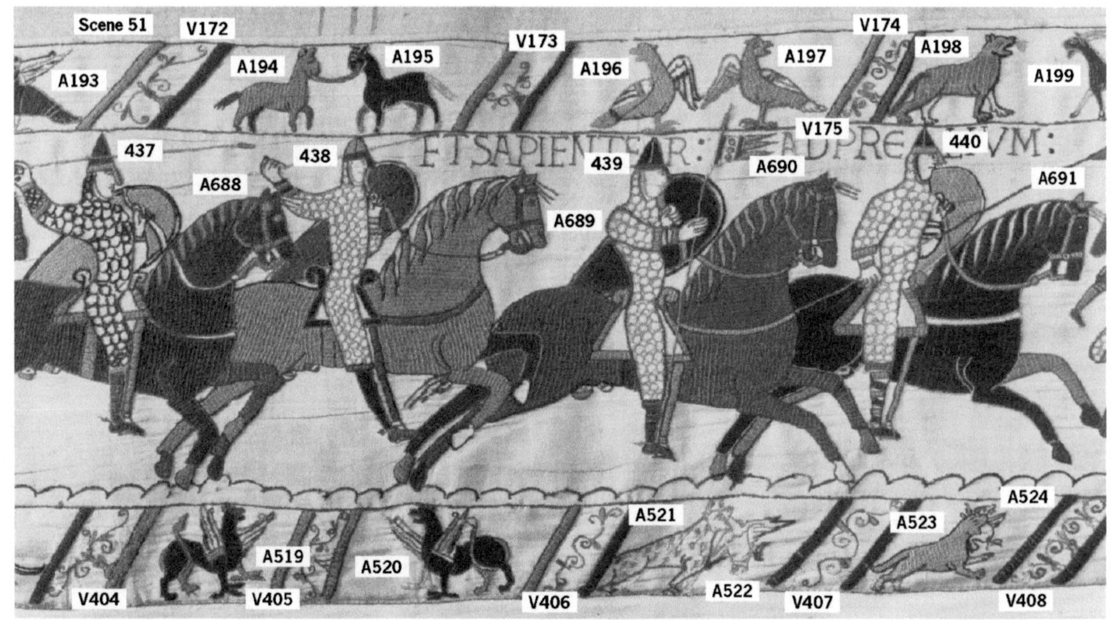

Scene 51
V172
V173
V174
V175
A193
A194
A195
A196
A197
A198
A199
437
A688
438
439
A689
A690
440
A691
ET SAPIENTI... R: ... AD PRE... VM:
A519
A520
A521
A522
A523
A524
V404
V405
V406
V407
V408

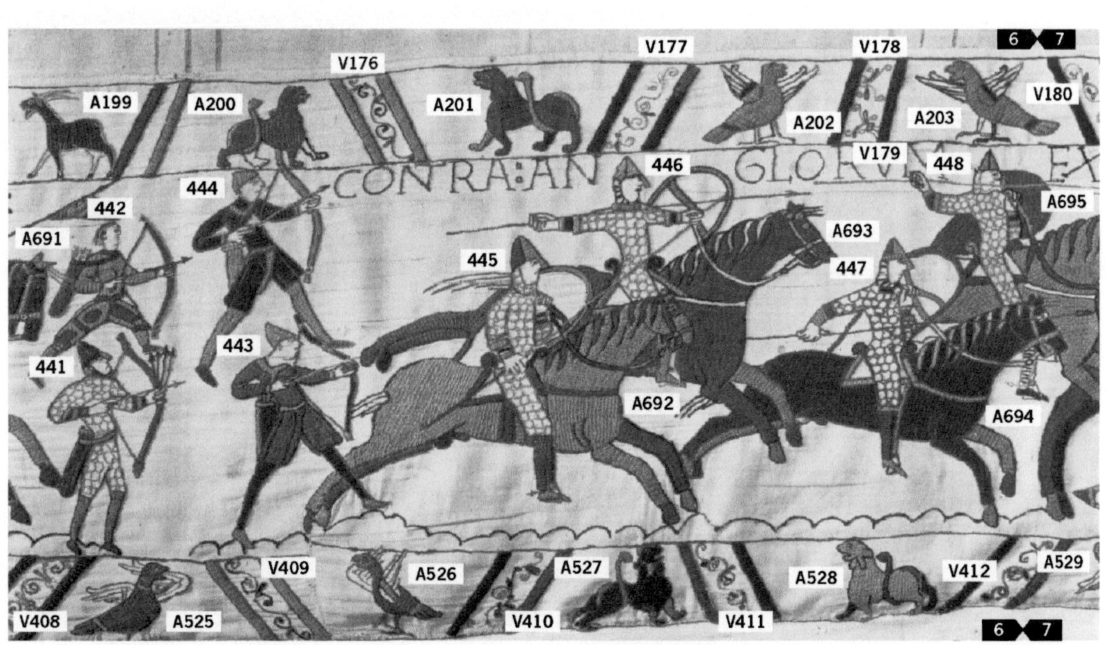

V176
V177
V178
V179
V180
A199
A200
A201
A202
A203
442
444
446
448
A691
A693
A695
441
443
445
447
A692
A694
CON RA AN
GLORV... EX
6 7
V408
V409
V410
V411
V412
A525
A526
A527
A528
A529
6 7

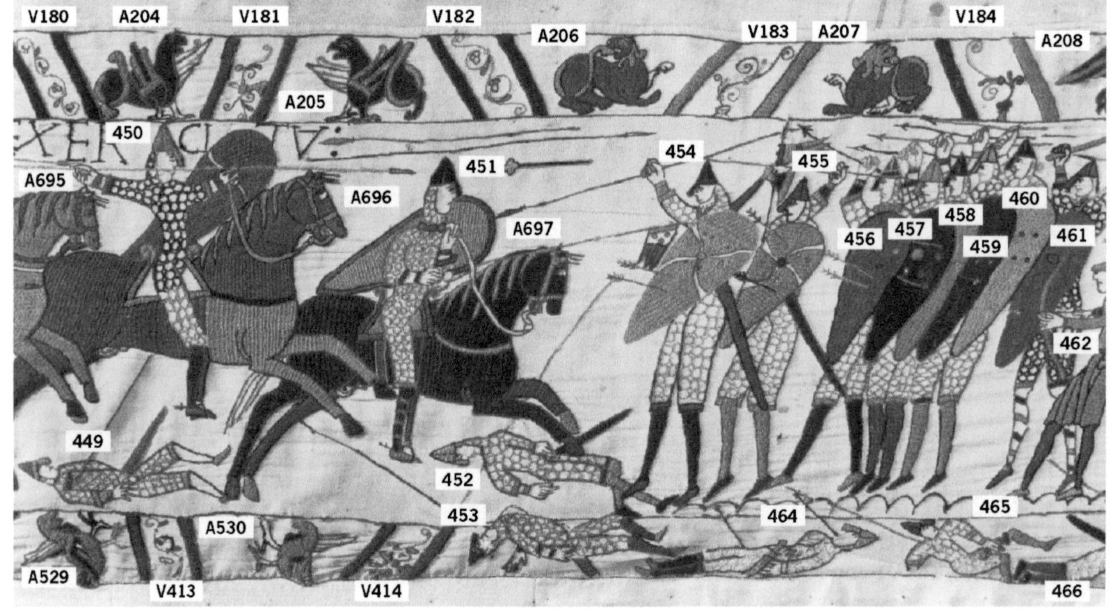
V180 A204 V181 V182 A206 V183 A207 V184 A208
A205
XER ACLU
450 454 455 458 460
A695 451 456 457 459 461
A696 A697
452 462
449 453 464 465
A530
A529 466
V413 V414

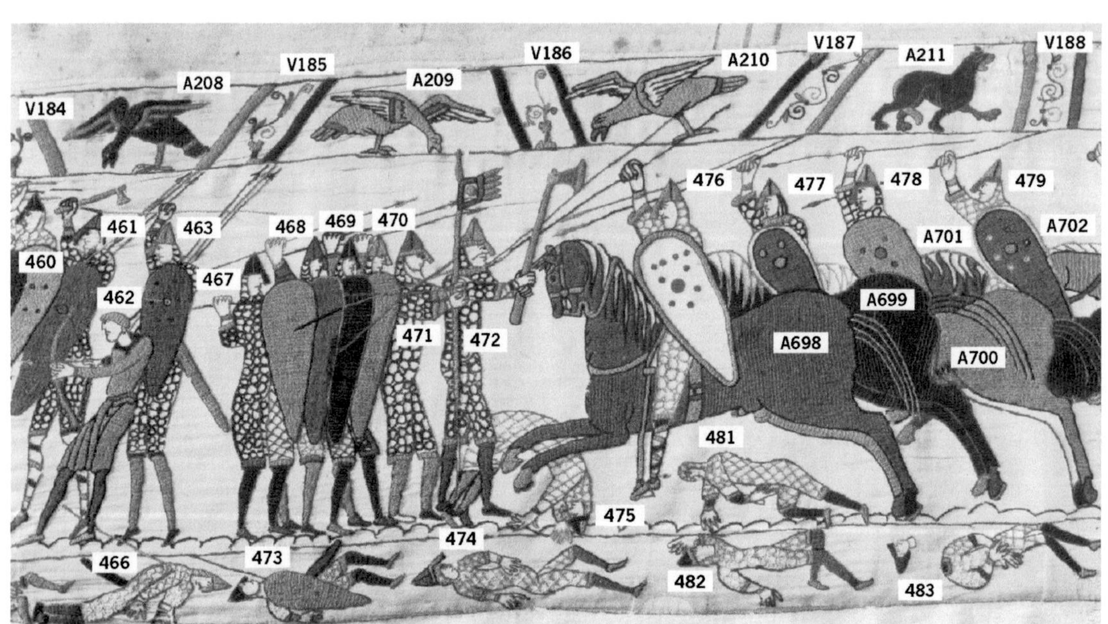
V185 V186 A210 V187 A211 V188
A208 A209
V184
476 477 478 479
461 463 468 469 470 A701 A702
460 467
462 A699
471 472 A698 A700
481
475
466 473 474 482 483

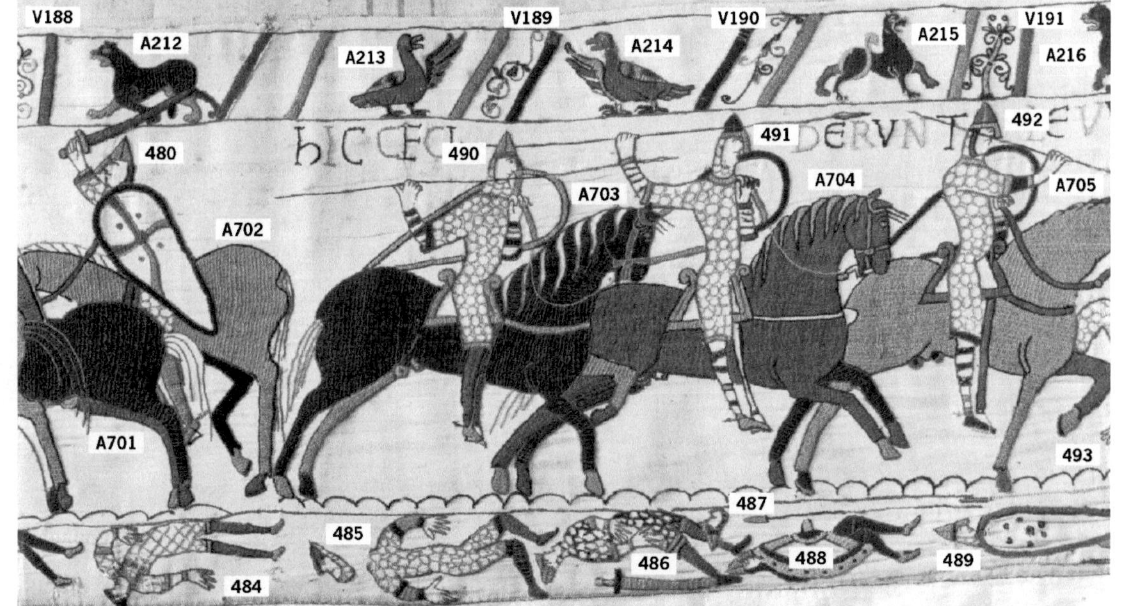

V188
A212
480
A702
A701
hICCEC
490
A703
V189
V190
491
A704
A215
V191
A216
492
A705
493
484
485
486
487
488
489
A213
A214
DERVNT

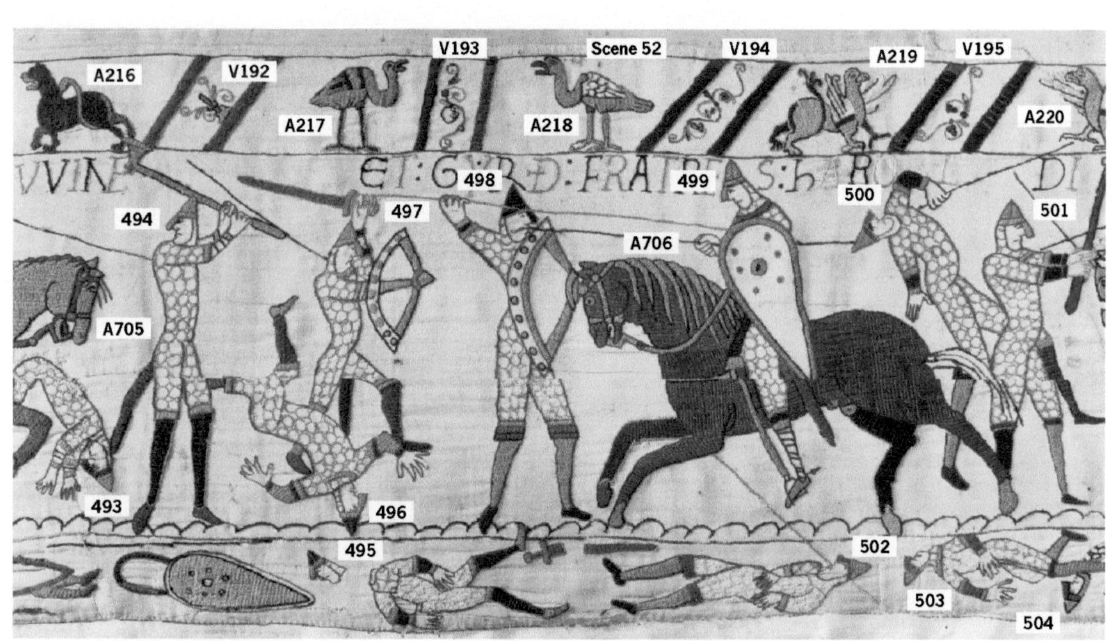

A216
V192
A217
V193
Scene 52
A218
V194
A219
V195
A220
VVINE
494
497
498
A706
ET:GYRD:FRATRES:HAROL
499
500
501
493
A705
496
495
502
503
504
EI:GYRD

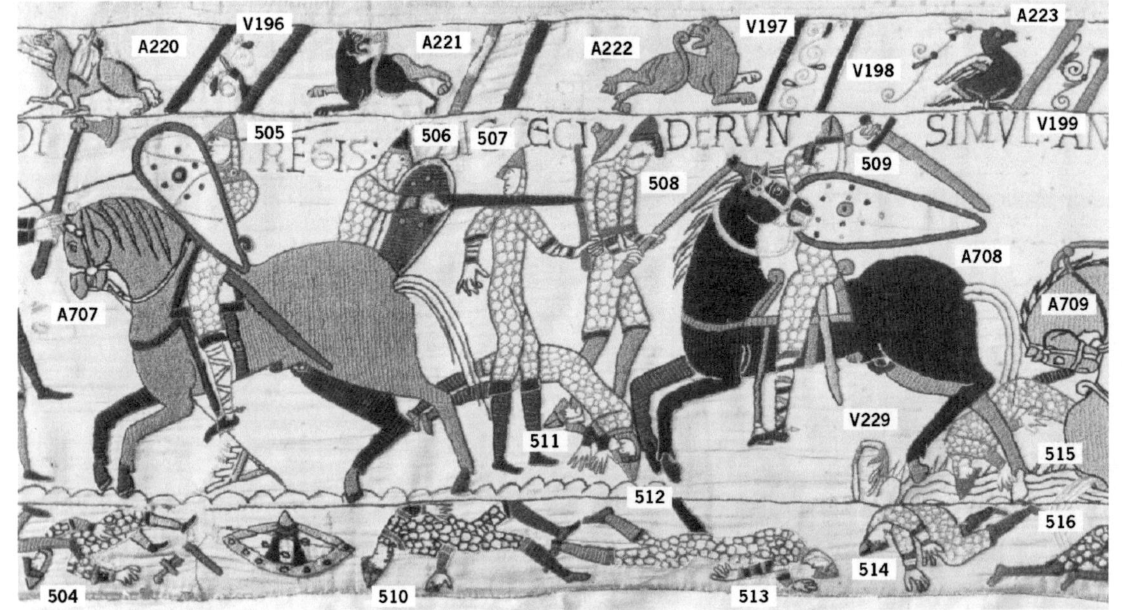

A220
V196
A221
A222
V197
A223
V198
V199
505
506
507
ECIVADERVNT A SIMVL·AN
508
509
A708
A707
A709
V229
515
511
516
512
504
510
513
514

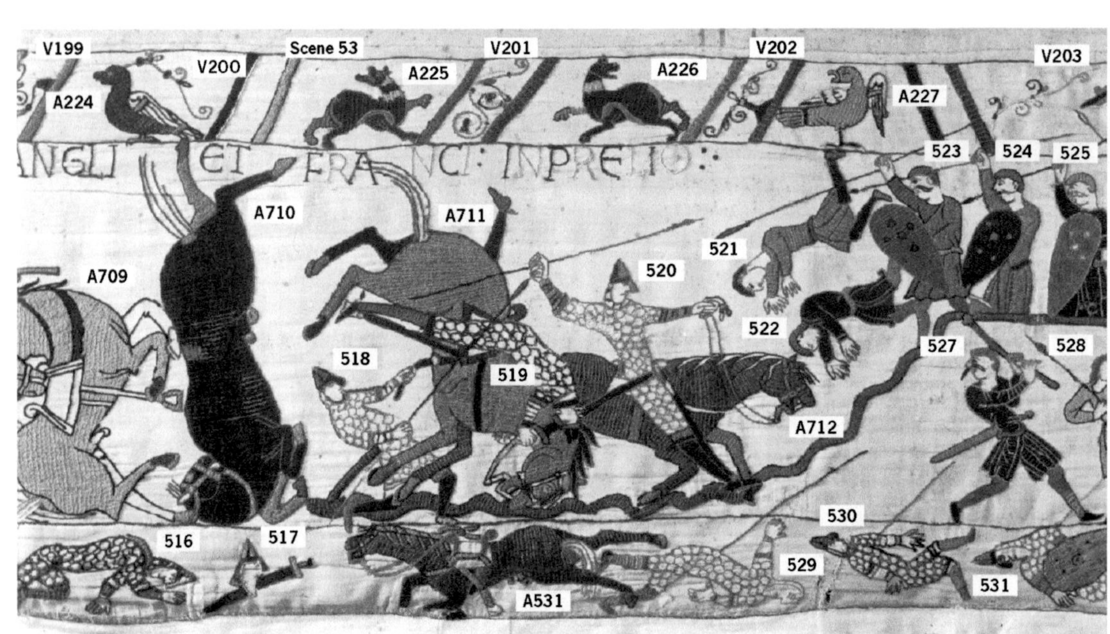

V199
V200
Scene 53
V201
V202
V203
A224
A225
A226
A227
523
524
525
ANGLI ET FRANCI: INPRELIO:
A710
A711
521
A709
520
522
518
519
527
528
A712
516
517
530
529
531
A531

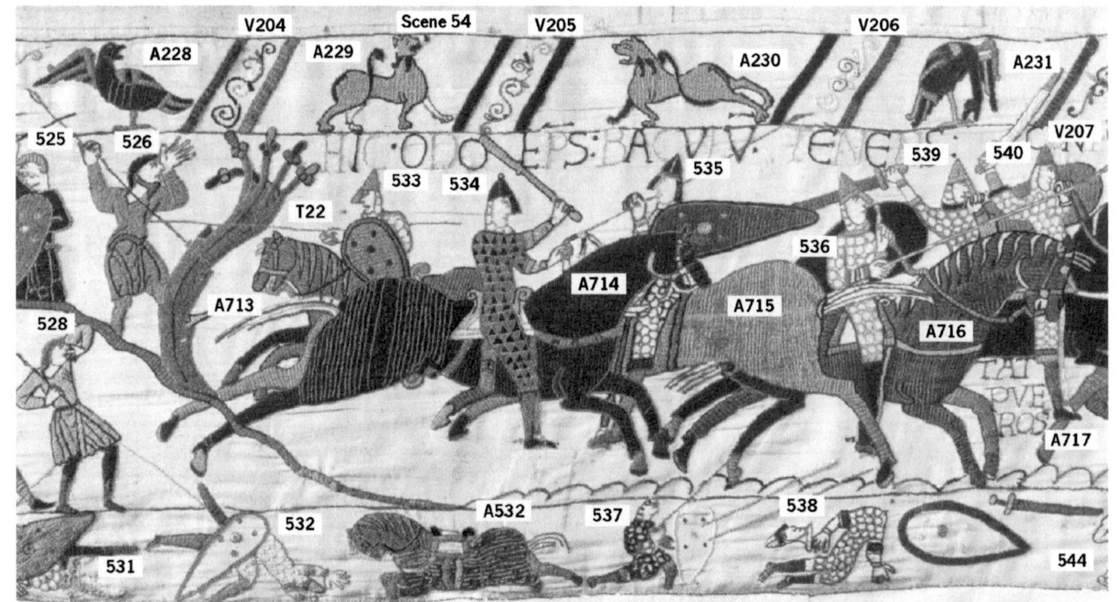

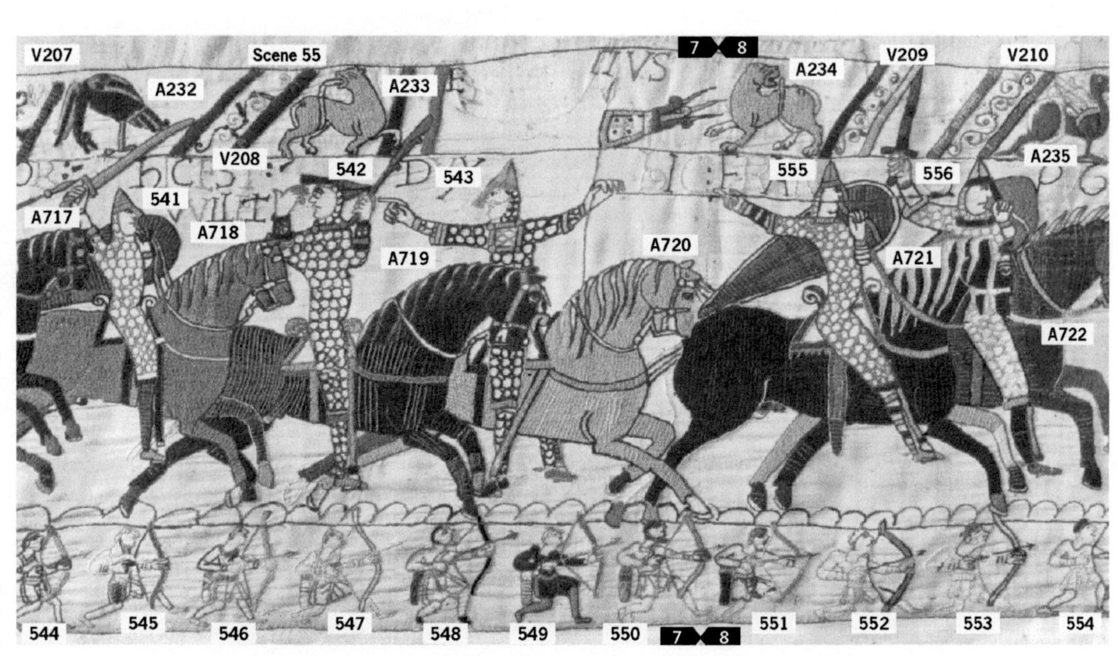

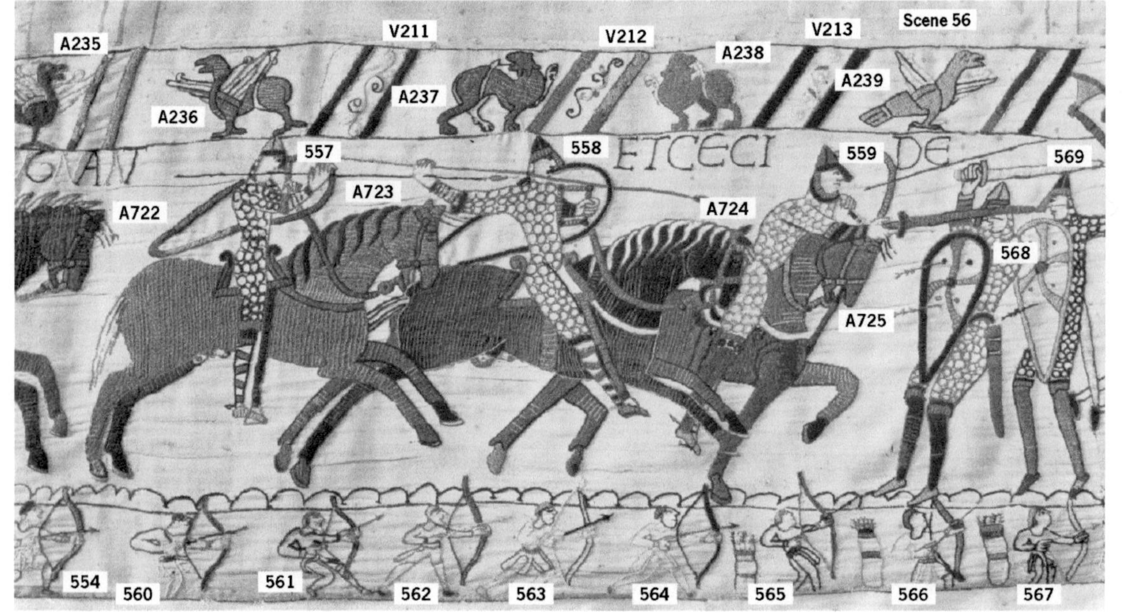

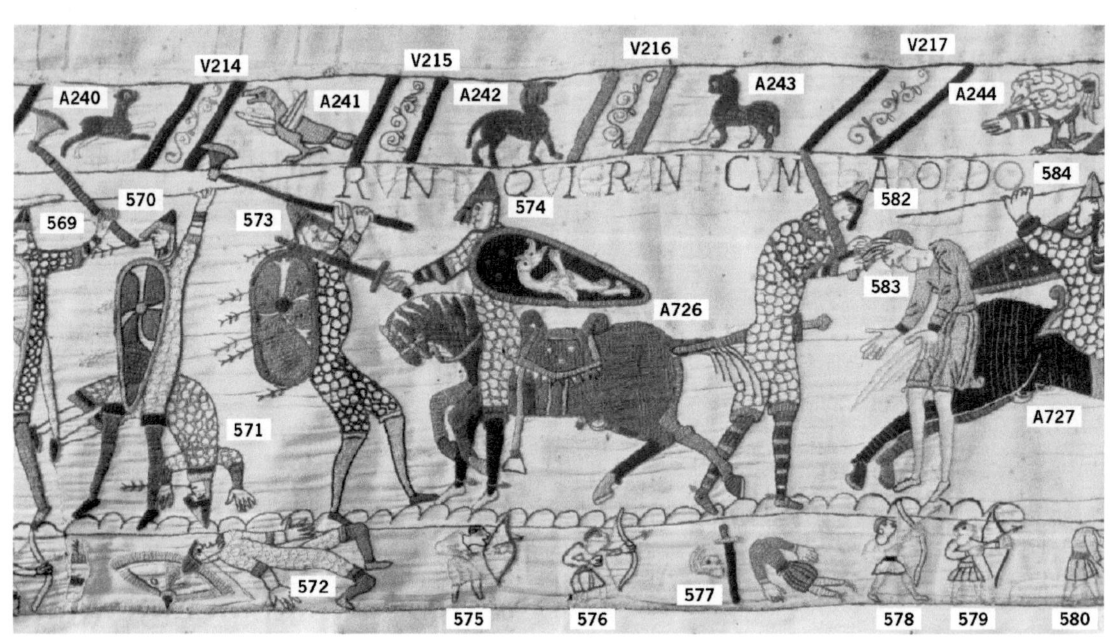

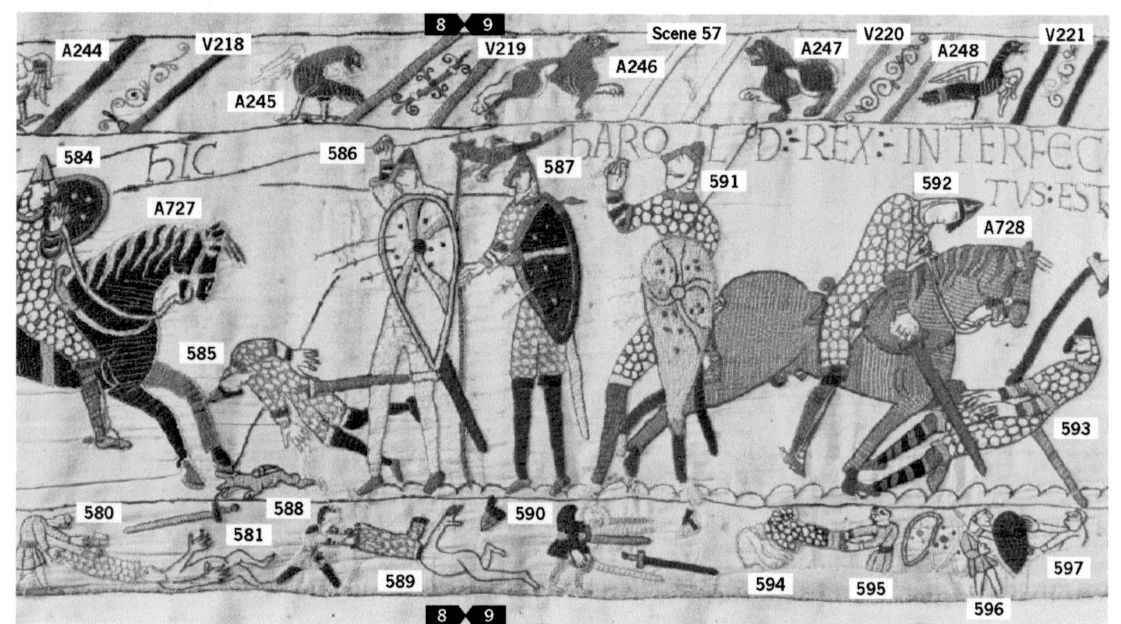

A244
V218
A245
8 9
V219
Scene 57
A246
A247
V220
A248
V221
584
hIC
586
587
hAROLD:REX:INTERFEC
591
592
TVS:EST
A727
A728
585
593
580
588
590
581
589
594
595
597
596
8 9

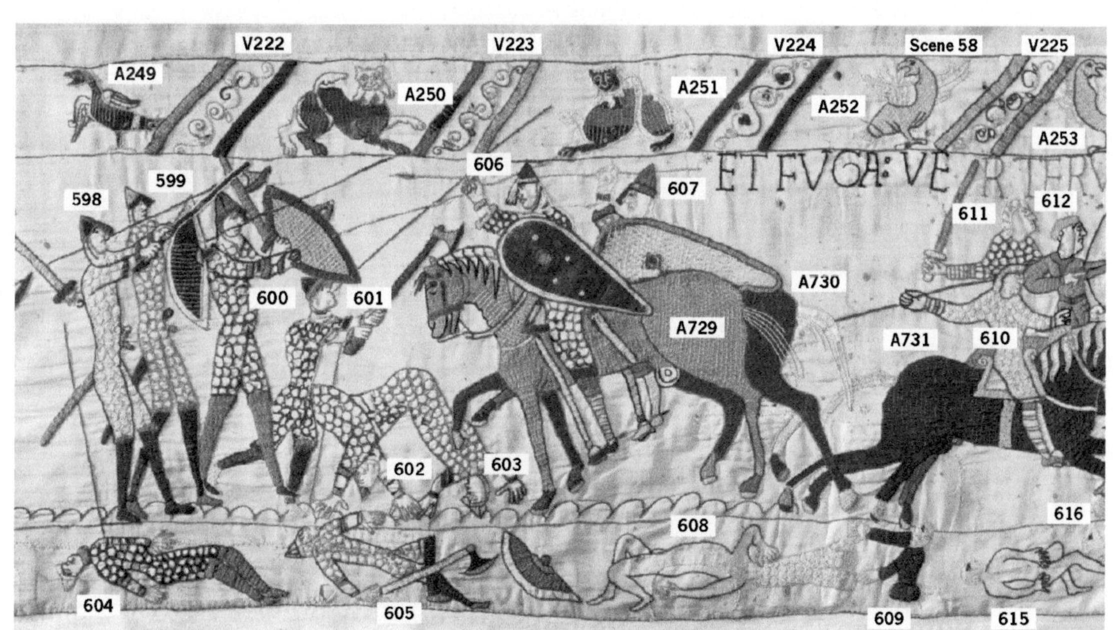

V222
V223
V224
Scene 58
V225
A249
A250
A251
A252
A253
599
606
607
ET FVGA:VE R TERV
611
612
598
A730
600
601
A729
A731
610
602
603
608
616
604
605
609
615

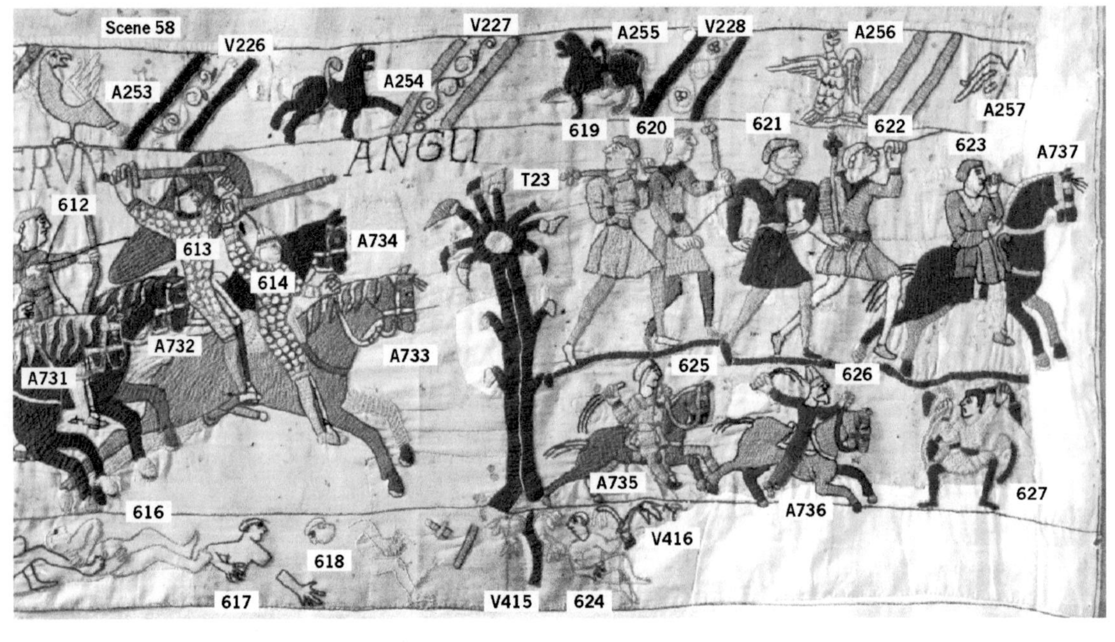

Scene 58
V226
A253
V227
A255
V228
A256
A254
A257
612
ANGLI
619
620
621
622
623
A737
T23
613
A734
614
A732
A733
625
626
A731
A735
627
616
A736
V416
618
V415
624
617

CHAPTER 5

THE REAL WORLD
OF THE TAPESTRY

The Bayeux Tapestry is one of few contemporary (or near contemporary) accounts of the events leading up to the Norman Conquest of England. As such, it is an important primary source for the events of 1064-6.

For the most part, the version of events shown in the Tapestry seems to be fairly reliable. While some elements broadly follow contemporary English accounts, it is nonetheless of interest that certain key episodes from the English perspective such as Harold's defeat of King Harald Hardrada at Stamford Bridge (25 September 1066) are omitted. As we have seen, it is also the case that some aspects of its story, such as the Ælfgyva incident (Scene 15) and the Breton campaign (Scenes 16-20), are uncertain or obscure. Since Odo is believed to be the Tapestry's patron, it is generally thought that he would commission a reliable account, but this view would seem to be over-simplistic. Unlike other contemporary accounts, the Tapestry is not an obvious apologist for either the Anglo-Saxon or Norman perspective. However, assuming the Tapestry was made for public display, and contemporaries familiar with the events depicted would have seen it, it seems likely that it is a broadly reliable account.

In view of the relative paucity of eleventh-century material culture, it is no surprise that historians and archaeologists have quarried the Bayeux Tapestry as a source for the appearance of contemporary artefacts. For many, such as H.E.J. Cowdrey (1988) and Shirley Ann Brown (1988), it remains the primary source for understanding the eleventh-century scene. However, scholars have rarely been sufficiently critical of its authority in this respect; Wolfgang Grape (1994), for example, was so convinced by the Tapestry's accuracy that he believed that the designer had a 'catholic interest in the contemporary scene' and that the Tapestry was 'a record of first-hand observation'.

MEDIEVAL ART HISTORICAL TRADITION

The task of understanding the 'contemporary scene' from medieval art is fraught with difficulties. First, there are few archaeological remains against which to test artistic

"

representations; this is particularly true for the eleventh century. Second, the medium used may limit the artist's scope for accurately recreating a particular artefact type, assuming this was the intention. Images on textiles are a clear case where simplification and stylisation is expected, and here special caution should be taken in any assessment of the visual imagery. Third, the fact it was customary for medieval artists to repeat pictorial formulae and reuse them in new contexts further complicates the matter. Charles Dodwell (1954) highlighted the fact that naturalistic, classical and semi-classical elements that appear in late Anglo-Saxon art were generally inspired by Carolingian art. The example par excellence is the Utrecht Psalter, which, as we have seen, was to have a profound influence on illuminations produced at Canterbury and beyond. The notion that the task of the artist is to do something new, though it is deeply embedded in modern cultural awareness, is a comparatively recent development. Much the reverse held true in the medieval period. Both J.J.G. Alexander (1992) and Martin Carver (1986) noted that it could be difficult for an artist to alter an accepted image or apply illustration to a text which had not previously been illustrated. In such a milieu, archaic representations of artefact types were common and probably deliberate. Moreover, the 'transmission' of pictorial model from exemplar to copy could lead to some corruption of the original image. Therefore, if the Tapestry designer behaved like most contemporary medieval artists, and used inherited formulae for artefacts, then the Bayeux Tapestry might not be as reliable a source for life in the eleventh century as has generally been assumed. The general dependence of late Anglo-Saxon artists upon earlier models should not be overstated; their work is rightly celebrated for its diversity and originality – iconographically, stylistically and technically. Yet this did not really extend to the depiction of events.

In order to assess the accuracy of the artefacts depicted in the Tapestry, it is necessary to compare them carefully with, on the one hand, those which survive archaeologically, and, on the other, with those depicted in art, most notably in manuscript illumination. The following discussion of architecture, arms and armour, ships, dress and clothing, birds and beasts, and vegetation aims to highlight the problematic nature of the Bayeux Tapestry for understanding the 'real world' of the eleventh century.

BUILDINGS AND ARCHITECTURE

The Bayeux Tapestry is rich in architecture. Most buildings depicted provide a physical or geographic context for a particular scene. Nonetheless, a few are principally scene dividers or embellishment; much like the Tapestry's trees, which will be discussed in due course. The diverse appearance of the buildings might suggest that the Tapestry designer intended the architecture to evoke the essence of a variety of contemporary structures. However, a detailed study of these buildings reveals that in many cases their architectural elements are fictive and borrowed from art; a view supported by Wolfgang Grape (1994) and Cyril Hart (2000).

Of the 33 buildings illustrated in the Tapestry, nine (Bosham Church, Guy's palace at Beaurain, Mont-Saint-Michel, Dol, Rennes, Dinan, Bayeux, Westminster Abbey and Hastings Castle) are named in the accompanying textual narrative. While this might lead the modern viewer to expect the depictions in question to resemble the actual structures they represented, Richard Krautheimer (1942) and Paul Lampl (1961) have demonstrated that early medieval practices were often different.

In the few instances where remains of named buildings survive, there is an opportunity to compare architectural fabric with the Tapestry illustrations. Where there is no corresponding fabric, or the buildings are not named, it must suffice to compare the designs with generic building types.

Churches

Rectangular buildings with trapezoid pitched roofs, the form shared by Bosham Church and Mont-Saint-Michel, are used elsewhere in the Tapestry for secular structures (such as Buildings 25-7 & 32), suggesting that the designer did not intend this form to be diagnostic of church architecture. It is only the small crosses on the roofs of these buildings that unequivocally indicate their true function.

Reginald Allen Brown (1989b) believed that the surviving early fabric at both Bosham and Mont-Saint-Michel reveals that the Tapestry designer may not have taken the appearance of the contemporary structures as the basis of his design. Even though the aisles, porch, and much of the chancel which dominate Bosham Church today are later additions (disguising much of the Saxon fabric), it is apparent that the ground plan of the original Saxon church has little in common with the building illustrated in the Tapestry (*13*).

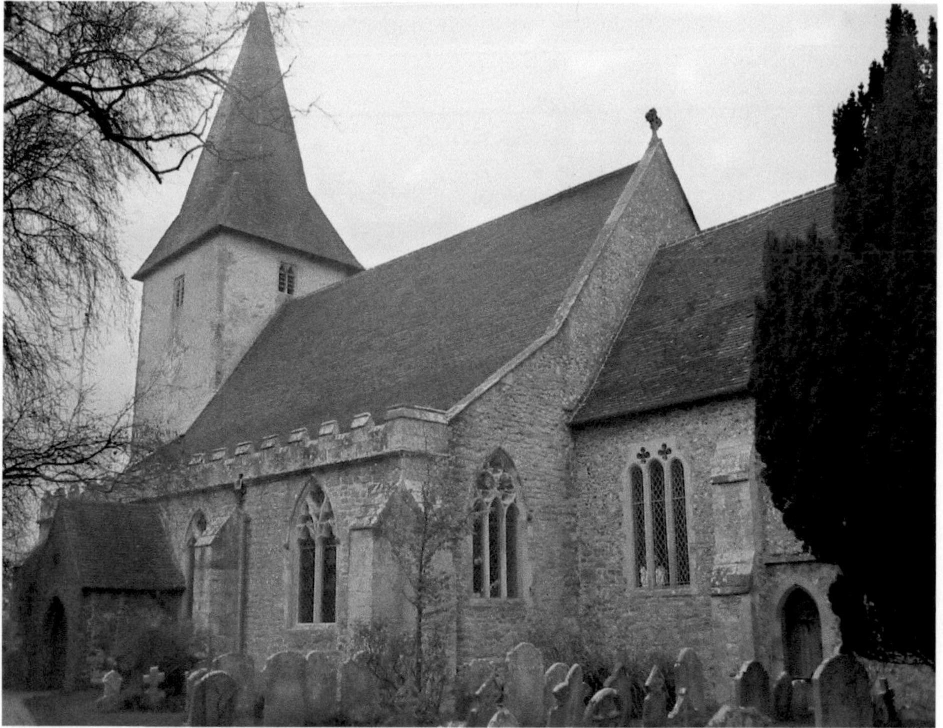

13 Bosham Church as it appears today

Lucien Musset (2002) suggested that the central 'doorway' shown in the Tapestry might represent Bosham's magnificent chancel arch (*14*); this would imply the depiction in the Tapestry shows both the inside and outside of the church. However, this ignores the fact that such rounded arches are not unique to this building. Any relationship between the surviving Anglo-Saxon parts of Bosham Church and the representation in the Tapestry could well be coincidental. The ground plan of Bosham Church (as shown in the Tapestry) seems to compare favourably with the extant remains of several Anglo-Saxon churches, such as Heysham in Lancashire and Thornage in Norfolk, and this may indicate that the designer took a standard Anglo-Saxon church form as the basis for his design. Moreover, one can move beyond the plan to compare individual aspects of the church in the Tapestry with for example the surviving fabric of St Laurence, Bradford-upon-Avon (*colour plates 23 & 24*), which has similar features and decoration. This is not to say that the Tapestry designer knew of this particular building first-hand, rather that the upper arcading, arched windows and doorway are typical features of many late Anglo-Saxon churches from which inspiration could have been drawn.

The Tapestry shows Mont-Saint-Michel on a hill, but there resemblance to the eleventh-century building ends. Maylis Baylé (2001) has noted that the Carolingian church, built in the tenth century, comprised a rectangular nave and square chancel built on the summit of the rock, with a lower sanctuary (the chapel of Notre-Dame-sous-Terre) on a terrace

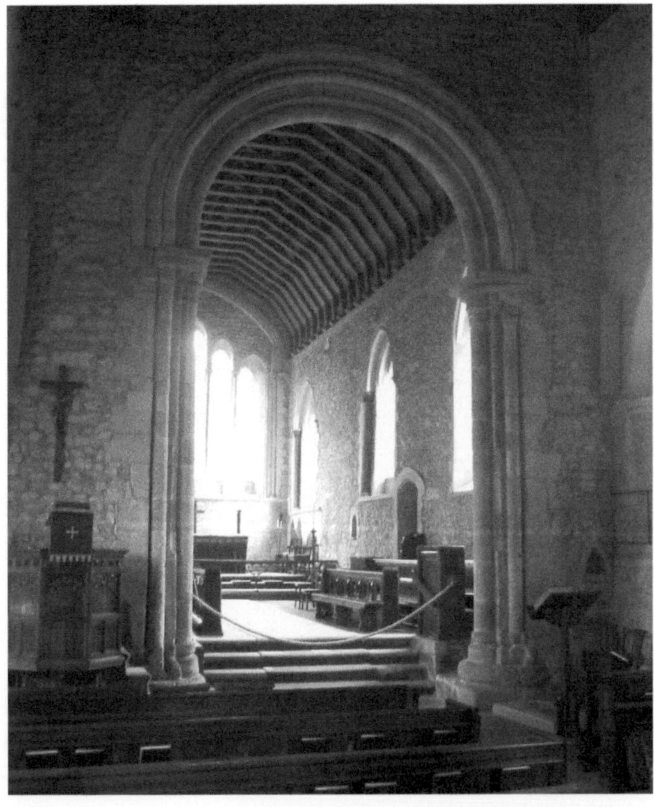

14 The chancel arch of Bosham Church

below. In about 1023, Abbot Hildebert II began work to replace (or incorporate) these buildings within an ambitious and complex Romanesque edifice. Although the structure in the Tapestry has some ancillary buildings, it is difficult to reconcile this depiction with the remains of the eleventh-century abbey complex (*15*). The nave, which consisted of seven bays, was not yet finished by 1085, and it is possible that the Carolingian church still survived when the Tapestry was produced; neither the new nave nor the earlier church is suggested in the Bayeux Tapestry.

It was art, not the real world, which informed much of the Tapestry's ecclesiastical architecture. Rectangular-shaped buildings, with trapezoid pitched roofs are commonly illustrated in contemporary illuminations, such as Junius 11, the Old English Hexateuch and British Library, Royal 15 A.xvi (*16*). It was these, as well as contemporary reliquary shrines – the latter highlighted by Cyril Hart (2000) – which probably influenced the Tapestry's depiction of both Bosham Church and Mont-Saint-Michel. This is especially likely given that such artistic creations will have been more immediately available to the designer, whatever

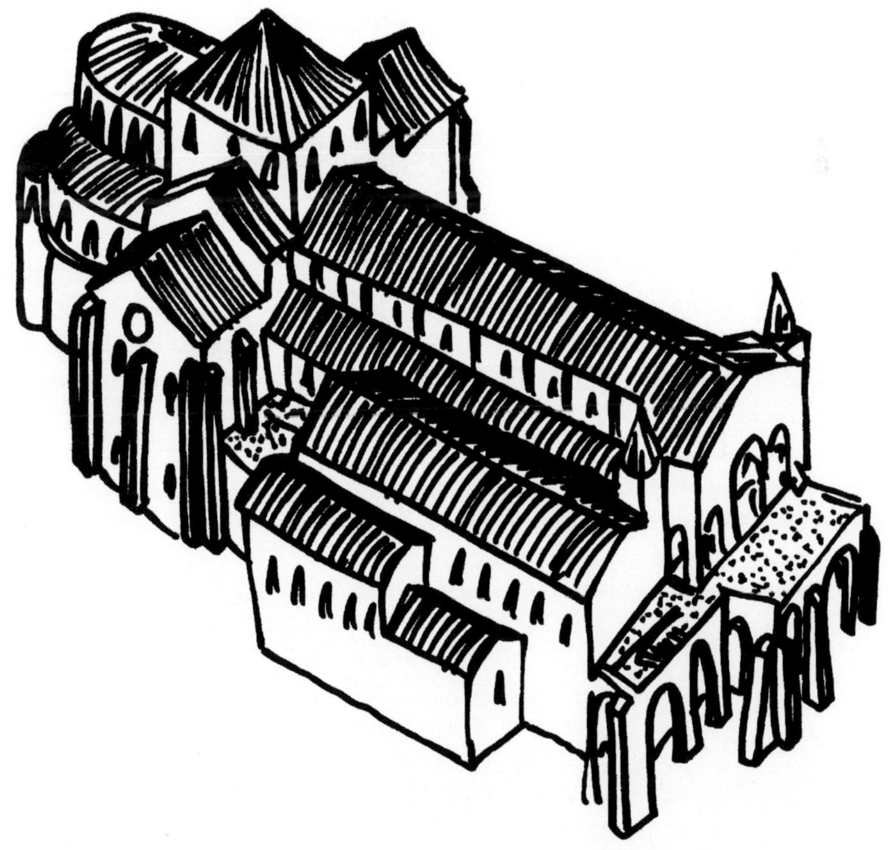

15 An artistic reconstruction of the Romanesque church of Mont-Saint-Michel based on extant architectural fabric and archaeological remains

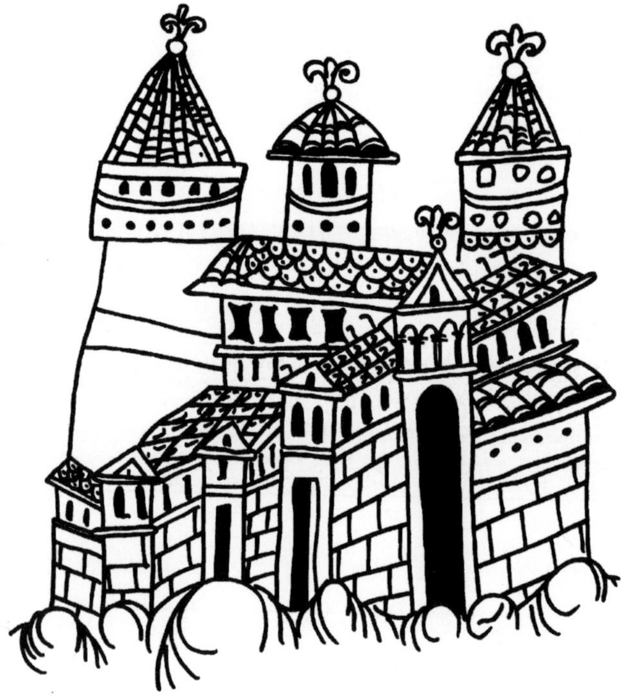

16 A building in British
Library, Royal 15 A.xvi
(folio 84)

their identity and circumstances, than the actual buildings themselves. Arched doorways
and windows are widespread in contemporary illuminations, as well as in surviving
architectural fabric. Arcading is also often found on religious structures in manuscript
art. Likewise, the association of the cross with church architecture is relatively common.

In contrast, Richard Gem (1981) has suggested that the Tapestry's depiction of
Westminster Abbey parallels both the surviving fabric and a description given in the *Vita
Ædwardi*; notable details in the most recent reconstruction of the extant remains are 'the
presbytery of two bays, the crossing tower with flanking turrets and with secondary turrets,
and the arcaded nave of five bays' (*17*). The appearance of Westminster Abbey in the Tapestry
displays many aspects of the Romanesque style, comparing well with the abbey church at
Jumièges; indeed, Richard Gem (1981) thought it possible that Westminster and Jumièges had
been designed by the same architect. It is therefore difficult to establish whether the Tapestry
depiction shows architectural features that were genuinely particular to Westminster, or
reflects generic Romanesque ecclesiastical architecture. On balance, if we believe the Tapestry
was produced in England, the latter seem less likely, since few English Romanesque buildings
would have been completed by 1070, about the time the Tapestry itself was probably produced.

Nonetheless, there are two aspects of the Tapestry's depiction of the Confessor's church
(Westminster Abbey) that are worthy of further discussion. First is the absence of the
western towers. It is likely that these were not completed by the time of the Tapestry's
execution. This theory has been supported by Tim Tatton-Brown (1995, personal
correspondence, 2004), who highlighted the fact that the Romanesque masonry surviving

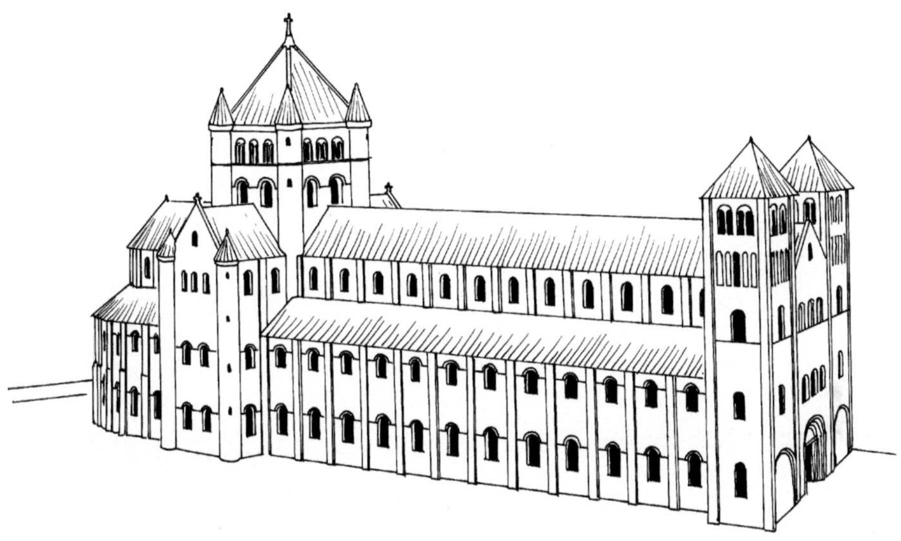

17 An artistic reconstruction of Westminster Abbey in the eleventh century. © *Dom Andrews*

within the towers is late eleventh century – that is to say they were a post-Conquest addition. Second, the Tapestry's depiction shows Westminster with a domed roof on its central-east tower, which most commentators agree would have been pointed, as shown in a reconstruction of the church published by Richard Gem (1981). Domed roofs, an intriguing feature of the Tapestry's architectural repertoire, are also commonly depicted in contemporary illuminations, such as the Harley 603 Psalter. The evidence for such roofs in early medieval western architecture is scant and hence it seems likely that this aspect must have been borrowed from art. This said, most other aspects of the Tapestry's depiction of Westminster Abbey seem to have been influenced by the appearance of the contemporary building, as demonstrated by the surviving fabric.

Defensive structures

Five of the six defensive structures depicted in the Bayeux Tapestry are named: Dol, Rennes, Dinan, Bayeux and Hastings Castle. They are shown as fortified structures upon defensive mounds, perhaps intended to represent 'motte and bailey' castles – defensive structures built on a mound (the motte) with an outer enclosure (the bailey). Although there are indications that such structures were being built in Normandy before 1066, the archaeological evidence remains inconclusive. Reginald Allen Brown (1976) and Eric Fernie (1999), amongst others, have even suggested that the origin of the motte is specific to the peculiar circumstances of the Norman Conquest. Whilst negative evidence should not be relied on too heavily, it is significant that to date none of these locations (apart from Hastings, perhaps) has yet produced the slightest trace of a fortified mound. Likewise, little remains of the early Norman castle of Hastings; excavation in 1968 of this much-altered feature was not able even to confirm that it was an early motte at all.

It seems unlikely (though not possible to prove) that the designer was trying to illustrate 'actual' castles in the places depicted, unless one suggests that the designer had seen these castles first-hand or had access to an accurate description of them. Indeed, most, including Reginald Allen Brown (1976) and David Wilson (1985), agreed that the designer represented these places by a type of castle which was visible in England in the 1070s on the assumption that, since this is how a 'Norman' castle looked in England, it was presumably the same in Brittany and Normandy.

Most of the Tapestry's defensive structures seem to be made of wood, including the upright members shown in the palisades at Dinan, Hastings and Rennes and the superstructure of Bayeux. This corresponds to what is known about fortifications built in England in the third quarter of the eleventh century. Ella S. Armitage (1912) noted that whenever a motte was first thrown up, the first castle upon it would have been wooden, as a stone structure could not be build immediately on loose soil. There is definite archaeological evidence for wooden structures upon mottes at a number of locations including Abinger in Surrey, Durham, and South Mimms in Hertfordshire.

The Tapestry also shows Hastings Castle upon a mound comprising several coloured bands, which suggested to Ella S. Armitage (1912) and Reginald Allen Brown (1989a) that it was formed from carefully differentiated layers of different material. Whilst this may not have been the case at the site believed to be Hastings (since excavations by P.A. Barker and K.J. Barton (1977) showed that the motte here was composed of different sorts of unstable and unstratified sand), examples of multi-composition construction are known at Bakewell in Derbyshire, Carisbrook on the Isle of Wight, Great Driffield in East Yorkshire, Hallaton in Leicestershire and York. Therefore, even if the Tapestry does not mimic the form of the early motte at Hastings it seems to embody a contemporary type.

Likewise, the building at Dinan is shown supported on timber pillars or stilts. This may have been an actual feature of contemporary defensive structures, perhaps designed to increase the space available to the defenders; Robert Higham and Philip Barker's (1992) interpretation of the excavated plan of the motte-top at Abinger rested heavily upon these considerations. Nonetheless, they could not imagine that the building depicted in the Tapestry was stilted, instead suggesting that the designer (wishing to show as much of the structure as possible) 'raised up in the air a building which in reality was on the ground'. This demonstrates the difficulties of paralleling the Tapestry's architectural depictions with the archaeological evidence.

Similarly, Robert Higham and Philip Barker (1992) thought the Tapestry's rendition of Dol to be somewhat enigmatic, though its motte, ditches, counterscarps and bridge with steps and gate are clear enough. The building's surface is shown constructed of small squares, which prompted Robert Higham and Philip Barker (1992) to suggest these are protective plates of hide or metal, for which there is documentary evidence. Even so, they thought that the structure on top of the motte to be very curious since it appears to be triangular in plan, which seems impossible. The structure at Bayeux, as depicted in the Tapestry, is also a strange looking building, especially as it has a domed roof. Charles Gibbs-Smith (1973) was certain it bore little resemblance to the actual structure, though there is no known extant remains to confirm one way or the other.

Whilst individual aspects of the Tapestry's defensive structures can be paralleled with the current knowledge of eleventh-century types, it seems apparent that some elements are stylised (perhaps invented) for artistic effect. Forts on defensive mounds rarely occur in contemporary illumination; the depiction of a walled town on an eminence in the Harley 603 Psalter (folio 13v), itself copied from the Utrecht Psalter, is the closest parallel. Whilst it is impossible to know if other now lost examples once existed in Anglo-Saxon times, it would be surprising if they did, given that such fortifications seem to be a phenomenon of the post-Conquest period.

Domestic dwellings

The Tapestry's domestic dwellings all share the same basic rectangular form, central doorway and trapezoid pitched roof. Building 32 is distinct, being a two-storey structure with pillars at ground level, which support a rectangular structure (very much like the domestic dwelling described above). Whilst none of these buildings is identified in the inscriptions, it is still possible to compare them with the archaeological evidence in general terms.

The rectangular ground plan of the Tapestry's houses can be paralleled with tenth- and eleventh-century buildings at Coppergate in York, Lincoln and Goltho in Lincolnshire, and elsewhere. The fashion whereby there is a doorway on the longest side of the building (normally one on either side) is predominately a rural phenomenon. Urban buildings, such as those excavated at Bow Lane, Botolph Lane and Milk Street in London, are often found with their gable ends fronting on to the streets, and this might be relevant to what is seen in the Tapestry.

Although the Tapestry does not clearly indicate the materials used to construct domestic buildings, the walls of Buildings 26 and 27 (Scene 41) seem to be constructed from horizontal wooden planks. Evidence from excavation in York shows that by the first half of the tenth century, post-and-wattle seems to have been the standard method of construction for domestic housing. However, post-and-plank construction was also used, so some of the Tapestry's houses might show this technique.

In contrast, the walls of Building 25 (Scene 41) are constructed of square blocks, which Simone Bertrand (1966) suggested was masonry. The fact that this building also has a 'scale' tile roof may also imply a stone structure below to support the weight of the roof (though, as Martin Carver (1986) has noted, scaled roofing in art could also represent wooden shingles). Indeed, scaled roofing is a common feature in early medieval art, and there are numerous Anglo-Saxon examples (*18*). This is not to say the designer would not or could not draw this element from life, but given that scale or square-tiled roofs were an established artistic convention, however representational, it might be expected that an artist would turn to the most familiar visual sources. It seems likely that most domestic dwellings, such as those at Coppergate in York and West Stow in Suffolk, actually had thatched roofs (*19*), and both Simone Bertrand (1966) and David Wilson (1985) have hypothesised that the diagonal patterned roof of Building 26 may be indicative of this.

The materials used in Building 32 (Scene 47) are difficult to identify; Lucien Musset (2002) has suggested that since the building is shown burning it might have been made of wood. It appears that the house has secondary flooring; the lower floor consists of long pillars, supporting a ceiling and the structure above. Evidence for early medieval examples of two-storey domestic houses are known; the *Anglo-Saxon Chronicle* (E) for 978 records that 'the leading councillors

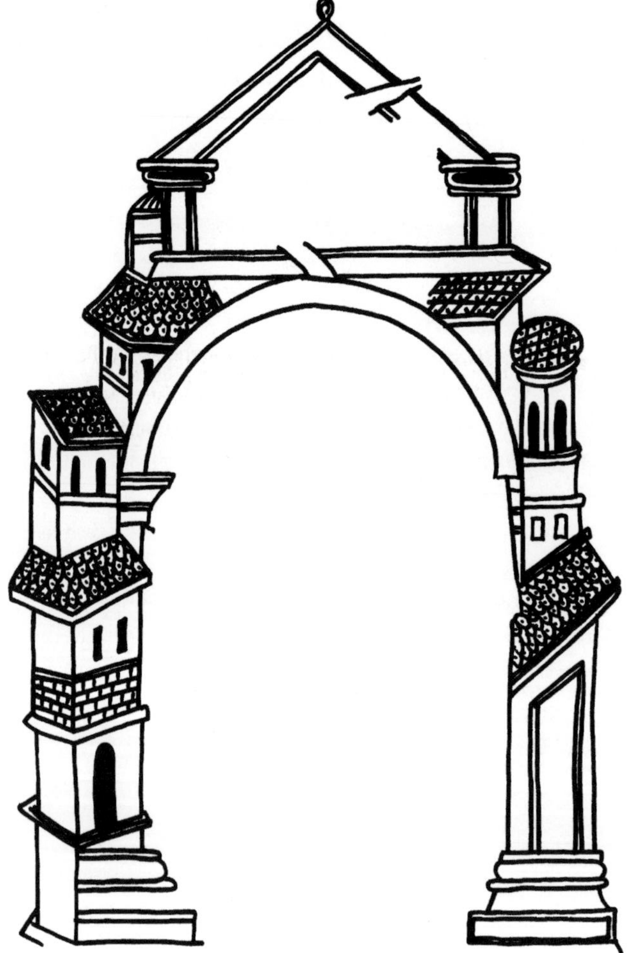

18 The scaled roofing fabric of a building in Pierpont Morgan Library M 869 (folio 83v)

of England fell down from an upper storey at Calne [in Wiltshire]'. However, the Tapestry's two-storey houses are also paralleled in art. These include buildings illustrated in the Junius 11 manuscript (pages 3 & 51), which show a multiple-tiered, rectangular building with a trapezoid pitched roof, supported on pillars (*20*).

High status domestic buildings

Of the all the Tapestry architecture, its high status domestic buildings (such as royal palaces) are the most overtly schematic and have been described as 'fantasy architecture' by Wolfgang Grape (1994). Unfortunately, there is no extant physical evidence for the eleventh-century high status domestic buildings in question to test the matter further. Whilst the designer makes good use of an interesting repertoire of basic architectural forms, such as towers, arches, pillars, domed and pitched roofs, it is apparent that none of these details is particular to the Tapestry's high status domestic buildings. Instead the emphasis, in most instances,

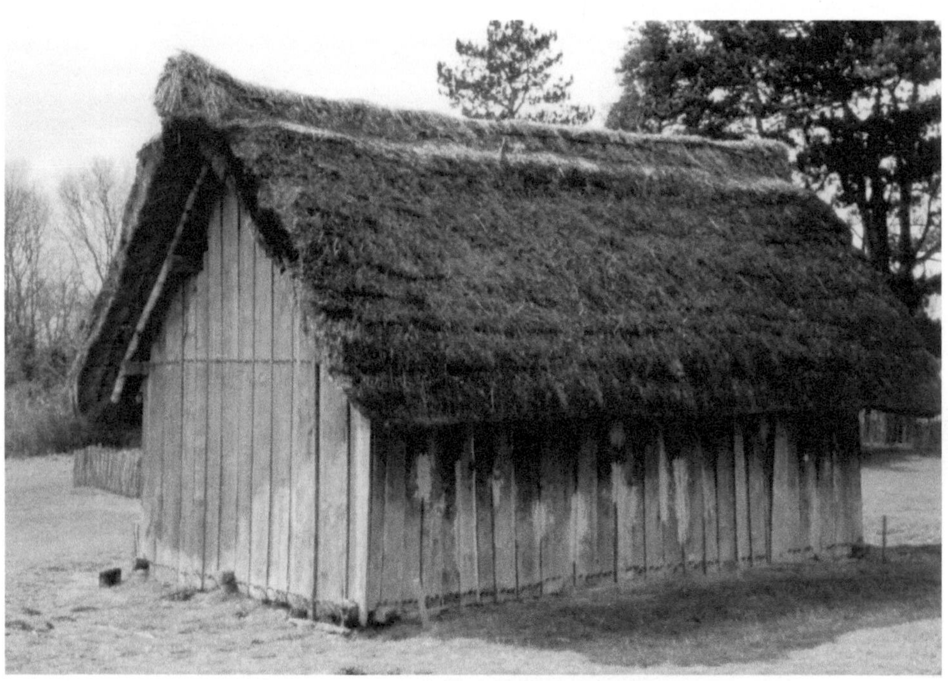

19 A reconstruction of an Anglo-Saxon house at West Stow in Suffolk

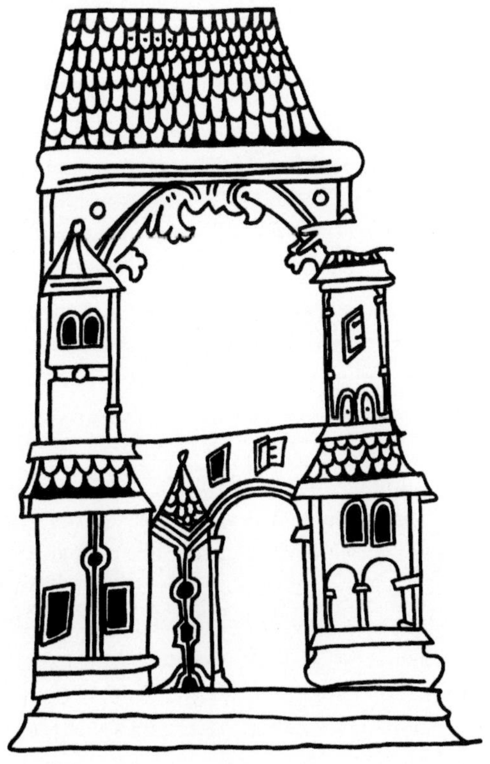

20 A two-storey building in
Junius II (page 3)

is upon the human characters who gesticulate below; the architectural elements are then designed to fit around them.

The Tapestry's high status domestic buildings are not depicted in a consistent manner, and this demonstrates their schematic nature. For example, the royal high status domestic building at Westminster seems to appear twice (Buildings 1 & 18), but the buildings themselves are quite distinct. Likewise, the three structures that we take to be William's high status domestic building at Rouen (Buildings 6, 8 & 23) seem to have little in common with each other.

John Blair (personal correspondence, 2004) suggested that the very striking differences between the representations of the halls at Westminster (Buildings 1 & 18) and that of Rouen (Building 8), of which the latter has a frieze of high-level arcading, may be seen as the designer's attempt to show a distinctively Norman type of building, and this arcading can be paralleled with extant Anglo-Norman remains at Westminster and Chepstow. However, similar arcading also occurs on (pre-Conquest) English buildings in the Tapestry, such as on Bosham church, and on extant Anglo-Saxon structures, for example St Laurence, Bradford-upon-Avon. Only in the case of Guy's high status domestic building at Beaurain (Buildings 4 & 5) do we see a similar basic form used twice for what we can assume to be the same structure. As far as the narrative is concerned, such idiosyncrasies are irrelevant, as is the fact that many of these buildings seem to be made of stone and are commonly depicted with classical features. In brief, rather than replicate actual domestic buildings, it seems that the designer has instead invented structures from a repertoire of architecture elements typical of contemporary manuscript art.

The point may be demonstrated by comparing the Tapestry's architecture with that of Junius 11. A significant number of architectural motifs are common to both the Tapestry and these manuscripts, including thin roofs supported by columns and towers. The thin roofs themselves can also be paralleled satisfactorily. For example, the curved arch of Buildings 1 and 23 in the Tapestry have the same basic form and similar central embellishment as structures in Junius 11 (pages 51, 54 & 56). Similarly, the mid-level pitched roofs, domed and pointed roofs, scaled roofing, arched windows and doors, and arcading found in the Tapestry are abundant in Junius 11. The same point could be made with reference to other extensively illustrated Anglo-Saxon manuscripts, such as the Old English Hexateuch or the Harley 603 Psalter. The latter, whose illustrations were copied from a remarkably archaising Carolingian model, is a reminder that the visual language in question derives ultimately from late antique and antique exemplars.

Summary

The buildings in the Bayeux Tapestry, like those in tenth- and eleventh-century manuscript illumination, are in the most part fairly schematic, their architectural form and constructional elements greatly simplified. This adds to the difficulty of differentiating between those attributes which may reflect 'the real world' and those which are either imaginative or traditional iconographic motifs, highlighted by Marla Schwartz (1994). Nevertheless, when parts of a building named in the Tapestry still survive, a more rigorous investigation is conceivable. With the possible exception of Westminster Abbey, the Tapestry designer does not seem to have been concerned to represent actual contemporary buildings. Even in the case of Westminster, architectural elements are illustrated that were not part of the fabric. In general, the designer seems to have created many of the buildings from a varied repertoire of basic architectural forms found in the visual arts. These forms, transmitted from classical times and preserved in art, cannot be thought to be typical of most contemporary buildings.

If the designer's basic architectural vocabulary was an inherited pictorial language, he nevertheless responded to certain aspects of the real world. Mottes, including some structural elements upon them, and Romanesque architectural elements, are notable cases in point. Yet even when responding to the 'real world', mistakes could still be made. Hence in the case of motted fortifications, Breton and Norman defensive structures are recreated on the assumption that they would match the new 'castles' being built in England. If it is the contemporary elements that are the most interesting aspects of the architecture in the Tapestry, they must still, evidently, be approached with circumspection.

ARMS AND ARMOUR

Arms and armour are widespread in the Bayeux Tapestry, which is hardly surprising given that warfare is fundamental to the narrative and is indicative of a time when Norman military capabilities were integral to the success and stability of their regime in England. Whilst Edgar Ætheling and much of the surviving elite soon submitted to the Norman invaders in 1066, resistance continued in parts of the country and at times was almost endemic. It would therefore seem astonishing if the Tapestry designer did not attempt to recreate accurately the arms and armour worn and used by contemporary fighting men. Although previous commentators, such as James Mann (1969) and Nicholas Brooks (1978), have generally agreed that this was the case, the archaeological evidence is less conclusive.

The largest concentrations of arms and armour in the Bayeux Tapestry appear during William's campaign in Brittany and during the Battle of Hastings. However, high status individuals, and members of their entourages, often carry or wear arms and armour in other scenes.

Helmets

Contemporary helmets provide good evidence that the Tapestry designer attempted to reflect elements of contemporary fashion within the design. Although few conical helmets survive, a tenth-century Polish example in the Royal Armouries, Leeds, and a tenth- or eleventh-century helm, from Northern France or the River Thames, in the Metropolitan Museum of Art, New York, compare well with the segmented helmets depicted in the Tapestry. Other examples of some relevance are the ninth- or tenth-century 'St Wenceslas' helmet' in Prague Cathedral, an eleventh- or twelfth-century helmet from Olmütz, Moravia, now in the *Kunsthistorisches Museum Hofjagdund Rüstkammer*, Vienna, and the (possible) eleventh-century Washingborough helmet, in the City and County Museum, Lincoln (*21*). Of these, only the Wenceslas helm has a nasal guard that is an original feature, though this has been doubted by some. This helmet also has a brow-band, a characteristic not found on any other surviving conical helmet (though the Olmütz and Washingborough helmets have holes around the lower edge, which may have held a brow band), but which is commonplace in the Tapestry. Nonetheless, whilst the archaeological evidence for individual aspects of the Tapestry helms may be slight, their basic conical form is consistent with the contemporary record.

Turning to pictorial representations, we find that, from about the tenth century, classical-style helmets and crested types give way to those of a conical type, suggesting that artists were responding to changing fashions in arms and armour. Conical helmets are found on Viking Age stone sculpture in Yorkshire, such as the tenth-century sculptures housed in Middleton Church, North Yorkshire (*22*), and it is not impossible (albeit hardly likely) that the Tapestry designer may have seen these, or similar works. A more plausible source of influence would have been contemporary manuscript illumination, where segmented conical helmets, such as that worn by Goliath in the Tiberius Psalter (folios 8v & 9r) are common (*23*). Nonetheless, it is a phenomenon of early medieval illumination that conical helmets are never shown with nasal guards. Indeed, since nasal guards are not found on conical helms in manuscript art until the twelfth century, their abundance in the Tapestry is particularly fascinating.

Another potentially significant visual source for the type of helmets depicted in the Bayeux Tapestry is eleventh-century coinage. 'Helmet type' coins of Cnut, dated to about 1024-30, and those of Edward the Confessor, of about 1053-6, seem to depict segmented conical helms with nasal guards (*colour plate 28*). However, it seems highly unlikely that the Tapestry designer was influenced by coinage design as neither type of coin was in circulation at the time the Tapestry was produced; a fact highlighted by Gareth Williams (personal correspondence, 2001).

In this case, the close correspondence between the design in the Tapestry and the known form of the contemporary artefact, allied to the circumstances that the visual tradition in manuscript illuminations was not as faithful to that form, strongly suggests that the designer was here responding to the 'real world'.

Armour

It is generally accepted that the armour shown in the Tapestry is a stylised representation of mail (*24*); both Simone Bertrand (1966) and James Mann (1957) have noted that mail, by nature highly intricate and complicated in structure, is difficult to represent in small scale. This offers a clear indication that the designer was prepared to use artistic motifs for some elements of the design, rather than try to emulate 'reality'. Besides the conventional circular and hatched types of mail commonly found in medieval art, the Tapestry designer also chose to illustrate, if somewhat infrequently, scaled armour and a strange form of armour with triangular plates, which Christopher Gravett (1996) thought may have intended to represent a padded coat. Neither type has been recovered archaeologically, which is not surprising, given we can presume the latter was organic.

Most intriguing is the fact that all the mail hauberks in the Tapestry are shown as trousered garments. This is particularly apparent in the scene where hauberks are carried on poles towards William's ships (Scene 37). Although it is plausible that soldiers may

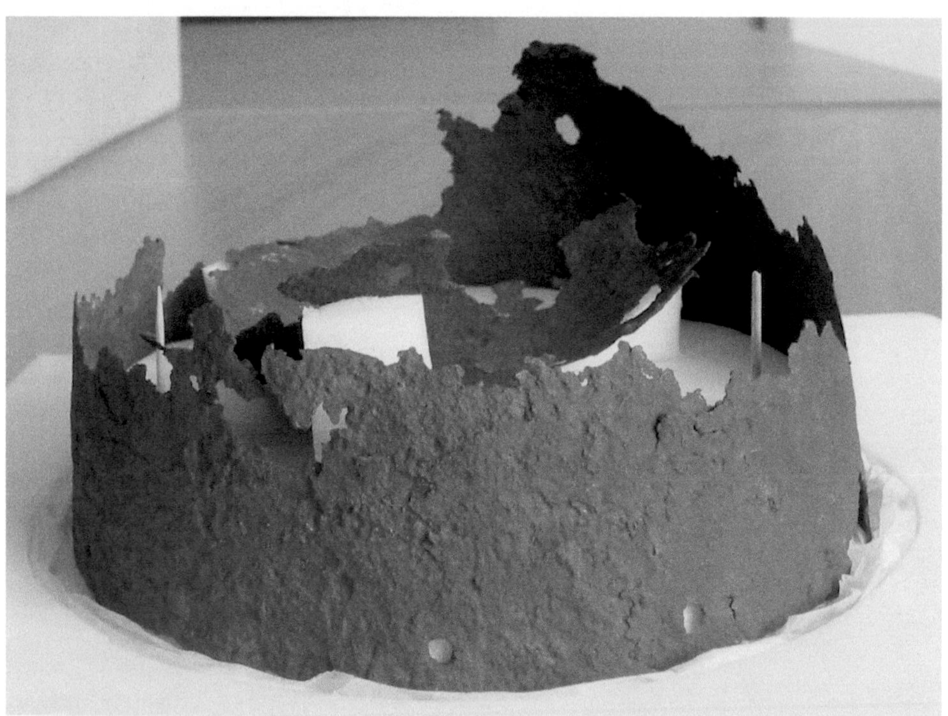

21 The Washingborough helmet

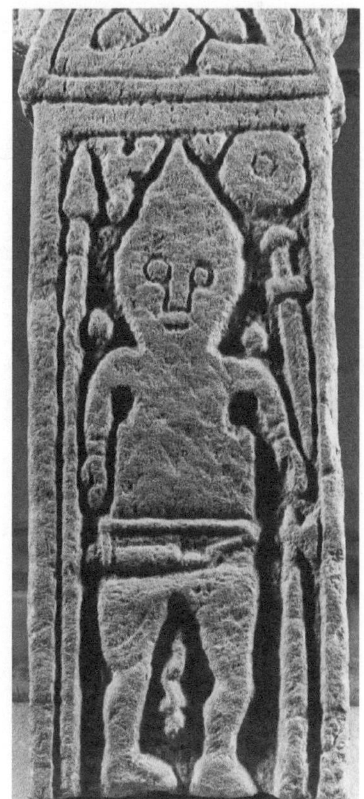

22 The warrior on stone sculpture (2A) in Middleton Church in North Yorkshire. © *Department of Archaeology, Durham University, Photographer T. Middlemass*

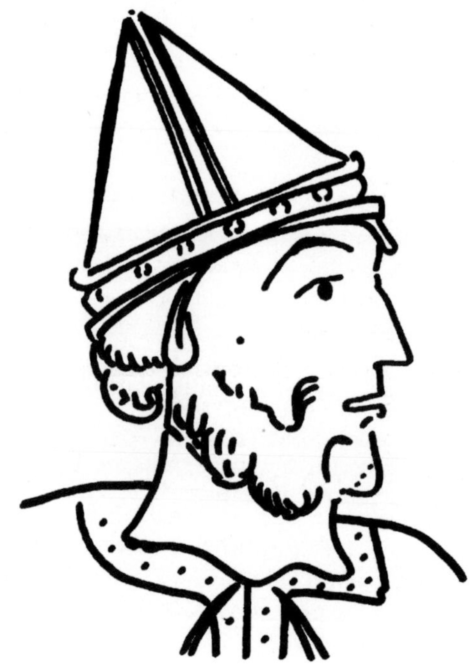

23 The segmented conical helmet worn by Goliath in the Tiberius Psalter (folio 9)

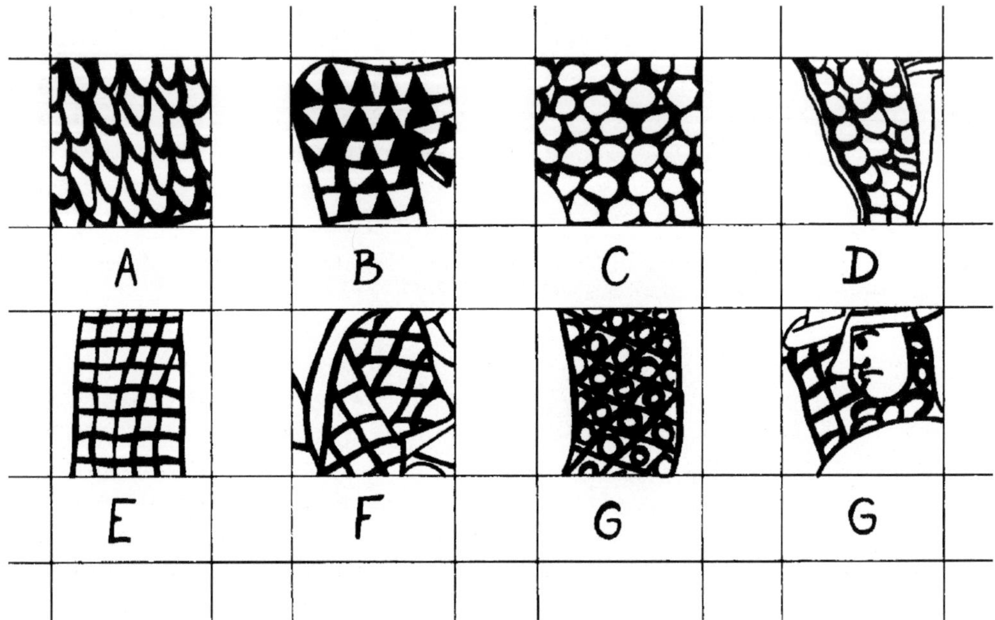

24 Different designs used to evoke armour in the Bayeux Tapestry: (a) scaled, (b) triangular/patterned, (c) circles, (d) half-circles, (e) crossed horizontal-hatch, (f) crossed diagonal-hatch, and (g) variations on types (c) to (g)

have fought in trousered armour on foot, it is generally accepted that horsemen could not without severe discomfort(!), unless parts of the garment was made of leather. Nicholas Brooks and H.E. Walker (1978) concluded that this 'blunder' was understandable since the Tapestry designer must have been an Anglo-Saxon, and thus unaccustomed to fighting upon horseback.

In 1055, the *Anglo-Saxon Chronicle* (C) recorded that Earl Ralph, the Norman nephew of Edward the Confessor, used English horsemen against the Welsh, though to little avail 'because they had been made to fight on horseback'. It is therefore enlightening that comparative examples are found in Anglo-Saxon art, not archaeology, including a king with trousered mail in the Old English Hexateuch (folio 24v) and a mailed figure in the Harley 603 Psalter (folio 73v) (*25*). Both illuminations were probably produced in Canterbury and therefore could have been available to the Tapestry designer.

The best example of trousered mail outside manuscript illumination is a carved stone fragment from Winchester (*26*), which Martin Biddle (1966) dated to the first half of the eleventh century, though George Zarnecki (1984) and Deborah Kahn (1992) thought it was post-Conquest; it is the most commonly cited example of trousered mail in English art. Whilst the origins of trousered hauberks are unclear, Simone Bertrand (1966) made the sensible proposition that it is more likely that this motif developed from an artist's misinterpretation or stylisation of a mailed skirt, perhaps strapped to the leg, than reflecting first-hand observation of the 'real world'.

Also peculiar are the horizontal and vertical lines, sometimes formed into a square, that are frequently depicted upon the chest of the Tapestry's hauberks. There is no conclusive explanation of their purpose, though they might be reinforced mail patches to protect the chest, or a lowered ventail or flap to guard the throat. Although they are mentioned in *La Chanson de Roland* (*Song of Roland*) of about 1170, nothing is known of ventails from the archaeological record until about the thirteenth century. Moreover, it seems unlikely that the designer took the motif from contemporary art since representations of ventails are infrequent, and those that occur, such as the mid twelfth-century sculptured capital at Notre-Dame-du-Port, Clermont-Ferrand, are (given their provenance and date) an improbable source of inspiration.

Swords

Swords in the Bayeux Tapestry compare well with the general typology of contemporary weapons; the form of the hilt, in particular, can be usefully compared with the archaeological evidence. Three types of pommel are depicted in the Tapestry, covering a wide chronology from the ninth century until the twelfth. First is shown a single, rather poor example of a 'three-lobed' pommel. In view of the archaeological evidence, James Mann (1957) suggested that by 1066 this type of pommel was going out of fashion, although it is commonly illustrated in late Anglo-Saxon manuscripts, such as the New Minster Liber Vitae and Cotton Tiberius B.v.

Second are illustrated tea-cosy pommels. The archaeological record attests to their popularity during the eleventh century, and they are of a type commonly illustrated in contemporary manuscripts, particularly those associated with Canterbury, such as Cotton Cleopatra C.viii and the Harley 603 Psalter.

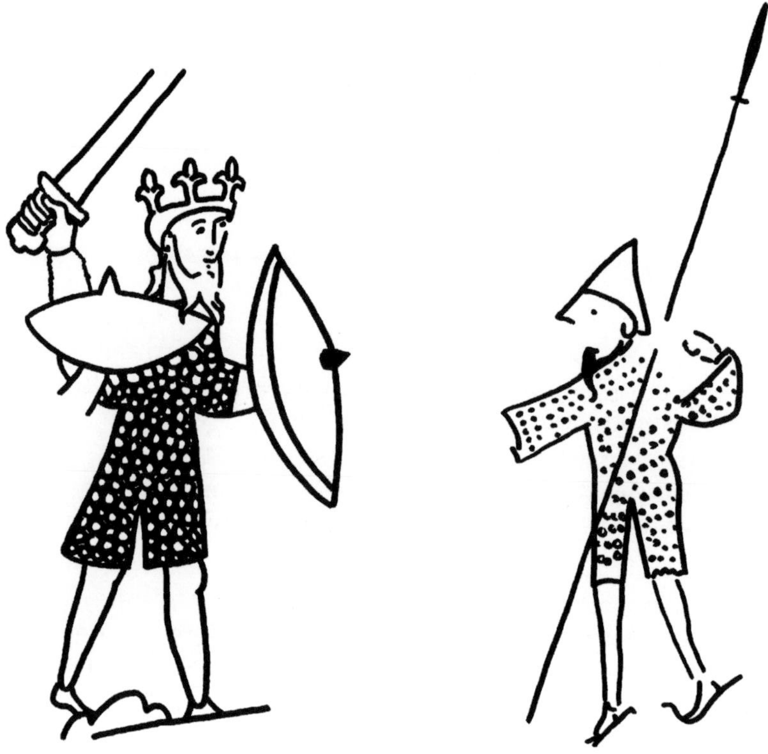

25 The trousered hauberks worn by a king in the Old English Hexateuch (folio 24v) (left) and a figure in the Harley 603 Psalter (folio 73v) (right)

Third are depicted disc pommels. Their occurrence in the Tapestry is more intriguing, since David Edge and John Miles Paddock (1988) thought that this type was introduced from southern Europe during the first two crusades (1096-9 and 1147-9). Given that this pommel type also appears in Late Anglo-Saxon manuscripts, such as Cotton Cleopatra C. viii and the Old English Hexateuch, there are grounds to question such a late date for its introduction into England. On the other hand, it is feasible that what appear to modern scholars to be disc pommels in late Anglo-Saxon manuscripts are irregularly drawn tea cosy or brazil nut pommels, and this is probably the case in the Bayeux Tapestry.

Short, straight cross-guards were favoured throughout the early medieval period, while curved forms were adopted in England from about the ninth century onwards. Accordingly, several cross-guards in the Tapestry seem to be curved. It is interesting that these sometimes curve away from the blade, towards the forearm, and this must be an error, as such a guard would channel a hostile weapon towards the defending swordsman's forearm. A similar phenomenon can be observed in contemporary illuminations, such as Cotton Tiberius B.v and the Tiberius Psalter, and this may well explain its occurrence in the Tapestry. Such idiosyncrasies, common to both the Tapestry and manuscript art, would seem to imply that the designer used manuscript exemplars for at least some aspects of the design.

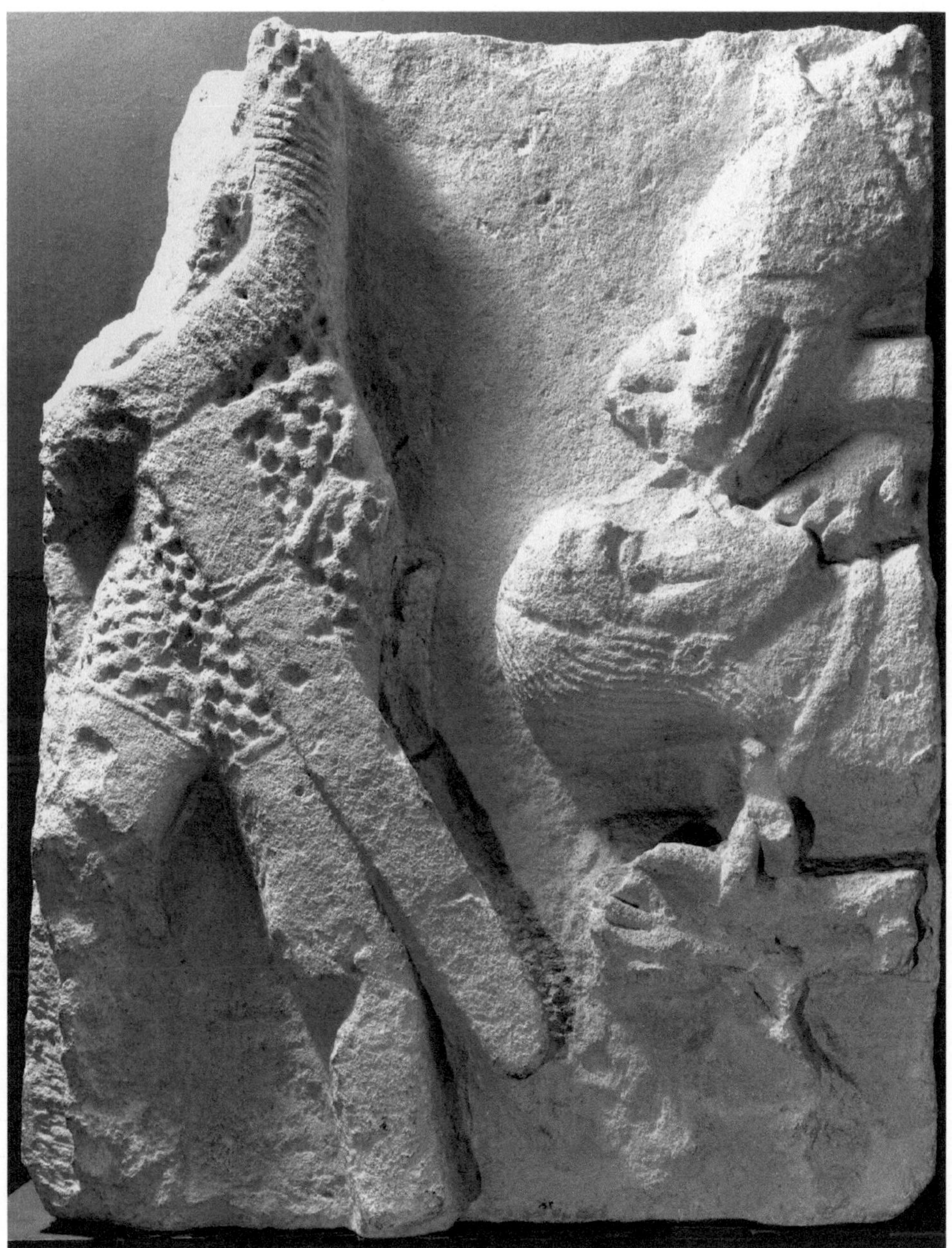

26 The trousered hauberk depicted on a stone sculpture fragment from Winchester. © *Winchester Excavations Committee*

Spears

Although the spears in the Tapestry are undoubtedly stylised, the spearheads themselves are broadly consistent with the archaeological record. However, it is interesting that several spears in the Tapestry have one or two sets of wings, a feature which S.H. Fuglesang (1980) argued was designed for hunting. It is noteworthy, therefore, that contrary to their intended function, such spears are repeatedly used in combat scenes. More importantly, some of these spears are also barbed, which makes little sense, as the wing would restrict the depth to which the spearhead could be thrust, whilst the barb would make it impossible to withdraw once used.

Both single- and double-winged spears are commonplace in early medieval illuminations. The former is predominately found in Carolingian manuscripts, such as the Vivian Bible (folio 215v), but also appears in the Canterbury-produced Bury Psalter (folio 36r), whilst the latter are shown in Cotton Cleopatra C.viii (folios 10v-11r) (*27*). It therefore is plausible that the designer appropriated winged spears from contemporary art.

Axes

Axes in the Tapestry are broadly similar to types that were commonly used in England and Scandinavia from about the tenth century. In the battle scenes, axes are nearly always associated with the English, and this is consistent with our understanding of Anglo-Saxon warfare. However, the Tapestry's axes have an additional iconographic significance. Excluding domestic scenes, it can be seen that the designer has used axes to denote persons of rank up to Scene 19, and thereafter to identify Anglo-Saxons in the mêlée of battle.

Though axes are not common in Anglo-Saxon illuminations, the depiction of a wood-worker felling a tree in Cotton Julius A.vi (folio 5v) provides a good parallel for the men cutting trees in the boat-building scenes of the Tapestry (*28*). Axes in other Canterbury manuscripts also show that the Tapestry designer could have taken inspiration from manuscript art, but this is by no means certain.

Bows

Bows are not prominent in the Bayeux Tapestry; archers only appear in Scenes 51, 55 and 58. Although their scale and linear form make comparison with contemporary weapons difficult, their small size does not compare favourably with the archaeological record for Western European bow staves, which Jim Bradbury (1997) noted, is characterised by a longer type. Illustrations of archers are rare in early medieval manuscripts, but when shown they are consistently depicted using a short, rather than long, bow; examples include Cotton Cleopatra C.viii and the Harley 603 Psalter. Likewise, the early eighth-century Ruthwell Cross, the Franks Casket of the first half of the eighth century (*29*), the mid ninth-century cross shaft from Sheffield, South Yorkshire, and an eleventh- or twelfth-century reliquary cross in the Victoria & Albert Museum, all depict short bows. Thus it seems that the Tapestry's bows are of a form fossilised in art.

The fact that arrows are incorrectly loaded onto bow staves (a right-handed archer would fire an arrow from the left-hand side of the bow stave) is also of interest, but may well be nothing more than an unintentional 'error', which has more to do with the designer's (or

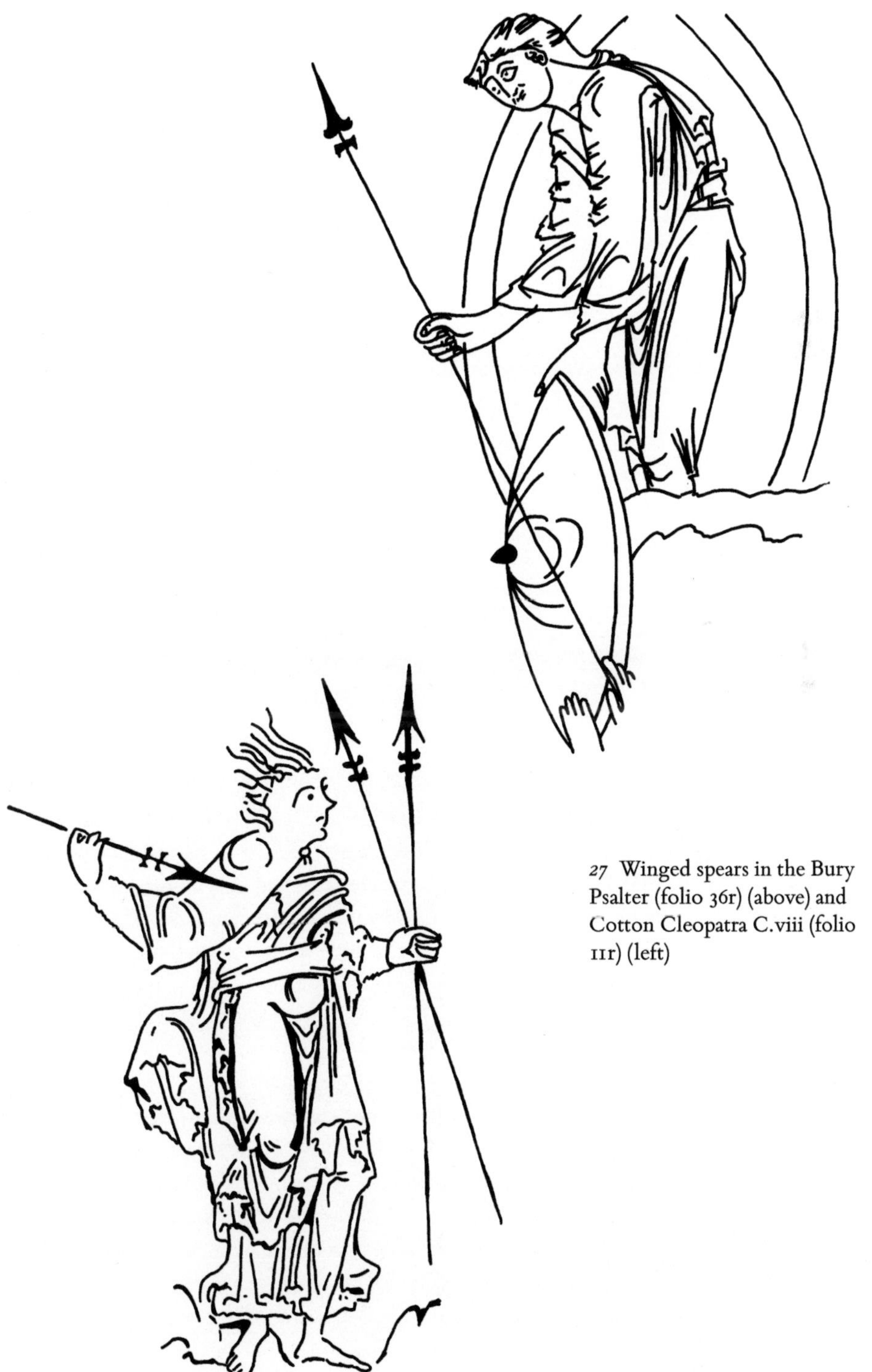

27 Winged spears in the Bury Psalter (folio 36r) (above) and Cotton Cleopatra C.viii (folio 11r) (left)

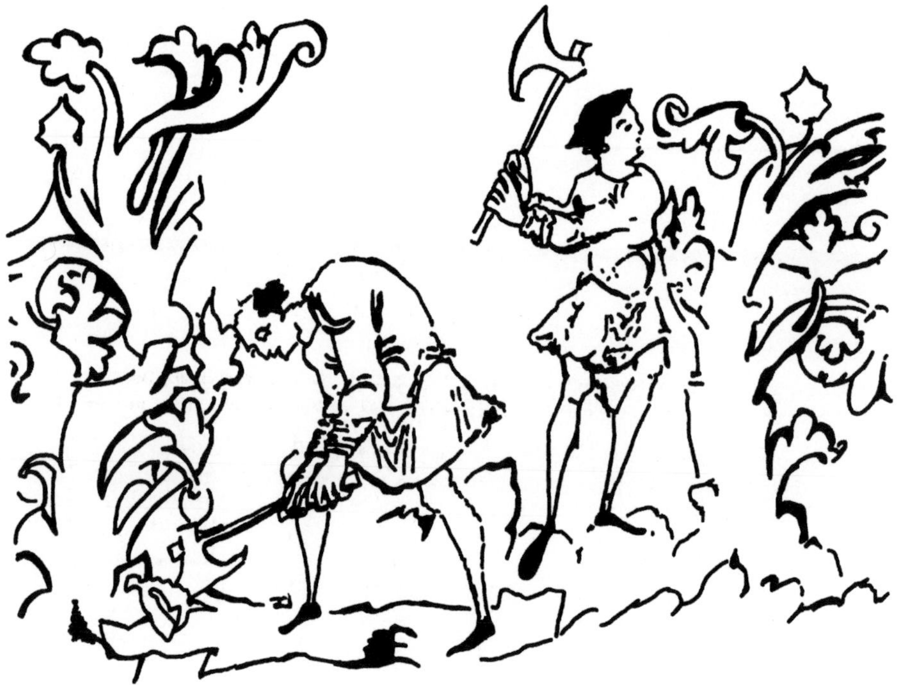

28 Woodworkers felling trees in British Library, Cotton Junius A.vi (folio 5v)

embroiderer's) method than with actual design (or knowledge). A plausible explanation for this error seems to be that the embroiderers first 'sewed in' the bow and then placed the arrow across it, whether the archer was facing right or left; indeed the only archer in the Tapestry facing left (Figure 462) correctly fires his arrow over the left-hand side of the bow stave. In point of fact, this phenomenon is found elsewhere in medieval art, where bowmen firing to the left are shown with arrows on the left side of the bow, as on the Franks Casket, whilst arrows fired right are shown across the right side of the bow stave, as on a sculpture fragment of the last quarter of the seventh century from Hexham, and the Sheffield cross shaft.

Round-shields

Round-shields provide some of the most conclusive evidence that the Tapestry designer borrowed aspects of the design from art. The majority of the round-shields in the Tapestry are shown in profile, revealing the form of the boss and showing that the board is convex. This contrasts with the archaeological evidence, notably the 32 round-shields recovered from the tenth-century Gokstad ship burial, which indicate that shield boards were probably flat.

There are many artistic parallels for convex round-shield boards, including the Franks Casket as well as numerous contemporary illuminations, such as Cotton Julius A.vi and the Tiberius Psalter. There is therefore clear evidence to suggest that in the case of

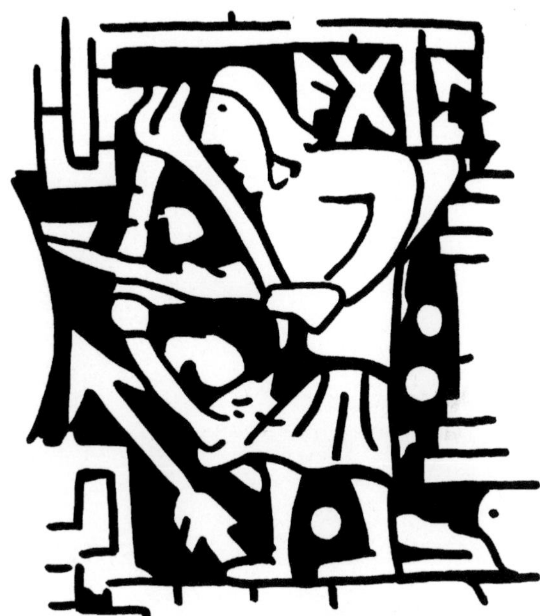

29 Archers on the Franks' Casket (right) and Ruthwell Cross (below). *Photograph © Department of Archaeology, Durham University, T. Middlemass*

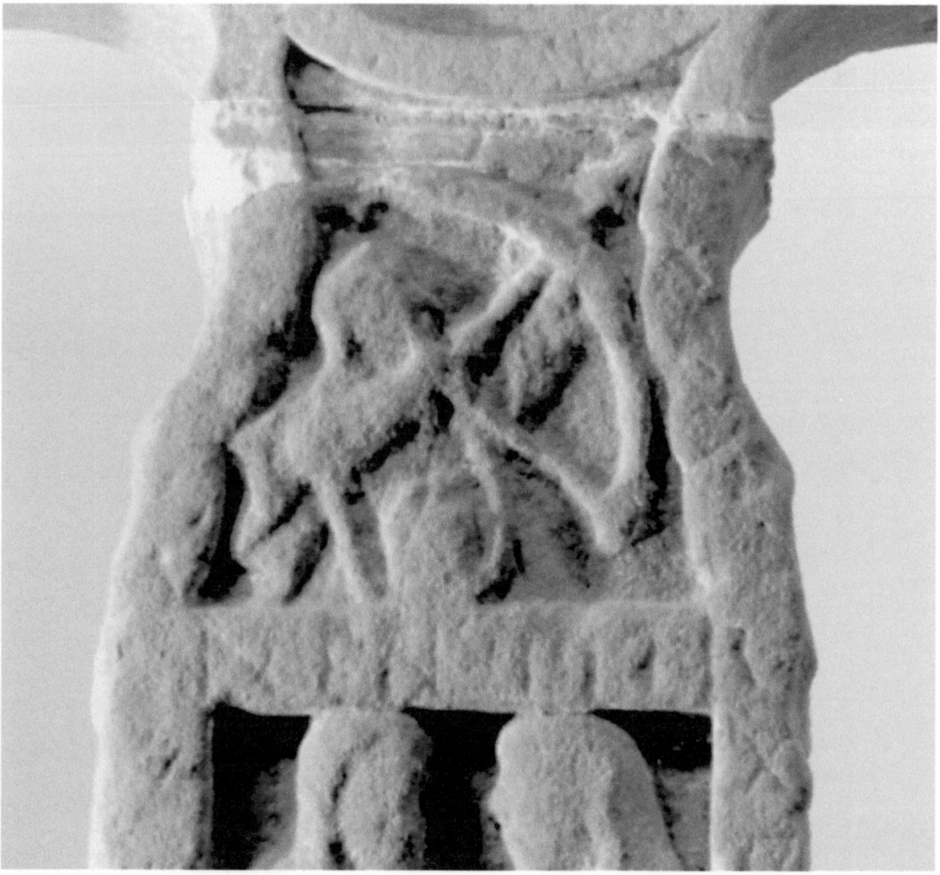

round-shields the Tapestry designer appropriated readily available artistic motifs, even though they did not correspond to the 'real world'. Depictions of convex shield boards seem to have derived from classical art, though the precise origins of such representations are obscure. Tania Dickinson and Heinrich Härke (1992) observed that to date Roman Iron Age bog deposits on the continent have only produced flat-shield boards.

Kite-shields

By the middle of the eleventh century, the kite-shield superseded the round-shield as the favoured defensive tool of the medieval warrior; it seems the kite-shield was favoured by the mounted knight. Kite-shields are more numerous than round-shields in the Bayeux Tapestry and this may provide evidence of the transition. It is interesting, therefore, that kite-shields only appear once in Anglo-Saxon art, in the work of 'hand F' of the Harley 603 Psalter (60r, 65v & 69r) (*30*), and are unknown in Norman illumination before the twelfth century. Intriguingly, artist F made his contribution to Harley 603 in the early eleventh century at Canterbury, so the Tapestry designer may have known his work. Whether influenced by F's hand or not, this undoubtedly reflects a contemporary trend in the Tapestry's repertoire.

That said, details of the design imply that art still exerted an influence. A majority of the Tapestry's kite-shields are illustrated with shield bosses, but unlike round-shields

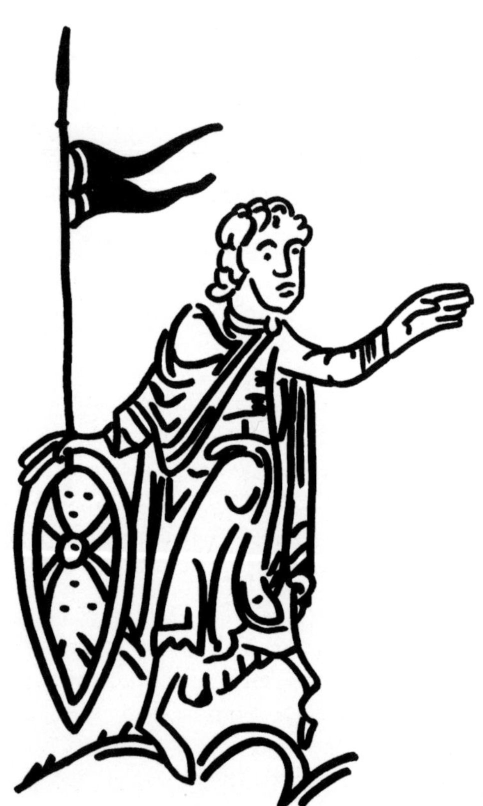

30 Kite-shields depicted in the Harley 603 Psalter (folio 29v). The kite-shield on this folio was not drawn by artist 'F', but an artist in the second half of the twelfth century

where the boss is functional (it is designed to protect the handgrip), bosses on kite-shields are unnecessary; kite-shields were held by an arrangement of straps, and hence metal bosses became redundant, though they could be used as an offensive weapon. Intriguingly, kite-shields with bosses continue to feature in art until about the thirteenth century, when flat-topped kite-shields become common; throughout the eleventh and twelfth centuries they are shown with and without shield bosses. Of course, it may have been the case that bosses remained in use as a decorative ornament, and that this is reflected in contemporary art. More likely, bosses were depicted on some kite-shields as a matter of artistic convention, since the boss was iconographically associated with the form of the shield.

Summary

Discreet idiosyncrasies in the Tapestry's depiction of arms and armour demonstrate that contemporary art did exert an influence upon the designer. First, there are 'errors', such as the trousered hauberks and convex shield boards. It is doubtful that these objects existed, and it is far more likely that such motifs were borrowed from contemporary art. Secondly, the designer consistently makes use of forms, such as particular pommel types and small bows, which (archaeologically) belong to an earlier period, but have been fossilised in art. Thirdly, the Tapestry depicts weapons, such as the winged spear, which have been borrowed for a context contrary to their intended function. Such motifs are clearly copied from contemporary art.

Nonetheless, the designer has chosen to illustrate some relatively recent innovations in arms and armour, such as conical helmets and kite-shields, which would seem to imply that not all of the military impedimenta were fallacious and out of date. Even so, this evidence must be viewed with caution. In many instances the archaeological record is weak, and near-contemporary art still offers good comparisons. Consequently, it seems probable that the Tapestry designer relied on motifs found in art for much of the arms and armour depicted.

SHIPS

Seafaring vessels were an integral part of warfare and defence in the eleventh century. The sea offered natural protection from invasion or attack, and was vital to trade and economic prosperity. Sea travel was also important politically, helping to maintain dynastic and religious ties between peoples across Europe and beyond. During the eleventh century, ports, harbours and beaches on both sides of the Channel must have been subject to considerable maritime activity.

As discussed previously, there is a presumption among modern scholars that the Tapestry designer would have wished to recreate the contemporary scene accurately, including the ships that operated within it. Accordingly, most commentators, including David Wilson (1985) and Lucien Musset (2002), have considered its ships to be faithful renditions of contemporary vessels. However, a systematic exploration of the relationship between the ships in the Tapestry, those depicted in contemporary manuscript illuminations, and the archaeological evidence, raises questions about the origins and authenticity of the Tapestry's depictions.

The basic form of the Tapestry's ships compares well with most early medieval ship finds. Particularly striking are the symmetrical hull forms, which have a curved keel and stem posts. These are characteristically 'Norse', typical of Scandinavian ships from the ninth to eleventh centuries and beyond. Vessels such as the early seventh-century ship from mound 1 at Sutton Hoo in Suffolk and the tenth-century boat from Graveney in Kent indicate that the Anglo-Saxons were familiar with a similar form of ship. As such, those in the Tapestry seem to conform to the broad scheme of contemporary north-west European boat building.

Horse transportation

The Tapestry's ships are shown fulfilling various functions. Those with horses aboard seem, by implication, to be cargo vessels. The designer does not (obviously or otherwise) make the distinction between cargo vessels and warships, as both appear broadly similar in form. Although archaeologists, such as Ole Olsen and Olaf Crumlin-Pedersen (1978) have paralleled the Tapestry's ships with the eleventh-century Skuldelev 5 in Denmark, such medium-sized warships would have had little room for storage or cargo.

Whilst a reconstruction of the tenth-century boat from Ladby in Denmark was put to sea with four horses, such a vessel could not have accommodated the large number of animals shown aboard ships in the Tapestry. Moreover, the Ladby exercise tested whether horses could embark (and disembark from) a shallow drafted vessel, rather than the sailing capabilities of a ship laden with up to ten horses and undertaking a Channel crossing. In any case, it is quite clear that the horses and ships in the Tapestry are not drawn to the same scale.

Gap amidships

Some ships are shown with a gap in the gunwale amidships, a feature which the designer possibly considered to denote the cargo hull of contemporary cargo vessels. Certainly, some vessels in the Tapestry do seem to compare well with the basic features of the Skuldelev traders (31), having the same hull form, central sail, cargo hold and (in three cases) oar ports both forward and aft. However, it is perplexing that in the Tapestry horses are never shown on ships with a gap amidships, while those ships with the gap (which we would naturally assume to be traders) are never shown with cargo. It is apparent that horses have a limited role in the earlier part of the Tapestry, and this might explain why they are not illustrated aboard vessels with a gap amidships. This begs the question, why, if cargo vessels are shown with a gap amidships in the earlier part of the Tapestry, are they not shown in the Norman invasion fleet?

The point at which the gap amidships appears within the Tapestry seems to be important in understanding its significance. Since in all but one instance the gap is associated with English vessels, it may be the case that the designer deliberately used this feature to differentiate between English and Norman ships.

It is also important to note that the English ship without a gap amidships (Ship 7) appears after one of the joins in the Tapestry (between Sections 2 and 3). It is possible that rather than representing a purposeful attempt to express characteristics of national identity, the

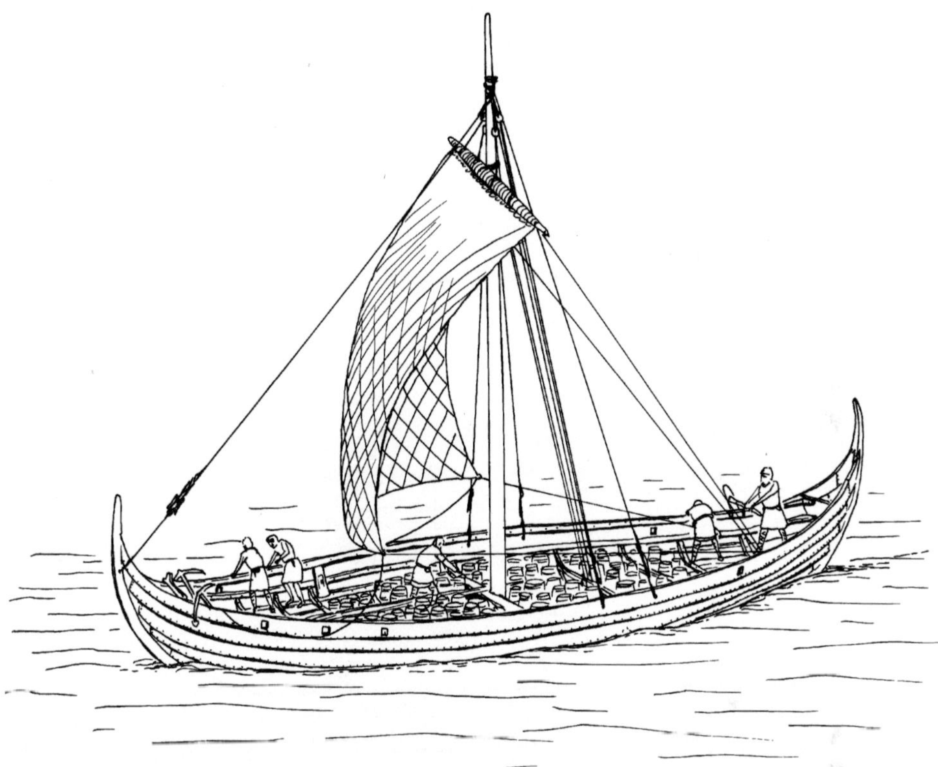

31 An artistic reconstruction of Skudelev 3 – one of the traders excavated from Roskilde fjord.
© *Dom Andrews*

distinction between the boats in the earlier part of the Tapestry and those depicted after Scene 24 is due to the tastes of different workshops or a simplification in the Tapestry design during construction.

Gaps amidships are rare in medieval art, but do seem to be depicted in both Junius 11 (page 68) and the Old English Hexateuch (folio 14r); in both, the Ark is shown with a doorway cut through the upper strakes (*32*). Hence, whilst it is possible that the Tapestry designer has used this feature in an attempt to convey the cargo hulls of contemporary traders, it is perhaps more likely that this motif was borrowed from art.

Figureheads and stem ornaments

The ornate figureheads of the Tapestry's ships are the most notable nautical feature, indicating the influence of artistic tradition as opposed to 'real life'. Imposing zoomorphic, anthropomorphic and decorative figureheads, commonly referred to in Scandinavian sagas, are traditionally associated with Viking longships; Karlhöfði, the ship of King 'Saint' Olaf II of Norway (1015-30), carried a king's head, whilst those of King Harald Hardrada of Norway (1047-66), Chief Raud the Strong of Salten, Norway, (about 997) and King Eystein

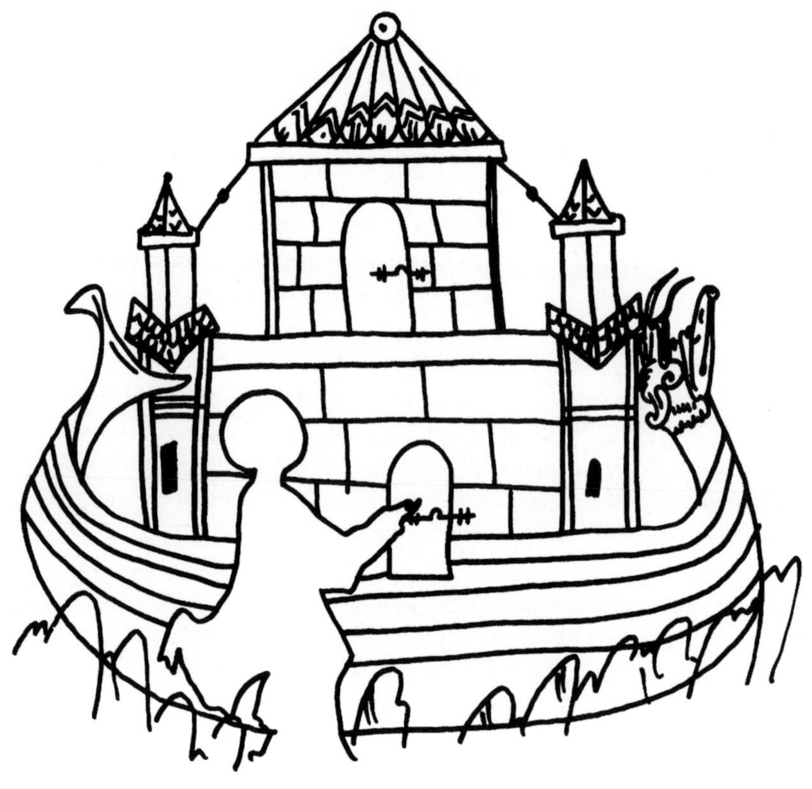

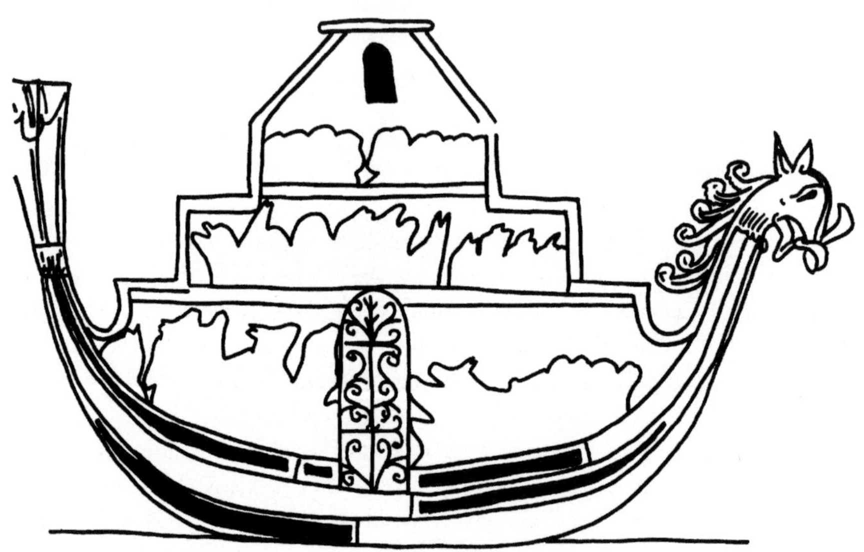

32 Vessels in Junius 11 (page 68) (top) and the Old English Hexateuch (folio 14r) (bottom) with gaps in the gunwale amidships

I of Norway (1103-23) all had ships with a dragon's head. However, mostly such literary sources date from long after the period in question; an exception is the *Encomium Emmae Reginae*, written between about 1037 and 1040, which describes the ornate figureheads of the ships of the Danish kings, Svein and Cnut, carved in the form of many kinds of animals and beasts.

Archaeologically, decorative figureheads are known from the time when the Anglo-Saxons first migrated to England, and elsewhere, as the examples from the River Scheldt at Zele (AD 69±180 years), Appels (AD 400±150) and Moerzeke (AD 350±70) demonstrate (*33*). Nonetheless, the suitability of these for display on the narrow, raking stems of Anglo-Saxon ships seems unlikely and has been doubted by John Haywood (1999); the Appels piece, in particular, had a massive tenon and the Zele figurehead was perhaps from a piece of furniture or cart. Although later examples are unknown, it is tempting to parallel the five zoomorphic carvings recovered from the Oseberg ship (which have handles to enable them to be carried, perhaps in a religious procession) (*colour plate 29*) with those described in the Scandinavian sagas. Even so, Thorleif Sjøvold (1957) convincingly argued that these were never tied or fixed to a Viking Age ship.

With no extant early medieval zoomorphic or anthropomorphic figureheads, it is necessary to examine surviving stem posts to see whether or not they might once have carried them. Such an investigation is difficult where the remains are fragmentary. The stem posts of Sutton Hoo (mound 1), for example, had rotted away prior to excavation, and although Rupert Bruce-Mitford (1975-83), who excavated the ships, hypothesised that a royal ship might be expected to have carried stem decoration, this was simply conjecture. Similarly, the height of the stem of the Gokstad ship could not be determined since the bow, stern and first two upper strakes had rotted away.

Surviving stem posts imply that early medieval ships had either square or, more commonly, pointed stem termination; the stem post recovered from Skuldelev 3 was pointed. Nicolay Nicolaysen (1992) and others have also suggested that figureheads may have been removable, and that boxed, square or flushed stems, commonly illustrated in the Tapestry, may have been slots designed to take a figurehead. There is later documentary evidence to support such a procedure; in 1221, Bishop Nicolas of Aaslo is said to have lent figureheads of his ship, *Skeggen*, to Duke Skule of Norway (*c*.1189-1240). The theory might have had more weight if all the Tapestry's beached ships had such slots, which they do not, and if slots did not also appear on some of the vessels sailing in William's invasion fleet. It seems unlikely that many of the newly constructed vessels of William's fleet would carry ornate stem decoration, as this would have tied up valuable time and resources. Whilst the 'Ship List', which Elisabeth (Liesbeth) van Houts (1988) believed was a contemporary text, states that William's flagship, the Mora, had a prow figurehead of a golden infant holding an ivory horn (also seemingly illustrated in the Bayeux Tapestry), it seems probable that many contemporary vessels, including most of those in William's fleet, would have had simple stem decoration or, more likely, none at all.

The diversity in the types of stem ornamentation depicted in the Tapestry is intriguing. Possibly the designer wished to evoke the diversity of William's grand fleet: requisitioned

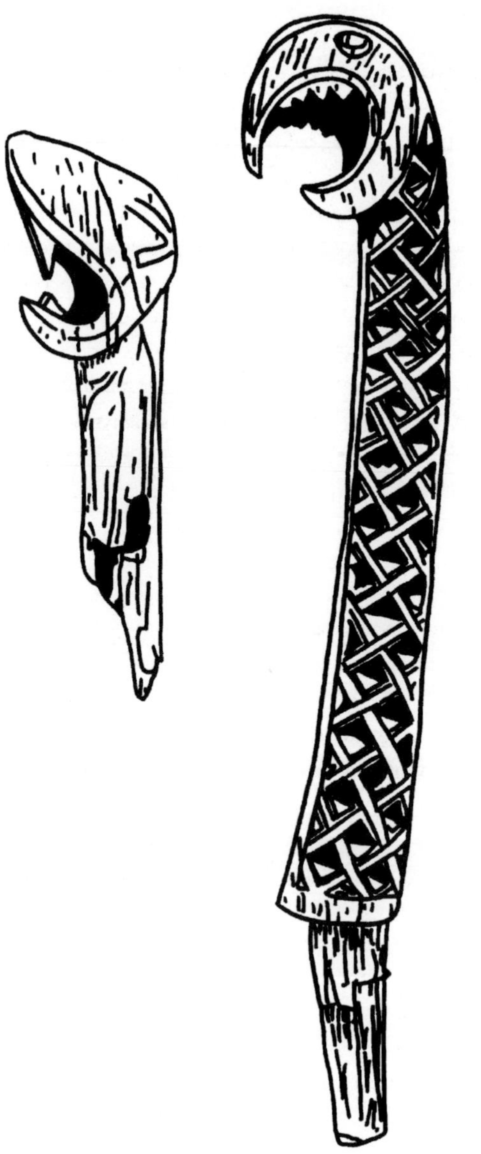
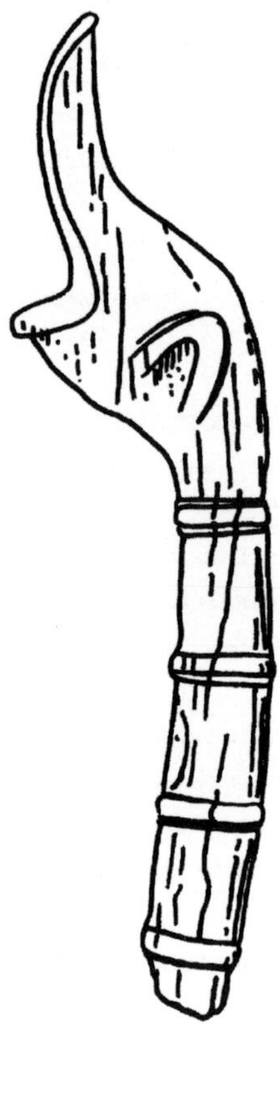

33 The decorative figureheads from the River Scheldt at Zele, Appels and Moerzeke

cargo ships, small boats, warships and specially constructed troop ships. This said, it seems likely that most working vessels in the eleventh century would have had pointed or square flush stems, so why does the Tapestry omit pointed stems, while ornate figureheads proliferate? The conundrum may be explained by iconographic tradition. Zoomorphic prow decoration can be traced back to prehistoric art, becoming common in the medieval period. Contemporary manuscript illuminations provide several parallels for the figureheads in the Tapestry, some of the closest being those in Junius 11 (pages 66 & 68) (2) and the Old English Hexateuch (folios 14r & 15r).

Planking

There are other vital clues of the extent to which the designer was concerned with recreating the contemporary scene. The strakes which form the hulls of the Tapestry ships are depicted in an array of multi-coloured bands. These could be purely decorative, like the stripes on the mound of Hastings Castle, but they might also represent clinker (or carvel planking, as suggested by Lucien Musset (2002). If the latter is true, then the number of strakes shown compares well with those found on early medieval wrecks. Nonetheless, the strakes of the Tapestry's ships are shown as single planks. Strakes of one-plank construction are known in the migration period, particularly in north-west Europe, but from the seventh century onwards ships, including Sutton Hoo (mound 1), Gokstad, Oseberg, Graveney and Skuldelev 1 to 6, were constructed of several planks scarfed together. Significantly, scarf joins frequently appear in manuscripts from the early twelfth century, such as Oxford, University College 165, but are less common before then. This said, Junius 11 (page 65) and the Old English Hexatueuch (folio 14r) provide good and early examples of hull planking with scarf joins, but even here this feature is atypical of ships in both manuscripts.

Shields along the gunwale

It has long been assumed that it was Scandinavian custom to hang shields along a vessel's gunwale when leaving or arriving in port. Five ships in the Tapestry have shields arranged in this manner, which compares well with the testament of Scandinavian sagas and was documented in the Gokstad funeral ship, where 32 shields were fixed along the gunwale of each side of the ship. Charles Gibbs-Smith (1957) and Arne Emil Christensen (1970) have argued that shields could not have lined the gunwale whilst a ship was underway, since oar ports would have been covered and therefore oars could not have been used to manoeuvre the vessel. This said, oars are not shown propelling any of the vessels with shields in the Tapestry. Also, an archaeological reconstruction of Skuldelev 5 was put to sea by oar with shields in the shield rack. However, most discussions have overlooked the fact that the shields on the ships in the Tapestry are not shown outboard, but are displayed from within the gunwale, contrary to the archaeological evidence.

Shields are depicted on ships in near-contemporary art, such as the eleventh-century stone from Ledberg, Sweden, and the Italian late twelfth-century Ebulo Codex (folio 120r), both of which show shields hanging along the outside of the gunwale. Of particular relevance to the Tapestry's illustrations (though they cannot have been known to the designer) are some early tenth-century coins from Spangerid, Vest-Auger, one of which seems to depict both round- and kite-shields from within the gunwale.

Illuminated manuscripts are less helpful in determining the origin of this feature, although the manner in which the halos of Christ and his companions line up against the side of the portside gunwale of the ship in the Hitda Codex (folio 117) offers an interesting analogy. The origins of this motif in the Tapestry are therefore uncertain.

Sails

There is extensive documentary evidence for the use of sails on Anglo-Saxon ships, but this is not paralleled in archaeology. Similarly, there is no direct evidence for the type of sails used on Anglo-Saxon or Norman ships. The bundle of yellowish woollen cloth (on to which red stripes were sewn) that was found in the Gokstad burial may be the vestiges of a sail, but this has been disputed by Nicolay Nicolaysen (1992), who thought it was part of a tent.

In the Tapestry, sails are shown with a curved triangular form which Wolfgang Grape (1994) reasonably supposed are stylised representations of the square sail. Grape also noted the strange form of the sail of Ship 3 in the Tapestry, suggesting that the designer was trying to show a wind-filled sail, which afterwards was simplified and stereotyped. However, this reading of the sail of Ship 3 is mistaken. Closer inspection reveals it to be an error; the bottom is shown with an outline stitch, but it has not been filled with laid and couched work.

Since the form of medieval sails is currently uncertain, it is difficult to be sure whether or not the renditions offered by the Tapestry designer depict those used by contemporary ships. However, most early medieval representations of ships show a forward-facing square or rectangular sail; examples are the tenth-century Gotland picture stones of Hunninge, Stenkyrka, and Lillbjärs and an undated graffito on an early Norman column in Upper Deal Church, Kent. Representations of triangular-form sails, like those in the Tapestry, become more common in twelfth-century illuminations, including Arundel 91 (folio 188) and Oxford, Corpus Christi College 157 (page 383). This motif also occurs in the Harley 603 Psalter (folio 51v). Whilst the Tapestry designer might have sketched the sails of ships as they visited a local harbour, as some have suggested, on balance it seems more likely that this triangular form was borrowed from contemporary art.

Cross at the masthead

The cross fixed high in the mast of the vessel that is believed to be William's flagship, the *Mora*, has been interpreted as a lantern or crossed pendant, perhaps the Papal banner (see Chapter 2). It is not known whether crosses were carried on the masts of contemporary ships, though they do appear in artistic depictions. Similar crosses are shown on early ninth-century coins from Dorestad, as well as on the twelfth-century Tournai font in Winchester Cathedral, though neither would have been known to the Tapestry designer.

Shipbuilding scenes

It has long been held that the shipbuilding scenes in the Bayeux Tapestry are of the utmost importance for understanding the use of woodworking tools in the early medieval period. Such a view presupposes that the tools and methods accurately reflect contemporary boat-building practice. Although the Tapestry seems to give an accurate rendition of eleventh-century woodworking tools, it is worth noting that diagnostic phases of contemporary boat construction are not depicted.

Men are shown felling trees with long-hafted, symmetrical, straight-bladed axes. A haft of up to 1m in length is believed to have been ideal for such a purpose and the axes depicted in the Tapestry seem to correspond to this view. The Tapestry also suggests that rough planks were smoothed with a T-axe, and this is also consistent with the archaeological evidence. Valerie Fenwick (1978), Ole Olsen and Olaf Crumlin-Pedersen (1967) have noted that the construction of the Graveney boat and the Skuldelev wrecks demonstrate that the axe was the principal tool of the medieval shipwright and was used in preference to the saw. Concordant with this, the Tapestry does not show carpenters working with saws. The other tools that are shown, such as breast-augers, hammers and side-axes, are similarly consistent with the archaeological evidence.

The trees in the boat-building scenes have tall straight trunks and are free of notches, providing excellent carpentry timber. They are also notably thinner and straighter than those depicted elsewhere in the Tapestry. In addition, the designer gives the impression that this timber was green, and as such would have been ideal for boat-building; Valerie Fenwick (1978) has highlighted the fact that green timber had practical advantages, as it could be easily cleft, without the log splitting, and conveniently worked. Although it is known that English shipbuilders used common/green oak for boat-building, while Scandinavians preferred pine (though some Old English texts associate them with ash), the designer (unsurprisingly) has made no obvious attempt to signal the type of trees being used.

As with all clinker-built vessels, the keel and stem posts were laid first. Next, the shell (the external timber planks) was fashioned, and then the frames were carved to fit. Whilst under construction, the vessel would be secured by a series of stakes. Using wedges, the medieval carpenter would have cleft tree trunks into usable planks, and these would have formed the strakes for the hull. Internal supporting timbers were cut, following the grain, from appropriately crooked trunks and branches. Given the generous amount of space that was allotted to the boat-building scenes, it is notable (though hardly surprising) that these important stages of clinker-build construction are not shown in the Tapestry. The designer clearly wished to evoke the enormity of the task of constructing the invasion fleet, rather than give a stage-by-stage account of contemporary carpentry methods which were incidental to the thrust of the narrative. Fundamental to understanding the boat-building scenes is the fact that the boats undergoing construction are not significantly different from the completed vessels shown elsewhere. Indeed, as the Tapestry only depicts phases of boat-building which are common to timber construction in general, there is little to suggest that the designer had an in-depth knowledge of contemporary boat-building practice, which was a specialised profession in the early medieval period.

Boat-building illustrations are extremely rare in Anglo-Saxon manuscripts; those that appear are associated with Noah's Ark. The parallels between the figure using an axe to smooth a timber plank in the Tapestry (Figure 269) and those engaged in constructing the Ark in both Junius 11 (page 65) and the Old English Hexateuch (folio 13v) are therefore particularly interesting, since both books may have been available to a designer with access to Canterbury illuminations (34). Inevitably, the availability of such motifs clearly lessened the need for the designer to sketch from personal observation.

Summary

The ship scenes in the Bayeux Tapestry are some of the most difficult to interpret with regard to the question of their sources. Analysis of individual elements raises serious doubts concerning the authority of various details of contemporary shipping depiction and it is apparent that the designer has effectively made use of motifs from contemporary manuscript art; examples include ships figureheads and the gap amidships. Further archaeological discoveries in this poorly understood area may yet refine our understanding; nevertheless, it is clear that the confidence hitherto placed in the designer's desire to accurately recreate the contemporary scene as regards ships and boat-building has been overstated.

DRESS AND CLOTHING

It is inconceivable that the Tapestry designer did not know what contemporary clothes looked like. Yet, some scholars, such as David Wilson (1985), have been less ready to accept the evidence of the Bayeux Tapestry at face value here than in other areas, since dress and clothing in the Tapestry 'is fairly standardized' and 'clearly related to that in contemporary art'.

As the only clothing to survive from the Anglo-Saxon and early Anglo-Norman period is highly fragmentary with the execption of shoes, it is of limited use for reconstructing the nature of whole garments. Excavations in York yielded the greatest selection of textile remains recovered from a Viking Age site in England, but only one garment (a sock!) was substantially complete. Similarly, John Nevinson (1957) and Gale Owen-Crocker (1986) observed that remarks about dress in contemporary literature are few, and of little help with regard to details of their form. Therefore, there is no firm basis of evidence against which to compare the Tapestry images, but some clues are offered by contemporary illuminations.

The majority of the 627 characters depicted in the Tapestry wear civilian clothing; from Scenes 1 to 40 (excluding the Breton campaign) the figures nearly always wear civilian clothing. Interestingly, most, including many of the elite and the clergy, wear the same basic outfit, comprising a long-sleeved tunic with belt, fitted trousers (sometimes gartered) and simple flat soled round-toed shoes. Gale Owen-Crocker (1986) noted that this contrasts to some manuscript illuminations where dress differs from one occupation to another, particularly in the case of male clothing. High status characters often wear cloaks, and a few, who are seated, are robed, highlighting their authority. Occasionally, both cloaks and robes are embellished with embroidery or, as in the case of William, decorative ribbons.

Whilst most ecclesiastics wear civilian dress and are distinguished only by their tonsure, some high-ranking clergy are shown in vestments. The three (clothed!) women all wear long-sleeved dresses (though the garments of the women fleeing the burning building (Figure 402) have longer hanging sleeves) and scarves covering the head. John Nevinson (1957) observed that the Tapestry also gives hints of material, pattern, folds, as well as border ornament and fastenings, but does not indicate seams or tailoring. Jewellery and dress accessories appear infrequently, with only functional round or square brooches and the occasional buckle depicted.

Elements of the clothing depicted in the Tapestry must be stylised, although how far this was due to the constraints of the medium remains uncertain. On the other hand, it is clearly

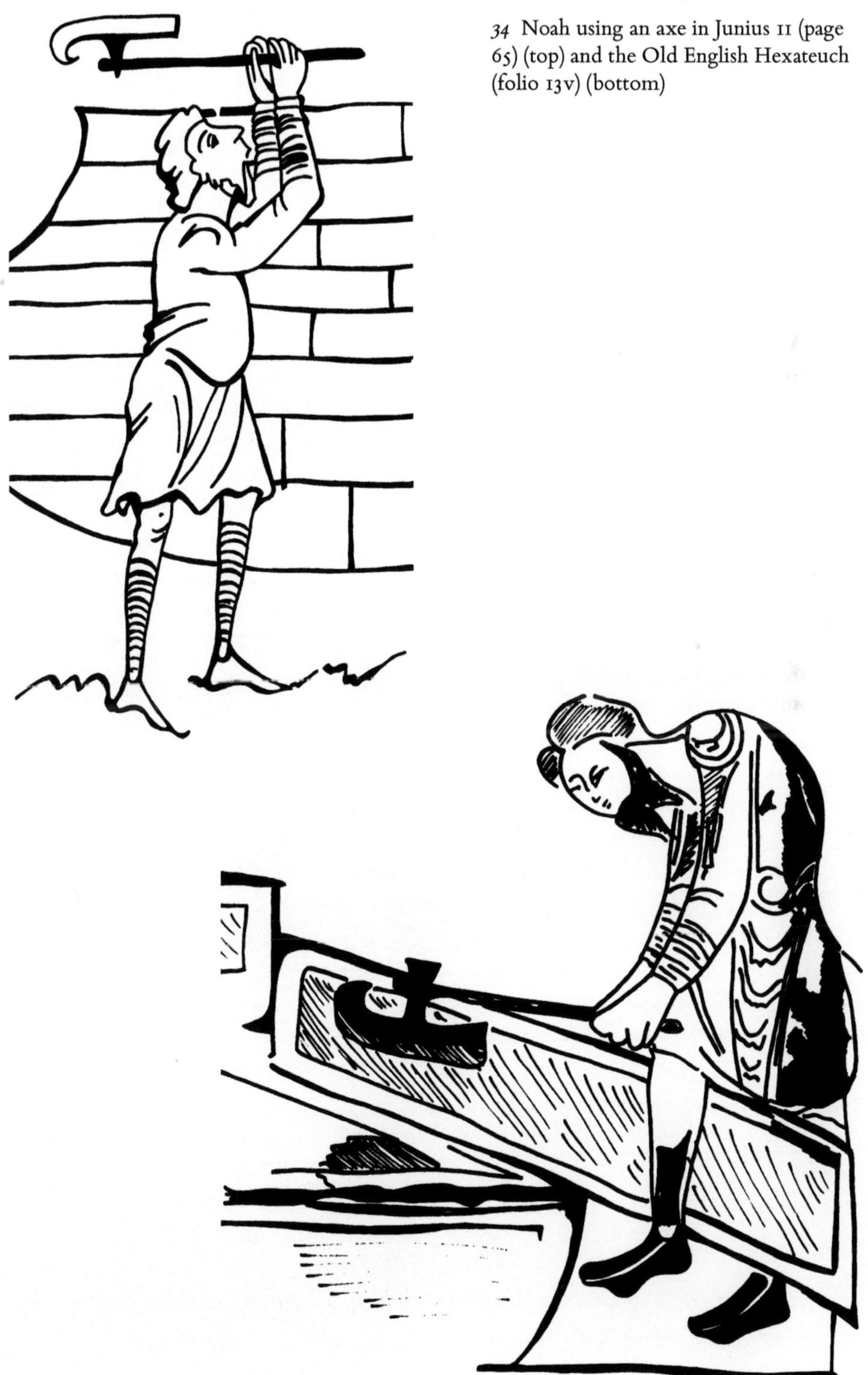

34 Noah using an axe in Junius 11 (page 65) (top) and the Old English Hexateuch (folio 13v) (bottom)

the case that the colours of the clothing in the Tapestry are life-like; the dyes available to the embroiderers would have also been accessible to contemporary tailors, though Gale Owen-Crocker (personal correspondence, 2007) highlighted the fact that smaller quantities would be needed for embroidery wool compared to actual garments, and this might have ensured the selective use of more expensive dyes in embroidery work. Excavations in York demonstrated that early medieval people may have worn brightly coloured garments, whose tones were produced using a range of natural dyes, along with imported silks and other textiles from the Mediterranean and the Near and Far East, though there is perhaps not enough evidence to suggest widespread use of such dyes.

Gowns

The loose-fitting gowns and 'classical' robes that are commonly depicted in early medieval manuscripts are less frequent in late Anglo-Saxon illuminations. Here, they are generally worn by royalty, the Divine and some religious figures. Correspondingly, such examples in the Tapestry are few; only 11 characters, all of high status, are clearly shown wearing long-sleeved, ankle-length gowns, while none wear classical robes.

In late Anglo-Saxon art, gowns are long-sleeved and tight-fitting. At times, gowned seated figures in the Tapestry also appear to wear an undergarment, sometimes of a different colour, which is suggested by a single diagonal line. This is also a common feature of gowns depicted in contemporary illuminations, including Cotton Titus D.xxvi (folio 75v) (35) and Cambridge, Trinity College B.15.34 (folio 1).

Gowns in the Tapestry, such as one worn by Edward (Figure 3), are occasionally embellished with plain or embroidered bands, which Gale Owen-Crocker (personal correspondence, 2007) suggested might be borders of an outer garment. The latter are normally found just below the knee of seated, high status individuals, and similar bands are also found in contemporary illuminations, such as Florence, Biblioteca Mediceo-Laurenziana, Plut XVII.20 (folio 1). Gowns are also occasionally embellished with other decorative elements. Thus, the geometric embroidered bands with associated quatrefoil motifs found on the gowns of King Edward in the Tapestry (Figure 3) can be paralleled with that of St John in Arundel 60 (folio 12v) (36). It is unlikely that the designer knew of this illumination and it therefore seems reasonable to suppose that these are two broadly contemporary reflections of the same fashion. Interestingly, Gale Owen-Crocker (1986) also compared some of the details of Edward's gown, which she suggested were unlike anything in Anglo-Saxon art, with the exotic dress found in tenth-century male burials at Birka, Sweden.

Tunics

Tunics in late Anglo-Saxon illuminations are shown to be about knee length, which is broadly consistent with those in the Bayeux Tapestry. Most tunics in the Tapestry are fastened with a belt, though this is less obvious in manuscript art.

Some tunics in the Tapestry are shown as culottes. John Nevinson (1957) identified these as a feature of working men, but they are in fact clearly worn by individuals of varying status and occupation. Gale Owen-Crocker (1994) suggested that the designer reserved trousered tunics for the Normans, but perhaps this association should be regarded

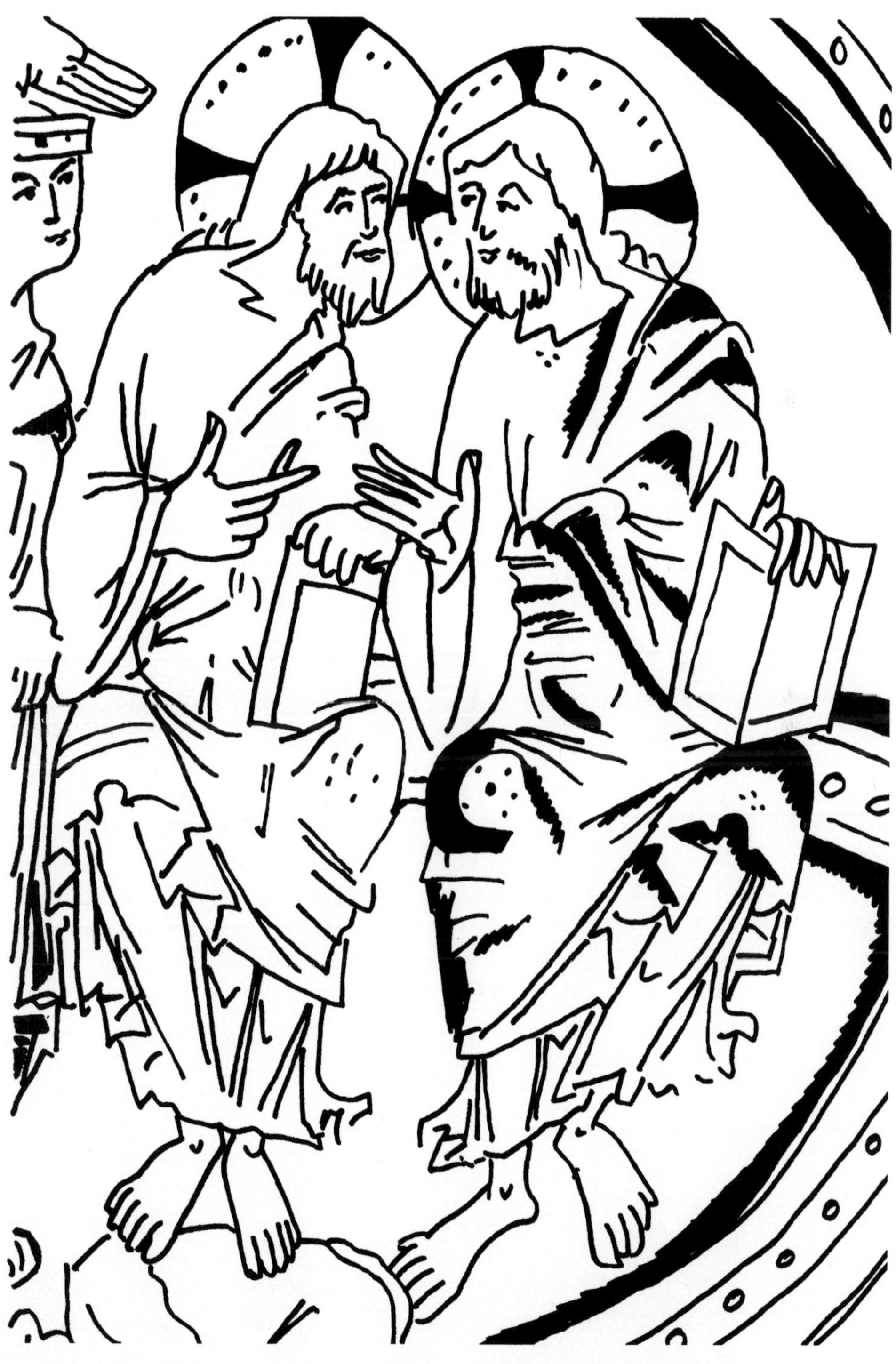

35 Gowns with a diagonal fold in British Library, Cotton Titus D.xxvi (folio 75v)

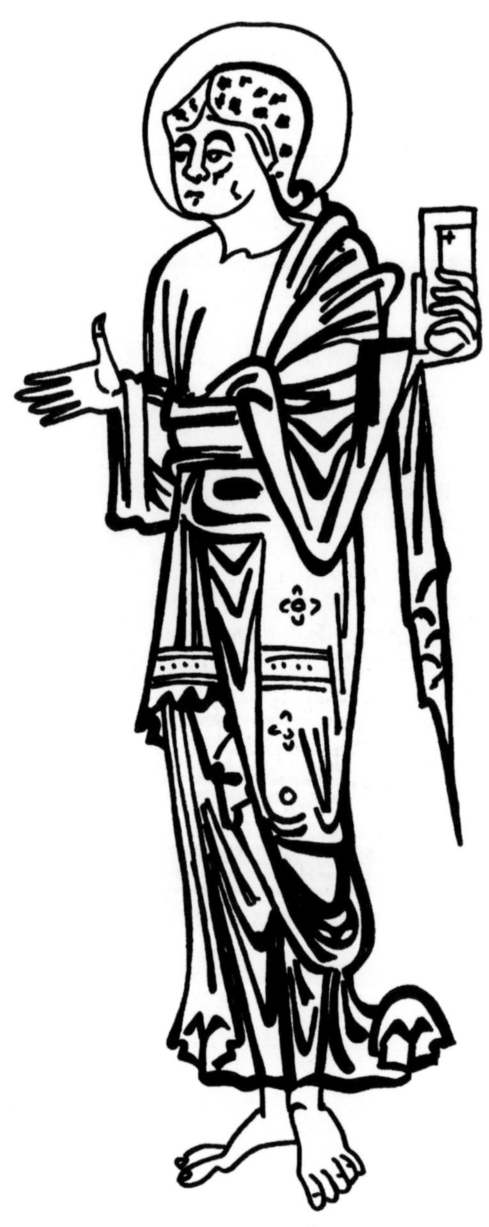

36 Embroidered bands and quatrefoil motifs on the gown of St John in British Library, Arundel 60 (folio 12v)

with caution since at least one Englishman (Figure 527) is also shown wearing them.

Trousered tunics are very rare in contemporary art; Gale Owen-Crocker (1994) noted that they 'were not part of the English iconographical tradition'. It is therefore intriguing that the culottes illustrated in the mid eleventh-century Tiberius Psalter (folio 13), like those worn by Figure 76 in the Tapestry, have banding on the inside leg (37). Unless the designer knew of this illumination, which was produced in Winchester, it is possible that these are two independent reflections of contemporary reality.

Baggy-trousered tunics (such as those worn by Figures 442 and 443) and those of one-piece construction (worn by Figure 117) are not found in manuscript art. Such garments in the Tapestry might therefore reflect a recent innovation in fashion, not known to earlier artists. John Nevinson (1957) suggested that trousered tunics of one-piece construction could not have been worn without some kind of opening, either at the front, rear or sides. The same is true of the trousered armour (see ARMS AND ARMOUR above), which is also seemingly of one-piece construction. Whilst we might not expect to see such an opening or fastenings in the Tapestry given its scale and the restrictions of the medium, it might alternatively be the case that the imagery represents a garment of two parts, but since both parts are shown of the same colour, the distinction between them is obscured.

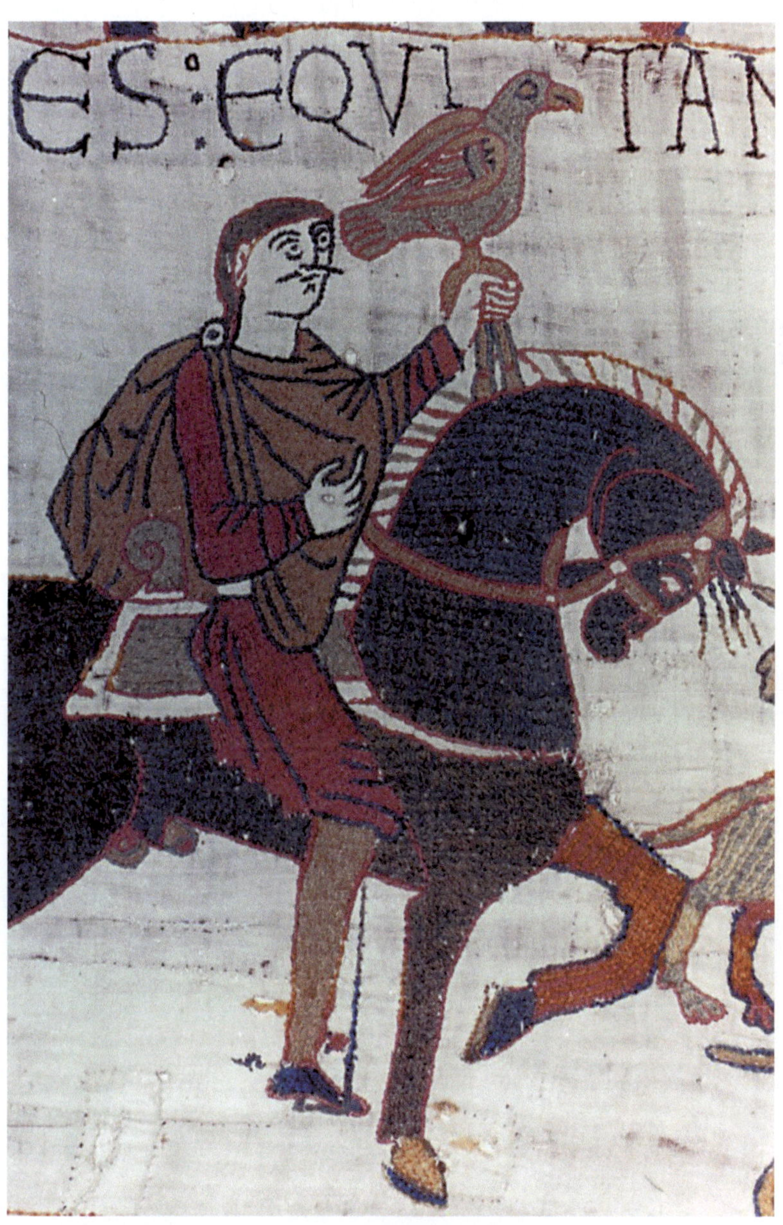

1 Harold (Figure 9) on horseback

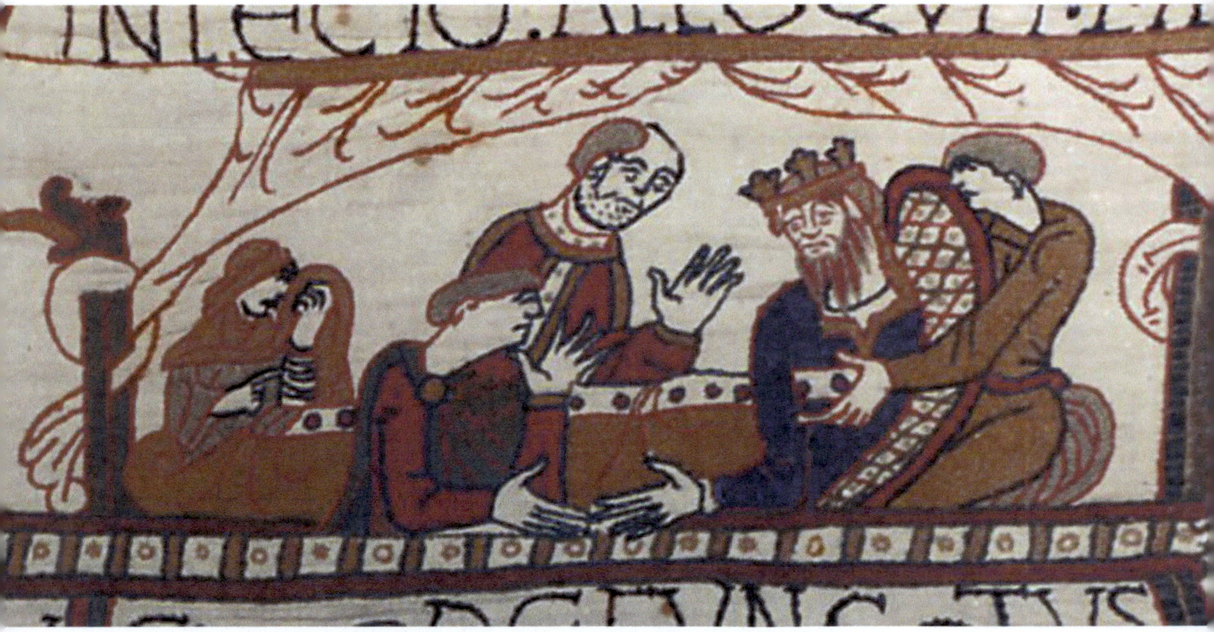

2 Edward (Figure 231) dying

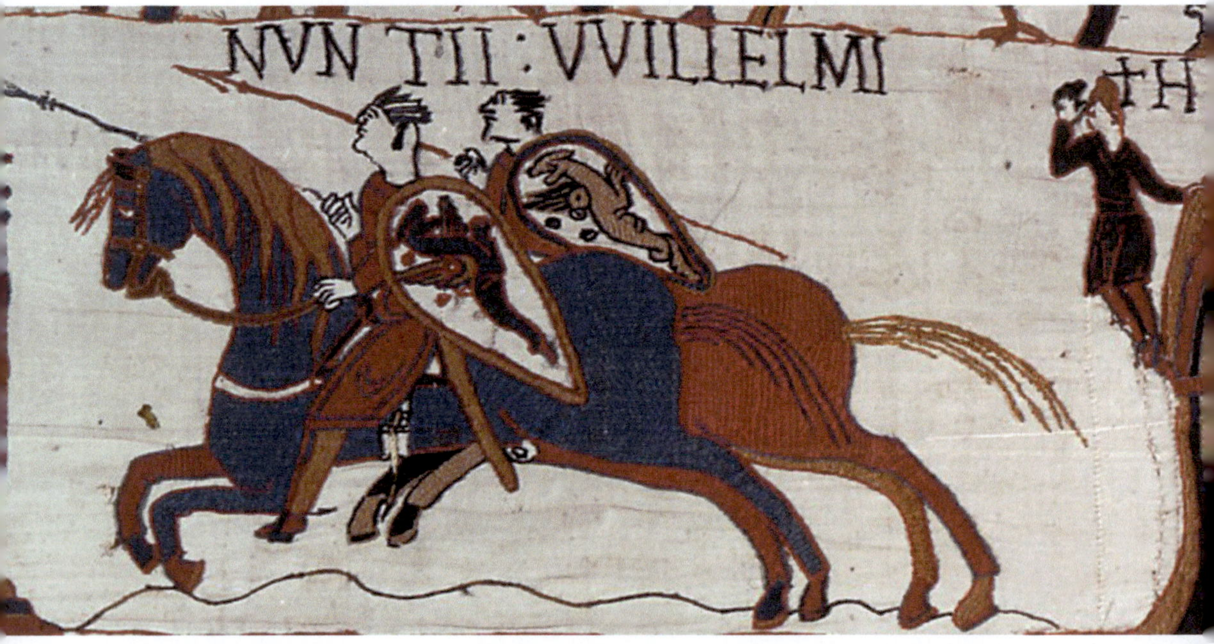

3 William's messengers (Figures 98-9)

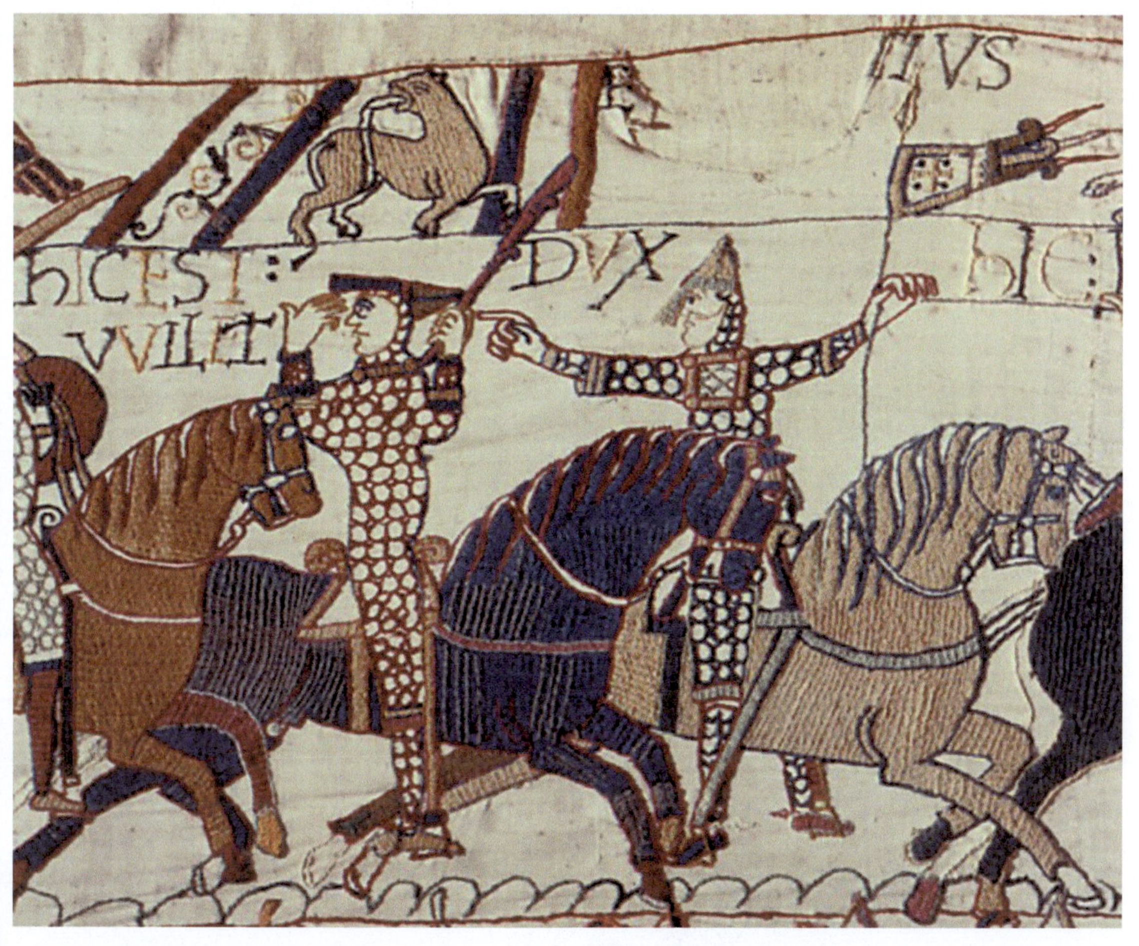

4 William and 'Eustace' (Figures 542-2)

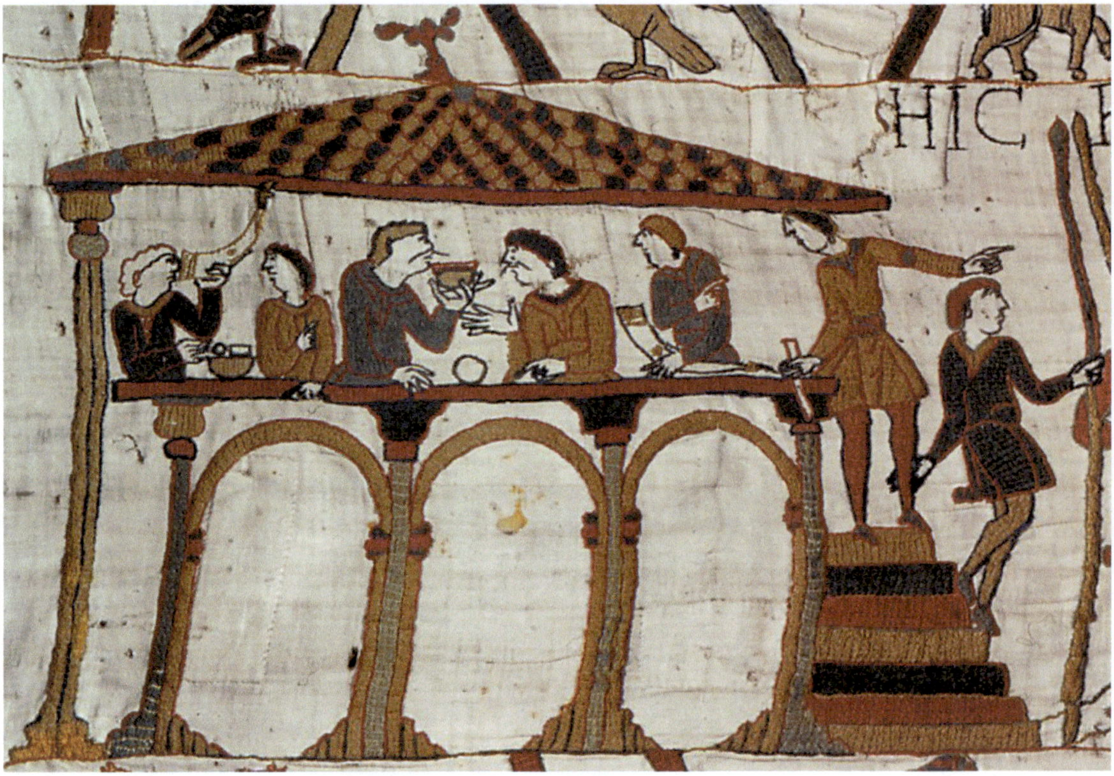

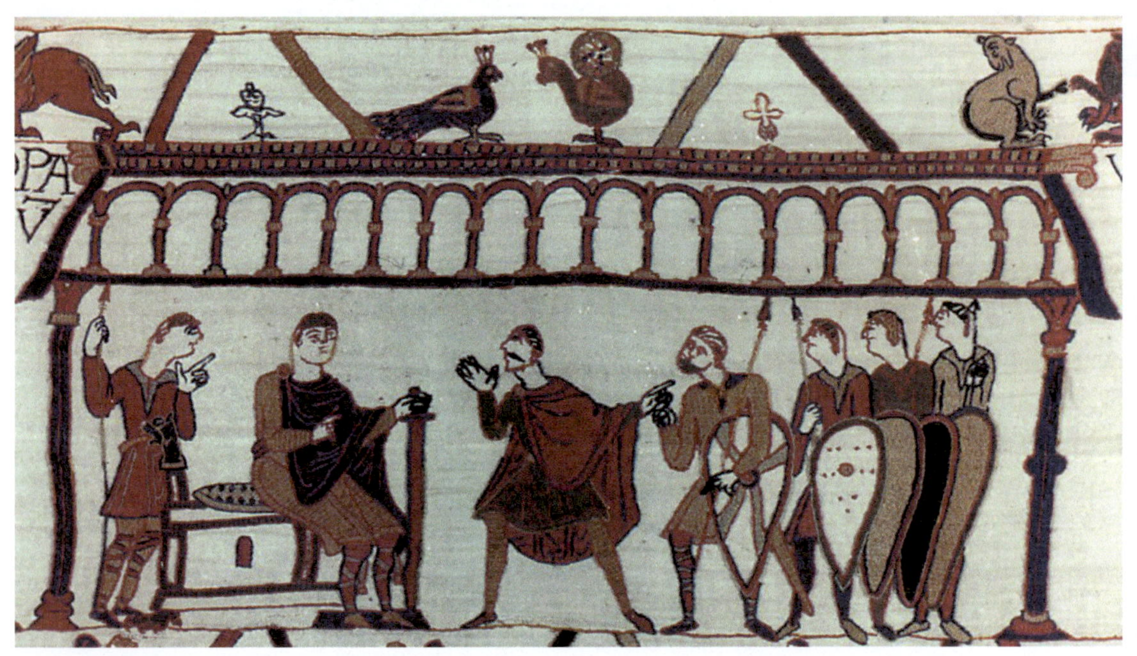

5 Harold's 'hall' at Bosham (Building 3)

6 William's 'palace' in Rouen (Building 8)

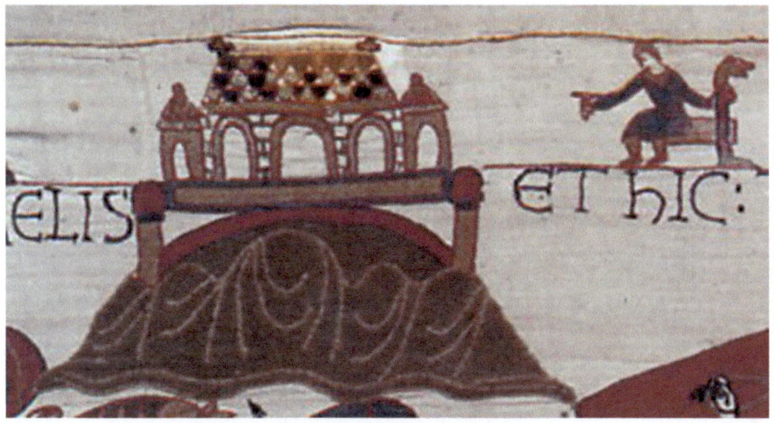

7 Mont-Saint-Michel (Building 11)

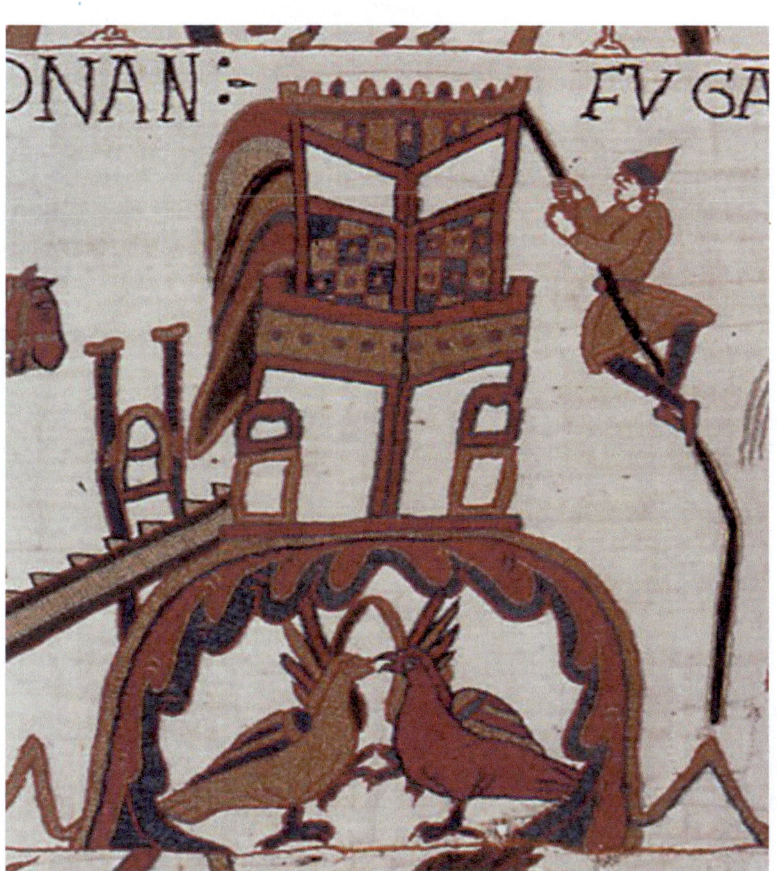

8 Conan (Figure 159) escapes from Dol (Building 12)

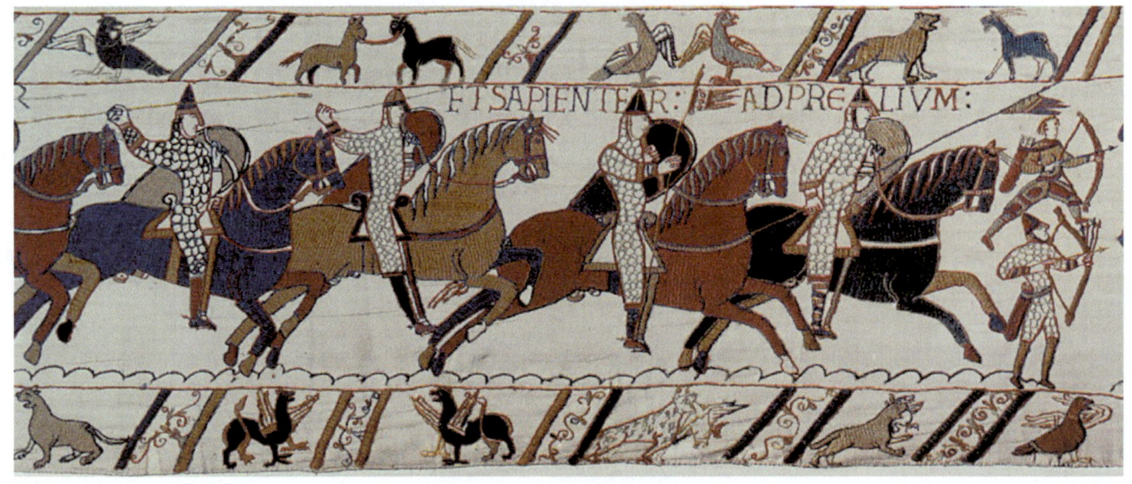

9 Norman cavalry (Scene 51)

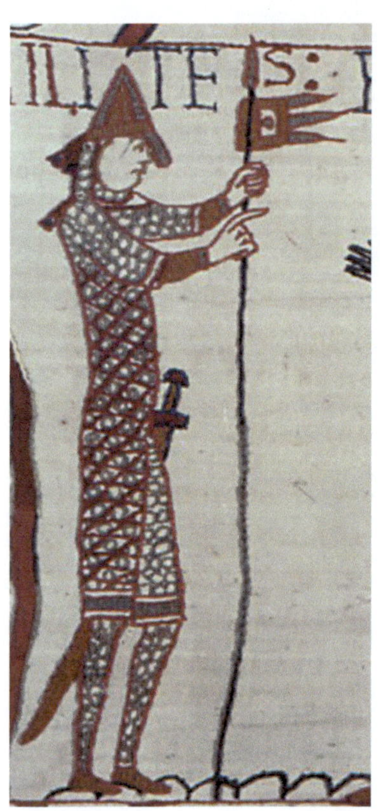

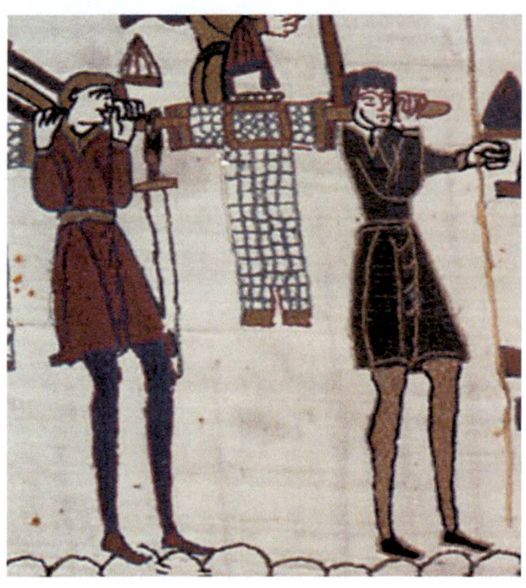

Left: 10 William (Figure 404) in armour

Above: 11 Mail hauberks being carried onto William's ships (Scene 37)

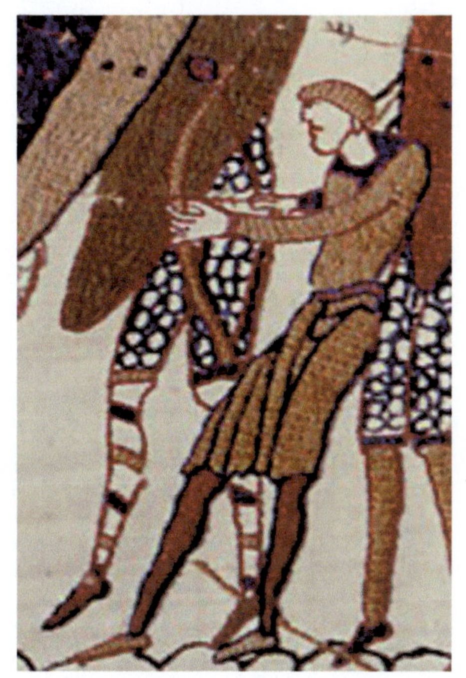

12 The lone English archer (Figure 462)

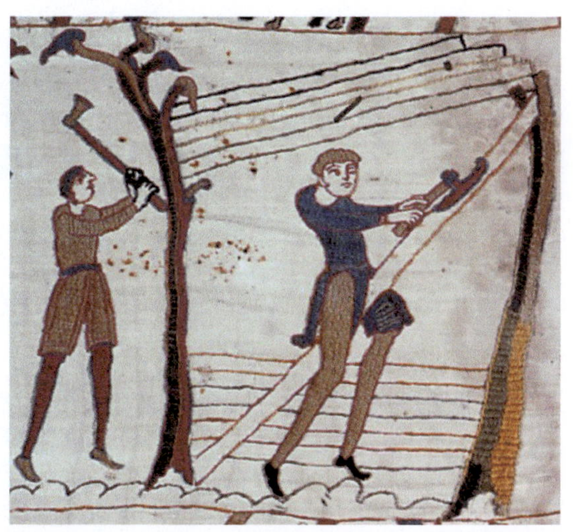

13 Woodcutters (Scene 36)

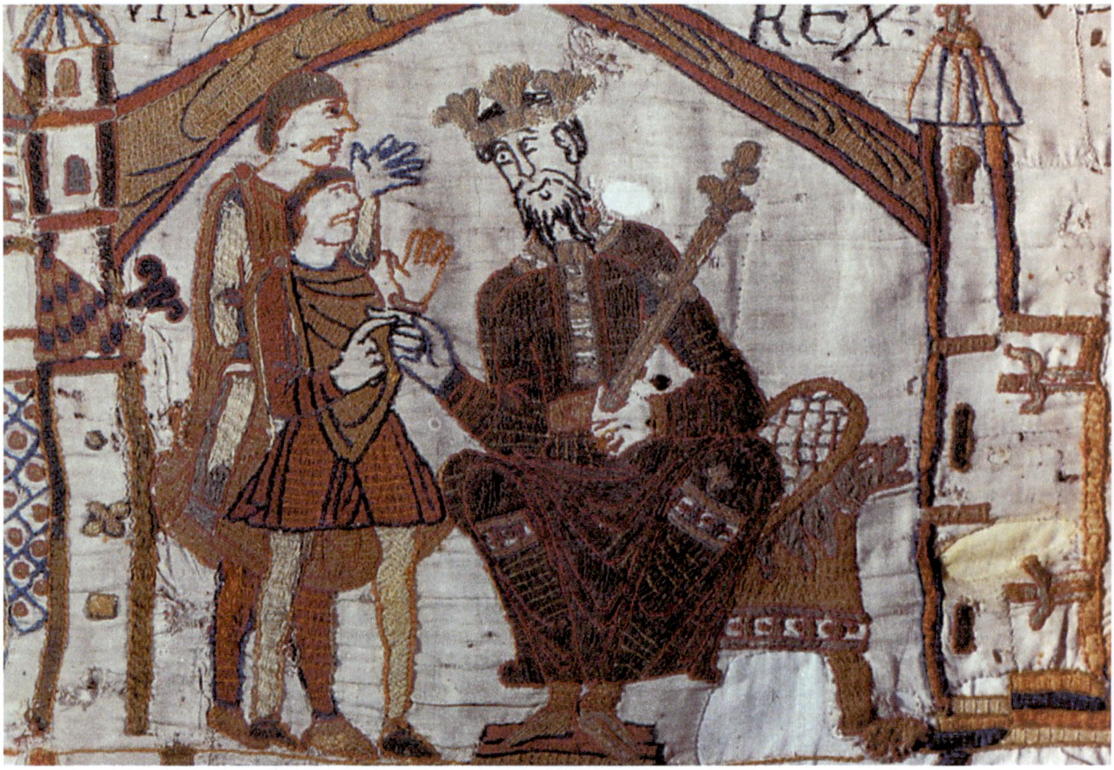

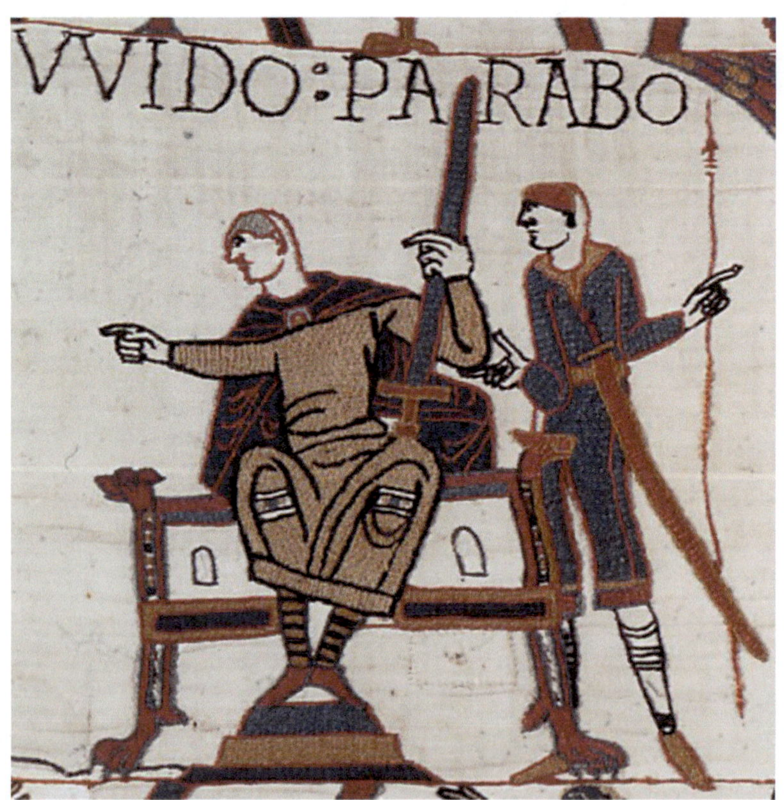

Above: 14 Edward (Figure 3) and Harold (Figure 1 or 2)

Left: 15 Guy (Figure 85)

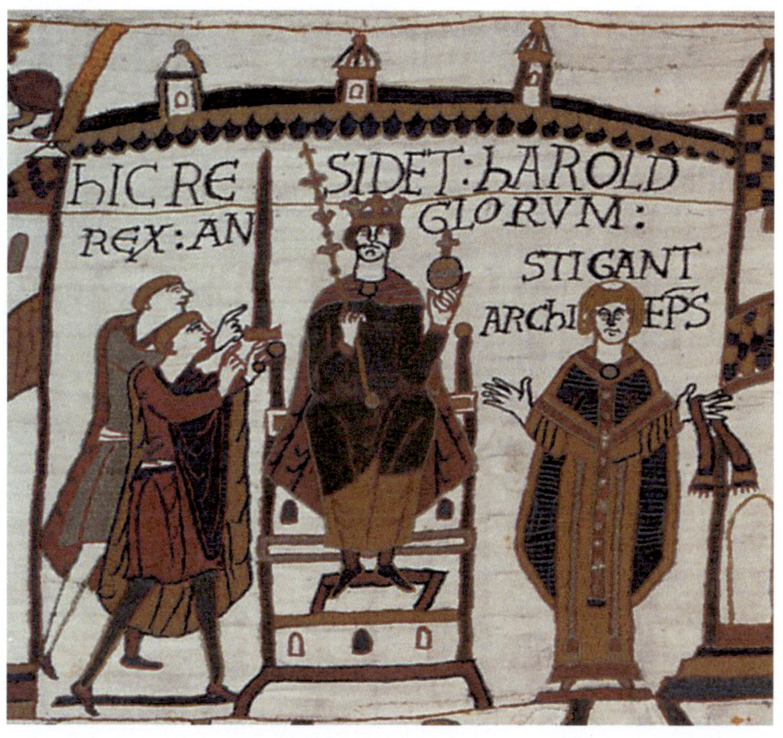

Above: 16 Harold's coronation
(Scene 30)

Right: 17 Harold (Figure 84)

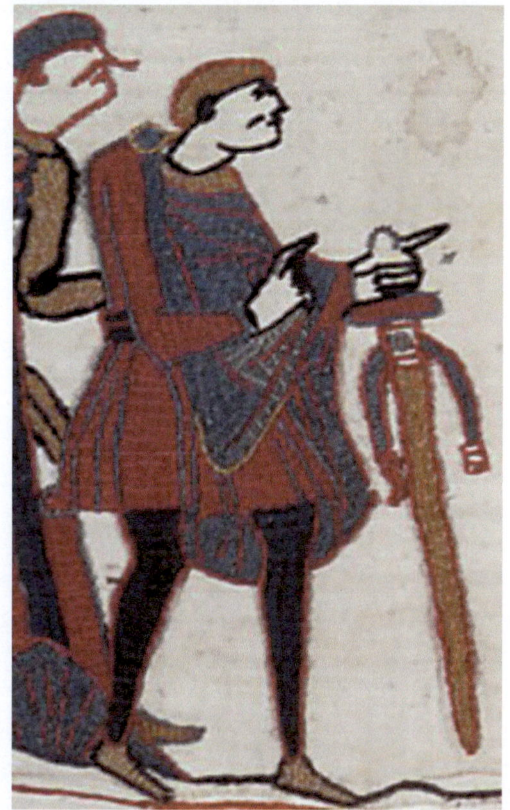

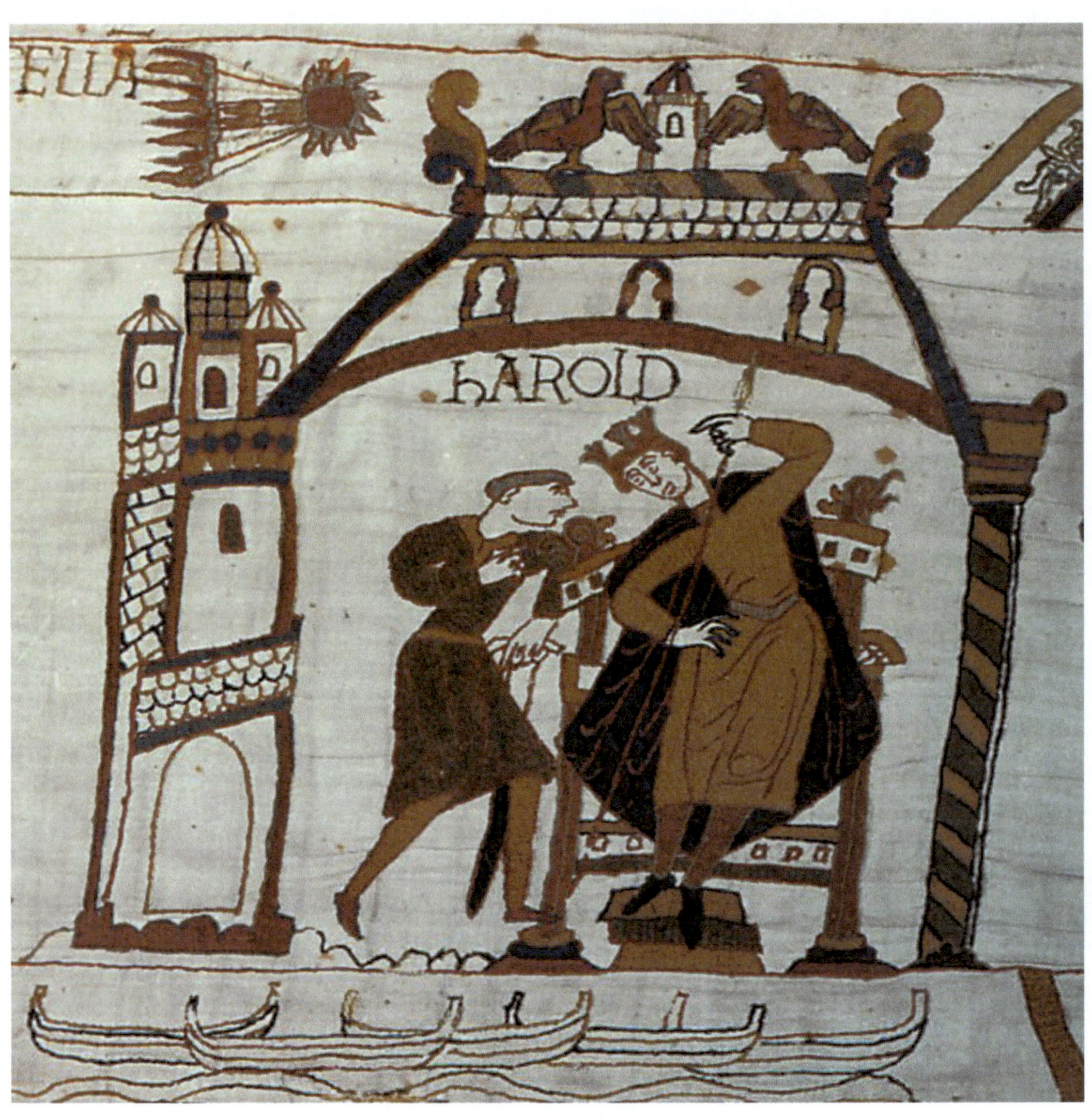

18 Harold (Figure 256) is told news news of the comet (Scene 33)

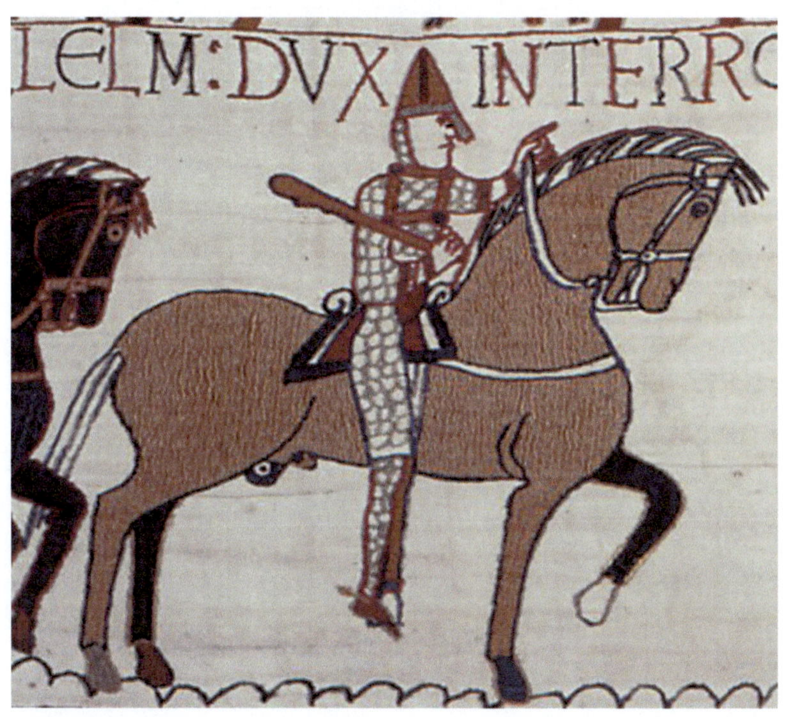

19 William (Figure 424) on horseback

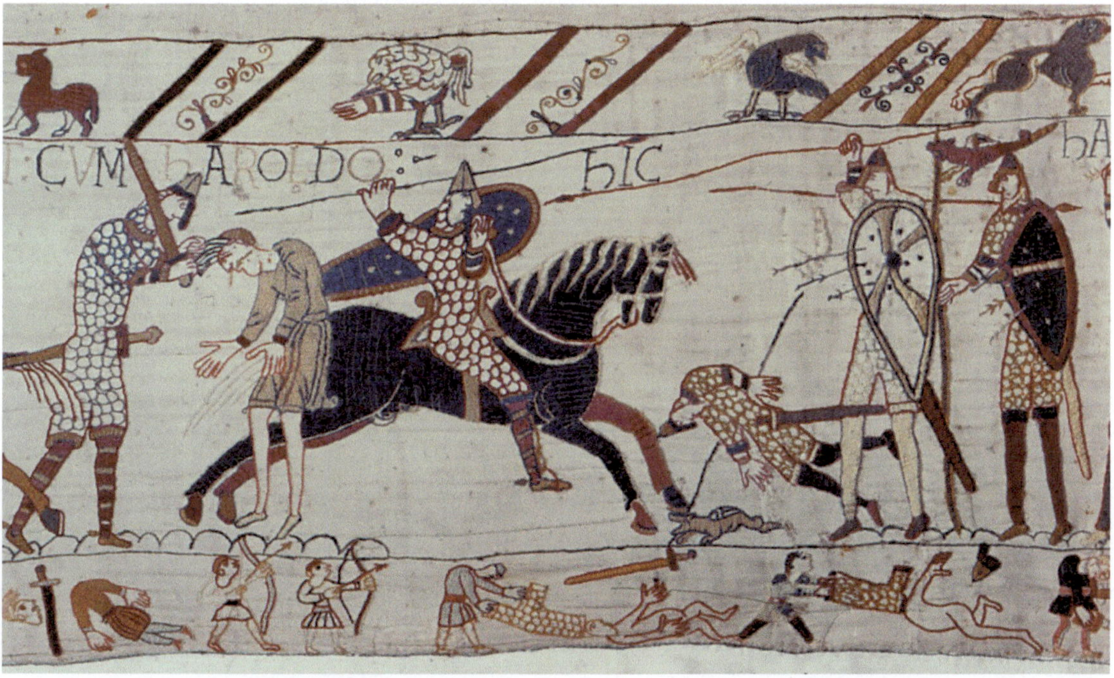

20 The turmoil of battle (Scene 56)

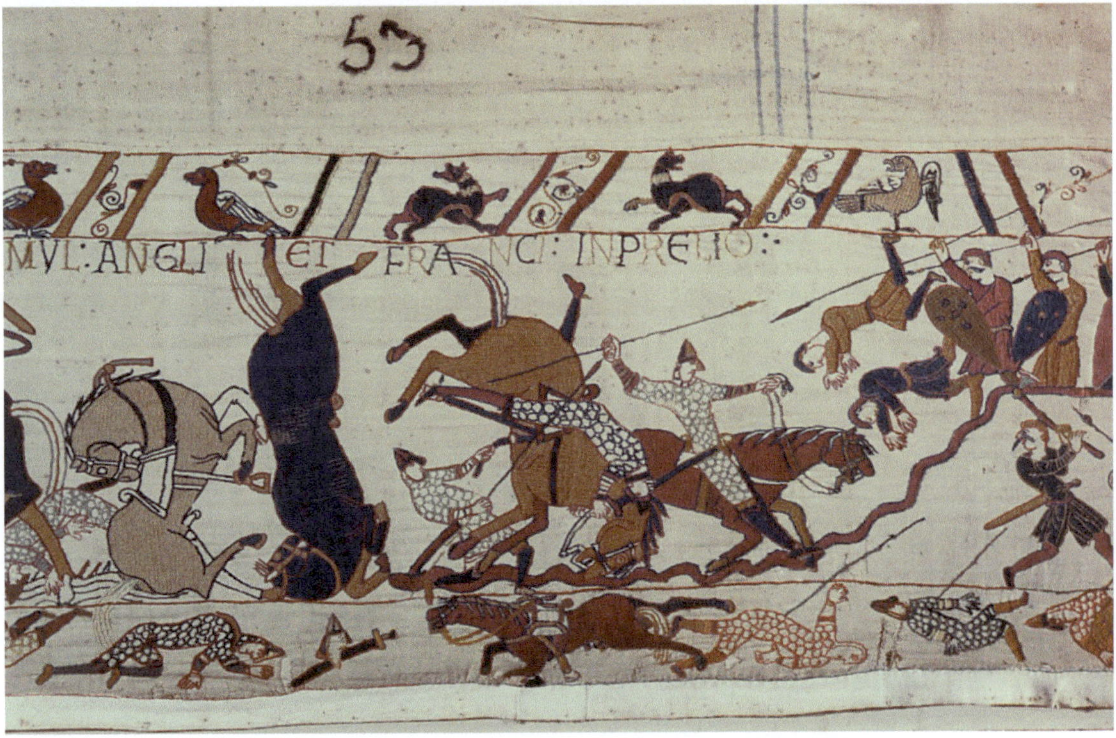

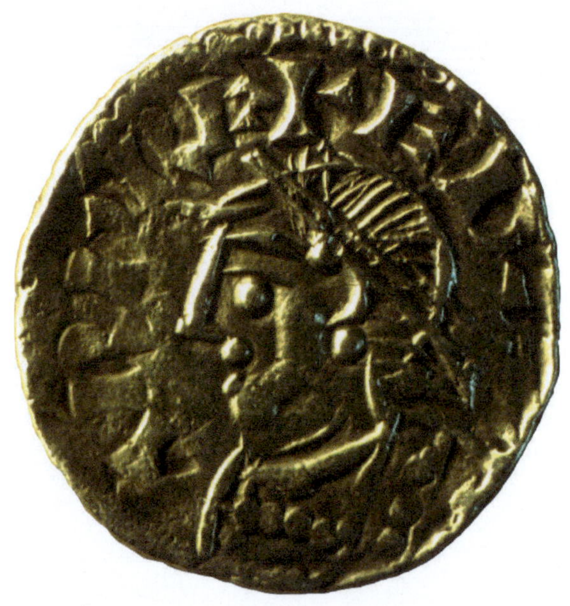

21 The turmoil of battle (Scene 53), showing the scene numbers on the backing cloth

22 Silver penny of King
Edward the Confessor.
*Courtesy of the Portable
Antiquities Scheme*

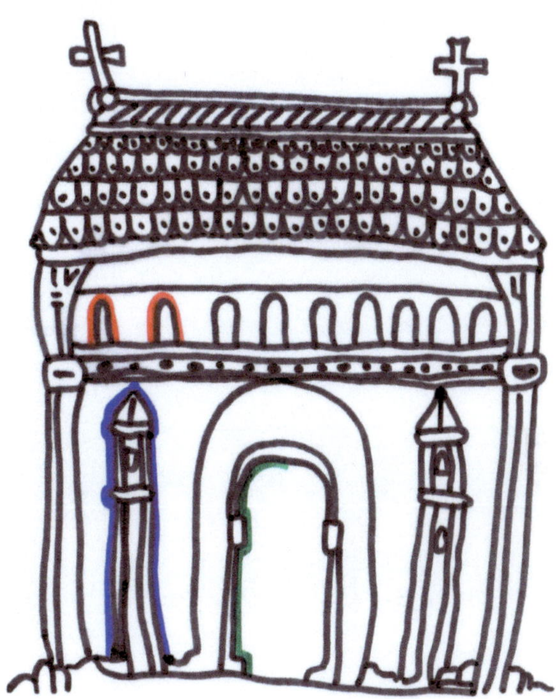

23 Bosham Church, as shown in
the Bayeux Tapestry

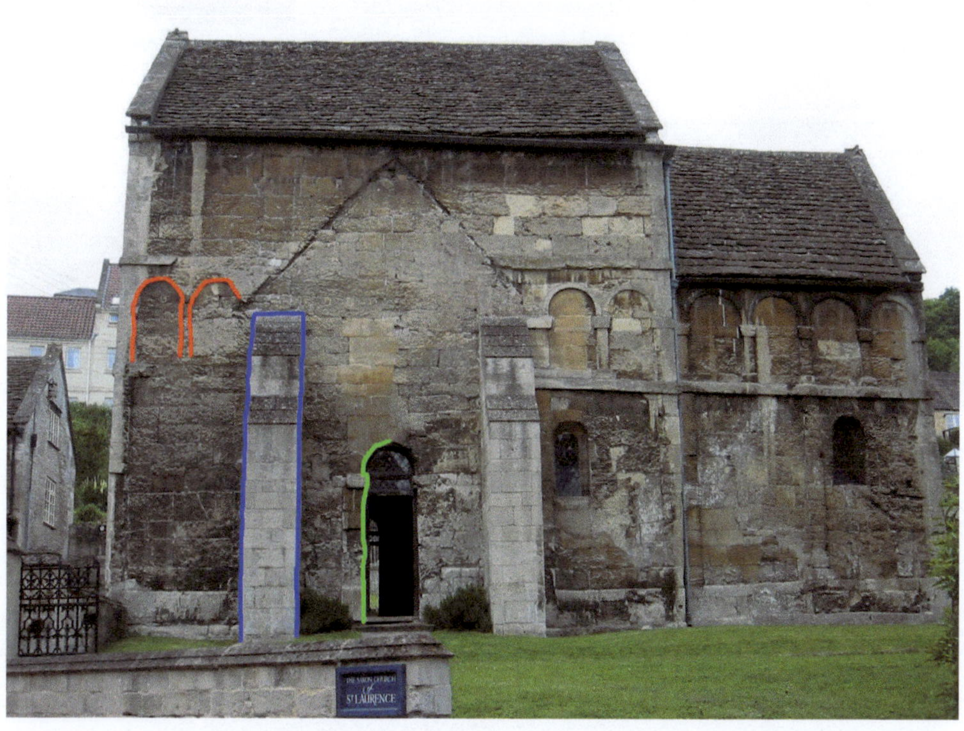

24 St Laurence's Church, Bradford-upon-Avon

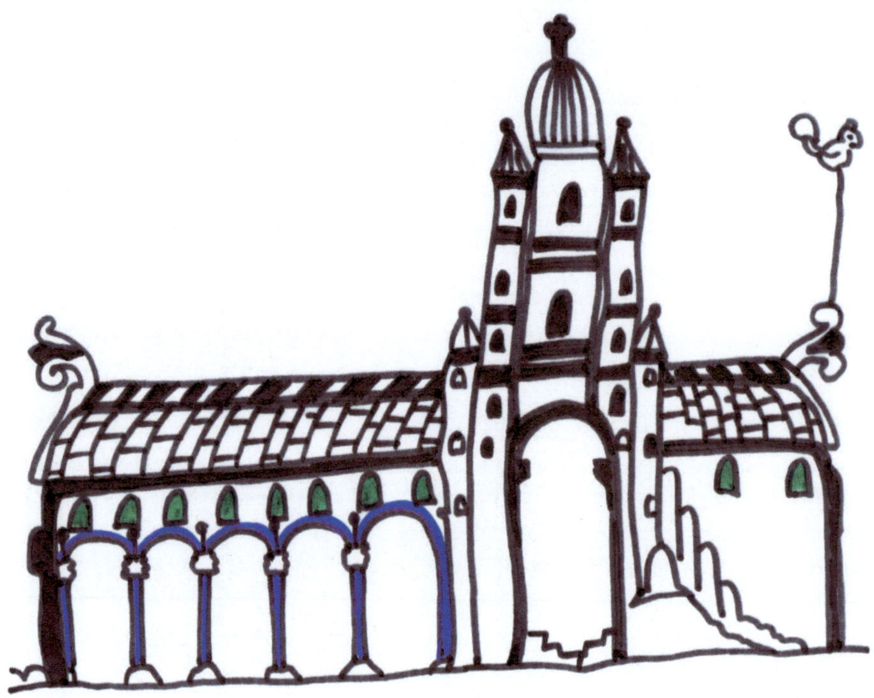

25 Westminster Abbey in the Bayeux Tapestry

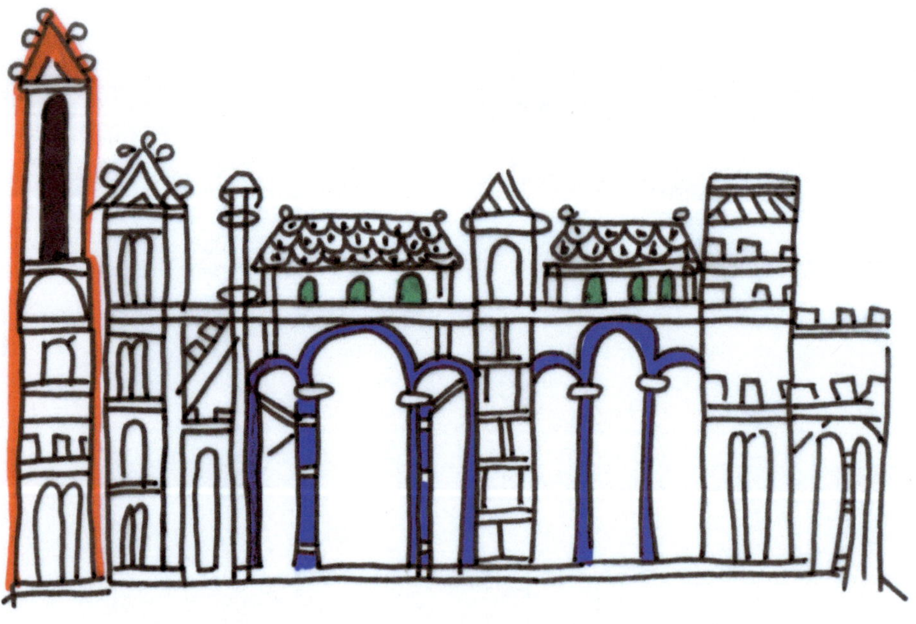

26 A building in British Library, Cotton Nero D.ii, which can be compared to *25* above

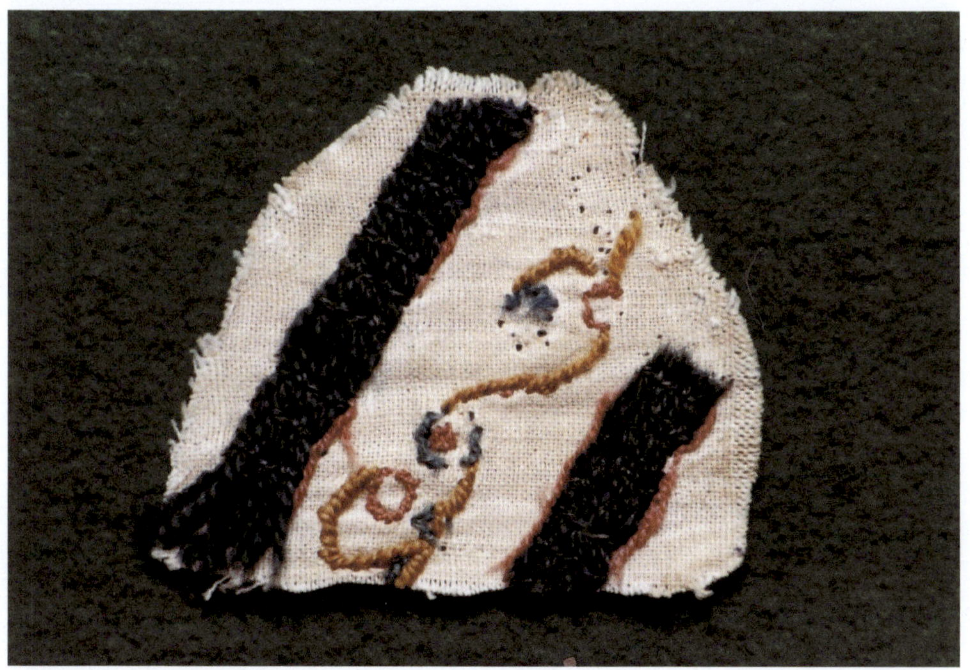

27 Fragment of the Bayeux Tapestry removed by Charles Stothard in about 1817. © *Bibliothèque municipale de Bayeux – Cliché Vincent Cazin*

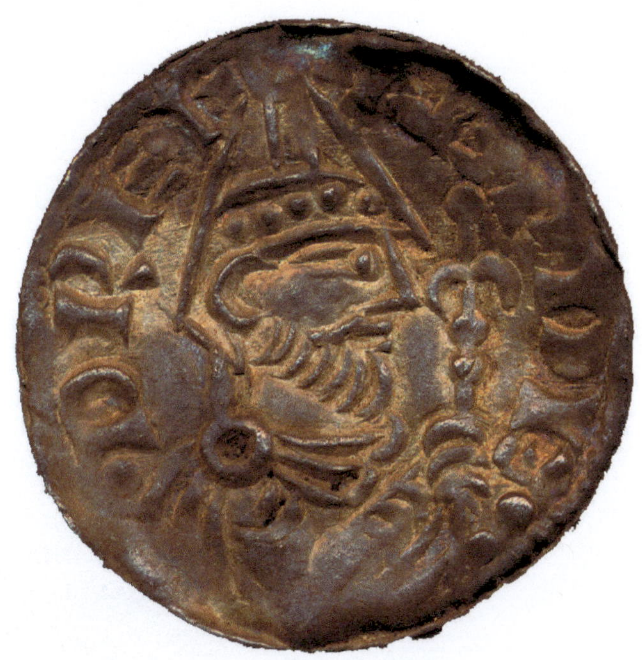

28 A conical helmet with nasal guard worn by Edward the Confessor on a silver penny of about 1053-6. © *Trustees of the British Museum, London*

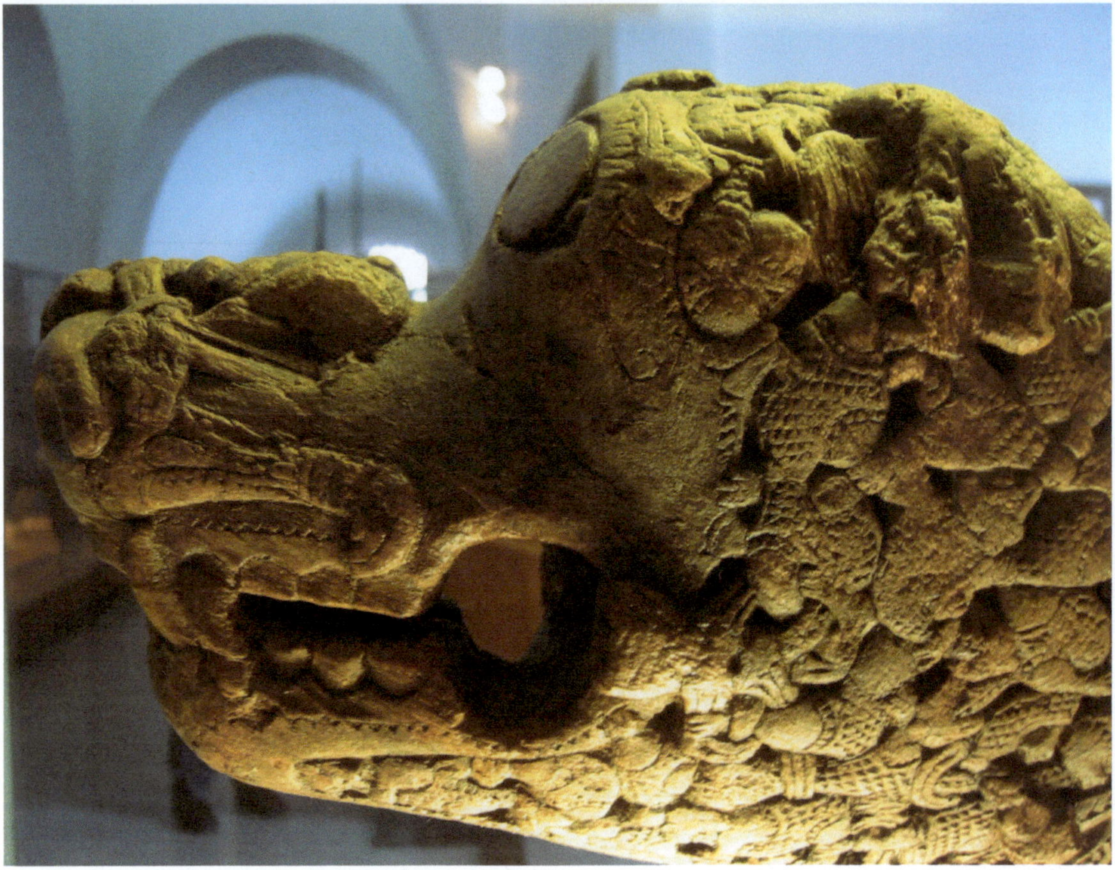

29 One of the zoomorphic carvings recovered from the Oseberg ship

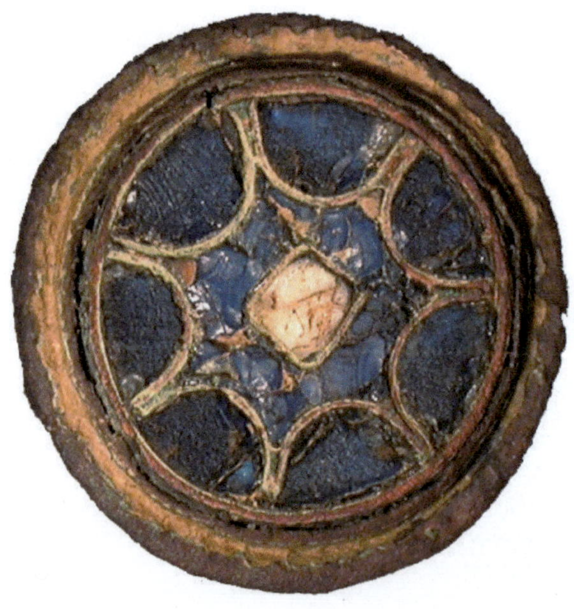

30 Late Anglo-Saxon disc brooche from Quidenham, Norfolk. *Courtesy of the Portable Antiquities Scheme*

Most tunics in the Tapestry have a rounded neckline, with slit front and v-shaped border. Alternatively, it might be that the contrasting colour might be due to one garment worn on top of another. This form rarely occurs in contemporary illuminations, where simple round or wavy necklines are most common. This said, there are striking parallels between the Tapestry depictions and the necklines of tunics in Cotton Tiberius B.v (folio 6v) (*38*) and the Tiberius Psalter (folios 9 & 11). Given that it is fairly unlikely that the designer referred to these illuminations and, moreover, that this feature is uncommon in art before the eleventh century, it seems reasonable to deduce that this motif reflected a contemporary form. This type of tunic neck form also seems to appear in Arundel 155 (folio 93) and Junius 11 (pages 53 & 59), but is shown with a more rounded v-shape.

In the Tapestry, and some contemporary illuminations, sleeves are typically long, reaching to the wrist; often these are shown with plain-banded cuffs and/ or hems. Whereas in many late Anglo-Saxon and Romanesque manuscripts, sleeves may be closely gathered on the forearm, as in the New Minster Charter (folio 2v), this feature is uncommon in the Tapestry, however embroidery work probably did not lend itself to the rendition of such detail.

Evidence that one aspect, at least, of the Tapestry's tunics was borrowed from art seems to be provided by the

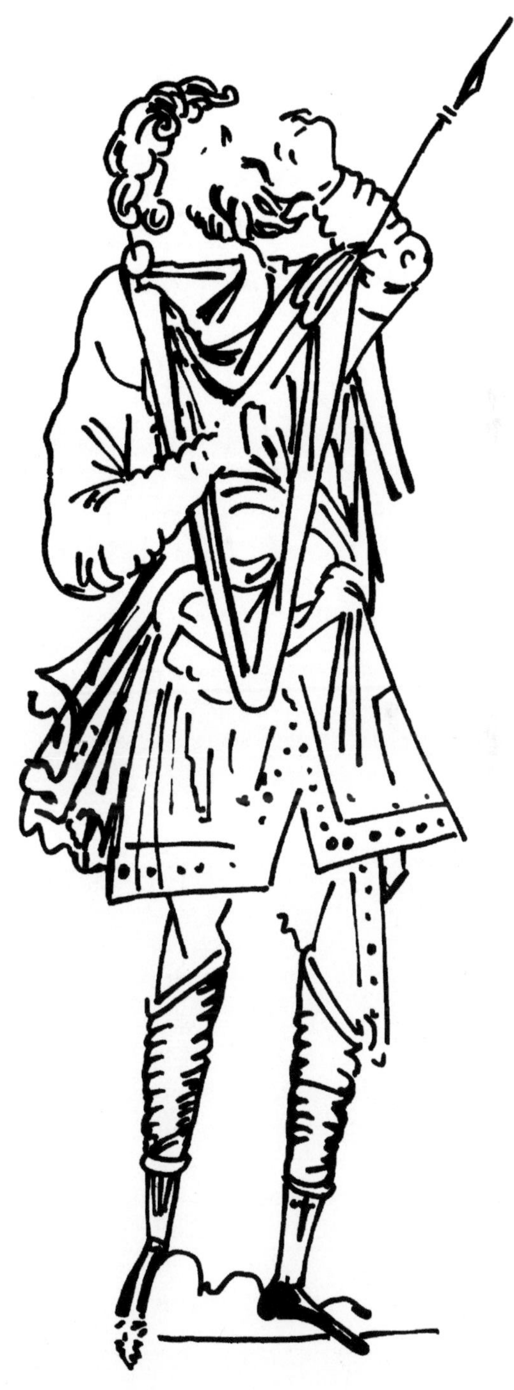

37 Culottes with banding on the inside leg in the Tiberius Psalter (folio 13)

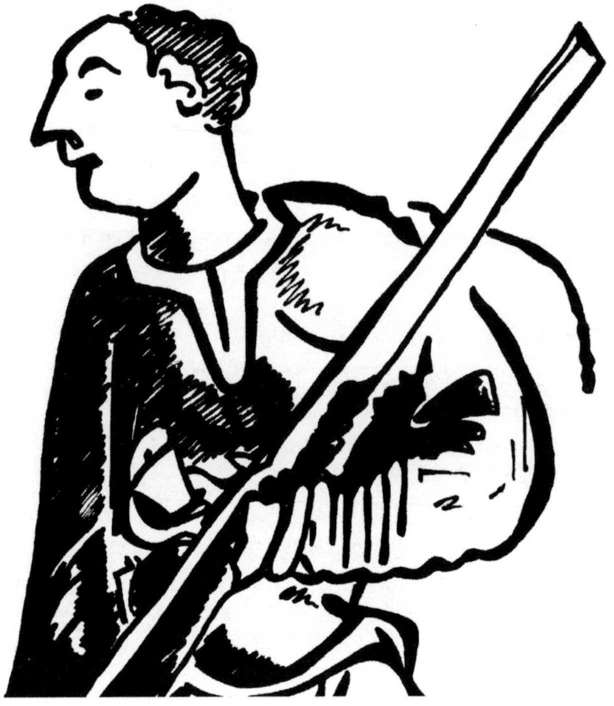

38 Necklines of tunics in British Library, Cotton Tiberius B.v (folio 6v)

occasional suggestion of a frill at the side of the knee, as in the tunics worn by Figures 266-7 and 269. However it seems unlikely that this was an actual feature of contemporary garments; it is more probably an artistic convention to indicate movement.

Cloaks and brooches

Several men in the Tapestry wear cloaks, which John Nevinson (1957) and others thought was indicative of rank. Cloaks worn by horsemen are quite short, hanging not much further than the waist, whilst those worn by other figures are significantly longer, often falling below the knees, sometimes almost to the ankles. This contrasts with cloaks shown in late Anglo-Saxon illuminations, including Cotton Julius A.vi (folio 4v) and the Tiberius Psalter (folio 13), which tend to be a little shorter. The notable exception is Cnut's cloak in the New Minster Liber Vitae (folio 6), which hangs well below the knees. Generally speaking, cloaks in Romanesque illuminations are approximately the same length as those in the Tapestry, and may reflect the post-Conquest fashion.

The cloaks in the Tapestry are mostly plain. The exception is one worn by William (Figure 118), which has ribbons towards the back of the neck and a decorated band at the hem. It is rare to find such ribbons associated with non-religious clothing in Anglo-Saxon drawings, though this is a prominent feature of Carolingian, Ottonian and Romanesque illumination. However, Cnut in the New Minster Liber Vitae (folio 6) is shown with a ribbon from his cloak. It is of course possible that William's cloak did actually have such ribbons, but given this is an established artistic convention, the designer may have instead coined this motif to denote William's status.

Both in the Tapestry and in illuminations, cloaks are frequently clipped with a simple brooch. Normally, brooches are worn on the right shoulder, leaving the sword arm free, though occasionally they are worn at the throat. Such brooches are generally circular, sometimes shown with a closed circle as a central motif, and similar examples can be found in contemporary art. It can safely be assumed that these are representations of disc brooches, a type typical of the late Anglo-Saxon period (*39 & colour plate 30*). On one occasion, the Tapestry illustrates a disc brooch (worn by Figure 56) with four (or five) inner segments, which may suggest decoration or its settings. Given that such detailed treatment is rare in art, Gale Owen-Crocker (1986) has suggested that this might reflect a brooch that had been admired first-hand.

Much less common are square or rectangular brooches. When they occur in manuscript art they are normally plain; examples can be found in the Boulogne Gospels (folio 11) and Cotton Tiberius A.iii (folio 117v). However, in the Tapestry they tend to have a central circle, dot (see Figures 117 & 136), or (sometimes off-centre) square (see Figures 85, 106 & 256). These types contrast with the ornate, rectangular brooch worn by Edward (Figure 207) in the Tapestry, which comprises a cruciform motif with central circle. An example with similar elements, though stylistically different, is worn by St Benedict in Arundel 155 (folio 133) (*40*).

Significantly, early English rectangular brooches are extremely rare archaeological discoveries (examples recorded by the Portable Antiquities Scheme include NLM194, SF178 and SF-D9EEA2), and continental examples are infrequently found in England. A possible explanation is that square brooches, being the prerogative of the richest and normally of gold or silver, are unlikely chance or archaeological finds. Even so, their rare survival suggests that few Anglo-Saxon artists would have observed such objects first-hand.

Alternatively, it is possible that the motifs in question are stylised representations of the square patches adorning ecclesiastical vestments, occasionally recreated in art, such as on the late eleventh-century Flemish gilt cover of Pierpont Morgan Library M.709. In this respect, it is therefore surely no coincidence that all the rectangular brooches represented in the Bayeux Tapestry (bar that on Figure 117) are shown joining a cloak either at the neck or at chest height, mimicking their position on ecclesiastical gowns. However, it seems likely that the Tapestry designer (and/or the embroiderers) turned these patches into brooches, as they are worn by high status secular figures, and one is worn on the shoulder.

Other small-scale dress fittings, such as strap-ends, pins, hook-tags and fasteners, which are well known from the archaeological record are in the most part unsurprisingly omitted from the Tapestry, as they are from most contemporary illustrations. Whilst the absence of these items does not impugn the accuracy of the Tapestry, it does provide further evidence that some elements of its illustrations were simplified.

Ecclesiastical dress

Three churchmen in the Tapestry (Figures 230, 234 & 243) wear formal religious dress, which consists of a narrow straight alb with long sleeves and a wide-fronted chasuble that

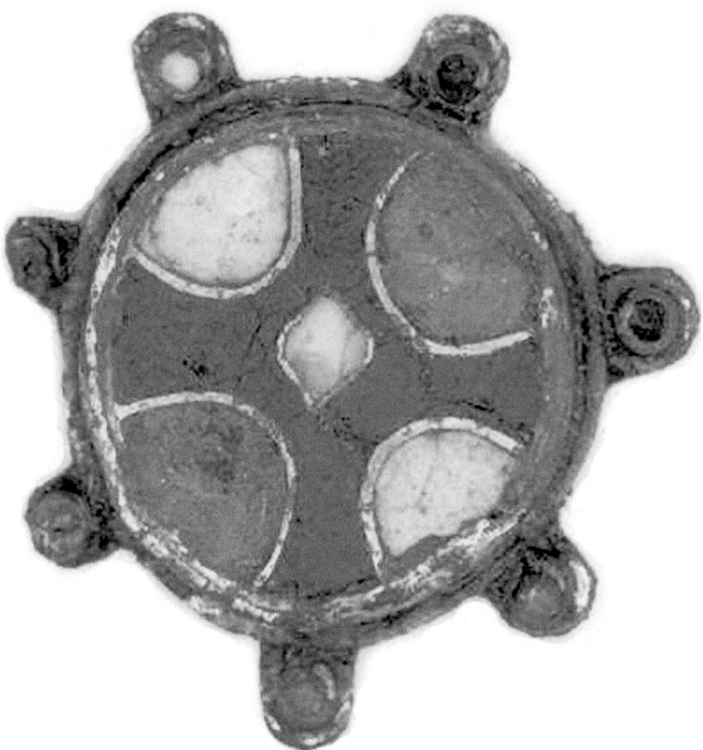

39 Late
Anglo-Saxon
disc brooch from
Quidenham,
Norfolk. *Courtesy
of the Portable
Antiquities Scheme*

falls in a v-shape covering much of the shoulders. The churchmen at Edward's deathbed (Figure 230 & 234, both probably Archbishop Stigand) wear chasubles with embroidered necklines and long palluims, whilst Stigand at Harold's coronation (Figure 243) is shown wearing a chasuble with plain banding, a plain stole, and a long palluim decorated with a dot and cruciform motif.

In some illuminations, the v-shape form of the chasuble is less pronounced, but those worn by Saint Dunstan in Cotton Tiberius A.iii (folio 2v) and by an anonymous ecclesiastic in the closely related image in Durham, Cathedral Library B.III.32 (folio 56v) are very similar to those in the Tapestry (*41*).

The survival rate of Anglo-Saxon and even Anglo-Norman ecclesiastical vestments is poor, and there is not really adequate material to compare with the depictions in the Tapestry. However, there is a marked increase in examples from about 1200, and these later vestments, such as the chasuble ascribed to St Thomas of Canterbury of the second half of the twelfth century, are broadly similar to the corresponding religious garments in the Tapestry, and also to those shown in late Anglo-Saxon illuminations, including Bodleian Library, Tanner 3 (folio 1v), the Tiberius Psalter (folio 18v) and Cotton Tiberius A.iii (folio 2v). Since ecclesiastical dress was fairly conservative, such comparisons prove useful.

At Edward's funeral (Scene 26), monks are shown wearing civilian clothing. This is not found in contemporary illuminations, where clerics will often be shown wearing

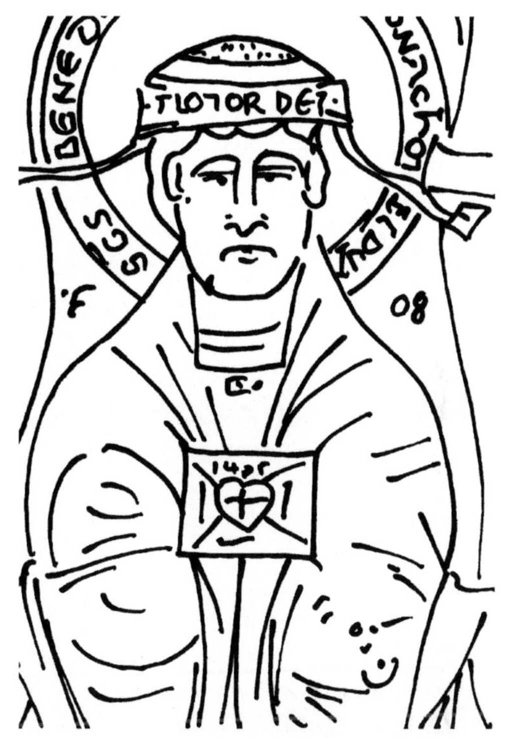

40 Rectangular brooch worn by St Benedict
in the Arundel 155 Psalter
(folio 133)

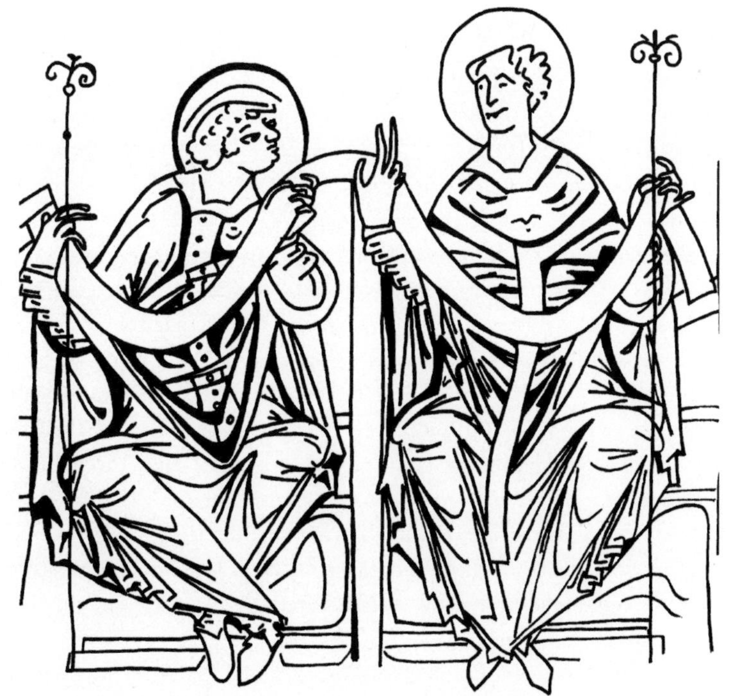

41 Ecclesiastical
vestments worn
by ecclesiastics in
Durham Cathedral
Library, B.III.32
(folio 56v)

ecclesiastical dress. It is perhaps significant that clergy in the Tapestry are always shown in lay dress, except where they appear in formal sacramental contexts, and are therefore vested.

Trousers

Most characters in the Bayeux Tapestry wear tight-fitting trousers (that might also be interpreted as stockings), which are also widespread in contemporary illustrations; only Turold (Figure 95) wears trousers with a loose cut.

Trousers in both the Tapestry and contemporary illuminations are often shown with horizontal banding (garters), normally only from the knee down; examples include British Library, Add. 24199 (folio 17), Junius 11 (page 74) and the Tiberius Psalter (folio 8v). Gale Owen-Crocker (1986) also noted close parallels between the garters worn by William (Figure 186) in the Tapestry and those worn by King Edgar in Cotton Tiberius A.iii (folio 2v).

At times, a diagonal band is shown just below the knees and this might be intended to represent leather strapping. This is clearly visible in both the Tapestry and the frontispiece to the New Minster Charter (folio 2v). Likewise, in Junius 11 (page 58) Malaleel's garters seem to unfurl, revealing the pattern of the banding. Gale Owen-Crocker (1986) noted that Normans in the Tapestry wear a wider selection of leg bands than Anglo-Saxons, and that at times this may have been used to distinguish between them. Such differences might also be coincidental. Gale Owen-Crocker (1994) also noted that cross-garters are prominent early in the second section of the Tapestry, but not thereafter. This may suggest that embroidering cross-garters took too long, or the embroiderer who favoured cross-garters only worked on a small section of the Tapestry.

Footwear

Footwear in the Tapestry is normally illustrated in profile, showing a narrow, often pointed, shoe with a rounded heel and toe; an exception is Edward's shoes (Figure 207), which are slippered, with an angular cut at the ankle. On a few occasions (see for example Figures 129, 136 & 187), the shoe upper is clearly depicted. In these instances the shoe widens gradually from the heel to a mid point then narrows sharply to a pointed toe. This contrasts with the majority of tenth- and eleventh-century shoes recovered in London. Frances Pritchard (1991) noted that in the tenth century most shoes had a rounded toe with the sides broadest across the tread tapering to a point (v-back) at the heel, whilst in the eleventh century the ankle boot becomes fashionable. By the end of the eleventh century the toe begins to increase in length. Although the Tapestry does seem to show a slight point to the toe, the ankle boot, typical of eleventh-century footwear, is clearly not depicted. These differences may suggest that the designer was recreating a form of shoes found in art, rather than those worn at the time.

Shoes are not particularly common in Anglo-Saxon illuminations; depending on the context, many characters are shown barefoot. Nonetheless, when they do appear, they generally compare better with those in the Tapestry than contemporary artefacts or shoes in Romanesque illuminations; Anglo-Saxon examples include Junius 11 (pages 57, 74, 84

& 87), Cotton Vitellius C. iii (folios 11v & 19) and the Old English Hexateuch (folios 15v, 32, 38 & 139v). Romanesque illuminations demonstrate a greater variety in form and style, with pronounced toes becoming a dominant feature. It is therefore interesting that the archaeological evidence shows a clear progression from blunt toes in the early tenth century to narrow pointed toes by the end of the eleventh. Around this time, excessively long, broad-based toes commonly appear, as do the first instep-waisted asymmetric soles, features highlighted by Francis Grew and Margrethe de Neergaard (1988) and Patricia Reid (2001), and these elements may be indicated in Romanesque drawings.

Shoes in the Tapestry are not shown stitched or laced, which is possibly due to their small scale and the limitations of embroidery. The only hint of embellishment is a red stripe that appears along the 'vamp' of one of Edward's shoes (Figure 3); Gale Owen-Crocker (1986) noted that vamp stripes depicted on shoes in manuscripts are very common, but normally white, Anglo-Saxon examples of which include Cotton Tiberius A.iii (folio 2v), the Tiberius Psalter (folio 9) and Cotton Caligula A.xv (folio 122v). Francis Grew and Margrethe de Neergaard (1988) highlighted the fact that vamp stripes are first recorded in (London) archaeological deposits of the late eleventh century, and barely outlived the twelfth. This detail therefore broadly reflects contemporary fashion. Decorated shoes occasionally appear in contemporary illuminations, such as the upper edge of King Cnut's shoes in the New Minster Liber Vitae (folio 6), which are decorated with bands of dots, and those of King David in the Winchcombe Psalter (folio 4v), which has fleurs-de-lys on the shoe uppers, while most are plain.

In the Tapestry, spurs are a distinguishing feature of footgear worn by horsemen. They are, however, uncommon in late Anglo-Saxon manuscripts, only being observed in the Hexateuch (folio 25v) and a few Romanesque drawings. It therefore seems reasonable to suggest that the designer had the Hexateuch, or a manuscript like it, as his exemplar. However, the form of the Tapestry's spurs better parallel the actual artefact than those in this manuscript, so it seems eminently possible that the designer drew upon first-hand knowledge of contemporary horse furniture.

Headgear

Only a few of the characters in the Bayeux Tapestry wear hats, and the same is true of those in contemporary illumination; Gale Owen-Crocker (1986) noted that men mostly appear bare-headed in art, even in winter! In the Tapestry, Conan (Figure 159) wears a pointed hat with large brow band, which is almost certainly a poor rendition of a non-segmented helm. Similar hats are worn by two archers (Figures 442-3), but are shown with a slight curve to the point. Though a little crudely rendered, these may be Phrygian caps, which are commonly found in contemporary manuscripts, such as the Sacramentary of Robert of Jumièges (folio 36v); other Anglo-Saxon examples include Bodleian Library, Douce 296 (folio 40v) and Cotton Tiberius B.v (folio 85v). The eastern origins of this type of hat are not disputed, hence if these are indeed Phygrian caps it seems likely that the designer borrowed this motif from art.

Women's dress

Women appear less commonly than men in manuscript illuminations and they are extremely rare in the Bayeux Tapestry; only three in the Tapestry (Figures 135, 228 & 402) are clothed. All the Tapestry's women seem to wear long ankle-length gowns, which sometimes trail on the ground. This is broadly typical of the form of dress found in contemporary art, where the subjects in question are generally biblical or saintly women; examples include Cambridge, Trinity College, O.3.7 (folio 1), the Old English Hexateuch (folio 15v) and Pierpont Morgan Library M.709 (folio 1v). The main difference between the women's clothes shown in the Tapestry and those in many illuminations is that the Tapestry's garments are long-sleeved and appear to flare at the cuffs (they do so particularly prominently on the gown of Figure 402), whereas most women in late Anglo-Saxon manuscripts wear loose-fitting overgarments or gowns with either straight sleeves or sleeves with a slight flare at the cuff. During the Romanesque period, sleeves protruded even further at the cuff (42), so it seems likely that the Tapestry designer, like contemporary illuminators, responded to this change in fashion, however Gale Owen-Crocker (personal correspondence, 1997) has identified such garments in the Harley 603 Psalter. Twice in the Tapestry, the form of such gowns is ambiguous; the sleeves trail by the sides of the robe, suggesting the robe is a sleeveless over-garment, rather similar to a pallium-like cloak, a feature also found in the Hexateuch (folio 76), but it is questionable whether this was intentional.

Women in both the Bayeux Tapestry and contemporary manuscripts wear a scarf

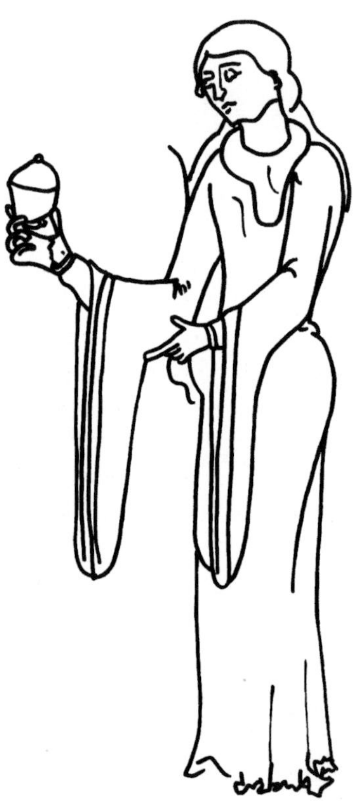

covering the head, neck and shoulders so that no hair is showing. In the Tapestry, such garments are rounded about the head, whereas some in Anglo-Saxon illuminations have angular hoods; rounded scarves are also found in Anglo-Saxon illuminations such as the Benedictional of Archbishop Robert (folios 21v & 54v), the Old English Hexateuch (folios 15v, 32, & 36) and Pierpont Morgan Library M.709 (folio 1v). Gale Owen-Crocker (personal correspondence, 2007) has suggested the head-dresses worn by women in the Tapestry are 'close fitting tie-on caps', which might have been worn under a wimple or scarf.

In the Tapestry, women's clothing is never decorated; the only embellishment of any sort is the plain-banded hem of Ælfgyva's dress (Figure

42 A woman in the Winchester Bible (folio 331v) wearing long-sleeved over-garments with flared cuffs

135). Much the same is true of female attire in contemporary illuminations; few clothes are decorated and such embellishments as appear are generally restricted to a plain hemline band. Interestingly, women in the Tapestry are never shown wearing jewellery, and the same is generally true of most contemporary art. This is in contrast to the archaeological evidence, which attests to fairly widespread use of jewellery. The reason simply seems to be that the small scale of such drawings calls for the simplification or omission of fine detail superfluous to the main design.

Summary

Contemporary costume is one area that any artist would surely know first-hand, hence one might expect to find some reflections of changing fashions in dress and clothing. This has particular relevance in the Bayeux Tapestry, given the number of people who may have been involved in its creation.

Ancient modes of dress, found in some contemporary art, are mostly omitted from the Tapestry, probably because the subject matter does not warrant it. Phrygian caps are the only (albeit ambiguous) remnant of classical attire. Nonetheless, in the Tapestry we still see a fusion of influences. On the one hand, there are elements of dress typical of late Anglo-Saxon art, such as ecclesiastical vestments, cloaks and shoes, which could either have been borrowed from art or observed first-hand. On the other, there are aspects of costume which apparently reflect up-to-date fashions, including tunics with a rounded neckline, slit front and v-shaped braided border, culottes and some elements typical of the post-Conquest period, such as women's long-sleeved dresses, with long cuffs. Also, there are some aspects of the Tapestry's dress and clothing which are essentially new, unparalleled in either the archaeological evidence or artistic tradition and are therefore difficult to understand; these include square brooches and trousered tunics.

It is apparent that the Tapestry designer was not concerned with certain smaller details, particularly in the case of dress accessories; such decorative embellishment as appears would seem to derive from artistic/visual tradition. Conversely, some details superficial to the narrative have been included, which might indicate the designer's knowledge of certain types of artefacts or activities; for example, spurs, which do not appear in much late Anglo-Saxon art, are shown in the Tapestry, and might suggest that the designer or patron had some equestrian knowledge. Furthermore, some elements of the Tapestry's dress and clothing also have an iconographic significance, indicating status or national affiliation, as in the case of gowns, cloaks and ribbons.

In general, therefore, the Tapestry seems to reflect accurately the dress and clothing worn by people in the late eleventh century, and, provided the evidence is interpreted with due care, can offer useful material for archaeologists and historians.

ANIMALS, BIRDS AND BEASTS

Consisting of 738 animals, zoomorphic images are the most prevalent type of motif in the Bayeux Tapestry. Although some creatures appear in the main panel, most are found in the borders; it is an issue of debate whether the latter are purely decorative, or symbolic and meaningful. The distinction between the role of creatures in the main frieze and that of those in the borders may also be relevant to the accuracy with which they are depicted; if animals are superfluous to the narrative then surely the artist has licence to draw from imagination, but in contrast it might be expected that animals are more realistically portrayed if their purpose were to add a naturalistic dimension to the design.

It is important to bear in mind that the medieval artist had a different understanding of what comprised a realistic portrayal of an animal than is the case today. A good example is the lion illustrated by Villard de Honnecourt in the Bibliothèque nationale de France, MS fr. 19093 (folio 48); the artist's inscription tells us it was supposedly drawn from 'real life', but, given the strong elements of stylisation and decoration, other factors than what he saw clearly came into play. Once again, therefore, it is necessary to assess each of the Tapestry's creatures on their own merits, examine how they compare with similar animals in art, and decide whether or not they seem to be a reasonable rendition of a creature we know today or one that existed in the eleventh century.

Main frieze

Horses

Of the 184 horses depicted in the Tapestry, all but seven are shown in the main frieze. They are clearly stylised, with their movements exaggerated, a point highlighted by Sarah Larratt Keefer (2005). Therefore, in Scene 54, Odo's horse (A714) runs with limbs outstretched far beyond the physical capability of such an animal. Likewise, their colouring is often imaginative and many carry anthropomorphic expressions. This said, the designer has taken time to illustrate the physique of horses, their manner, furniture and fittings, and has chosen to differentiate between mares, stallions and geldings.

Horses appear in various late Anglo-Saxon manuscripts, including some that were produced at Canterbury. Those in Cambridge, Corpus Christi College 23 (folio 2) are broadly similar in form and also have a comparable arrangement of harness fittings (43). Likewise, the form of one of William's horses in the Tapestry (A664) mimics a beast in the Old English Hexateuch (folio 69r). Of course, it is not certain whether the designer took these drawings as his model, copied from another, now lost, exemplar, or even sketched from the 'real world' around him. However, such motifs would have been accessible to a designer working from Canterbury illuminations.

Dogs

Dogs, of which there are 24 in the Tapestry, are characterised by a narrow body and long, thin tail; all wear collars. It is perhaps significant that all but one (A440) appear in Sections 1 and 2. Although clearly canine, because of their features, W. Brunsdon Yapp (1987) rightly suggested that the Tapestry designer did not attempt to differentiate between the types of hunting dogs used in the medieval period. This might indicate that the designer satisfied the scope of the commission with one generic type of dog, rather than any specific breed.

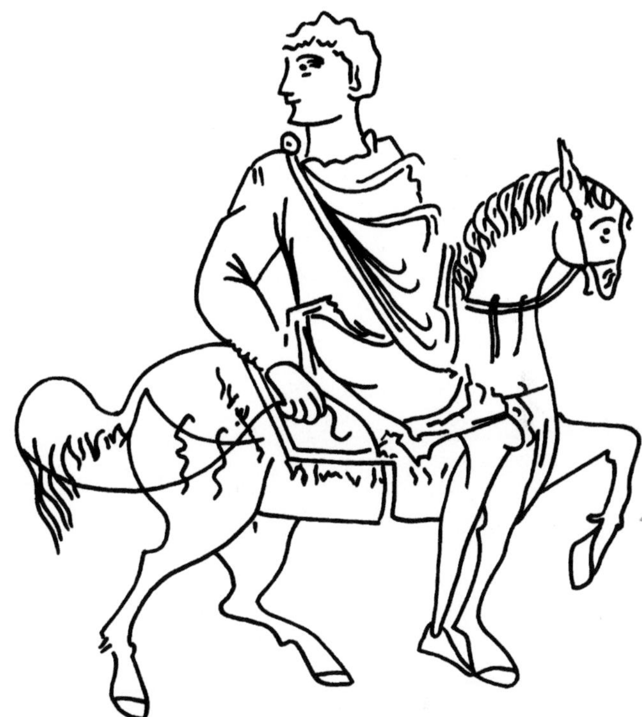

43 Horse and horse furniture depicted in Cambridge, Corpus Christi College 23 (folio 2a)

Dogs are not common in contemporary art, but when shown are often characterised by their thin athletic body and collar, as they are in the Tapestry. Good parallels include the dogs in Cotton Tiberius B.v (folio 42r), and others highlighted by Cyril Hart (2000 & 2005). On this basis it seems probable that the designer based his dogs on art rather than life.

Hawks

Of the ornithological varieties depicted in the Tapestry, birds of prey, presumably hunting hawks, are most recognisable, and are characterised by their large eyes and rounded beak. These appear from Scenes 2 to 14 and are shown on the wrist of Guy (A559 & A573), Harold (A539, A547, A561 & A571) and William (A581).

Although these hawks might reflect the form of real life creatures, their colours, like so much in the Tapestry, are clearly imaginative, and it might be useful to look for comparisons in art. However, hawks are uncommon in art, not least because of the dearth of early medieval hunting and other secular books; later examples include the mid thirteenth-century falcon book of the Holy Roman Emperor Frederick II (r.1212-1250) and the early fifteenth-century hunting book of Gaston Phebus. Nonetheless, a good parallel for the Tapestry's hawks, one of which is even handled by a mounted huntsman, appears in Cotton Julius A.vi (folio 7v) (*44*). Given that this illumination was possibly produced in Canterbury, it may well have been available to the designer. However, it is just as likely that the Tapestry designer took the basic characteristics of a bird of

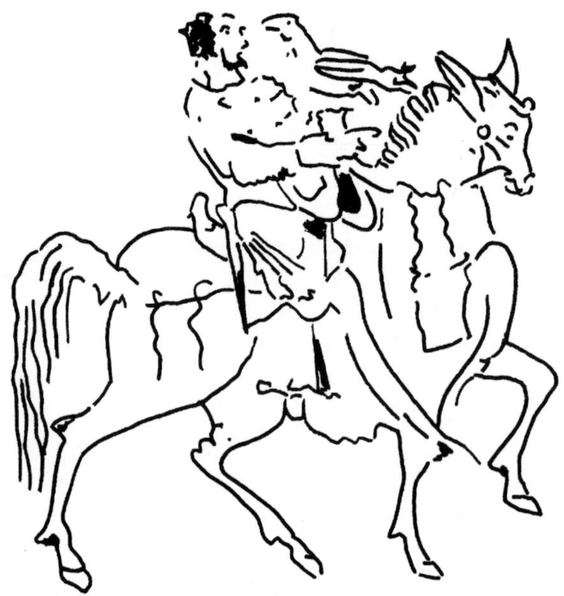

44 A mounted huntsman in British Library, Cotton Julius A.vi (folio 7v)

prey from knowledge of the Evangelist symbol for St John – an eagle, of which plentiful examples survive.

The Borders

The Fables
Many of the creatures illustrated in the Tapestry's borders are not species that appear in the main frieze. While a few are instantly recognisable, most are difficult to identify with certainty.

Some of these short stories seem to represent well-known fables, such as the raven and the fox, and the crane and the wolf. Therefore, it should be possible to tell which creatures the designer intended to recreate, and whether these are 'accurately' illustrated.

The fable of the raven and the fox is shown on three occasions (A102-3, A272-3 & A343-4), but there is little consistency in the manner in which either animal is depicted. On one occasion, the raven is shown, unrealistically, multi-coloured (A272), rather than black, on another its form is more like that of a blackbird (A344). Similarly, some foxes look little like the animal we know. One (A273) has an uncharacteristically long thin tail (which W. Brunsdon Yapp (1987) thought was more like that of a wolf), whereas another (A343) is shown with floppy ears. Indeed, the 'foxes' in the Tapestry are not greatly distinct from what we take to be a bear (A280) or wolf (A282) in other scenes. Here then, the accuracy of detail seems of little importance to the designer. Even so, the 'raven' is shown clearly as a bird, and hence the tale is identifiable. Likewise, in other fables, such as that of the crane and the wolf, only certain (often single) characteristics seem to be of any significance. For example, of two cranes depicted (A101 & A281), neither reflects accurately the form of the species. What actually seemed to matter to the designer is the essential feature of the bird's long neck, which was fundamental to the narrative and understanding of the tale.

Scenes of agriculture and everyday life

Agricultural scenes are found in the lower borders. Of particular interest is the donkey and horse shown pulling a plough and harrow (Fables 15 & 16). Although scholars, such as J. Clutton-Brock (1976) did not believe that horses were used for ploughing in the Anglo-Saxon period, as the horse collar does not seem to have been invented, it is plausible the creatures themselves could have be taken from 'real life', as both are broadly representative of the actual beasts. Francis Wormald (1957) paralleled these depictions of ploughing in the Tapestry with contemporary calendar illustrations representing occupations of the month, including Cotton Julius A.vi (folio 3) (45) and Cotton Tiberius B.v (folio 3). However, it is apparent these drawings were not the specific source of what is shown in the Tapestry, though this should not exclude the influence of art. Indeed, there are strong parallels between the Tapestry's depictions and Canterbury-produced illuminations, such as the Junius 11 manuscript (page 54) and the Harley 603 Psalter (folio 21r).

Similarly, Fable 17 shows a man (Figure 97) scaring birds (A317-8), which are multi-coloured and clearly schematic. Moreover, here (as seen earlier) the influence of art is clear; Francis Wormald (1957) noted that the Tapestry's depiction replicates a scene in the Old English Hexateuch (folio 26v). He observed that the basic form of the birds is similar and that the Tapestry designer even emphasised the outstretched claws of the original.

The Tapestry also depicts a scene of bear-baiting. Clearly stylised, this bear (A321) is by no means a convincing rendition. Again, art offers a close comparison in the form of a near-contemporary initial in Arundel 91 (folio 47b), a manuscript from Saint Augustine's Abbey, Canterbury.

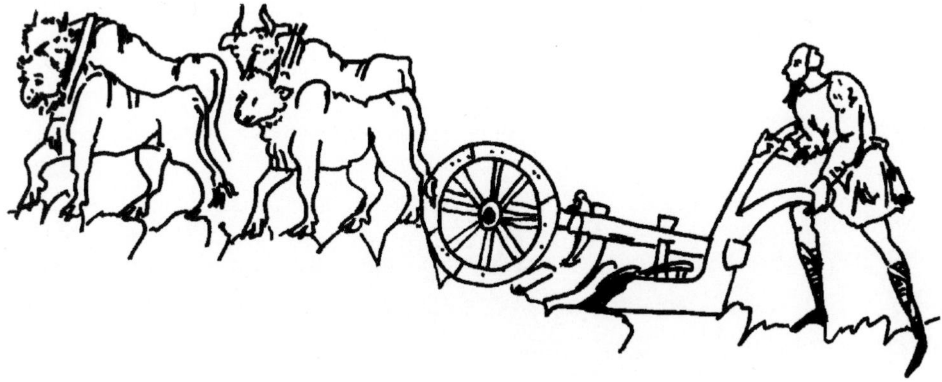

45 Oxen pulling a plough in British Library, Cotton Julius A.vi (folio 3)

Farm animals

Apart from Scene 40, farm animals are confined to the borders. Some are depicted in symmetrical pairings, whilst others are participants in the Tapestry's fables. The farm animals in the main frieze (A659-61) relate to those seized as provisions described in the inscription, providing a 'naturalistic' setting for the narrative.

The sheep in the Tapestry are shown with a solid body and have round horns and a stubby, slightly curved, tail. These characteristics can be likened to the actual creatures, but also compare well with those in contemporary illustrations, such as Cotton Julius A.vi (folio 5) (*46*) and the Hexateuch (folios 14r & 67v), which could well have been available to the designer.

A pair of hogs (A75-6) occurs in the Tapestry's upper border. They are shown with a sub-oval body, hairy crest along the back and curled tail. Again, these animals parallel the appearance of actual beasts, but also, in general terms, those in contemporary art. Examples include the illustration of the Miracle of the Gadarene Swine in Getty Museum 9 (leaf 1) and on a tympanum of the first quarter of the twelfth century from St Nicholas' Church, Ipswich. Either the real world or art could have provided the designer with a model.

The same is true of the goats, which are characterised by their pointed narrow horns and tufty beard; they are also often shown with rounded backs and small stubby tails. As with other farm animals in the Tapestry, they have characteristics of 'real-life' goats, and also compare well with depictions in contemporary illuminations, such as Cotton Vitellius C.iii (folio 19) and the Hexateuch (folio 15v, 26v, 48v, 49r & 84v).

Two bovines occur in the Tapestry: one (A304) is depicted in Fable 13, the other appears in the main frieze (A660). These creatures are characterised by their inward turning horns, sub-rectangular shaped body, bumpy back and long tail of two strands. Both animals adopt the same canter-style pose, with head shown in portrait; David Wilson (1985) likened them more to a drunken Evangelist symbol than a serious milk-producing creature. A similar example is found in the Trinity Gospels (folio 16r)

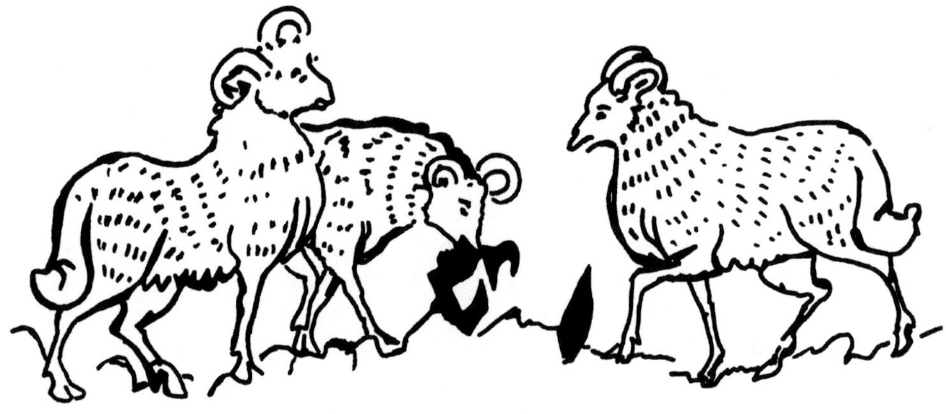

46 Sheep in British Library, Cotton Julius A.vi (folio 5)

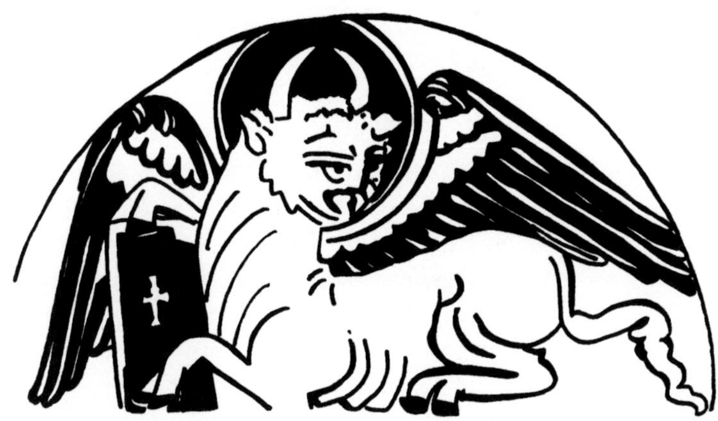

47 An Evangelist symbol for St Luke in the Trinity Gospels (folio 16r)

(*47*). Even when compared with illustrations of bovines in other manuscripts, such as the Old English Hexateuch (folios 66r, 67r & 67v), the Tapestry's animals are notably stylised.

Birds

There are 222 birds (including hawks) in the Tapestry, most of which are in the borders. The majority of these appear in symmetrical pairings, placed between beasts. At face value, their purpose seems purely decorative.

The birds in the Tapestry are clearly stylised, and therefore drawing parallels with real world ornithology is problematic. For example, most birds are shown with only two toes, surely a convention for front toes and back toe. Although the characteristics of some birds are accentuated, they do not seem to reflect a particular type. Their sizes vary, though the majority are quite large. Most are shown rounded, plump, and have long necks and small heads (such as A50). Others are thinner, with large wings, and a small neck (such as A73). This said, some are clearly poultry, shown with a crest and rounded tail feathers (such as A41-2). A pair of peacocks is also illustrated (A61-2), shown with distinctive crests and colourful tails.

Parallels for the Tapestry birds and their posture are found in art; Carola Hicks (1993) noted they are relatively common, especially in manuscript initials. For example, many different varieties of birds are shown in the Hexateuch (folios 3v, 4r, 6r, 14r, 15r, 15v & 115v), depicted in flight as well as walking. In some instances birds are even shown in symmetrical pairings, for example in the Kederminster Gospels (s.n.), as well as in sculpture and metalwork.

In manuscripts, this feature is common above arcades, and dates back to at least the ninth century – it is shown, for example, in the Ebbo Gospels (folios 10r-15v). As with the Tapestry's birds, they often bite their borders and gesticulate. Similarly, birds with a single raised wing are common in both the Tapestry and other art works, which W. Brunsdon Yapp (1987) paralleled with sculptures on the mid twelfth-century south doorway of Kilpeck Church, Herefordshire. Some birds in the Tapestry can be favourably compared with particular examples in art. For example, the birds beneath Dol (A598-9) can be paralleled with illustrations in Cotton Tiberius B.v (folio 82v), whilst the Tapestry's peacocks (A61-2) compare well with birds in the Trinity Gospels (folio 9v).

Rabbits

The Tapestry seems to illustrate rabbits (A441 & A493), which can be distinguished from hares by their relatively short ears, though some, such as Naomi Sykes (personal correspondence, 2005) believes it is actually hares that are shown in the Tapestry. This idea is strengthened by the view that rabbits were first introduced to England after the Norman Conquest, perhaps even as late as the late twelfth century. However, similar short-eared creatures also appear to be shown in the Old English Hexateuch (folio 4r) and Cotton Vitellius C.iii (folio 19), indicating the availability of visual models for the Tapestry's 'rabbits'. Indeed the Tapestry's rabbits compare particularly well with those in the Hexateuch, sharing their form of motion and extended hind feet, as well as the characteristic ears.

Lions

Among the identifiable land-based animals in the Tapestry, lions are particularly prevalent, being shown on at least 66 occasions. Lions occur only in the upper and lower borders and are more common at the beginning of the Tapestry. All but two (A305 & A308) are shown as symmetrical pairings.

The Tapestry's lions differ in details, but most are characterised by their wavy or ruffled manes; those of A258-9 appear striped. Most are shown in profile (only the heads of A97-8, A250-1 & A486-7 face forward), sometimes with mouths open and/or tongues hanging out; their rounded backs, slender waists and toned bodies are emphasised. These characteristics might be compared with those of living beasts, though it is highly improbable that the designer had ever seen a lion. Closer inspection reveals that the lions in the Tapestry are stylised and were probably borrowed from art; Carola Hicks (1993) noted that lions are a popular motif of the Canterbury school of illumination. Whilst most are shown with a widening tip at the tail, some (such as A21-22, A87-8, A154-5 , A190-1, A313-4 & A367-8) have a decorative trefoil ending. Similarly, their tails are normally shown between the legs and wrapped around the body; this has been termed by W. Brunsdon Yapp (1987) as the 'Bayeux tail', though it is found elsewhere in art. Some are even shown biting their own tails, and commonly a foreleg is raised. This form of lion rampant, with tail curling between its legs and around its body, is uncommon in Anglo-Saxon illumination, but is found in Junius 11 (page 11) (*48*) and contemporary metalwork, such as 'class 11a' stirrup-strap mounts. Further, the association of the lion with a winged beast (normally a dragon), prevalent in the Tapestry, is also common in Canterbury illuminations, such as the Arenberg Gospels (folio 13v).

Camels

Camels are only shown once in the Tapestry, as a symmetrical pairing (A51-2) in the upper border. Their presence is intriguing since it is improbable that the designer knew of such animals first-hand. Although David Wilson (1985) thought the Tapestry's camels

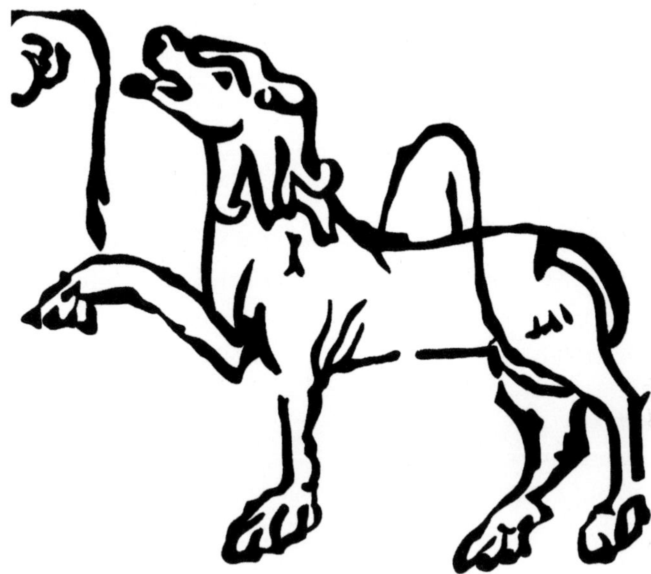

48 Lion in Junius 11 (page 11)

to be 'unconvincing' they do share attributes with actual beasts, and are characterised by their two humps, long, thin, crooked neck and small head with pointed ears. Good parallels for the Tapestry's camels do occur in contemporary manuscripts, notably the Hexateuch (folios 4r, 22v, 23r, 39r, 39v, 46r, 48r, 48v, 49r & 84v), where they are relatively common. As this work was probably executed in Canterbury, it is possible that the Tapestry designer actually knew these drawings, or their source, and may have used them in the work.

Mythical beasts

Some of the beasts depicted in the Tapestry are mythical, and clearly could never have been observed by the designer; the general view is that these would have been borrowed from art. Griffins, of which there are 41, are the most common. Dragons (nine), centaurs (five) and winged horses (two) are also illustrated. All are found in the Tapestry borders, most in symmetrical pairings. Such arrangements are also found in manuscript initials; the best examples appear in Romanesque drawings such as British Library, Royal 6 B.vi (folio 23) and Harley 624 (folio 93v).

Griffins are a cross between a beast and a bird. In the Tapestry, they are characterised by their large outstretched wings, and often have a rounded beak and talon-shaped forefeet. Hind legs normally end in paws, and may also have claws. All griffins are shown with tails, which often curl between the hind legs and around the body, as with the Tapestry's lions. Some of the griffins in the Tapestry are probably copies of winged lions representing the Evangelist St Mark, commonly found in art, a view supported by W. Brunsdon Yapp (1987). While griffins proper are rare in late Anglo-Saxon illuminations, examples can be found in Junius 11 (page 13) and the Trinity Gospels (folio 10v), both possibly produced in Canterbury.

Dragons (which also appear on some of the kite-shields in the Tapestry), like griffins, are shown winged, but are bipedal and have a long, thick tail. Their tails either arc over the back or trail behind; some are even shown knotted. Dragons are illustrated with a small head and pointed ears. Often they are shown with a forked tongue and may have fire protruding from their mouths. Dragons are an extremely common motif in late Anglo-Saxon art, and strong parallels can be drawn between the dragons in the Tapestry and, for instance, those in the contemporary Tiberius Psalter (folios 60 & 72) (*49*). These not only share the same basic form, but also have small wings and knotted tails. Other examples include British Library, Royal 5 F. iii (folio 2v), Cambridge, Corpus Christi College, 41 (page 246 & 410), and Bodleian Library, Douce 296 (folios 10 & 40v).

Summary

Although many of the animals depicted in the Bayeux Tapestry could have been drawn from real life, it seems more likely that most were borrowed from art. Animals in the main frieze appear to illustrate actual beasts, though the repertoire of types is relatively small, including just horses, dogs, hawks and a few farm animals. Although the designer is likely to have had first-hand experience of such animals, artistic models would have been conveniently available; the best evidence for their use is the Tapestry's stylised cow (A660), which must have been inspired by an Evangelist portrait.

In the cases of animals that are not represented in the main frieze, the degree of accuracy varies. The designer seems to exaggerate features of beasts that were useful to the narrative, at the expense of those that were not. This is particularly evident in the fable of the wolf and crane, where only the length of the bird's neck is fundamental, rather than an accurate portrayal of the actual beast.

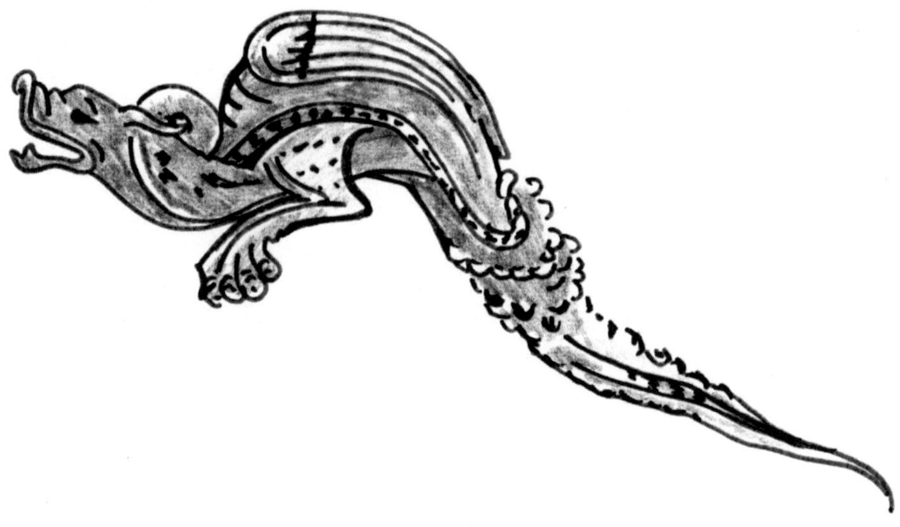

49 Dragon in the Tiberius Psalter (folio 72)

Elsewhere in the borders (outside narrative sequences) most creatures seem to be highly stylised, offering decorative embellishment only. Indeed, some of these, such as the mythical creatures, must have been taken from art, since they did not exist. It may be that animals such as horses, dogs and farm animals seem realistic just because they are expected to be accurate portrayals, whilst others, such as mythical creatures, do not, because they are known never to have existed. Certain other creatures have attributes that are recognisable today, such as the lion's mane and camel's humps, but it seems unlikely that the designer observed these first-hand. Further, there are many creatures in the Tapestry which cannot be identified with any degree of certainty, the forms of which would surely have perplexed even the eleventh-century viewer.

Considered together, the birds and beasts in the Bayeux Tapestry provide little clue to the designer's understanding of the world. Although many of the creatures could have been sketched from 'real life', most in all probability were borrowed from art. Nonetheless, there is a general distinction between the depiction of animals that had a narrative function, and those that did not. This is crucial for understanding the Tapestry's creatures.

VEGETATION

The vegetation depicted in the Bayeux Tapestry has attracted little scholarly comment. Drawing on a limited range of parallels, such discussions, including those of Francis Wormald (1957) and David Wilson (1985), tend to examine the vegetal ornament as further proof that the Tapestry was produced in England shortly after the Norman Conquest. However, in the present context, the vegetation should be considered with regard to the extent to which the designer drew from 'real life' or borrowed from contemporary art. Although no one has seriously suggested that the Tapestry's vegetation is a product of first-hand observation (even the 'naturalistic' English herbals of the eleventh century, of which three surviving examples are illustrated, are copies of ancient models) it is essential to evaluate its nature and status in some detail as another very prominent indication of the designer's visual language and attitudes to representing the real world.

Vegetation in the Bayeux Tapestry

The vegetal ornament in the Bayeux Tapestry can be divided into two main types: first, trees, which are common in the main frieze; second, 'cruciform' and 'scrolled' leaf-work, which are typical of the borders. Relatively few trees occur in the borders and leaf-work is only seldom found in the main frieze.

Trees

Trees in the Tapestry (of which there are 24 in the main frieze) normally comprise a single trunk and a number of branches. Often, branches will entwine with one another, in many instances forming a hatched effect or simple interlace pattern. In other instances, branches fan outwards, or lean to one side, as if they were blowing in the wind. Some branches,

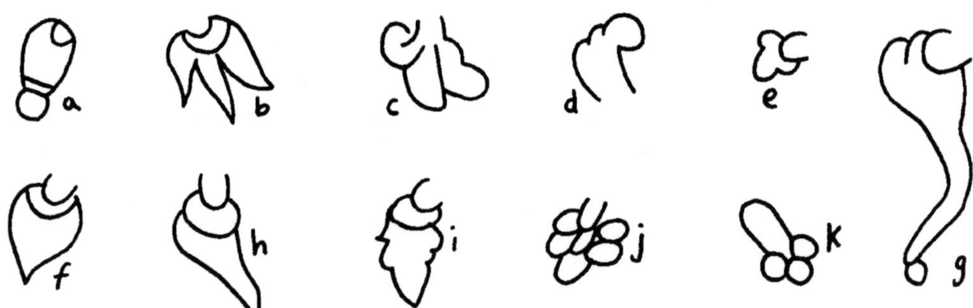

50 Decorative leaves or fruit on trees in the Bayeux Tapestry: (a) oval leaf with lobed terminal, (b) trifoliate pointed leaf, (c) trifoliate acanthus leaf, (d) single-sided acanthus leaf, (e) trifoliate rounded leaf, (f) heart-shaped leaf, (g) aroid leaf with lobed terminal, (h) chilli-shaped leaf, (i) serrated leaf, (j) multi-lobed leaf, and (k) oval-lobed leaf

often the lower ones, are short and stubby. In one instance (Tree 13) all the branches are cut. Most trees have decorative leaf or fruit terminals, of which 11 distinct types can be identified: (a) oval leaf with lobed terminal, (b) trifoliate pointed leaf, (c) trifoliate acanthus leaf, (d) single-sided acanthus leaf, (e) trifoliate rounded leaf, (f) heart-shaped leaf, (g) aroid leaf with lobed terminal, (h) chilli-shaped leaf, (i) serrated leaf, (j) multi-lobed leaf, and (k) oval-lobed leaf (*50*).

Trunks usually consist of vertical multi-coloured stripes, each leading to different coloured branches. When added to the hatched or interlaced branches, the effect, which Francis Wormald (1957) considered to be a 'characteristic' of the Tapestry's trees, is strikingly decorative. In some instances, trunks have trapezoid horizontal bands (here termed 'stumps'), which often appear staggered. Sometimes these also appear at the top of tree trunks (termed 'trapezoid nodes'). In three instances (Trees 16, 21 & 23) these nodes are rounded, but one (Tree 19) appears as a wavy band.

Trees in the borders, of which there are at least 20, have the same basic characteristics of those in the main frieze. However, since they are smaller they are also greatly simplified with fewer branches, leaves or fruit.

Vegetal border ornament

There are broadly two groups of vegetal leaf-work found in the Tapestry's borders: first (type 1), 'cruciform' or 'quasi-cruciform'; second (type 2), 'scroll' form. The former is mostly rigid and upright, whereas the latter is suspended and normally curls in sporadic spirals. Occasionally these types merge into a cruciform variant with scrolled protrusions (type 3) (*51*).

Cruciform vegetal ornament is predominately found in the earlier part of the Tapestry (until about Scene 35), are which scrolled ornament is common. This division is interesting since it may reflect a change in procedure, or workshop, which will be examined further in Chapter 6.

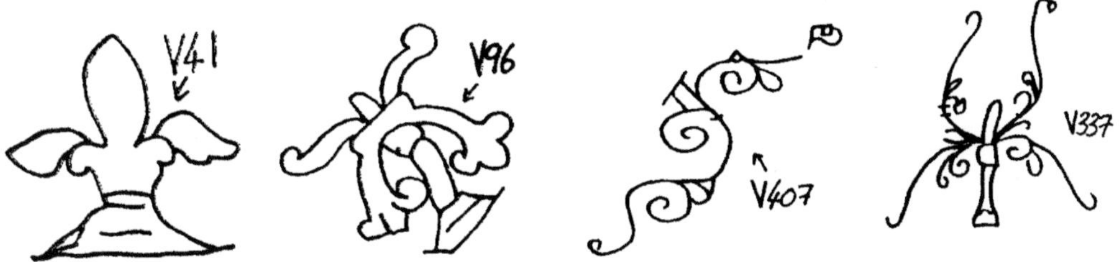

51 Types of vegetal ornament found in the borders of the Bayeux Tapestry (left to right): type 1 (cruciform), type 1 derivative (quasi-cruciform), type 2 (scrolled), and type 3 (cruciform variant)

Parallels for the trees in the Bayeux Tapestry

General similarities between the trees in the Tapestry and those in the Hextateuch have long been recognised. Of particular interest are the parallels noted by Francis Wormald (1957) between Trees 18 to 20 and those on folio 36v of the Hextateuch, which have similar 'strand-like trunks', 'tangle of branches' and leaves 'ending in bunches of trefoil acanthus and teat-like buds'. David Wilson (1985) observed similar comparisons with trees in the Tiberius Psalter (folio 7), which perhaps better reflect the rigid form of those in the Tapestry. Other good, but rather general, parallels are found in British Library, Cotton Julius A.vi (folio 5v) and Junius 11 (pages 11 & 41).

It is rare that the Tapestry can be compared with another Anglo-Saxon textile, but the fragment, now in the the Museo di Sant'Ambrogio, Milan (52), offers such an example, and it is here that particularly good parallels are found. Although the individual strands of the trees in the Bayeux Tapestry are thicker and fuller than the Milan fragment, their general form is similar. The trees in the Milan fragment are also symmetrical, like those in the Bayeux Tapestry, and have scrolled branches similar to the ornament found in the Tapestry borders. Further, the long, tall trunks of the Milan fragment, with a few strands at a low level, and a trapezoid node at the top of the trunk (discussed below) is also matched in the Bayeux Tapestry.

Interlace

Hatched or interlace ornament, characteristic of some of the Tapestry's trees, is also found in some late Anglo-Saxon illuminations. Thus, the loose plait of Tree 5 can be paralleled in the Junius 11 manuscript (page 24) (53). Similarly, the intertwining branches of Trees 6 and 7 can be favourably compared to Junius 11 (page 39), Harley 603 Psalter (folio 7r), the Trinity Gospels (folio 11v), the Bury Gospels (folio 11v) and Pierpont Morgan Library M.709 (folio 26v). Here, there are striking similarities in the curvature of the plaits and associated leaf ornament. Further, Wolfgang Grape (1994) paralleled the trunk of Tree 3, which 'curls round in an oval loop framing an elaborate interlace pattern', with that in the Old English Hextateuch (folio 7).

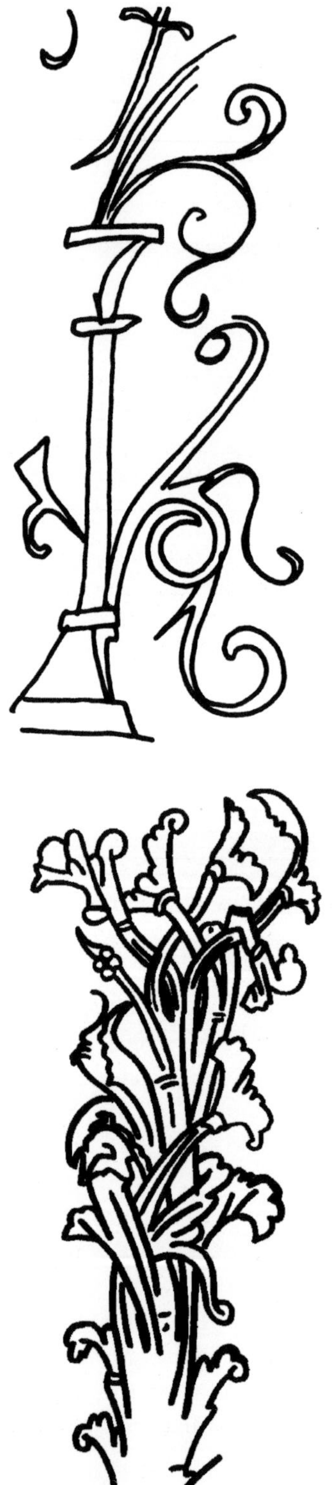

52 Trees in the Museo di Sant' Ambrogio textile fragment

53 Loose plait of trees in Junius 11 (page 24)

Occasionally, the interlacing of the Tapestry's trees is fairly tight, quite unlike that of trees in contemporary illumination. A particularly good example is Tree 1 (other examples are Trees 2, 3, 15 & 18), which was commented upon by both David Wilson (1985) and Wolfgang Grape (1994). However, such interlace decoration is found in initials and upon architectural elements depicted in contemporary illuminations; examples include the capitals of a building in Junius 11 (page 57) and the initials in Arundel 155 (folios 12, 53 & 93). Such examples could have provided the basis of this motif in the Tapestry.

Wolfgang Grape (1994) considered the Tapestry's interlace to be Ringerike in style. He made convincing comparisons between the Tapestry's ornament and tenth-century commemorative stone sculpture at Jelling in Denmark and Vang in Norway; Ringerike-type elements are found elsewhere in the Tapestry, such as on the figureheads of ships, which were discussed above (SHIPS).

Trapezoid nodes

The trapezoid node at the tops of some tree trunks (such as that of Trees 15, 17 & 19) is an intriguing feature of both the Tapestry and the Milan textile fragment. It also appears on trees in Junius 11 (page 78). Although not found in other narrative contexts, it is a common feature of capitals depicted in architecture and canon tables, both of which would have been known to the designer.

Staggered stumps

Trees with stumps or cut lower branches, shown in the Tapestry, are also found in some contemporary illuminations, including the frontispiece of Pierpont Morgan Library M.709 (folio 1v) where it represents the tree-trunk cross. Whilst the motif might echo some 'real life' phenomenon once observed by contemporary artists, such as the felling of lower branches for tinder, by the late eleventh century it was an established convention in art. Occasionally, these tree stumps have sub-circular protrusions, which may be intended to be fungi. In the Tapestry, such depictions are rare, but can be found on Trees 2 and 6. These also appear in art, such as London, Lambeth Palace, 3 (folio 6).

Leaf varieties

The foliage in the Tapestry better reflects that found in art than that of first-hand observation. Particularly common in the Tapestry are 'trifoliate acanthus' (type c) and 'single-sided acanthus' (type d) leaves, which are typical of ornament found in contemporary illuminations. For example, type c is found in British Library, Royal 1, D. ix (folio 11), British Library, Royal 15, A. xvi (folio 84), and Cambridge, Trinity College, O.2.51 (folio 46); type d is found in Cotton Julius A.vi (folio 5v), the Winchcombe Psalter (folio 4v) and the Trinity Gospels (folio 15r). Also popular in the Tapestry are 'trifoliate pointed' (type b), 'trifoliate rounded' (type e), 'heart-shaped' (type f), 'serrated' (type i), 'multi-lobed' (type j), and 'oval-lobed' (type k) leaf varieties which are, likewise, common in both Anglo-Saxon and Romanesque illuminations. For example, type b is found in the Harley 603 Psalter (folios 2 & 25r), Cotton Cleopatra C.viii (folio 23v), and the Hereford

Gospels (folio 3v); type e appears in the Eadwig Gospels (folio 10), Cambridge, Pembroke College 301 (folio 10v), and Cambridge, Trinity College, O.4.7 (folio 48v); type f is found in British Library, Royal 12, C.xxiii (folio 6v), the Leofric Missal (folio 154v) and Cotton Julius A.vi (folio 5v); type i is found in Harley 5431 (folio 54v), Bodleian Library, Bodley 718 (folio 1), and Bodleian Library, Douce 296 (folio 40); type j appears in the Æthelstan Psalter (folio 120v), Junius 11 (pages 13 & 41), British Library, Stowe 2 (folio 1); type k is found in Bibliothèque nationale de France, lat. 6401 (folio 57v). However, 'chilli' (type h) leaves are only found in pre-Conquest illuminations, such as the Æthelstan Psalter (folio 10v), Bodleian Library, Rawlinson C.570 (folio 44v), and Cotton Vitellius C.iii (folio 56v), while other types, such as 'oval leaves with lobed terminals' (type a), are only found in the Romanesque illuminations studied, such as the Winchester Psalter (folio 9), placing the design at the watershed of pre- and post-Conquest traditions. 'Aroid leaves, with lobed terminals' (type g) seem to be particular to the Tapestry, suggesting the designer also developed original motifs.

Trees in the borders

Trees in the borders (V150-1, V231-43, V246, V249 & V415-6), and those which appear in the first part of the Tapestry, like those in the main frieze, can be paralleled in illumination. However, unlike the trees in the main frieze, these have a more fluid form, akin to the acanthus scroll that is found elsewhere in the borders. One tree stands out from the rest, as it has symmetrical branches that spout outwards along the length of its trunk (V234), a motif that is not found in manuscript art until the twelfth century; examples can be found in British Library, Add. 37472 (I)v, Cotton Nero C.vii (folio 46), and the Bible of Saint-Bénigne (folio 148).

Parallels for the vegetal ornament in the Bayeux Tapestry

Both forms of vegetal ornament depicted in the borders of the Tapestry can be favourably compared with the 'conventional leaf-work' found on eleventh-century textiles, such as those of the mid eleventh-century from Bamberg, which display zoomorphic motifs and diagonal line dividers, and contemporary manuscript illumination.

Cruciform vegetal ornament (type 1)

The Tapestry's cruciform vegetal ornament is highly stylised, but some sub-classes (typically types 1b, 1c & 1e) appear to derive from acanthus leaf ornament, which is common in art; for example type 1b is found in the Æthelstan Psalter (folio 21r), the Harley 603 Psalter (folio 64r) and the Bury Psalter (folio 62); type 1c appears in the Eadwig Gospels (folio 247v) and Arundel 155 (folio 93). Perhaps more indebted to acanthus leaf motifs is type 1e, which is found in Paris, Bibliothèque nationale de France, lat. 987 (folio 41), Junius 11 (page 7) and the Tiberius Psalter (folio 60). In general, the remaining sub-classes of type 1 (types 1a, 1d, 1f, 1g & 1h) ornament are less widespread, but are found as decorative embellishment to architectural structures, canon tables and as general border decoration. Type 1a is found in Cambridge, Corpus Christi College 183 (folio 1v); type 1d is found in the Tiberius Psalter (folio 72); type 1f is found in Bodleian Library, Bodley 579 (folio 154v); type 1g is found in Cambridge,

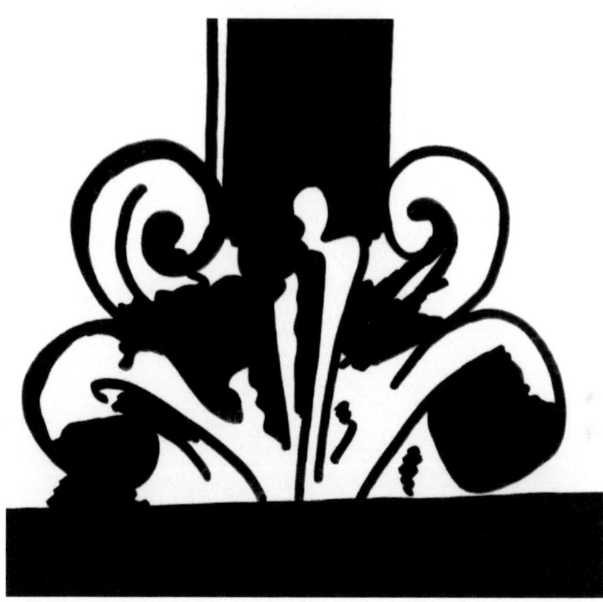

54 Cruciform vegetal ornament
depicted in the Cambridge,
Pembroke College 301 Gospels
(folio 5v)

Pembroke College 301 (folios 5v, 70v & 71) (*54*); type 1h is found in the Sacramentary of
Robert of Jumièges (folio 72). It may be that the rigidity of some cruciform ornament in the
Tapestry is due to the limits of the medium.

Acanthus scroll

Occasionally, the vegetal ornament in the borders has thick strands which spiral haphazardly
with sporadic twists and turns. This decoration compares better with the more robust trees
of the Tapestry than with the delicate plant ornament found elsewhere in the borders (such
as V1, V286, V301 & V303).

Francis Wormald (1957) made favourable comparisons between V390, which has leaves
that 'stretch out and curl up tightly at the end' and the 'stringy acanthus ornament' of
the Winchcombe Psalter (folio 5). Also similar are the acanthus elements of Junius 11
(pages 7 & 9) (*55*) and V150 and V151 in the Tapestry. Of particular note is the tube-like
neck of the stem and the tendril stumped lower strands. Even the strands themselves have
the same characteristic gentle twist. However, such ornament is also found in many other
contemporary illuminations, such as Bodleian Library, Bodley 577 (folio 1v), Warsaw,
Biblioteka Narodowa, I. 3311 (folio 15), and Monte Cassino, Archivo della Badia, BB.
437, 439 (pages 126 & 127).

Near the end of the Tapestry, a figure (Figure 627) appears in 'foliage scroll', a motif
which is quintessentially Romanesque; comparable examples include Madrid, Biblioteca
Nacional, Vit 23-8 (folio 15) and Bodleian Library, Auct. E. inf. 1 (folio 304). This foliage
scroll is also found on contemporary metalwork, including Benward's candlestick, which
dates to the early eleventh century, and the early twelfth-century Gloucester candlestick.
Nonetheless, whilst uncommon in late Anglo-Saxon art, this motif may have had its roots
in the 'gripping beast' motif, which is typical of pre-Conquest metalwork.

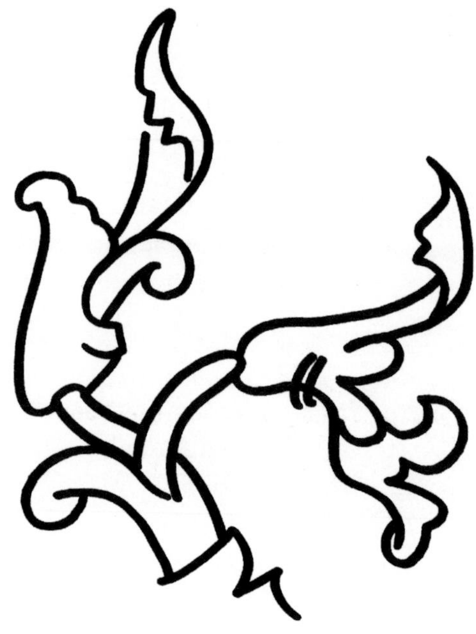

55 Acanthus elements of vegetal
ornament in Junius 11 (page 7)

Scrolled vegetal ornament (type 2)

The Tapestry's scrolled vegetal ornament (type 2) is much more fluid and sporadic than
the cruciform varieties (type 1). It also has numerous associated decorative elements, such
as leaves, buds and fruit, which parallel those of 'vine scroll' in both stone sculpture,
such as Lastingham 8A (Lastingham Church, North Yorkshire) of the eighth century and
Kirkdale 7A (St Gregory's Minster, North Yorkshire) of the late eighth or early ninth
century, and illuminations, such as British Library, Add. 47967 (Fly-leaf iii) and Pierpont
Morgan Library M.708 (folio 43r).

More often than not, these are highly stylised derivatives of standard ornament
types. Particularly good parallels with the Tapestry's 'type 2' scrolled ornament can be
found in an early eleventh-century herbal, Cotton Vitellius C.iii (folio 11v) (*56*). Such
ornament also appears on textiles, including those from Bamberg and the fragment
in the Museo di Sant'Ambrogio, Milan. This allows comparison of medium. The
Tapestry's scrolled vegetal ornament can also be paralleled with the filigree ornament
of the jewelled binding of (the probably Flemish) Pierpont Morgan Library M.709.

Cruciform-scrolled derivative vegetal ornament (type 3)

Type 3 vegetal ornament also features in contemporary illumination, as in Cotton
Cleopatra C.viii (folio 24r) and Junius 11 (page 7) (*57*). Both were probably produced in
Canterbury, and may well have been available to the designer of the Tapestry. This type
of ornament is not found in Anglo-Saxon stone sculpture, which may be explained by its
delicate form and by the general paucity of southern late Anglo-Saxon sculpture.

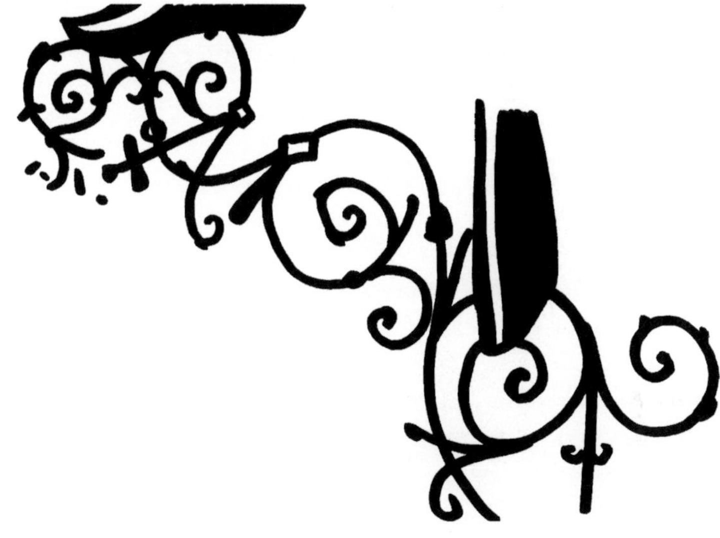

56 Scrolled vegetal
ornament depicted
in British Library,
Cotton Vitellius
C.iii (folio 11v)

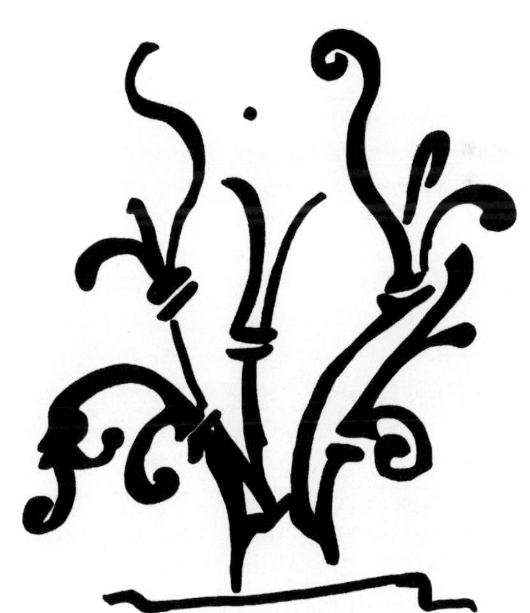

57 Cruciform-scrolled
derivative vegetal ornament
depicted in Junius 11 (page 7)

Leaf and bud types

Vegetal ornament in the borders is embellished with fewer leaves, buds and fruit than that in the main frieze. In part this may be due to their narrow size and the limited space available. This is particularly true for 'cruciform' ornament, where foliage is confined to vegetal tendrils and acanthus type ornament. Similarly, the 'acanthus scroll' in the Tapestry borders does not have leaves, buds or fruit.

This contrasts with 'scrolled' vegetal ornament, which is occasionally embellished with leaves and fruit. Leaf types are commonly oval (such as V105 & V407), whilst a tri-lobed variety becomes popular in Scene 51 (for example V180 & V189). Both leaf varieties are found in contemporary manuscripts, such as the Hereford Gospels (folio 9r). Similarly, some leaves appear pointed but may be just elongated oval varieties (such as V200). At times, buds are indistinguishable from leaves, normally sprouting from a node or stem. Mostly, these are oval, but elongated, almost pointed, varieties are also depicted (such as V192, V369 & V393). The nodes themselves may be square, oval or sub-circular in shape (for example V187 & V381). Similar nodes are found in contemporary illuminations, such as Junius 11 (page 13), Cambridge, Trinity College, B.11.2 (folio 4), Cotton Vitellius C.iii (folio 11v) and the Hexateuch (folio 36).

Function and landscape

Trees in the main frieze

Francis Wormald (1957) noted that trees in the Tapestry's main frieze act as punctuation marks, which divide one scene from another (as in the case of Tree 1, which divides Scenes 2 and 3, for example) and 'by this means the Tapestry's characters are able to turn in the opposite direction without too abrupt an interruption of the action'. Though eleventh-century parallels are not numerous, such a usage had a venerable ancestry; trees appear as scene dividers in classical paintings, and the practice was adopted by some Carolingian artists, such as in the Grandval-Moutier Bible (folio 5v) and the Vivian Bible (folio 10v).

However this is not the function of all the Tapestry's trees. For example, Trees 8 to 13, shown being felled by Norman woodsmen, illustrate some of the practicalities involved in realising Duke William's invasion plans. In this scene, therefore, they actively participate in the narrative. Perhaps significantly, these trees are thin and narrow, with little foliage and few low branches, and hence ideal for shipbuilding.

Further, some trees appear in the middle of narrative sequences, and therefore cannot be understood as scene dividers. Examples include Tree 14, which, although it appears towards the end of the boat-building scene, is not used to divide it from the next; a building performs this function. Instead, Tree 14 covers the aft of Ships 11 to 14. Its positioning is important since it simplifies this scene, allowing the narrative to flow forward; with only the forward parts of the boats showing, the viewer is guided towards the next scene. Similarly, Tree 23 almost impedes the charge of four Norman horsemen, who chase the fleeing English from the battlefield. In this instance, the tree conveniently allows the main frieze to be divided into two: Englishmen (Figures 619-23) cautiously make their way home in the upper section, whilst below, Norman horsemen (Figures 625-7) torture a captive.

The fact that a few trees seem to bow has attracted comment. Wolfgang Grape (1994) has suggested that Tree 14, which occurs at the end of the shipbuilding scene, is a 'salute to the completed ships', stressing the speed in which they have been completed. Similarly, he believed that Tree 3 'draws attention to the arrival of William's emissaries', that Tree 4 'bows in obeisance' before William, and that Trees 6 and 7, which flank an English ship, were designed to emphasise the importance of this scene. These views are difficult to substantiate. As some trees bow to the right, they might simply suggest the direction of the narrative. This is particularly evident in the case of Tree 4, where the tree divides two scenes within which characters move in different directions. This tree follows the action moving from left to right, and as such alerts the 'viewer' that the narrative will now continue in the normal direction.

Other trees (Trees 1, 6-7 & 12) seem purely decorative; the narrative flows irrespective of their presence. These are surely just space fillers. On some occasions, the designer has even shown two or more trees standing together, when one would suffice if it were to be purely functional (see for example Trees 15-7 & 18-20).

Trees in the borders

Trees in the borders are mostly associated with the Tapestry's fables, which are particularly prominent in the first few sections of the lower border (between Scenes 1-18). It is possible that these function as scene dividers within the smaller narrative sequences (see for example V237-8). Of more significance are the trees in Scene 58 (V415-6), which seem to be associated with the torture of the English who flee the battle, and thus help to convey the events in the main narrative.

Vegetal ornament in the main frieze

In only two instances is vegetal ornament, other than trees, found in the main frieze. V229 appears alone (and thus is easily missed) as a wilting plant, in the thick of battle, beneath the caption 'at the same time, both English and French fell in battle'. Next to this plant are a few wavy lines, possibly representing a short expanse of water or a marsh, which Lucien Musset (2002) described as a watery grave for a knight (Figure 515) who falls from his horse. V229 may be a marshland plant, which emphasises the boggy nature of the battlefield. Alternatively, since it is shown with a drooping stem, it could be a metaphor for the death and destruction taking place above.

Similarly, V230 is clearly functional rather than purely decorative. This plant appears as a vine leaf scroll, and restrains a man (Figure 627) undergoing torture. It seems likely that this figure is an Englishman, as two men on horseback (it is normally Normans who ride horses) attack him. This motif therefore clearly relates to the events in the narrative, rather than just being decorative. It may be the case, though it is impossible to be certain, that this figure is associated with Christ 'the true vine' (John 15: 1-17).

Vegetal ornament in the borders

The cruciform and scroll vegetal ornament in the Tapestry's borders seems purely decorative. However, the positioning of the different types of ornament is of some interest. Most cruciform (type 1) vegetal ornament is depicted in the earlier parts of the Tapestry: from Scene 2 to 35 in the upper border, and Scene 13 to 35 in the lower border. In contrast, scroll (type 2) ornament is found in the mid to later parts of the Tapestry: from Scene 35 to 58 in the upper border and Scene 35 to 51 in the lower border. Whilst it is tempting to hypothesise that this change in ornament reflects events in the main frieze – marking the point (Scene 35) at which Duke William learns that Harold has taken the English crown – it seems more likely that these changes reflect different embroiderers or workshops, or even the circumstances in which the commission was produced.

Summary

In the most part, vegetation in the Bayeux Tapestry has not been drawn from the 'real world'; rather these elements are traditional motifs borrowed from art. The plants and foliage in the Tapestry parallel those found in contemporary illumination, including work which was produced in Canterbury and hence would have been available to an artist working there. However, the significance of these motifs must not be overemphasised, as a majority of the Tapestry's vegetal elements are common in earlier and later illuminations, produced elsewhere in England and abroad. Whilst some aspects of the vegetal ornament in the Tapestry are typically Anglo-Saxon, others are more popular after the Norman Conquest. It is difficult to identify particular sources used by the designer. Whether this is due to differences in medium, the character of the work, the artist's style, or even the non-survival of the relevant works is debatable. However, it seems probable that the designer was indebted to a number of influences, mainly artistic. There are indications of improvisation, but the designer may have also responded to some 'real world' observations. This is perhaps most evident in some of the trees in the boat-building scenes, where their tall, narrow appearance helps convey realism to the narrative.

It is inconceivable that the designer did not have first-hand knowledge of contemporary plant types. Nonetheless, it is clear that the designer was more interested in the decorative qualities of traditional vegetal motifs than in producing an accurate rendition of familiar trees and plants; even in the case of herbals, which are assumed to be naturalistic, artists have borrowed from art rather than life. In this respect, the Tapestry artist was influenced by a range of artistic conventions. This provides a sobering counterbalance to the view of the designer as a proto-realist, and is a useful reminder of the many other factors, apart from visual reality, that affected the choice of how to depict the eleventh-century world.

CHAPTER 6

THE DESIGN AND PRODUCTION OF THE TAPESTRY

Little is known for certain about how the Bayeux Tapestry was designed and produced, but research in recent years has offered some tantalising clues. The following draws upon this evidence and attempts to give an account of who the Tapestry designer might have been, his (for it seems likely the designer was a man) relationship with the patron, thought to be Bishop Odo of Bayeux, and the design and production of the Tapestry.

THE BAYEUX TAPESTRY DESIGNER

To a greater or lesser extent, the Tapestry's artefacts (discussed in Chapter 5) enable us to build a profile of the designer, and explore his relationship to his pictorial models and to the 'real world'.

A designer familiar with south-east England

The depiction of the real world in the Bayeux Tapestry suggests that its designer was familiar with south-east England. The best evidence for this is the likelihood that the designer was acquainted with manuscripts produced at Canterbury, highlighted in Chapter 5 and discussed further below. However, at least one aspect of the design suggests that the designer might have travelled further afield. Notwithstanding some anomalies and a reliance on certain artistic motifs, the relative accuracy of the depiction of the Romanesque Westminster Abbey (discussed in Chapter 5) suggests that the designer knew the building or had access to reasonably accurate depictions of it, though it is also possible that he based his illustration upon a verbal or written account. It seems likely that all the major clerics would have been summoned to Edward's funeral and the coronations of Harold and William, all in Westminster Abbey. Assuming the designer was based in Canterbury, it is quite possible that he made the trip to London to see the abbey itself.

A designer familiar with lay society

It has been noted that the Bayeux Tapestry offers a reliable and convincing portrayal of contemporary dress. It is certain that the designer, whether lay or cleric, would have known the form of contemporary garments. More importantly, the realism of his response to many articles of contemporary lay clothing, such as the form of tunics and culottes, is greater than is generally the case in art of the period. This may suggest he himself was a member of the laity or at the very least that he was interested in lay fashion. It is possible that the designer was a cleric who wore lay dress, like the clerics he depicts. Both Gale Owen-Crocker (1986) and John Blair (personal correspondence, 2004) thought that there was nothing implausible about English secular clergy at this time wearing lay dress. The fact that late Anglo-Saxon texts urge priests not to wear lay clothing suggests some did. For example, in Ælfric's first Old English letter for Wulfstan of about 1006, it is stated that a mass-priest 'may never be clothed with lay clothing'. Likewise, in his pastoral letter for Wulfsige II, Ælfric says 'the priest is not to wear a monk's garb or that of a layman'. However, the implication must be that most did not wear lay attire as it was considered wrong to do so.

It is also of note that, in contrast to many of his contemporaries, the Tapestry designer demonstrates a good understanding of post-Conquest female fashion, for example the long-sleeved dresses with flared cuffs, which were typical of the time. It is likely that the embroiderers were women. William of Malmesbury's *Gesta Regum Anglorum* records that Edward the Confessor's wife, Edith, embroidered the robes he wore at festivals. Likewise, Domesday Book contains at least two references to secular embroideresses: Leofgyth of Knook, Wiltshire 'made and makes the gold fringe of the king and queen' and Ælfgyth of Oakley, Buckinghamshire, who held land 'on condition of her teaching' Godric, the sheriff's 'daughter gold embroidery work'. It can therefore be imagined that they might have instructed the designer, or corrected his work, had he erred in his depiction of female costume. However, there is no reason to assume that he did so; it is simpler to presume that he was familiar with the garments in question. This would indicate that the designer was accustomed to the company of women, including those of the higher echelons. Of course, clerics may have been familiar with female clothing and there is documentary evidence to support this. In the Northumbrian Priest's Law, dated to between 1008 and 1023, it is stated that 'if a priest leaves a woman and takes another, *anathema sit*!' – implying, therefore, that some Northumbrian priests had female partners. However, the rules governing close contact with women seem to have been strict. Ælfric's first Old English letter for Wulfstan says that 'no bishop and no mass-priest, deacon or minster-priest, is to have living in his dwelling nor in his house any women, unless it is his mother or his sister, father's sister or mother's sister'. Ælfric also states 'that he who takes a widow or a deserted wife is never afterwards to be a deacon or mass-priest'.

A designer familiar with the clergy

Whether he was a cleric or a layman, the Tapestry designer certainly knew how ecclesiastics dressed. His depictions are as accurate and detailed as those found in contemporary illuminations; parallels include Rouen, Bibliothèque Municipale, A.27 (368) (folio 1v), the Tiberius Psalter (folio 18v) and Cotton Tiberius A.iii (folio 2v). This is not surprising, given

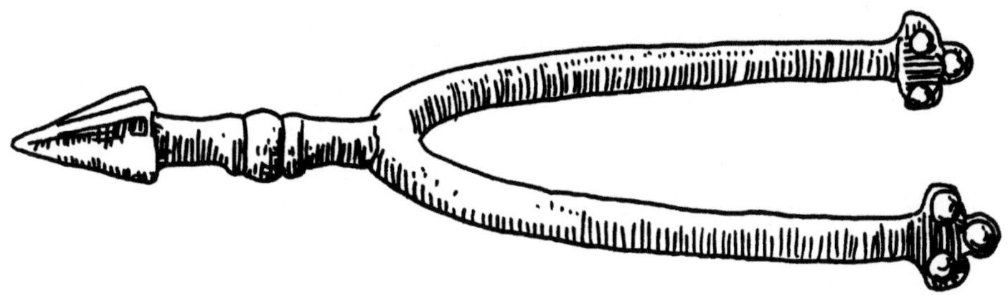

58 An eleventh-century spur from Winchester

that the Church had a prominent role both in society as a whole and in the illustrations of manuscripts, known to have been among the designer's sources. More intriguing is the fact that the designer, in contrast with his contemporaries, also shows tonsured clerics wearing lay clothing (comprising tunics and tight fitting trousers), such as at the funeral of Edward the Confessor (Scene 26). This must be of some significance, though its meaning is lost nowadays.

A designer familiar with the highest social echelons

The designer used clothing to distinguish men of rank from the lower echelons of society (discussed further below). He used decorative or intricate motifs to emphasise the quality of garments and jewellery worn by high status characters; for example William's cloak (Figure 118) has an embroidered hem, and Edward's brooch (Figure 207) is shown with 'jewelled' cells. This indicates that he was aware of contemporary social distinctions, as one would expect.

Likewise, the creatures drawn with the greatest degree of accuracy are horses, dogs and hawks. Particularly interesting is the fact that the designer shows horsemen wearing spurs (*58*); he even seems to illustrate stirrup-strap mounts. Since these artefacts are rarely depicted in contemporary art, they may suggest the designer had some first-hand equestrian knowledge. Although it is also possible that the designer borrowed this motif from manuscripts such as the Hexateuch, the form of the spurs in the Tapestry better reflects the actual artefact. Horses and hawks were certainly kept by men of rank, including Edward and Harold. Whilst there is no evidence to suggest that the designer owned such animals himself, he clearly knew them. This is perhaps indicative of his interaction with high status individuals, including, we may presume, Bishop Odo.

A designer familiar with art and other crafts

Given that the Tapestry designer borrowed from contemporary illuminations, we can presume that he was au fait with a range of manuscript art. Indeed, he may himself have been first and foremost an illuminator, a possibility examined below.

It has been noted that the designer used decorative motifs to emphasise the quality of garments and jewellery. Whilst similar motifs appear in manuscript art, the designer clearly delighted in utilising such forms. This perhaps reflects his knowledge of embroidery and jewellery-making, the former being implicit in the nature of the work under consideration. It is inevitable that the designer witnessed other craftsmen at work.

Likewise, the Tapestry's woodworking scenes reveal that that the designer was familiar with contemporary carpentry methods, though seemingly not specifically with the work of the shipwright. Woodworking would have been a common sight in most towns and villages; wood was certainly readily available and affordable, and was worked to produce a great range of different structures and artefacts.

The artist, his model and the 'real world'

The relationship between the artist, his model and the 'real world' is complex. It is clear that, for most aspects of the work, the designer used art-based motifs. Like contemporary artists, he borrowed 'traditional', sometimes archaic, motifs for aspects of the 'real world' which he surely knew first-hand. A good example is the Tapestry's vegetation, which is pure fantasy. Here, there was little need to reflect 'real life', as vegetation, with the possible exception of the trees in the shipbuilding scenes, is incidental to the main thrust of the narrative. Likewise, much of the architecture in both the Tapestry and contemporary illuminations appears to be of a sub-classical style; possible exceptions include the plan of Christ Church waterworks in the Eadwine Psalter (folios 284v-5 & 286r) and sections of a building in Bodleian Library, Bodley 494 (folios 115v, 156, 158 & 162v). When the designer responded to 'real life', such as for Westminster Abbey and the mottes, it was because the structures in question were particularly important within the narrative.

For certain other aspects, the designer selected the artistic schema that most accurately reflected contemporary reality, even though the narrative did not dictate it. For example, in the Bayeux Tapestry, the influence of contemporary garments seems more pronounced than in most eleventh-century illuminations. Yet dress and clothing was, of course, one aspect that every beholder could evaluate. Hence, as well as accurately depicting artefacts that had a narrative role, the designer might have also reflected the contemporary scene in areas that interested him or where the likely knowledge of his prospective audience required that he did so.

THE DIRECTION OF THE TAPESTRY'S PATRON

It has been shown that the case for Odo's patronage is substantial. It seems unthinkable that a man as powerful and resourceful as Odo would not have imposed his mark on the work, and the Tapestry's artefacts might offer clues to reflect this.

Odo the warrior

At a crucial moment in the battle, Odo (Figure 534) is shown rallying the 'boys' (Scene 54). Considering the Bishop of Bayeux is believed to have had a military role at Hastings, it is interesting that some of the Tapestry's arms and armour are less than accurate, and many seem to reflect ancient types. This said, whilst Odo was increasingly involved in military affairs from 1080, it is significant, as David Bates (1975) has suggested, that 'he played no discernable part in the warfare of 1067 to 1071 which completed the Conquest'. In fact, the Tapestry is the only contemporary source that ascribes an important military role to Odo

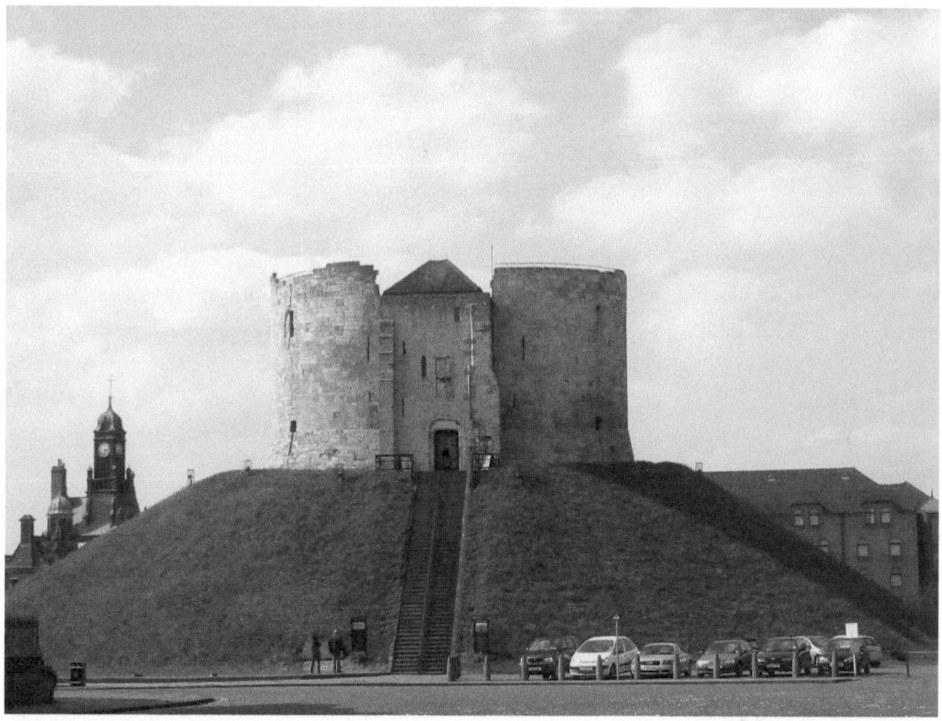

59 Clifford's Tower, York

at Hastings, which quite possibly could be exaggerated. Perhaps the patron accepted the limitations of art for depicting the 'real world', or that he was not much involved with the design process.

On the other hand, it is notable that the Tapestry's mottes, especially Hastings Castle, seem to reflect the actual structures that were being built when the Tapestry was commissioned. In this connection, it is perhaps significant that they had a direct association with Odo; the *Anglo-Saxon Chronicle* (D) for 1066 records that 'Bishop Odo and Earl William… built castles far and wide throughout the land, oppressing the unhappy people, and things went ever from bad to worse' (*59*). This is not to say that Odo commented on the accuracy of the Tapestry's mottes, but rather that the designer was probably very conscious of their importance in the context of his work, and made a special effort to depict them.

Odo the lord

Pre-eminent amongst the nobility, Odo was clearly a man of great wealth; Domesday Book records that his landholdings in England were only second to that of the king. David Bates (1975) noted that he had estates in 22 counties, exceeding a value (in 1086) of about £3050.

It is therefore notable that whilst the Tapestry uses hawks and dogs besides other attributes to indicate status (such animals accompany Guy, Harold and William), none is associated with Odo. The omission is perhaps coincidental; the hawks and hounds are only found in the earlier parts of the Tapestry, whereas Odo first appears at a much later point

(Scene 35). Indeed, elsewhere the designer highlights Odo's status in a variety of ways: he is identified with a tonsure (Figures 264, 380 & 384); he is shown at the head of the table (Figure 380) – the position of Christ at the Last Supper; and in Scene 54 he is shown wearing a triangular patterned hauberk and holding a baculum (Figure 543), which David Bates (1975) identifies as 'a symbol of authority and direction'.

Odo the ecclesiastic

It is certain that Odo knew Westminster Abbey; he attended William's coronation there on Christmas Day 1066 and that of Matilda on 11 May 1068. Odo also had an interest in church architecture. He was currently rebuilding his own cathedral at Bayeux, for which some scholars, such as Frank Stenton (1957), believe the Tapestry itself may have been commissioned. David Bates (1975) noted that Odo was also a benefactor to other institutions and later in life also became further involved with affairs of the Church; he is surrounded by his clergy in witness lists of 1092 and 1093, he attended the council of Clermont in November 1095, and in 1096 he travelled around Normandy with the papal legate, Abbot Gerento of St Bénigne of Dijon, presumably to preach the Crusade, on which he went.

Odo's status and interest in the Church might also therefore explain the apparent accuracy of the depiction of Westminster Abbey in the Tapestry. On balance, it seems unlikely that Odo would have instructed the designer about Westminster's appearance or indeed have been overly concerned with such detail, especially since no such interest is apparent in relation to structures in Normandy that were more relevant to the ducal family, most notably his own cathedral church at Bayeux. David Bates (1975) noted that 'in spite of his English interests, Normandy, and Bayeux cathedral in particular, remained the focal point of Odo's life'. Yet in the Tapestry, perhaps surprisingly, these structures in Normandy are highly stylised.

Earlier, it was noted that the accuracy of the Tapestry's ecclesiastical garments suggests the designer was familiar with clerical dress. However their accuracy might be better explained by the direction of the patron. Against this possibility is the fact that Odo himself is never shown in religious vestments. Is seems unlikely that he would insist on accuracy for others, yet never take advantage of it to flaunt his own ecclesiastical status.

In brief, artefacts which we might reasonably identify with Odo, such as certain types of arms and armour, do not reflect those of the real world of the eleventh century, whereas those that appear realistic, such as ecclesiastic garb, are (strangely) never associated with the Bishop of Bayeux. It may be concluded therefore that the artefacts give little indication that the putative patron was involved in the details of the design.

THE PRODUCTION OF THE BAYEUX TAPESTRY

Although the Bayeux Tapestry presents a new and, as far as we know, original picture cycle, there is good evidence that much of its design is based on pre-existing artistic motifs. These provide vital clues to the range and nature of the sources that influenced the designer.

Elements typical of art in general

Whilst it is clear, given the nature of the surviving evidence, that manuscript art appears to have been the primary influence upon the designer, he was clearly familiar with a wider spectrum of visual culture. Some of the Tapestry's motifs are of an established type, with a long tradition in Anglo-Saxon art commonly found not only in illumination but also on stone sculpture, antler, bone, leather and metalwork. It also seems likely that such motifs would have commonly occurred in textiles and wall paintings. The vegetal ornament, predominately found in the Tapestry's borders, is a case in point, as are the Tapestry's beasts. Although some may have been sketched from life (albeit quite unlikely) most are indebted to artistic motifs that were widely available in the eleventh century.

Elements typical of manuscript art

The Tapestry's classical-style architecture, typical of late Anglo-Saxon and post-Conquest illuminations, is perhaps the clearest evidence that the designer was influenced by manuscript art; for example C.A. Ralegh Radford, E.M. Jope and J.W. Tonkin (1973) noted that the buildings in the Harley 603 Psalter 'are shown as stone-built, with tiled roofs' as 'they belong to the Mediterranean tradition' upon which the illustrations of this manuscript and its continental model are based. As previously discussed, in the most part the Tapestry's buildings are composed of generic architectural elements, assembled in different combinations to create a variety of distinct structures. This is commonplace in manuscript art, as too is the manner in which architecture is used to provide a physical environment, either as the settings for scenes, or to divide them. This is not particular to Canterbury illuminations – it also occurs, for example, in some Carolingian illuminations, such as the Grandval-Moutier Bible (folio 5v). Whilst it is difficult to identify specific exemplars that may have been drawn upon by the Tapestry designer, the best parallels for the variety of forms and quantity of architecture is found in Canterbury illuminations, discussed below.

Also typical of manuscript art are many aspects of the Tapestry's arms and armour. Barbed spears with wings, short bows and convex shield-boards (types absent from the archaeological record) are common in both English and continental illuminations from at least the ninth century; Martin Carver (1986) noted that barbed spears, for example, are inherently a Carolingian invention fossilised in Ottonian and Anglo-Saxon art. Likewise, the frill found beside the knee on some of the Tapestry's tunics is a common convention used to indicate movement in illuminated manuscripts, such as Junius 11 (page 74), Cotton Caligula A.xv (folio 123) and the New Minster Liber Vitae (folio 7).

Elements typical of Canterbury illuminations

The strongest parallels with the Tapestry illustrations occur in manuscripts that were certainly or probably produced in Canterbury, of which three (the Harley 603 Psalter, the Hexateuch and Junius 11) are of particular interest. The numerous parallels between motifs in these manuscripts and the Tapestry provided good evidence that the designer knew and used them, or manuscripts like them.

The Harley 603 Psalter, a copy of the Utrecht Psalter produced at Christ Church by at least seven artists, mostly during the first half of the eleventh century, provides good general parallels for the Tapestry's architecture, arms and armour, clothing and vegetation. Significantly, this manuscript (hand F) offers the first and only parallel for a depiction of a kite-shield in Anglo-Saxon art; there are also striking similarities between the geometric designs on some of the Tapestry's shields and those in the Harley 603 Psalter (folios 29v & 30v), but these were drawn in the twelfth century (*30*). Further, this manuscript (see folios 27v & 51v) parallels the way in which the Tapestry designer foreshortens the sail of the ships, giving them their triangular form.

The Old English Hexateuch, which was probably produced at St Augustine's Abbey in the first half of the eleventh century, provides parallels for several complete motifs found in the Tapestry, such as the illustrations of an Israelite spy escaping from Jericho down a rope (folio 141v, Scene 10), Abraham slinging at birds (folio 26v, Scene 18) (*1*), a servant waiting at a table (folio 57v, Scene 36), and a woodworker (Noah) using a T-axe (folio 13v, Scene 43) (*34, bottom*).

Besides these complete motifs, similar forms of artefacts (or elements thereof) occur in both the Tapestry and the Hexateuch. Of particular interest is a figure wearing a trousered hauberk (folio 24v) (*25, left*) which, it seems, is the earliest representation of this type of armour in Anglo-Saxon illumination; other parallels include the Harley 603 Psalter (folio 73v) (*25, right*), which seems to be a twelfth-century addition, and the (probable Romanesque) stone fragment from Winchester Old Minster (88A) (*26*). Similarly, the ships in this manuscript (folios 15 & 24v), particularly their figureheads, are similar to those in the Bayeux Tapestry. There are also general parallels with the Tapestry's boat-building scenes, architecture, dress and clothing, vegetation and beasts.

Junius 11 may have been produced at Christ Church, Canterbury, in the late tenth century. Its ships parallel those in the Tapestry; of particular note are their figureheads and the gap amidships (pages 65, 66 & 68). Like the Tapestry and the Hexateuch, it also shows boat-building (page 65). Junius 11 also offers good general parallels for the Tapestry's architecture; specific elements include the steps leading up to a building (page 84), which are similar to those leading up to Bosham Church (Scene 3) and the two-storey house in the Tapestry (Scene 47). It includes vegetal interlace and acanthus elements akin to those in the Tapestry; the trapezoid nodes found on some of the Tapestry's trees, for example, only otherwise occur in Junius 11 (page 78) and an Anglo-Saxon textile fragment in the Museo di Sant'Ambrogio, Milan. There are also general parallels in arms and armour, clothing and beasts, as discussed in Chapter 5. Of special note are Junius 11's lions rampant shown with their tails between their legs (*48*) and griffins (pages 11 & 13), which are uncommon in pre-Conquest art.

Notable parallels found in other Canterbury illuminations for the type of trees, and the men cutting them, include Cotton Julius A.vi (folio 5v) (*28*) in which is also to be found generic parallels for the 'occupations of the month' and some of the Tapestry's creatures (see folios 4v, 5 & 5v). In Cotton Cleopatra C.viii, there is a match for the 'man with a coil' (folio 27), discussed by Francis Wormald (1957), and for the cruciform scroll (type 3) ornament (folio 24r). In Arundel 155, the brooch worn by St Benedict (folio 133) (*40*) parallels the centrally fastened neck brooches in the Tapestry, while ecclesiastical vestments similar to those in the Tapestry are depicted in Cotton Tiberius A.iii (folio 117v) and Durham, Cathedral Library, B.III.32 (folio 56v) (*41*). The Tapestry's horses and the arrangement of their harness fittings are paralleled by those in Cambridge, Corpus Christi College 23 (folio 2a), a late tenth-century copy of Prudentius' Psychomachia (*43*). Further, the sixth-century Italian St Augustine's Gospels (folio 125r) (*3*), which were certainly at St Augustine's Abbey by the eleventh century, seem to have been the model for the Tapestry's feast scene (Scene 43).

Whilst the strongest parallels are found in manuscripts from St Augustine's Abbey, the Tapestry also shares a large number of motifs with Christ Church illuminations. It therefore seems probable that both scriptoria had an impact on the designer. Although Odo was in litigation with Christ Church over land, this seems unlikely to have restricted the designer having access to whatever he needed. Indeed, it is plausible that the Tapestry designer compiled a sketchbook of relevant motifs from illuminations housed by both communities.

Elements typical of Romanesque illuminations

Whilst many of the closest parallels are found in late Anglo-Saxon art, the Tapestry is (of course) a post-Conquest work. Therefore, it is unsurprising that it shares various affinities with Romanesque art. To date, it has not been possible to identify specific exemplars that the designer knew, and it is perhaps doubtful that this will ever be known. The clearest parallels with Romanesque art, such as some of the leaf types, are too general and widespread to permit the identification of a particular model, while in the case of clothing it is unclear whether the parity reflects a debt to Romanesque art or to real life. Likewise, it has already been noted that the Tapestry shows horsemen using spurs, which are more common in post-Conquest illuminations, but this may similarly reflect his personal equestrian knowledge.

THE DESIGNER'S WORKING PRACTICES

It has been shown that illumination had a profound influence upon the designer, and it can be confidently suggested that he sketched from manuscript exemplars. It is also possible, perhaps likely, that the textile tradition was as prolific as the manuscript one; manuscripts for certain scriptoria survive, whereas textiles hardly ever do – even the manuscripts that survive are likely to be a relatively small proportion of those that were produced. John Blair (personal correspondence, 2004) thought it possible that the traditions of illumination and embroidery, amongst other arts forms, had long existed side by side, influencing each other. Nonetheless, it seems certain that the Tapestry designer was a trained illustrator, and, unless we presume that he specialised exclusively in textile design (which seems unlikely), it is probable that he contributed to the decoration of some eleventh-century manuscripts, though, to date, specific examples are unknown (or at least unidentified).

It might also be assumed that the designer was a cleric. Whilst Michael Gullick (1998) highlighted evidence for the involvement of professional (lay) scribes in the production of manuscript books at ecclesiastical centres in England during the late Anglo-Saxon and Romanesque periods, such as at St Albans (by the end of the eleventh century) and Abingdon (in the early twelfth century), examples are scarce. That said, in the eleventh century, monastic scriptoria produced books for each other and non-monastic clients. Also, lay participation was potentially important since these 'professionals' may have been able to work longer hours than cloistered members of the communities, which would directly affect the speed with which libraries were built up, a point also made by Michael Gullick (1998). He further noted that they might have worked at more than one centre, and this, therefore, would have been a means by which new ideas and decoration were transmitted from one centre to another. As such, it is quite possible that our designer could have used and been familiar with manuscripts held by local religious communities, whether he was a cleric or not.

Inception

Although the terms of his commission are not known, it can be imagined that the designer would have had a basic, possibly detailed, design concept, which may have been based upon a written or oral narrative account; some scholars, such as Bernard Bachrach (1988), have hypothesised that the Tapestry follows a lost *Gesta* or *Chanson de geste*. However, Richard Gameson (1997) found this model 'altogether too simplistic' and instead suggested that since 'the narrative flows so well… we should credit him [the designer] with a proactive and not merely a passive role in the formation of this particular version of the story'. It is likely that the designer was given some instruction concerning events and elements that should be included or omitted. It is also possible that the Tapestry's account was composed especially for the purpose of this commission. The apparent fact that Odo did not contribute his knowledge of the contemporary scene to the visual depictions does not automatically mean he did not have a role in forming the narrative. On the contrary, since Odo has such a prominent role in the Tapestry, it is eminently plausible that he (or his agent) did.

Richard Gameson (1997) believed it was likely that the designer had the 'freedom to select and mould the material according to his own style and art'. The above discussion of the relationship between the designer and patron supports this; whilst the designer was clearly influenced by contemporary art, he showed both ingenuity and originality in accomplishing his pictorial narrative. At the same time, the fact that the artistry becomes simpler after Scene 24 (discussed further below) also suggests a degree of flexibility during the process of creation, especially at the embroidery stage.

The Tapestry's inscriptions appear to be squeezed between the pictorial imagery, hence some commentators, such as George Wingfield Digby (1957), have suggested that they were an afterthought, added at a late stage of the design process or even upon the completion of the work. However, Richard Gameson (1997) viewed this as 'an erroneous twentieth- [and twenty-first-] century perception, presupposing the modern neat delineation between picture and caption… its inappropriateness is underlined by many early medieval book illuminations which include inscriptions within the picture space'.

Design

It has been noted that the Tapestry designer borrowed complete motifs from known exemplars, and it seems highly probable that he knew the libraries where these were kept. Although the artefacts depicted in the Tapestry suggest that the designer primarily consulted material in Canterbury, it is also possible that he had his own collection of drawings, a model book, which he used for his design. This could have been compiled from a number of sources over a period of time. It is interesting, therefore, that some elements of the design most commonly appear in Winchester books; an example is the distinctive form of the Tapestry's tunics, which are found in Cotton Tiberius B.v (folio 6v) (*38*) and the Tiberius Psalter (folios 9 & 11). Of course, it is possible such motifs did also appear in Canterbury manuscripts, which are now lost. Alternatively, these motifs may provide evidence that the designer consulted other libraries, though perhaps in this instance what we have instead are independent reflections of contemporary reality. It is also important to emphasise that whilst the designer almost certainly used Canterbury illuminations, this in itself does not prove the Tapestry was actually produced there; sketches (and memories) were portable, and wherever the design was done, the embroidery could have been done elsewhere.

Production

The designer would have sketched out his design onto linen, possibly by squaring up – overlaying a grid onto a sketch, and using this to help transfer an image from the sketch to the original. Richard Gameson (1997) thought it seemed likely that the design would have been sketched as an outline drawing, with perhaps only the most important scenes being drawn in detail.

It is not known where the Tapestry was embroidered, but it must be assumed it was produced in a workshop accustomed to embroidery work. Jan Messent (1999) believed that 'individual professional embroiderers' would more usually have worked 'in workshops under royal patronage to ensure that accommodation, wages and the purchase of... materials was met'; for example, in 802, Eanswitha, an embroiderer of Hereford, was granted by the Bishop of Worcester a lease of land on condition that she carried out textile work for the priests of the cathedral church. The fact that particular artefacts or attributes (such as moustaches, gaps amidships and certain types of flowers and fauna) found in the earlier parts of the Tapestry do not continue throughout the work may suggest that the design was not sketched in full before embroidery began, but rather was developed as work progressed. Alternatively, and perhaps more likely, the designer may have sketched a full version of his design, but allowed the embroiderers an element of independence in the treatment of minor motifs. The embroiderers would presumably have been experienced in transferring a design onto linen, and could have copied border motifs from a model-book; Kay Staniland (1991) has highlighted evidence of this later in the medieval period.

Although Jan Messent (1999) and others have suggested that the nine lengths of the Tapestry were embroidered in different workshops, there is no evidence to support this. Certain regularly appearing motifs, which would be difficult to standardise across a variety of centres, such as the geometric designs used to evoke mail, provide evidence that it was probably worked by a single team. A variety of motifs were used, but most types appear throughout the Tapestry. Therefore, we might imagine one team of embroiderers working systematically through the whole Tapestry, from left to right, though invariably some embroiderers would have worked on the design from above (upside down); a view supported by Jan Messent (1999). The use of one team would have had time implications; the fact that the design becomes greatly simplified, particularly after Scene 24, may reflect this.

Errors in the Tapestry, which are examined below, suggest that the designer did not monitor the progress of his work throughout the embroidery stage. The fact that these remained uncorrected implies that he may never have seen the finished product, if indeed the work ever was fully completed.

The embroiderers' work and the design

Mistakes in the Tapestry are few, but they have nonetheless altered the appearance, and hence our understanding, of some artefacts. They were referred to individually in the discussion above; however, it is now worth examining them collectively since they shed light on the work of the embroiderers.

The sail of one ship (Boat 3, Scene 5) was rendered in outline, but not in-filled using laid-and-couched work, as is the convention elsewhere in the Tapestry, and consequently it looks square rather than triangular. Wolfgang Grape (1994) was convinced that the form was intentional, but, as we have seen, the effect is almost certainly the result of oversight on the part of the embroiderers.

Likewise, the Tapestry shows some men wearing culottes and a tunic of matching colour, giving the appearance of a one-piece garment. Whilst this may have been intentional, it seems unlikely that contemporaries wore such clothing. It is worth recalling in this context that mail hauberks are shown trousered, which is also incorrect. Perhaps, then, the embroiderers misunderstood the designer's intent, believing that, like the mailed hauberks, these garments were of one-piece construction.

The Tapestry shows right-handed archers firing arrows from the right hand side of the bow stave, when they would have been fired from the left side, as highlighted by Jim Bradbury (1997). This follows an artistic convention that when archers are illustrated facing right, the arrow is shown crossing the bow stave on its right hand side, whereas when an archer is depicted facing left the arrows cross the left hand side of his bow stave; examples of depictions of archers firing arrows from the wrong side of the bow stave include the Ebbo Gospels (folio 15v) and Harley 2826 (folios 4v, 5r & 6v). The significance of this in the present context is that it suggests, unsurprisingly, that the embroiderers had little understanding of archery.

It is also the case that the embroiderers show a majority of the Tapestry's sword hilts with disc-shaped pommels, a type, according to David Edge and John Miles Paddock (1988), unlikely to have been commonplace before the end of the eleventh century. Although this form of pommel also occurs in contemporary illuminations, it seems likely that the embroiderers intended to depict the 'walnut type' (more common at the time the Tapestry was produced) but, perhaps due to the limitations of the medium, it was misrepresented. Similarly, women in the Tapestry never wear jewellery, though it is evident on the basis of surviving material culture that they did. The explanation would seem to be limitations of the embroidery medium for such small-scale detail.

It was noted above that some of the embroiderers were probably working upside down, and a few errors reflect this. An example is the mailed hood (Figure 432) shown superimposed over a conical helmet. Strangely, the nasal guard is shown, even though the lower part of the helmet is omitted. Such cases illustrate lapses in the embroiderers' concentration. Indeed, Jan Messent (1999) believed that some of these errors and lesser quality embroidery was the work of 'less-skilled hands' or 'assistants'. More significantly, the designer did not spot them, which provides further evidence that he was not available (or able) to make corrections at the embroidery stage.

Variations in the motifs depicted in the individual lengths of the Tapestry

The Tapestry was constructed of at least nine pieces of linen of varying lengths. Some features are particular to specific sections and this has led certain commentators, such as Albert Levé (1919), to suggest that the lengths may have been worked by different teams of embroiderers, perhaps in different workshops. However, these variations are probably best explained by the fact that the design was simplified in its later parts, perhaps to save time, money or both.

This point is illustrated by the moustaches and hairstyles, which were initially used to distinguish between the English and Normans. Moustaches are most frequent in Section 1, becoming less so from Section 2. In Scene 25, even Harold is clean shaven! From this point onwards, only the occasional figure is moustached. When Normans first occur (in Scene 8), many are shown with the backs of their heads shaven; however, by Scene 17, during the Breton campaign, this feature has been discontinued. Although this may be partially explained by the fact that much of Section 3 is in England, whilst from Section 6 most Normans wear helmets, so their hair is covered, nevertheless, a discrepancy remains.

Likewise, hawks only appear in the early part of the Tapestry (between Scenes 2 & 14), disappearing early in Section 2; ships with a gap in their gunwale amidships only occur in the first two lengths (between Scenes 4 & 24), and cross-garters are prominent in the second section of the Tapestry, but thereafter are mostly shown as horizontal bands. There is also a distinctive change in the Tapestry's form of vegetation from about Scene 35; here the 'cruciform vegetal ornament' typical of the earlier sections of the Tapestry gives way to a 'scrolled' variety. Further evidence is provided by the fact that square or rectangular brooches are confined to the first three sections of the Tapestry (from Scene 9 until 33) although brooches are only worn by cloaked figures, which are themselves less prominent in the latter part of the Tapestry. All brooches in the latter part of the Tapestry are round (depicted from Scene 33), the explanation being that a circle would have been easier to stitch than a square.

It has already been noted that the same range of motifs for depicting armour was used throughout the Tapestry, providing evidence that the same team of embroiderers worked on all its extant lengths. However, whilst at the outset the different armour types are clearly distinguishable, the distinction blurs as the narrative continues, suggesting that the work was accelerated as it progressed.

We therefore see two distinct phases in the manufacture of the Tapestry: in phase one, the first two sections, there is a high degree of detail and ornament, and in phase two this is reduced. The second phase of the Tapestry begins at Section 3, where square brooches disappear and the ornament in the borders is simplified. The division is also reflected in a change of pace in the narrative. The scene-numbering system that was added to the backing-cloth is a testament to this. Most of the individual scenes (phases of actions) occur in the first three sections (Scenes 1-37), accounting for about 60 per cent of its scenes in about 40 per cent of its length. The weight of evidence therefore suggests that the rate of production increased as work progressed, and that all the sections were produced by the same team of embroiderers.

The artefacts and the date of the Tapestry

It is possible that the depicted artefacts shed light on the date of the Tapestry. Although the designer seems to have recreated contemporary garments, these cannot be precisely dated. The episcopal garments best parallel depictions in some late Anglo-Saxon illuminations, but twelfth-century examples of such vestments also survive. Likewise, parallels for the Tapestry's female dress are found in Romanesque illuminations, and therefore these elements must have been current after the Conquest. They cannot be dated more specifically, however; although their long sleeves and flared cuffs become prominent in the twelfth century, some examples are known from the second quarter of the eleventh.

Conical helmets with nasal guards point to a date no earlier than the second half of the eleventh century, on the basis of when they first occur in manuscript illumination. Similarly, the Tapestry's kite-shields are unlikely to have been current much before the Norman Conquest, although they do appear in some Ottonian illuminations, such as the Codex Aureus of Echternach (folio 78), and they were still in use until at least the twelfth century.

More problematic are the 'disc-shaped' pommels shown on many of the Tapestry's swords. According to David Edge and John Miles Paddock (1988), these were introduced into England from southern Europe during the first two crusades, which, superficially, would date the Tapestry to the late eleventh century at the earliest. However, as discussed, the disc-shaped pommel is unreliable dating evidence for two reasons. First, this type of sword pommel also occurs in late Anglo-Saxon manuscripts, which undermines the 'received' late date for its introduction into England. Secondly, it is possible that 'disc' pommels are merely irregularly drawn 'tea-cosy' or 'walnut' pommels; both types were current in the eleventh century.

The Tapestry's depiction of Mont-Saint-Michel further demonstrates the limited value of its 'artefacts' for precisely dating its production. The seven bays of the late eleventh-century nave, which we know were not finished by 1085, are not shown in the Tapestry. However, neither is there any indication of the earlier Carolingian church, which was removed to construct the new nave. The depiction of a Romanesque Westminster Abbey is more specific. The abbey was one of a few buildings constructed in the style in England before about 1070, but of course this only confirms the *terminus post quem* that we know from the historical events depicted. Likewise, the Tapestry's motted fortifications suggest a post-Conquest date, but not one that has a rigid chronology. In brief, whilst the exact dates of many of the Tapestry's real world elements are difficult to establish in detail, their general chronology ties in (if somewhat broadly) with the traditional dating of the work outlined in Chapter 1.

SYMBOLISM AND ICONOGRAPHY OF ATTRIBUTES

The designer makes good use of symbolism and iconography to highlight particular individuals and important phases in the narrative. Besides using conventional motifs he innovates, employing new artefact types, to ensure the narrative flows and is understood.

Affiliation

The designer uses specific attributes to distinguish between the Normans and English. Moustaches are used to denote Englishmen, though these are less in evidence after the Breton campaign (Scenes 16-21). Axes, excluding woodworking tools, are typically used by the English and this confirms our understanding of Anglo-Saxon warfare; only Guy (Figure 91) is otherwise shown holding an axe. Similarly, round-shields are used to identify the English (Figures 488, 497-8, 504, 510, 572-3, 599-600 & 603), especially in confused battle scenes; they only occur during the Hastings campaign, where they are used to distinguish between the opposing armies.

Normans are sometimes identified by their shaven hairstyles. It is not known whether this was a contemporary fashion, though it seems to be unique to the Tapestry; David Wilson (1985) likened the bare-necked Normans of the Tapestry to a description in Oxford, Bodleian Library, Hatton 115, but this refers to the shaven necks of Danes, not Normans, and the Normans were descended from Norwegian (not Danish) Vikings. The Tapestry designer also identified archery with Norman warfare, perhaps on the basis of his understanding of the role of archery at Hastings; in the Tapestry archers only appear at Hastings, and all but one of them (Figure 462) are Norman. The Tapestry also closely associates the horse with the Normans; apart from Harold, Englishmen only ride horses in England. As with archery, it is likely that the designer understood that horses played a fundamental part in William's success at Hastings.

Although other artefacts in the Tapestry have been interpreted as symbols of national identity, their association with either the English or Normans is coincidental. For example, Gale Owen-Crocker (1986) noted that the Normans display variation in their leg bands, which might distinguish them from the Anglo-Saxons. It has been noted that cross-garters are prominent in the second section of the Tapestry, but thereafter are mostly shown as horizontal bands. A likely explanation of this is that embroidering cross-garters took too long and hence was abandoned after the first phase, which of course recounts events in Normandy. It is thus coincidental that more Normans than English wear this type of leg band; indeed, Harold (Figure 187) and William (Figure 183) wear the same type of leg bands. Gale Owen-Crocker (1986) also identified culottes with the Normans, and it is certainly the case that it is predominately they who wear them. Nonetheless, some figures with moustaches (such as Figure 527), who are therefore English, also wear culottes. Hence, it seems unlikely that this attribute was intentionally used to differentiate between 'nationalities'. Indeed, it is a general feature of the Tapestry that there is no obvious national distinction in the clothes worn, though one may have existed in real life. Indeed, Orderic Vitalis in his *Historia Ecclesiastica* noted that, after the Conquest, 'you could see many villages or town markets filled with displays of French wares and merchandise, and observe the English, who had previously seemed contemptible to the French in their native dress completely transformed by foreign fashions'. Further, it is coincidental that all but one English ship is shown with a gap amidships. This feature occurs in the earlier parts of the Tapestry, and is discarded in the simpler later parts.

Status

Some artefacts indicate status, highlighting important figures. Clothing is a prime example; only the elite wear gowns or cloaks, which, to some extent, may have reflected real life. These garments are sometimes worn by those surrounding the focal figure, magnifying his or her importance. Likewise, jewellery is rare in the Tapestry. Brooches, for example, are only worn by cloaked figures and further indicate their status; they may be round, square or rectangular, and the quadrangle types seem to be reserved for the highest echelons, such as Guy (Figure 85), William (Figure 106), Edward (Figure 207) and Harold (Figure 239).

On many occasions, William is shown with ribbons hanging from his clothes; these are first shown tied to the feet of hawks (see A559 & A561), but they are probably just jesses. Thereafter, William has ribbons hanging from his knees (Figure 106), a braided cloak (Figure 118) and helmet (Figures 179 & 404). Such ribbons help identify the primacy of his status, especially in scenes where he is depicted alongside other high status characters or where he would otherwise be difficult to recognise. The clothing of other members of the highest echelons is also embellished with embroidery. For example, Edward (Figure 3) is once shown with vamp stripes on his shoes, and has quatrefoil motifs on his gown. Likewise, William (Figure 85) once wears a gown with embroidered bands just below the knees. Distinctive armour is used to the same end; a scaled type of mail (type a) is only worn by Guy (Figure 91), and a triangular patchwork mailed coat (type b) only by William (Figure 143) and Odo (Figure 534).

The designer also used animals, notably hawks and dogs, to highlight status. Hawks are mostly held by, or on behalf of, Harold, but are also associated with Guy and William. It is revealing that once Guy hands over Harold to William, only the duke is shown with a hawk; at the very moment when Harold's grasp on power begins to slip away, he loses this emblem of status. Hunting dogs (see Scenes 2 & 14) are also primarily associated with Harold, highlighting his status. Likewise, when Englishmen ride horses, they indicate the status of their rider; Harold is the main character distinguished in this manner (such as in Scenes 2, 24 & 50).

Some artefacts, though symbols of affiliation, also have additional iconographic significance. The designer used axes, for example, to denote persons of rank up to Scene 19, and thereafter to identify Anglo-Saxons in the mêlée of battle. Interestingly, the axe does not necessarily need to be held by the high status character but can be wielded by a companion nearby; examples are Figure 90 (Guy), Figure 205 who accompanies Figure 206 (Harold), Figure 208 who stands behind Figure 207 (Edward) and Figure 238 who holds an axe towards Figure 239 (Harold). Axes are also held by Figure 287 and associated with English positions during battle, such as Figures 497-8 who stand before the mortally wounded Leofwine, and Figures 599-600 who stand before Harold in the scene of his death. Similarly, round-shields are often held by companions of the English elite who are dead or dying, such as Figures 497-8 who stand before the fatally injured Leofwine, in the lower border of Scene 52 below 'regis', Figure 573, in the lower border of Scene 56, below 'cecidervnt', Figures 599-600, who stand before the mortally wounded Harold, and below, in the lower border of Scene 57.

Symbolism and narrative

The evidence suggests that it was not necessary for the artefacts used by the designer to highlight national affiliation or status to actually reflect real life. Their primary purpose was to ensure that the narrative flowed and could be clearly understood. Verisimilitude could be incidental to this function. Indeed, in certain circumstances it could impede it, while exaggeration might facilitate it.

For example, although it is impossible to be sure whether Englishmen generally wore moustaches or that most Normans shaved the back of their heads, it might be suggested with some confidence that this feature reflected real life, otherwise it would have been nonsensical to the contemporary viewer. At the same time, however, it should be expected that such characterisations are exaggerations and generalisations in the service of visual clarity. Likewise, whilst we have seen that the designer associates weapons with either the English or Normans on the basis of his understanding of how the opposing armies fought at Hastings, these attributes may have been overstated for visual lucidity. Indeed, we might imagine that round-shields, which in the Tapestry are only associated with the English, were also used by some Normans.

Clothing is the most realistic of the Tapestry's devices for indicating status. The gowns that distinguish men of high status perhaps reflect garments worn at the time. It is less likely, however, that cloaks and brooches would have been worn only by the elite. It is known that high status figures would have worn expensive jewellery made of gold and silver, perhaps also embellished with semi-precious and precious stones. The less well-off people would have worn base-metal replicas made of copper-alloy or pewter, recreating the appearance of gold or silver. Such distinctions would have been difficult to show in embroidery, and hence the designer seems to have chosen to indicate status by showing the elite wearing cloaks with brooches, and the lower echelons without them.

Embellishment of clothing, with vamp stripes and embroidery, reflects real-life attributes affordable to the elite, though the less well-off may have copied high status fashion in lesser quality materials. As with jewellery, distinguishing fabric quality would have been difficult in two-dimensional art. Perhaps more significant is the fact that embellished clothes would have signalled their quality to the contemporary, and this was used by the designer to highlight particular characters. The designer has used scaled and triangular types of armour in a similar manner.

Symbolism in the Tapestry and contemporary art

It is valuable to consider if artefacts are depicted as a mark of affiliation or status, as they might have been in contemporary art.

Unlike the Tapestry, most surviving works of art recreate well-defined biblical or spiritual events, whose characters often act within established iconographies and outside human time. Therefore, whilst the Tapestry designer has used contemporary or at least non-archaic attributes to indicate the national affiliation or status of his contemporary figures, the same would hardly be expected of much eleventh-century art.

It is rare elsewhere to find personal characteristics used to denote national affiliation. The depiction of Normans with shaven hair seems to be unique to the Tapestry; significantly, this feature does not seem to occur in illuminations, even those from Normandy. Similarly, in Anglo-Saxon illumination, such as Cotton Cleopatra C.viii (folios 9v & 12v) and Junius 11 (pages 44, 54 & 58), only bearded figures have moustaches, and there is no evidence to suggest they have been used to distinguish 'nationality'. This confirms the fact that the designer exaggerates the currency of moustaches for the purposes of his narrative.

Likewise, although the Tapestry designer associates particular types of weapons with 'national' identity, this does not seem to occur elsewhere in contemporary art. Whilst in the Tapestry, axes and round-shields are largely reserved for Anglo-Saxons, in pre-Conquest illuminations they are used by people on both sides of a conflict. Thus, in the Harley 603 Psalter (folio 8v), the opposing armies of Psalm 16 both carry the same type of round-shield, while in Psalm 53 (folio 29v), the psalmist carries a kite-shield, as do his enemies in Psalm 54 (folio 30r). Similarly, in Cambridge, Corpus Christi College 23 (folios 18r), two figures with round-shields fight one another.

Although contemporary artists, in contrast to the Tapestry designer, do not seem to have used artefacts to indicate national affiliation, the reverse is true in regard to status. Thus, a robed Moses stands before Israelites in tunics in the Hexateuch (folio 139v), and a robed Christ greets the people of Jerusalem who wear tunics in the Tiberius Psalter (folio 11). Similarly, the cloak, together with its brooch fastener, is used to identify the elite. The ancestors of Christ in the Boulogne Gospels (folios 11r & 11v) for example, are shown wearing cloaks and brooches. Likewise, in Junius 11 (page 54) Abraham is shown cloaked, while Tubal-Cain is not. Ribbons of the sort seen on William's clothes in the Bayeux Tapestry, which highlight his status, also occur in Carolingian and Ottonian art. They are, for example, associated with the Emperor Lothar in the Lothar Gospels (f.1v). This said, in some Ottonian illustrations they are worn by lesser mortals, such as the Romans in the Codex Egberti (folio 22), and an inhabitant of Jericho in the Pericopes Book of Reichenau (folio 119). Such ribbons are less common in Anglo-Saxon illuminations, but are clearly used as a symbol of status; an example is the ribboned cloak of King Cnut in the New Minster Liber Vitae (folio 6). Further, it is common elsewhere in contemporary art, as in the Tapestry, for the elite to wear ornate garments, embellished with embroidery and jewellery; such as the ornate clothes of King Edgar in Cotton Tiberius A.iii (folio 2v), and the embroidered robes of Aldhelm in London, Lambeth Palace, 200, (folio 68v) and St Benedict in Arundel 155 (folio 133).

In other respects, the designer shows greater innovation in using artefacts to highlight status than contemporary artists. Patterned armour like that of William, Odo and Guy, for example, is seemingly not used for this purpose in Anglo-Saxon illuminations; an example of patterned armour in Anglo-Saxon art appears in Bodleian Library, Douce 296 (folio 40v), though here the armour is not used to highlight status. A Romanesque parallel might be Boethius in Cambridge, University Library, Ii.3.12 (folio 61v), who wears a gown patterned in scales, similar to the decorated armour of Guy in the Tapestry. Neither do hawks or dogs tend to be symbols of status. These differences are explained by the dominance of biblical and hagiographical subject matter in early medieval art, where such creatures have different, or little, iconographic meaning.

Uniqueness and naturalism

The uniqueness of the Tapestry, and the fact that it is a new picture-cycle narrating a recent historical event, impresses its 'naturalism' upon the modern viewer, to a greater extent than any other example of eleventh-century art. Yet, the break with established conventions is actually much less than is generally assumed. Significantly, however, the designer does expand traditional methods of pictorial narrative.

The designer takes time to illustrate the progression from one scene to the next, whereas in most eleventh-century art this is merely implied. In Junius 11 and the Old English Hexateuch, for example, the act of shipbuilding is largely implicit, but in the Tapestry (Scenes 35-6) the process is shown in more detail; in Junius 11, Noah is shown building the Ark on page 65, but by page 66 it is shown complete with animals aboard. Likewise, the Hexateuch shows the Ark being built (folio 13v), but it is complete thereafter (folios 14v-15v). Hence, the Tapestry gives the impression that its designer was familiar with every detail depicted. This encourages exaggerated confidence in the accuracy of these illustrations.

The fact that the Tapestry's visual narrative continues at one level, rather like a modern day cartoon, and is, in the most part, chronological, makes it seem naturalistic (especially to the twenty-first century mindset). In contemporary art, even in contemporary narrative art, this is less common.

Of further interest are the Tapestry's incidental details of everyday life that give the impression that the designer observed such elements first-hand, though this is unlikely to have been the case. For example, in Scene 45, two men (Figures 390-1) are shown fighting or play-fighting with spades. Likewise, in Scene 53, a soldier (Figure 518) unseats a knight by unfastening the girth of his saddle. Further, in Scene 25/6, one of the Tapestry's characters (Figure 209) places the weather vane on top of Westminster Abbey. Although such flourishes are typical of Anglo-Saxon art, especially manuscript initials (for example, an armed figure menacingly grabs another by his leg in Bodleian Library, Tanner 10, folio 115v), the Tapestry seems to have a naturalistic edge, since these details are used to embellish a contemporary event.

Identity and emphasis

The designer was an expert at using attributes to highlight significant characters, some of whom are identified by the use of established iconography. For example, Edward (Figure 3), Guy (Figure 85), Harold (Figure 242), Odo, Robert and William (Figures 384-6) are all shown enthroned, indicating their importance. This convention is commonplace in contemporary art; examples include David in the Tiberius Psalter (folio 30r) and Cain enthroned in Junius 11 (page 57) (60). Likewise, as we have seen, Odo in the feast scene (Figure 380) is shown at the centre of a semi-circular table, paralleling the representation of

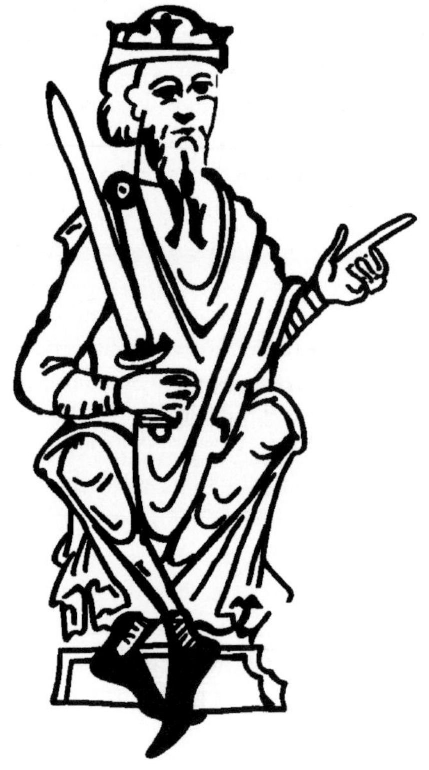

60 Cain enthroned in Junius 11 (page 57)

Christ at the Last Supper in the St Augustine's Gospels (folio 125r). Similarly, many of the Tapestry's important characters, such as Edward (Figures 3 & 207) and William (Figure 385), are shown larger than their companions. Comparisons in contemporary art are common, and include King Edgar in Cotton Vespasian A.viii (folio 2v) and Enoch in Junius 11 (page 58). Likewise, the small size of the character traditionally believed to be Turold (Figure 95) serves to highlight him; parallels for identifying a character in this particular way (perhaps ironically) have not been found in contemporary art.

It is also apparent that while some of the Tapestry's artefacts are not indicative of status in their own right, the designer has innovatively used them to draw attention to important characters. For example, although, as has already been seen, round-shields are used to identify the English, particularly during the mêlée of battle at Hastings, they also help to highlight the death of significant characters, such as Gyrth (Figures 497-8) in Scene 52 and Harold (Figures 591 & 593) in Scene 57. Specifically, it is the isolation of particular artefacts in the Tapestry that makes them significant. For example, a cloak worn by a high status character amongst other cloaked figures, such as Harold (Figure 9) and his entourage in Scene 2, is not a distinguishing attribute. In contrast, a cloaked character shown in isolation, such as Harold (Figure 74) in Scene 8, stands out. Where an artefact alone does not necessarily indicate status, the designer employs other attributes to highlight his most important characters. For example, in Scene 2 where the cloak does not distinguish Harold from his companions, the earl (Figure 9) is also shown wearing spurs, holding a hawk, and accompanied by dogs.

The designer also contrived scenes to emphasise important people. For example, in the aforementioned Scene 2, where Harold (Figure 9) is shown on horseback leading a hunting party, the designer has used specific features to distinguish the earl from his companions. In terms of the main narrative, this scene is of little significance. Hence, it seems that the designer has conceived this scene specifically for the purpose of introducing Harold to the viewer and highlighting the fact that he is a character of status and importance. It is hardly a coincidence that his name appears for the first time in the accompanying inscription. Similarly, the feast scene (Scene 43) showing Bishop Odo (Figure 380) blessing the food and drink is designed to emphasise his importance within the narrative. By using established iconography to liken Odo to Christ, it emphasises his spiritual role in the Norman Conquest of England.

CHAPTER 7

CONCLUSION

As stated in the introduction, this book is neither intended to offer a comprehensive study of the Bayeux Tapestry, nor to summarise the scholarly debate this most famous embroidery has attracted over the past few centuries. Indeed, so much has been written on the Tapestry that such a task is almost impossible, though Shirley Ann Brown's 1988 bibliography (and the forthcoming sequel) of Tapestry studies offers an invaluable start. Instead, I hope I have provided the reader with a general introduction to the Bayeux Tapestry and highlighted some of the most interesting and informative aspects of this fascinating and unique example of medieval art. To this end I have concentrated on aspects of the Tapestry that most interest me, in particular the extent to which the embroidery reflects the real world of the eleventh century and the influence of contemporary art and art-historical tradition upon its designer. I think that this area of study is particularly important because it impacts on our general understanding of life at the time of the Norman Conquest.

The Bayeux Tapestry is perhaps the best-known contemporary source and illustrated narrative of that time and, as such, it is invaluable for historians, archaeologists and art-historians – especially if its story, both imagery and words, is considered accurate. It is impossible to be a hundred per cent certain about many aspects of history in the late Anglo-Saxon or early Norman period, but the subject matter of this study reminds us that, as with any historical source, it is best to be cautious when drawing upon the Tapestry for an understanding of life in the eleventh century. That is not to say the Bayeux Tapestry should be ignored or its historical value underestimated, but its true potential can be recognised and utilised only by asking simple questions of it (such as who, when, where, and why). The answers will hopefully allow a better understanding of the influences and biases that may have affected it, for better or for worse.

WHO, WHEN, WHERE AND WHY?

Although we do not know the identity of the Tapestry's designer, most historians believe its patron to be Bishop Odo of Bayeux, half-brother of William the Conqueror.

It is impossible to ever know the exact relationship between the two men (patron and designer), but we might assume that the patron would have had at least some initial input into the design; perhaps Odo just outlined or suggested the basic thrust of the Tapestry's narrative. Indeed, study of the artefacts depicted in the Tapestry and other aspects of the work suggest Odo was little involved with any detail in the Tapestry, including the depiction of individual characters or even its major scenes. Likewise, Odo probably had very little to do with the design of the work once it had been commissioned. Moreover, it seems probable that even the designer himself did not work on the Tapestry on a day-to-day basis, and may have never seen the final product. Instead, the embroidery was left to embroiderers, and consequently the design was likely to have been improved, altered and amended. This would have mostly been purposeful, but not always, as there are obvious embroidery errors. If the patron had offered any clear ideas about the Tapestry's purpose, message (assuming it had one) and what it should show, these may have been lost in the interpretations of the designer and thereafter his team of embroiderers.

Given that Odo is believed to have been the Bayeux Tapestry's patron, it seems likely that it was produced in England, probably by an English designer and almost certainly English embroiderers. As discussed in Chapters 1 and 5 the Tapestry ties in well with Canterbury-produced illuminated manuscripts, though much of its design and style compare well with contemporary art of the eleventh century in general. As Odo was Earl of Kent he would have been in an ideal location to commission such a work, though it is conceivable that if the designer referred to drawings in Canterbury libraries (Christ Church and St Augustine's) then it is plausible the embroidery could have been done elsewhere; favourite suggestions include Wilton and Winchester.

Considering the evidence, it seems likely that the Bayeux Tapestry was produced soon after the events it depicts, thus making it one of the earliest records of the Norman Conquest of England. If Bishop Odo was its patron, it is likely to have been manufactured prior to his death in 1097, and most likely before 1082, when he was imprisoned by William. Whilst Odo was released from prison upon William the Conqueror's death in 1087, he was shortly thereafter banished by William Rufus. Furthermore, the suggestion of a date range of 1072 to 1077 by Richard Gameson (1997) is based on the notion that Abbot Scotland of St Augustine's Abbey (formerly of Mont-Saint-Michel) may have influenced the depiction of Mont-Saint-Michel. The year 1077 was also a momentous date, as it coincided with the consecration of Odo's cathedral at Bayeux, so perhaps the Tapestry was made for that (though many modern scholars are now unconvinced that this was the case).

The dating of the Tapestry is important, as an earlier date implies that its designer was more familiar with the events depicted, and obviously those that viewed the Tapestry would also be aware of the accuracy or otherwise of the Tapestry's tale. However, both literary and artistic conventions in the eleventh century differ from those today; indeed, it would have been acceptable to present a record of real-life events in a way that was contrary to reality (as today's observer would see it) especially if circumstances suited it, or events demanded it.

No contemporary record exists to explain why the Bayeux Tapestry was produced, and it is unlikely that this will ever be known for sure. However, if Odo did commission the Tapestry for his cathedral in Bayeux, then many things begin to make sense. It would explain why Odo and 'his men' have such an important role in the Tapestry, especially when compared to other contemporary sources. It would reveal why Bayeux itself also has a central role in the Tapestry's narrative, the place where Harold 'makes a sacred oath' to William. It would explain why the Tapestry was almost certainly produced in Canterbury and eventually came to be rediscovered in Bayeux. It would also clarify why some events important to the English perspective of the events leading to the Norman Conquest are absent from the Tapestry, such as the defence of the English coast and Harold's defeat of Harald Hardrada.

Traditionally, the Bayeux Tapestry has been seen as a piece of blatant Norman propaganda, glorifying Odo and the Normans at the expense of the English. Indeed, there seem to be many parallels between the Tapestry's story and Norman apologists, such as William of Poitiers, William of Jumièges, and the *Carmen de Hastingae Proelio*. However, in recent times this view has been revised with the idea that the propaganda aspect has perhaps been overemphasised in the past. Historians have observed that the Bayeux Tapestry, unlike contemporary Norman sources, recognises Harold as king – he has the title *Rex* and is shown in full regalia. He is depicted as a great lord, a man of wealth and power. He demonstrates bravery – rescuing men from the River Couesnon – and has a religious conscience. Such 'pro-English elements' have suggested to some scholars, such as David Bernstein (1986) and Bernard Bachrach (1988), that the Tapestry narrative might have meant different things to different audiences, and even contained subversive messages; perhaps English embroiderers used this commission as an opportunity to snipe at the Normans and ridicule their leaders.

It seems entirely plausible that if the Tapestry was manufactured in England, there was potential for the work to reflect the opinions and ideas of 'Englishmen'. Whilst it is possible that the English designer or embroiders might have inserted details of jest or comedy into the Bayeux Tapestry (as illuminators of contemporary manuscripts did) it seems a rather dangerous art, especially given the status and reputation of the Tapestry's patron, to risk life and limb by using such a work to make a political statement. It is all too easy to become sidelined by conspiracy theories, which can never really be proven or solved. This said, it is important to bear in mind that any interpretation or understanding of the Tapestry must consider that it is now believed to be an English work produced for a Norman patron.

FROM CANTERBURY TO BAYEUX

Since the Bayeux Tapestry is in fact embroidery, and most probably produced by a Canterbury designer, then it might be best described as the 'Canterbury Embroidery'. However, to again use Shirley Ann Brown's (1988) words, 'to call it by another name…would seem pedantic'. Indeed, the probability that the Tapestry was commissioned by the Bishop of Bayeux, and the fact that it was rediscovered in Bayeux, where it is now exhibited, means that it makes sense that the Tapestry is prefixed with the town's name, even if some people who are unfamiliar with the work assume that it was also made there.

Whilst we do not know how the Bayeux Tapestry ended up in Bayeux, it seems plausible that it was sent there by Odo, perhaps for the consecration of his cathedral in 1077, or after he was banished from England in 1088. Whilst the Tapestry survives today as a great 'icon' of medieval art, it is easy to suppose that this must also have been the view in the second half of the eleventh century, which might not actually have been the case. The (almost certainly fictitious) tapestry described by Abbot Baudri of Bourgueil was a much more impressive and expensive affair than the Bayeux Tapestry, said to consist of silver, gold and silk threads and embellished with gems and pearls. Shirley Ann Brown and Michael Herren (1994) believed that Baudri must have known of the Bayeux Tapestry, though this can never be proven. It is not known if other works similar to the Bayeux Tapestry, or that invented by Baudri, actually existed, but it is known that richer and finer works were created at the time. Extant examples, though fragmentary, include richly decorated embroideries interred with St Cuthbert (who had died in 687), which date to the tenth century.

If the Bayeux Tapestry was made for Odo's cathedral then it is difficult to see how it was exhibited. It has been traditionally believed that it was hung around the nave of Bayeux Cathedral, as described in the 1476 inventory of the cathedral's 'Treasures', which seems to have been the practice in later years. If this was the case then it would have been dwarfed in the present cathedral, and probably that of Odo's. Anyone viewing the Tapestry could not have easily seen any of its detail or read the inscriptions (assuming they were literate) though this was perhaps typical of most works of art exhibited in a great church. Shirley Ann Brown (1988) has also noted that Odo's Romanesque cathedral would have been even darker than the Gothic structure that survives today. It is also the case that hanging such a textile in the cathedral for long periods of time would have caused irretrievable damage to the embroidery. Perhaps the Tapestry may have only been displayed periodically, which seems to tie in what we know of how it was exhibited in the later medieval period.

Albert Marginan (1902a) seems to have been the first to propose that the Tapestry was not made for display in Bayeux Cathedral, but was instead made for a secular residence, such as a great hall in a palace or a castle – a theory advocated by Charles Dodwell (1966). Dodwell, like Otto Wekmeister (1976) and Shirley Ann Brown (1977), expressed concern that the Tapestry's subject matter, particularly its lewd imagery, made it inappropriate for display in an ecclesiastical building. This theory makes little sense, however, as the demarcation between secular and religious art was not as obvious in the medieval world as today; indeed, the Church authorities in the fifteenth century clearly did not have a significant problem with displaying the Bayeux Tapestry in a church. Of course this is not to say that the Tapestry was unsuitable for display in a secular residence. Indeed, its form may have suited it. Gale Owen-Crocker (2005) has noted that the juxtaposition of certain scenes in the Tapestry suited display in a rectangular structure. This theory was advanced by Chris Henige (2005), who even suggested possible buildings in which the Tapestry may have been displayed, including the keeps of Rochester and Dover Castles. It is perhaps little appreciated that wall hangings, like furniture, were portable and could be moved by their owner from one place to another. It seems unlikely, therefore, that a textile hanging would have been made to fit into a particular place within a particular edifice. From this perspective, if the Tapestry was made for Bayeux Cathedral, then it seems unlikely the structure of the cathedral actually dictated its design.

Displaying the Bayeux Tapestry has also proved a problem in the modern era. The Tapestry's long, narrow size has made it tricky to display it satisfactorily in a modern building. The most unsuitable method was employed during the early nineteenth century, when the Tapestry was shown to its visitors at Bayeux Town Hall by winding it out using a contraption which Hudson Gurney (1817) likened to something 'which lets down the buckets to a well'. Thereafter, from 1842, the Tapestry was displayed as a single length and at eye level in the Municipal Library. This was a vast improvement, though it seems the Tapestry was folded backwards and forwards (in a zigzag fashion), because of the size limitations of the exhibition room. In 1913, the Tapestry was moved, for conservation reasons, to the upper floor of the Hôtel du Doyen (formerly the Old Episcopal Palace), where it was displayed in a less suitable space. Here, in order to view the Tapestry, visitors followed its story around the outside sides of a square display, before going through a gap in the display to examine the remainder of the Tapestry from within. No doubt, as interest in the Tapestry increased, this display method would have inhibited proper viewing of the Tapestry and caused something of a bottleneck for people visiting (or who had visited) the final half of the exhibit. Here it remained until the outbreak of the Second World War, when it was taken off display. Following the liberation of France, the Bayeux Tapestry was displayed at the Louvre from 10 November to 15 December 1944, where it was possible to view the Tapestry as a continuous length. This proved to be a major advantage for the visitor, and later inspired the Bayeux authorities to remodel the Hôtel du Doyen to allow better viewing of the Tapestry. Whilst the new gallery was being prepared, there was a strong desire to have the Tapestry on display, so it was provisionally agreed to reinstall the famous embroidery in its old exhibition case in the Hôtel du Doyen and thereafter in the Chapel of the Municipal School, where it was exhibited between 28 March and 31 May 1948. On 6 June 1948, the Tapestry's new home was inaugurated, apparently offering an excellent viewing experience for visitors and was easily accessible. However, as the Bayeux Tapestry became more popular it was realised the exhibition was increasingly inadequate and unsafe, so again the Bayeux authorities began the search to find a new display space. By the mid 1970s it was agreed to remodel the Grand Seminary to home the Tapestry. Between 2 November 1982 and 6 February 1983 the Bayeux Tapestry was removed from display and conserved prior to exhibition in the Centre Guillaume le Conquérant, which is where the Tapestry remains housed to this day. In this current exhibition, the Tapestry is viewed at eye-level on the outside of a u-shaped case, in a secure environment. The gallery lighting is subdued so visitors have an excellent view of the textile and its detail. Ideally, the Tapestry would be viewed in a single length, but few 68m+ rooms exist in Bayeux and the costs of again building such an exhibition space would no doubt need to be justified.

DISCUSSION AND DEBATE

Upon the rediscovery of the Bayeux Tapestry in the early eighteenth century, the first scholars interested in the work deliberated its possible date, provenance and patron. In this respect, it is interesting that within the first hundred years of Tapestry studies, theories were first proposed that are more or less established as fact today (that is to say, the Tapestry is broadly contemporary with the events it depicts, and it was probably produced in England on the orders of Bishop Odo of Bayeux). However, there was always dissenting opinion, and there will always be.

It has already been noted that it was local tradition that the Bayeux Tapestry was produced by Queen Matilda, and until relatively recently it was known as 'Matilda's Tapestry'. Hence, many of the Tapestry's earliest scholars believed the embroidery was fairly contemporary with the events it depicts, though some, such as Lord Lyttelton (1769) and the Abbé de la Rue (1811), dated it to the twelfth century; Bolton Corney (1836) even suggested an early thirteenth-century date. Whilst the earliest scholars generally accepted the tradition that Matilda had the Tapestry made, even suggesting she might have worked it with her own hands, Antoine Lancelot (1732) recognised, early on, that Odo had an important role in the Tapestry, beyond what one might expect. However, it was more than 90 years later that Honoré François Delauney (1824) first presented the hypothesis that Bishop Odo was the Tapestry's patron. So convincing was Delauney's theory that subsequent research has mostly built upon his conclusions, rather than offering any compelling challenge. However, John Gosling (1990) and Carola Hicks (2006) recently proposed the Tapestry was made on the orders of Queen Edith, whilst Andrew Bridgeford (2004) has suggested Eustace of Boulogne was the patron. It seems most unlikely that either hypothesis will become established.

Likewise, although the first Tapestry scholars believed the work was made in Normandy, an English provenance was soon proposed. A letter written by 'S.L.' (1803) to the *Gentleman's Magazine* noted the fame of English embroidery in the eleventh century and soon after Francis Douce (1814) stated the Tapestry itself was actually of English manufacture. However, it was not until the theory that Odo was the Tapestry's patron became established that the link with England made much sense. For a long time, there was little consensus on exactly where the Tapestry may have been produced, assuming it was made in England. Some, such as William Lethaby (1917), and more recently David Wilson (1985), have favoured Winchester, whilst John Gosling (1990) considered Wilton. Édélestand du Méril (1862) even suggested Waltham Abbey (which was founded by Harold). However, the general consensus is that the Tapestry was made in Canterbury for the reasons outlined in the introduction; a theory supported by Frank Stenton (1957), Richard Gameson (1997), and Cyril Hart (1997, 2000 & 2005), amongst others. This said, an English provenance was not universally supported. Eugène Anquetil (1907) and Wolfgang Grape (1994) believed the Tapestry was made in Bayeux. Likewise, Albert Levé (1919) thought the Tapestry was produced in Normandy, perhaps by a designer from the Abbey of Saint-Bertin at St Omer. Similarly, George Beech (2005) recently proposed that the Bayeux Tapestry was produced at St Florent, Saumur, in the Loire Valley, though it seems unlikely this theory will favour much support.

The characters depicted in the Bayeux Tapestry have also attracted a great deal of scholarly attention. Much of this has attempted to explain who certain characters are and why they appear in the Tapestry. Perhaps the most famous of these is the lady identified as Ælfgyva (Figure 135) in the inscription, who is shown being touched on the face by an unnamed cleric. The fact that the nude figure (Figure 137) in the lower border replicates the pose of the cleric above (Figure 136) clearly has the whiff of scandal, though what this might be continues to perplex historians. Numerous theories have been proposed. Some scholars, such as Denis Butler (1966), believe Ælfgyva in the Tapestry to be a daughter of William who was to marry Harold, whilst Henri Prentout (1921-2) even suggested Ælfgyva might have supervised the work. The fact of the matter is no one knows for sure, since no surviving historical source refers to the enigmatic scandal.

Another of the Tapestry's mysterious figures is the figure first identified by Charles Stothard (1819) as Eustace of Boulogne (Figure 543). The inscription (E[...]TIVS) only gives a partial reading of this figure's name, but Eustace fits and seems to make sense within the historical content. Although Eustace was out of favour with William soon after the Conquest after partaking in a rebellion against him, the two men seem to have been reconciled before 1075 or 1077; their friendship is referred to by William of Poitiers. However, recently David Spear (2007) proposed that the figure could actually be Robert of Mortain. Whilst this is an interesting alternative to the Eustace theory, it has not yet become mainstream thinking amongst Tapestry scholars.

Bolton Corney (1836) first identified Turold, Wadard and Vital, who are named in the inscription, as vassals of Odo – a theory developed further by others, including Daniel Rock (1870) and Hirokazu Tsurushima (1985). The fact that these three men are mentioned in association with Odo in Domesday Book has proved crucial in the establishment and acceptance of this theory. However, it still remains to be discovered why, in particular, these three individuals were chosen to appear.

Bizarrely, some of the Bayeux Tapestry's unnamed characters seem easier to identify. For example, it is pretty much accepted that the characters at Edward's deathbed include Earl Harold (Figure 229), Edith (Figure 228), Archbishop Stigand (Figure 230) and Robert fitz Wimarch (Figure 232). Whilst there is little in the Tapestry to independently confirm the identity of these figures, the Tapestry's imagery ties in well with historical accounts of Edward's death described by the *Vita Eadwardi*, and this is the basis for identifying the characters depicted. That said, most of the Tapestry's characters are anonymous, deliberately so.

Several historians and archaeologists, many of whom have been mentioned above within the context of analysing the extent to which the Bayeux Tapestry reflects the real world of the eleventh century, have examined the Tapestry's detail in the hope of learning more about everyday artefacts and structures. In earlier years of Tapestry scholarship, such aspects were examined in the context of wider observations of the textile, but increasingly scholars have examined individual aspects in detail; important in this respect was the work of Simone Bertrand (1966) and Lucien Musset (2002). Other aspects concentrated on specific details, and the Battle Conference on Anglo-Norman Studies established in 1978 has been important in this respect. Individual aspects attracting scholarly attention include the Tapestry's flags, which have been studied by Gilbert French (1857), E.M.C. Barraclough (1969) and Derek Renn (1993), the Tapestry's buildings, by Urban Holmes (1959), Vivian Mann (1975) and Marla Schwartz (1994), the Tapestry's castles, by Reginald Allen Brown (1989b), Arnold Taylor (1992) and others, and details of the Tapestry's ships, by André Sleewyk (1981) and Owain Roberts (1981). There have also been grand tomes that have attempted the impossible task of trying to examine the Bayeux Tapestry as a whole, including those of Frank Stenton (1957), David Wilson (1985 – thankfully reprinted in 2004) and Lucien Musset (2002).

The relationship between the Bayeux Tapestry and French epic poetry – known as *chanson de geste* – has attracted some discussion, including that of Gaston Paris (1902), and particularly Charles Dodwell (1966). Three particular sources have been studied in this respect in relation to the Tapestry; *La Chanson de Roland*, Wace's *Roman de Rou* of about 1170, and the *Carmen de Hastingae Proelio*. However, the late date of *chansons de geste* and the relatively early date of the Tapestry make it unlikely that the Bayeux embroidery is of the same genre, unless it is an early prototype. Similarly, Gale Owen-Crocker (1998) has compared the Tapestry's story with the heroic Old English poem *Beowulf*. Instead, perhaps, the Bayeux Tapestry is best seen as a visual record in the same vein as contemporary written accounts, such as William of Poitiers, William of Jumièges and Eadmer, and the parallels and differences have been endlessly discussed by historians, from the earliest days of Tapestry studies.

The hidden meanings of the Bayeux Tapestry, alluded to above, have attracted much discussion, particularly in recent times. The most famous of these studies was that of David Bernstein (1986) which explored *The Mystery of the Bayeux Tapestry*. Bernstein was convinced that the Tapestry's Anglo-Saxon designer was using the embroidery to subtly insert his own interpretation of history, and that Old Testament iconography was the prime source influencing the Tapestry's design. Likewise, Bernard Bachrach (1988) essentially argued that the English cunningly inserted hidden meanings in the Tapestry that would have been obvious to Anglo-Saxons, but missed by a Norman audience. As Shirley Ann Brown (2004) has noted, given that England in the post-Conquest period was essentially an Anglo-Norman society, it is not obvious that such a clear demarcation between the English and Normans actually existed in reality.

In a similar vein, historians have studied the relationship between the Bayeux Tapestry's main frieze and its borders. Many scholars, including Hélène Chefneux (1934), Léon Herrmann (1939) and Francis Wormald (1957), highlighted the apparent similarities between some of the Tapestry's border details and Aesop's fables. This has given rise to the hypothesis that these images convey messages that relate to the events in the main frieze. Advocates of the view that there was a profound relationship between the Tapestry's borders and the main frieze include James Bard McNulty (1989), David Bernstein (1986) and Dan Terkla (1995); Bernstein was keen on inferring particular meaning in the Tapestry's individual creatures, not just those in the 'fables'. This contrasted with the views of Carola Hicks (1992), amongst others, who believed the borders are 'decorative' and 'that it is not part of their function to contribute to the message of the central text'. However, she was clear that 'pure ornament does not imply ornament without meaning'. Indeed, it seems reasonable that border motifs, such as the Tapestry's fables, were selected as they broadly complemented the main thrust of the messages in the main frieze, whilst others were typical of those that commonly decorated eleventh-century embroidery.

Likewise, the relationship between the Bayeux Tapestry's inscriptions and the main frieze has been studied at length. It seems logical to suppose the inscription was added to clarify the visual narrative and identify certain characters, though it is apparent there is no consistency as to when text is added or omitted. Occasionally, the lack of text can be frustrating for the scholar; a few words here and there might have given clues to certain conversations or identified certain figures. Some scholars, such as Jan Messent (1999) believe the text was added later, perhaps as an afterthought. The inscriptions provide crucial evidence supporting the view that the Tapestry was made in England – a view supported by most. It has also been noted that the inscriptions may be significant in advancing the understanding of how the Bayeux Tapestry was designed and made. However, also of interest to scholars are the sources upon which the Tapestry's textual narrative may have been based. The Tapestry's visual narrative has been reasonably paralleled with the accounts of William of Poitiers, William of Jumièges and Eadmer, in particular, but in reality all of these sources will, at times, parallel one another, since they describe the same historical event. However, this does not prove one way or another whether or not the designer knew or used any other extant contemporary source. Indeed, Bernard Bachrach (1988) believed the Tapestry's inscriptions were an abbreviated form of a longer text, now (unfortunately) lost; of course it is a theory that can never be proven or disputed. In contrast, Richard Brilliant (1991) thought the text was deliberately abbreviated, but may have offered prompts for a jongleur, using the Tapestry as a prop for telling a tale.

In a similar manner, some scholars, such as Andreas Kuhn (1992) and Gale Owen-Crocker (2007), have studied the gestures of characters depicted in the Tapestry, in an attempt to interpret their meaning and dialogue. Such theories are interesting, and stimulate further debate, but are ultimately relatively theoretical, as it is impossible to have a comprehensive understanding of the medieval mindset.

In recent times, it has become fashionable to explore the Bayeux Tapestry in new and imaginative ways. Advances in philosophy, gender studies, filmic theory and other studies have seen Tapestry research take new, sometime obscure, directions. For example, Gerald Bond (1995) interpreted the scene of Ælfgyva and a cleric (Scene 15) as the subjection of female sexuality to male dominance. Likewise, Rouben Cholakian (1998) uses Freudian and Marxist principles to understand the Tapestry, and sees class struggle, the suffering of women and pacifism as key messages within the narrative. Suzanne Lewis (1999) attempted to explore 'how the Tapestry tells its story and shapes the responses of reader-viewers'. In essence, her theory proposes that the Tapestry invites different interpretation depending on the audience, though was primarily designed to convince an Anglo-Saxon audience of the inevitability of the conclusion – the Norman Conquest. In general, such theories are impossible to prove and opinion is divided on how much this adds to the advancement of our understanding of the Tapestry.

The history of the Bayeux Tapestry has also attracted some attention. Particularly useful in this respect are the works of Simone Bertrand (1957), Shirley Ann Brown (1988) and Carola Hicks (2006). Also intriguing is the history of the Tapestry during the Second World War, first recorded by René Dubosq (1951), but expanded upon by Sylvette Lemagnen (2004) and Carola Hicks (2006) following the discovery of important documentary evidence, which was handed over to the authorities of Bayeux by the widow of Herbert Jankuhn (who headed the German team that studied the Tapestry) on 18 November 1994.

Opportunities to study the material composition of the Bayeux Tapestry have been few and far between, and hence there are few works that offer a comprehensive technical analysis of the Tapestry's fabric. In 1864, Alfred Darcel, though examining another textile showing the life of St Martin, did make some observations on the Tapestry's embroidery work, including the stitching, wools and dyes used. More recent studies were undertaken by Simone Bertrand (1957 & 1960). Likewise, some scholars, such as Desirée Koslin (1990) and Gale Owen-Crocker (1994), have investigated how the Tapestry may have been made, and it is hoped major advances in this respect will be made in the future.

It was not until 1982 that scholars had the opportunity to analyse the Tapestry fabric, when it was removed from display (between 2 November 1982 and 6 February 1983) for conservation prior to exhibition in the Centre Guillaume le Conquérant. At a Colloquium at Cerisy in 1999 this research became known to a wider audience, and was subsequently published in 2004. It reported on how the project was set up and organised, revealing that the Tapestry's fabric and dyes had been analysed to a level not previously seen and commenting on the restoration of the embroidery. The researchers also analysed the Tapestry's 'modern' backing fabric, showing it to be formed from reused cloth. They also published the results of scientific texts, revealing how the woollen threads used in the Tapestry were spun and which colorants were used in the fibres, in adddition a microbiological analysis of the Tapestry's fabric was undertaken.

In the nineteenth century, the Bayeux Tapestry was heavily restored, and these restorations were studied by Charles Dawson (1907). Recently, David Hill and John McSween (forthcoming, 2008) have been using Bernard de Mountfaucon and Charles Stothard's facsimiles of the Bayeux Tapestry, and images of the reverse of the textile, to identify restorations in the Tapestry in order to gain a better understanding of how the work originally appeared. This research offers a tantalising opportunity to learn more about how the work was designed and produced.

FUTURE STUDY

It might be reasonable to believe that all that could be said about the Bayeux Tapestry has been said, and therefore it is unlikely that much more will be written about it. However, for better or worse, the reality is probably very different. The fact that the Tapestry is so famous, and that there is such a public interest in it, makes it certain that more will be written, much of it adding little more to what is already known. However, some research will be new. It is also important to inform the general reader of such developments – one of the purposes of this study.

So, what might be expected from future Bayeux Tapestry research? Of course, this is an impossible question to answer, as it cannot be predicted what might be revealed through examination of the relevant and various sources or any possible investigations of the Tapestry fabric itself. It is also impossible to know what new sources might come to light, or might be revealed from a subsequent analysis of them. So, perhaps it is better to ask what is desirable to know (that is not already known)?

Firstly, it would be great to have some confirmation that the basics are right. Scholars are probably right to be fairly confident that the Bayeux Tapestry was made in England in the second half of the eleventh century by a designer using Canterbury manuscripts, and that Bishop Odo of Bayeux was the Tapestry's patron. However, it would be wonderful to know this for sure. Possibly further scrutiny of manuscript illuminations will reveal the actual exemplars the designer used, and this in turn might reveal further clues about who the designer was, where he worked and what libraries he visited. From this perspective it would be intriguing to learn more about the designer, such as who he was, whether he also illuminated manuscripts (as has been suggested in this study), and whether he was involved throughout the project, or just provided a design from which the embroiders worked (another theory presented here).

It would also be interesting to discover more about where the Bayeux Tapestry might have been displayed, as this might reveal further clues about the Tapestry's purpose and function. It would be good to know if the Tapestry was merely a decorative record of a historical event recognising the role of its patron (as seems logical) or if it really had hidden meanings and messages. Obviously the intended audience would differ depending on where the object was displayed; theories that it would have one message for the Normans and another for Anglo-Saxons only really make any sense at all if the Tapestry was displayed in England, as few Anglo-Saxons would have seen it in Bayeux.

The opportunity to learn more about the Tapestry's enigmatic characters, such as Ælfgyva, Turold, Wadard and Vital, would also be useful. Perhaps vital information might be revealed from a careful study of existing sources. However, given that these are relatively well known, and many scholars have studied them, this seems extremely unlikely. Likewise, it is wishful thinking that a new source will be rediscovered and provide vital clues about who these characters are. Perhaps there is still hope, however, as in recent times scholars have come up with new theories that have some substance.

What is certain is that scholars will use new techniques in theory to attempt to learn more about the Bayeux Tapestry. It is easy to be sceptical about the use of such techniques as they often presuppose a particular mindset, which might be very different from that of the medieval mind. Often such theories are impossible to prove and are not particularly objective. However, they do offer food for thought to the open-minded historian, and it is always useful to try and interpret a source in different ways in the hope of gleaning more information.

In a similar respect, interdisciplinary research can often be revealing. Scholars who have similar training and backgrounds, and therefore knowledge and experiences, are likely to interpret things in similar ways, and hence research can become stagnant. However, broadening the appeal of a subject to a wider audience brings in people with different skills and experiences, and increases the opportunities for identifying new opportunities for research and investigation. The Bayeux Tapestry has a wide public appeal and most will have some thoughts on it, which can be interesting. Experience shows that scholars who are open to suggestions and interpretations of the 'non-expert' or student often benefit in the long run, so it is vital academics are open to such ideas and encourage debate and dialogue. In my experience as an archaeologist there have been many benefits from working closely with metal-detectorists, re-enactors and suchlike, rather than dismiss their views and experiences, as was often the case in the past.

It must be hoped that much will be learnt about the Bayeux Tapestry from further detailed examination. There have been some important developments in this respect in recent years, such as highlighted in this study, of the extent to which the Tapestry reflects the real world of the eleventh century. Of course, many scholars have analysed the Tapestry in great detail, but it is amazing how much can be overlooked. Gale Owen-Crocker's (2007) study of gesture, for example, has shown similarities between certain gesticulations of the Tapestry's characters which have hitherto not been spotted. Whilst it is apparent that interpreting the meaning of these gestures is more problematic, such investigations do offer further opportunities for research.

It must be hoped that one day, further study can be made of the Tapestry's fabric. The difficulty of course is that the Bayeux Tapestry is on permanent display, so opportunities to study it further are limited. This is not helped by the fact that the Tapestry is hung on a backing strip, so the reverse of the embroidery is hidden. There is still much more to learn about the scientific analysis undertaken in 1982/3, and it must be hoped that further information in this respect is soon published. For example, the analysis of the dyes and wool used in the Tapestry might be traced by forensic archaeologists to particular plants and breed of animals, and this could somehow inform more about where and when the Tapestry was produced. Likewise, perhaps radio-carbon 14 dating might be used to date the Tapestry more precisely, though perhaps the textile is so contaminated that this is impossible. There are certain to be more questions a scientist could ask.

Similarly, a closer visual inspection of the fabric might allow a greater understanding of the Bayeux Tapestry. Much of David Hill and John McSween's (forthcoming, 2008) research has made use of the photographs of the reverse of the Tapestry, but few of these have been published. These photographs might allow further advances in Tapestry studies. Indeed, surely much more could be learnt about the design and production of the Tapestry by a closer examination of the fabric. Perhaps, with new scientific techniques, it might be possible to see if the cartoon (followed by the embroiderers) still survives on at least part of the fabric. Perhaps analysis of the individual strands of the threads used might offer clues on how many embroiderers worked on the Tapestry, or even identify different hands, as is regularly possible in the study of manuscripts. It also seems plausible that such work could shed light on whether the individual lengths of the Tapestry were worked in a single workshop, as has been suggested in this book, or in different places.

Finally, whilst one would not like to suggest the current display of the Bayeux Tapestry is substandard, as in many ways it is clearly not, it is obvious that it would benefit from being displayed as a single length. The economics of such a gallery probably make little sense, but it would be wonderful to stand in front of it, and be able to stand back from it, to see the work in its entirety. Also, dare I suggest, it would be fantastic to see the Bayeux Tapestry on display in England, so more people in this country could benefit from learning more about this magnificent example of medieval art, which is also such an important document of the history of the English people.

APPENDIX A

THE TAPESTRY'S INSCRIPTIONS

The Tapestry's Latin inscriptions are for the most part in square upper case, though the letters 'e' and 'h' are commonly shown rounded and as lower case, as are 'd' and 'm', to a lesser extent. In the earlier part of the Tapestry (up to Scene 42) the letters are worked in black, but thereafter alternate in various colours.

Abbreviations are not numerous. However, the final 'm' from case endings has been omitted a number of times – its absence normally indicated by a horizontal line over the preceding letter. Likewise some words and personal names have been abbreviated; examples include *sancti* to '*sci*', *archiepiscopus* to '*archieps*' and *Wilelmus* to '*Wilel*'. '7' is sometimes used for *et* (and) and the Old English letter forms '-' (th) and 'æ' (a) also occur, though infrequently.

Following are the Tapestry's inscriptions (translation in brackets):

EDVVARD REX (King Edward)

VBI hAROLd DVX ANGLORVM ET SVI MILITES EQVITANT AD BOShAm (where Harold, duke of the English, and his knights ride to Bosham)

ECCLESIA (the church)

HIC hAROLD MARE NAVIGAVIT (here Harold sailed the sea)

ET VELIS VENTO PLENIS VENIT IN TERRA VVIdONIS COMITIS (and with the wind full in his sails he came to the country of Count Guy)

HAROLD (Harold)

hIC APPREhENDIT VVIDO HAROLDV[M] (here Guy seizes Harold)

ET DVXIT EVM AD BELREM ET IBI EVM TENVIT (and led him to Beaurain and kept him there)

VBI Harold 7 VVIDO PARABOLANT (where Harold and Guy talk)

VBI NVNTII VVILLELMI DVCIS VENERVNT AD VVIDONE[M] (where the messengers of Duke William came to Guy)

TUROLD (Turold)

NVNTII VVILLELMI (William's messengers)

HIC VENIT NVNTIVS AD WILGELMVM DVCEM (here comes the messengers to Duke William)

HIC WIDO ADDVXIT hAROLDVm AD VVILGELMVM NORMANNORVM DVCEM (here Guy brought Harold to William Duke of the Normans)

HIC DVX VVILGELM CVM hAROLDO VENIT AD PALATIV[M] SVV[M] (here Duke William comes with Harold to his palace)

VBI VNVS CLERICVS ET ÆLFGYVA (where a clerk and Ælfgyva)

hIC VVILLEM DVX ET EXERCITVS EIVS VENERVNT AD MONTE[M] MIChAELIS (here Duke William and his army came to Mont Saint-Michel)

ET hIC TRANSIERVNT FLVMEN COSNONIS (and here they cross the River Couesnon)

hIC hAROLD DVX TRAhEBAT EOS DE ARENA (here Duke Harold dragged them out of the sand)

ET VENERVNT AD DOL ET CONAN FVGA VERTIT (and they came to Dol and Conan turned to flight)

REDNES (Rennes)

hIC MILITES VVILLELMI DVCIS PVGNANT CONTRA DINANTES (here Duke William's soldiers fight against the men of Dinan)

ET CVNAN CLAVES PORREXIT (and Conan offered up the keys)

hIC WILLELM DEDIT hAROLDO ARMA (here William gave arms to Harold)

hIE WILLELM VENIT BAGIAS (here William came to Bayeux)

VBI hAROLD SACRAMENTVM FECIT VVILLELMO DVCI (where Harold made an oath to Duke William)

hIC hAROLD DVX REVERSVS EST AD ANGLICAM TERRAM (here Duke Harold returned to English soil)

ET VENIT AD EDVVARDV REGEM (and came to King Edward)

hIC PORTATVR CORPVS EADWARDI REGIS AD ECCLESIAM S[AN]CI[I] PETRI AP[OSTO]LI (here is the body of King Edward carried to the church of Saint Peter the Apostle)

hIC EADVVARDVS REX IN LECTO ALLOQVIT[VR] FIDELES (here King Edward in bed harangues his faithful friends)

ET hIC DEFVNCTVS EST (and here is he dead)

hIC DEDERVNT hAROLDO CORONA[M] REGIS (here they have given the king's crown to Harold)

hIC RESIDET hAROLD REX ANGLORVM (here sits Harold the king of the English)

STIGANT ARChIEP[ISCOPU]S (Stigand the archbishop)

ISTI MIRANT STELLA[M] (there men marvel at the star)

hIC NAVIS ANGLICA VENIT IN TERRAM WILLELMI DVCIS (here an English ship came to the land of Duke William)

hIC WILLELM DVX IVSSIT NAVES EDIFICARE (here Duke William ordered them to build ships)

hIC TRAhVNT[VR] NAVES AD MARE (here the ships are dragged to the sea)

ISTI PORTANT ARMAS AD NAVES ET hIC TRAhVNT CARRVM CVM VINO ET ARMIS (these men are carrying arms to the ships and here they are dragging a cart laden with wine and arms) hIC VVILLELM DVX IN MAGNO NAVIGIO MARE TRANSIVIT ET VENIT AD PEVENESÆ (here Duke William in a great ship crossed the sea and came to Pevensey)

hIC EXEVNT CABALLI DE NAVIBVS (here are the horses leaving the boats)

ET hIC MILITES FESTINAVERVNT hESTINGA VT CIBVM RAPERENTVR (and here the soldiers have hastened to Hastings to seize food)

HIC EST VVADARD (here is Wadard)

hIC COQVITVR CARO ET hIC MINISTRAVERVNT MINISTRI (here is the meat being cooked and here the servants have served it up)

hIC FECERVNT PRANDIVM ET hIC EPISCOPVS CIBV[M] ET POTV[M] BENEDICT (here they made a banquet and her the bishop blesses the food and drink)

ODO EP[ISCOPV]S (Bishop Odo)

WILLIAM (William)

ROTBERT (Robert)

ISTE IVSSIT VT FODERETVR CASTELLVM AT HESTENGA (this man has commanded that a castle should be thrown up at Hastings)

CEASTRA (castle)

HIC NVNTIATVM EST WILLELMo DE hAROLD (here news is brought to William about Harold)

hIC DOMVS IN CENDITVR (here a house is burned)

hIC MILITES EXIERVNT DE hESTENGA ET VENERVNT AD PRELIVM CONTRA hAROLDVN REGE (here the soldiers went out of Hastings and came to the battle against King Harold)

HIC VVILLELM DVX INTERROGAT VITAL SI VIDISSET EXERCITV[M] HAROLDI (here Duke William asks Vital whether he has seen Harold's army)

ISTE NVNTIAT HAROLDVM REGE[M] DE EXERCITV VVILELMI DVCIS (this man gives news to King Harold about Duke William's army)

HIC WILLELM DVX ALLOQVITVR SVIS MILITIBVS VT PREPARARENT SE VIRILITER ET SAPIENTER AD PRELIVM CONTRA ANGLORVM EXERCITV[M] (here Duke William exhorts his soldiers that they prepare themselves manfully and wisely for the battle against the English army)

hIC CECIDERVNT LEVVINE ET GYR- FRATRES hAROLDI REGIS (here fell Leofwine and Gyrth the brothers of Harold)

hIC CECIDERVNT SIMVL ANGLI ET FRANCI IN PRELIO (here English and French fell together in battle)

HIC ODO EP[ISCOPV]S BACVLV[M] TENENS CONFORTAT PVEROS (here Bishop Odo holding a mace cheers on the young men)

hIC EST DVX VVILEL[MUS] (here is Duke William)

E(VSTA)TIVS (Eustace)

hIC FRANCI PVGNANT ET CECIDERVNT QVI ERANT CVM hAROLDO (here are the French fighting and those who were with Harold have fallen)

hIC hAROLD REX INTERFECTVS EST (here King Harold has been killed)

ET FVGA VERTERVNT ANGLI (and the English have turned in flight)

APPENDIX B

MANUSCRIPTS CITED

Key to dates:

x/xi	late tenth century/early eleventh century
xi	eleventh century
xi^{in}	early eleventh century
xi^{1}	first half of the eleventh century
xi$^{1/4}$	first quarter of the eleventh century
xi$^{2/4}$	second quarter of the eleventh century
xi^{med}	middle of the eleventh century
xi^{2}	second half of the eleventh century
xi$^{3/4}$	third quarter of the eleventh century
xi$^{4/4}$	fourth quarter of the eleventh century
xi^{ex}	end of the eleventh century

Æthelstan Psalter – London, British Library, Cotton Galba A.xviii, x$^{2/4}$ (Winchester, Old Minster).

Arenberg Gospels – New York, Pierpont Morgan Library, M 869, x$^{4/4}$ to xi^{in} (Canterbury, Christ Church).

Arundel 60 – London, British Library, Arundel 60, xi$^{3/4}$ and xi$^{4/4}$ (Winchester, ?New Minster).

Arundel 91 – London, British Library, Arundel 91, xii$^{1/4}$ (Canterbury, St Augustine's).

Arundel 155 – London, British Library, Arundel 155, xi$^{1/4}$ (Canterbury, Christ Church).

Benedictional of Archbishop Robert – Rouen, Bibliothèque municipale, Y. 7 (369), x$^{4/4}$ (Winchester, New Minster).

Bible of Saint-Bénigne – Dijon, Bibliothèque municipale, 2, xii$^{2/4}$ (Saint-Bénigne, Dijon).

Bibliothèque nationale de France, lat. 987 – Paris, Bibliothèque nationale de France, lat. 987, x$^{4/4}$ (Winchester).

Bibliothèque nationale de France, MS fr. 19093 – Bibliothèque nationale de France, MS fr. 19093, xii$^{2/4}$ (Northern France).

Bibliothèque nationale de France, lat. 6401 – Paris, Bibliothèque nationale de France, lat. 6401, x$^{4/4}$ (English hand at Fleury).

Bodleian Library, Auct. E. inf.1 – Oxford, Bodeian Library, Auct. E. inf. 1, xii^{med} and xii$^{4/4}$ (Winchester).

Bodleian Library, Bodley 494 – Oxford, Bodleian Library, Bodley 577, xii$^{3/4}$ (uncertain).

Bodleian Library, Bodley 577 – Oxford, Bodleian Library, Bodley 577, x/xi (Canterbury, Christ Church).

Bodleian Library, Bodley 579 – Oxford, Bodleian Library, Bodley 579, ix^{ex} (?Arras or Cambrai), later additions x1-2+ (Canterbury, Christ Church) and xi^{med+} (Exeter).

Bodleian Library, Bodley 718 – Oxford, Bodleian Library, Bodley 718, xi^{in} (Canterbury and Exeter).

Bodleian Library, Douce 296 – Oxford, Bodeian Library, Douce 296, xi$^{2/4}$ (?Crowland).

Bodleian Library, Rawlinson C.570 – Oxford, Bodleian Library, Rawlinson C. 570, x^2

Bodleian Library, Tanner 3 – Oxford, Bodleian Library, Tanner 3, xi$^{2/4}$ (?Worcester).

Bodleian Library, Tanner 10 – Oxford, Bodleian Library, Tanner 10, x^1 (uncertain).

Boulogne Gospels – Boulogne-sur-Mer, Bibliothèque municipale, 11, x^{ex} (English artist at Saint-Bertin).

British Library, Add. 24199 – London, British Library, Add. 24199, x^{ex} (uncertain).

British Library, Add. 37472 (I)v – London, British Library, Add. 37472 (I), xii$^{2/4}$ (Canterbury? Christ Church).

British Library, Add. 47967 – London, British Library, Add. 47967, x$^{2/4}$ and x^2 (Winchester).

British Library, Royal 1, D.ix – London, British Library, Royal 1 D. ix, xi$^{1/4}$ (Canterbury, Christ Church).

British Library, Royal 5 F.iii – London, British Library, Royal 5 F. iii, ix/x (Mercia?).

British Library, Royal 6 B.vi – London, British Library, Royal 6 B.vi, xii^1 (Rochester).

British Library, Royal 12, C.xxiii – London, British Library, Royal 12 C. xxiii, x^2 (Canterbury, Christ Church).

British Library, Royal 15, A.xvi – London, British Library, Royal 15, A.xvi, xi$^{2/4}$ (Canterbury, St Augustine's).

British Library, Stowe 2 – London, British Library, Stowe 2, xi$^{3/4}$ (Winchester? New Minster).

Bury Gospels – London, British Library, Harley 76, xi^1 (Canterbury, Christ Church).

Bury Psalter – Vatican City, Biblioteca Apostolica Vaticana, Reg. Lat. 12, xi$^{2/4}$ (Canterbury, Christ Church).

Cambridge, Corpus Christi College 23 – Cambridge, Corpus Christi College, 23, x^{ex} (Canterbury? Christ Church).

Cambridge, Corpus Christi College 41 – Cambridge, Corpus Christi College, 41, xi^1 (uncertain).

Cambridge, Corpus Christi College 183 – Cambridge, Corpus Christi College 183, $x^{2/4}$ (unknown).

Cambridge, Pembroke College 301 – Cambridge, Pembroke College, 301, $xi^{1/4}$ and $xi^{2/4}$ (uncertain).

Cambridge, Trinity College, B.11.2 – Cambridge, Trinity College, B. 11. 2, $x^{3/4}$ (Canterbury, St Augustine's).

Cambridge, Trinity College B.15.34 – Cambridge, Trinity College, B. 15. 34, xi^1 (Canterbury, Christ Church).

Cambridge, Trinity College, O.2.51 – Cambridge, Trinity College, O. 2. 51, xi^2 (Canterbury, St Augustine's).

Cambridge, Trinity College, O.3.7 – Cambridge, Trinity College, O. 3. 7, $x^{3/4}$ (Canterbury, St Augustine's).

Cambridge, Trinity College, O.4.7 – Cambridge, Trinity College, O. 4. 7, $xii^{1/4}$ (Rochester Cathedral Priory).

Cambridge, University Library, Ii.3.12 – Cambridge, University Library, Ii. 3. 12, $xii^{2/4}$ (Canterbury, Christ Church).

Codex Aureus of Echternach – Nürnberg, Germanisches Nationalmuseum, 156.142/KG1138, $xi^{2/4}$ (Echternach).

Codex Egberti – Trier, Stadtbibliothek, 24, x^2 (Reichenau).

Cotton Caligula A.xv – London, British Library, Cotton Caligula A. xv, $xi^{3/4}$ (Canterbury, Christ Church).

Cotton Cleopatra C.viii – London, British Library, Cotton Cleopatra C. viii, x^{ex} (Canterbury, Christ Church).

Cotton Julius A.vi – London, British Library, Cotton Julius A. vi, xi^{in} and xi^{med} (Canterbury? Christ Church).

Cotton Nero C.vii – London, British Library, Cotton Nero C. vii, xii^1 (Canterbury, Christ Church).

Cotton Tiberius A.iii – London, British Library, Cotton Tiberius A. iii, xi^{med} (Canterbury, Christ Church).

Cotton Tiberius B.v – London, British Library, Cotton Tiberius B.v, $xi^{2/4}$ (Winchester?).

Cotton Titus D.xxvi – London, British Library, Cotton Titus D. xxvi and xxvii, xi^1 (Winchester, New Minster).

Cotton Vitellius C.iii – London, British Library, Cotton Vitellius C. iii, xi^{in} (Canterbury, Christ Church).

Durham, Cathedral Library B.III.32 – Durham, Cathedral Library, B. III. 32, xi[med] (Canterbury, Christ Church).

Eadwig Gospels – Hanover, Kestner Museum, WM XXIa 36, xi[1/4] (Canterbury, Christ Church).

Eadwine Psalter – Cambridge, Trinity College, R. 17. 1, xii[med] (Canterbury, Christ Church).

Ebbo Gospels – Épernay, Bibliothèque municipale, 1, ix[1] (Hautvillers Abbey, near Reims).

Ebulo Codex – Bern, Burgerbibliothek, Cod. 120. II, xii[ex] (Italian).

Egerton 3314 – London, British Library, Egerton 3314, xi[ex] (Canterbury).

Florence, Biblioteca Mediceo-Laurenziana Plut. XVII.20 – Florence, Biblioteca Mediceo-Laurenziana, Plut. XVII.20, xi[1] (Canterbury, Christ Church).

Getty Museum 9 – Los Angeles, Getty Museum, MS 9, x/xi (?Canterbury).

Grandval-Moutier Bible – London, British Library, Add. 10546, ix[2/4] (Tours).

Harley 603 Psalter – London, British Library, Harley 603, x/xi and xii[2/4] (Canterbury, Christ Church).

Harley 624 – London, British Library, Harley 624, xii[1] (Canterbury, Christ Church).

Harley 2826 – London, British Library, Harley 2826, ix[med] (Reims).

Harley 5431 – London, British Library, Harley 5431, x[4/4] (Canterbury, St Augustine's).

Hereford Gospels – Cambridge, Pembroke College, 302, xi[med] (uncertain).

Hitda Codex – Darmstadt, Hessische Landesbiblithek, 1640, xi[1/4] (Cologne).

Junius 11 – Oxford, Bodleian Library, Junius 11, x[ex] (?Canterbury, Christ Church).

Kederminster Gospels – London, British Library, Loan 11, xi[1/4] (?Canterbury, Christ Church).

Leofric Missal – Oxford, Bodleian Library, Bodley 579, ix[ex] (Arras? or Cambrai), later additions x1-2+ (Canterbury, Christ Church) and xi[med+] (Exeter).

London, Lambeth Palace, 200 – London, Lambeth Palace, 200, x[ex] (Canterbury, St. Augustine's).

Lothar Gospels – Paris, Bibliothèque nationale de France, lat. 266, ix[med] (Tours).

Monte Cassino, Archivo della Badia, BB. 437, 439 – Monte Cassino, Archivo della Badia, BB. 437, 439, xi[med] (uncertain).

New Minster Charter – London, British Library, Cotton Vespasian A. viii, x[3/4] (Winchester, New Minster).

New Minster Liber Vitae – London, British Library, Stowe 944, xi[2/4] (Winchester, New Minster).

Old English Hexateuch – London, British Library, Cotton Claudius B. iv, xi[2/4] (Canterbury? St Augustine's).

Oxford, Corpus Christi College 157 – Oxford, Corpus Christi College, 157, xii[2/4] (Worcester Cathedral Priory).

Oxford, University College 165 – Oxford, University College, 165, xii$^{1/4}$ (Durham Cathedral Priory).

Pericopes Book of Reichenau – Munich, Bayerische Staatsbibliothek, Clm. 4454, xi^{in} (Reichenau).

Pierpont Morgan Library M.708 – New York, Pierpont Morgan Library, M.708, xi$^{2/4}$ (?household of Judith).

Pierpont Morgan Library M.709 – New York, Pierpont Morgan Library, M.709, xi$^{2/4}$ (household of Judith of Flanders?).

Rouen, Bibliothèque Municipale, A.27 (368) – Rouen, Bibliothèque Municipale, A.27 (368), xi$^{2/4}$ (Wessex).

Sacramentary of Robert of Jumièges – Rouen, Bibliothèque Municipale, Y. 6 (274), xi$^{1/4}$ (uncertain).

St Augustine's Gospels – Cambridge, Corpus Christi College, 286, vi^{2} (Italian).

Tiberius Psalter – London, British Library, Cotton Tiberius C. vi, xi^{med} (uncertain).

Trinity Gospels – Cambridge, Trinity College, B. 10. 4, xi$^{1/4}$ (?Canterbury, Christ Church).

Utrecht Psalter – Utrecht, Universiteits Bibliotheek, 32, ix^{1} (Hautvillers Abbey, near Reims).

Vivian Bible – Paris, Bibliothèque nationale de France, lat. 1, ix$^{2/4}$ (Tours).

Warsaw, Biblioteka Narodowa, I. 3311 – Warsaw, Biblioteka Narodowa, I. 3311, x/xi and xi$^{2/4}$ (uncertain) – Evangeliary

Winchcombe Psalter – Cambridge, University Library, Ff. I. 23, xi$^{2/4}$ (?Winchcombe Abbey).

Winchester Bible – Winchester, Cathedral Library, 17, xii^{2} (Winchester, Cathedral Priory of St Swithun).

Winchester Psalter – London, British Library, Cotton Nero C. iv, xii^{med} (Winchester? Cathedral Priory of St Swithun).

BIBLIOGRAPHY

PRIMARY SOURCES

Anglo-Saxon Chronicle (see Garmonsway)
Chronicle of Battle Abbey
Eadmer, *Historia Novorum* (see Bosanquet)
Encomium Emmae Reginae (see Campbell)
Gilbert Crispin, *Vita domini Herluini abbatis Beccensis*
Goscelin, *Vita Sancti Augustini*
Guy, Bishop of Ameins, *Carmen de Hastingae Prolio* (see Moron and Muntz)
Henry of Huntington, *Historia Anglorum*
John (Florence) of Worcester, *Chronicon ex Chronicis* (see Stevenson)
Orderic Vitalis, *Historia Ecclesiastica* (see Chibnall)
The Battle of Maldon (see Bradley)
Vita Eadwardi (see Barlow 1992)
William of Jumièges, *Gesta Normannorum Ducum* (see van Houts)
William of Malmesbury, *Gesta Regum Anglorum* (see Mynors, Thomson and Winterbottom)
William of Poitiers, *Gesta Guillelmi ducis Normannorum et Regis Anglorum* (see Davis and Chibnall)

SECONDARY SOURCES

Alexander, J.J.G., *Norman Illumination at Mont St Michel 966-1100* (Oxford, 1970)
Alexander, J.J.G., *Medieval Illuminators and their Methods of Work* (New Haven and London, 1992)
Amyot, T., 'Observations on an Historical Fact Supposed to be Established by the Bayeux Tapestry', *Archaeologia* 19 (1819), 88-95
Amyot, T., 'A Defence of the Early Antiquity of the Bayeux Tapestry', *Archaeologia*, 19 (1819), 192-208
Anquetil, E., 'La Telle du conquest d'Angleterre', *Annuarire des cinq departments de la Normandie* 73 (1907), 449-77
Armitage, E.S., *Early Norman Castles of the British Isles* (London, 1912)
Backhouse, J., Turner, D.H. and Webster, L. (eds), *The Golden Age of Anglo-Saxon Art 966-1066* (London, 1984)
Bachrach, B.S., 'Some Observations on the Military Administration of the Norman Conquest', *Anglo-Norman Studies* 8 (1986), 1-26

Bachrach, B.S., 'Some Observations on the Bayeux Tapestry', *Cithara* 27 (1988), 5-28

Barker, P.A. and Barton, K.J., 'Excavations at Hastings Castle, 1968' *Archaeological Journal* 134 (1977), 80-100

Barlow, F., *The Feudal Kingdom of England 1042-1216* (London, 1988)

Barlow, F. (trans.), *The Life of King Edward who rests at Westminster* (Oxford, 1992)

Barlow, F., *Edward the Confessor* (London, 1997)

Barlow, F. (ed. and trans.), *The* Carmen de Hastingae Proelio *of Guy Bishop of Amiens* (Oxford, 1999)

Barlow, F., *The Godwins* (Harlow, 2002)

Barraclough, E.M.C., 'The Flags in the Bayeux Tapestry', *Armi Antichi* (1969), 117-28

Bates, D.R., *Odo Bishop of Bayeux 1049-1097* (unpublished PhD thesis, Exeter University, 1970)

Bates, D.R., 'The Character and Career of Odo, Bishop of Bayeux (1049/50-1097)', *Speculum* 50 (1975), 1-20

Bates, D. (ed.), Regesta Regum Anglo-Normannorum, *the* Acta *of William I* (Oxford, 1998)

Bates, D., *William the Conqueror* (Stroud, 2001)

Baxter, R., *Bestiaries and Their Users in the Middle Ages* (Stroud, 1998)

Baylé, M., 'Architecture et enluminure dans le monde normand', in P. Bouet and M. Dosdat (eds), *Manuscripts et enluminures dans le monde normand (Xe-XVe siècles)* (1999), 51-68

Baylé, M., Bouet, P. et al, *Le Mont-Saint-Michel* (Paris, 1998)

Baylé, M. and Bouet, P. (eds), *L'Architecture Normande au Moyen Age*, 2 vols (Caen, 2001)

Bédat, I. and Girault-Kurtzeman, B., 'The Technical Study of the Bayeux Embroidery', in P. Bouet, B. Levy and F. Neveux (eds), *The Bayeux Tapestry: Embroidering the Facts of History* (2004), 83-109

Beech, G., *Was the Bayeux Tapestry Made in France? The Case for Saint-Florent of Saumur* (New York, 2005)

Bennett, M., 'Poetry as History? The Roman de Rou of Wace as a Source for the Norman Conquest', *Anglo-Norman Studies* 5 (1983), 21-39

Bernstein, D., 'The Blinding of Harold and the Meaning of the Bayeux Tapestry', *Anglo-Norman Studies* 5 (1983), 40-64

Bernstein, D.J., *The Mystery of the Bayeux Tapestry* (London, 1986)

Bertrand, S., 'The History of the Tapestry', in F. Stenton (ed.), *The Bayeux Tapestry* (1957), 76-85

Bertrand, S., 'Etude sur la Tapisserie de Bayeux', *Annales de Normandie* 10 (1960), 197-206

Bertrand, S., *La Tapisserie de Bayeux et la manière de vivre au onzième siècle* (La Pierre-qui-Vire, 1966)

Biddle, M., 'Excavations at Winchester, 1965, Fourth Interim Report', *The Antiquaries Journal* 45 (1966), 308-332

Bond, G., 'Arresting Subjects: Aelfgyva and the Colouring of History', in G. Bond (ed.), *The Loving Subject: Desire, Eloquence and power in Romanesque France* (Philadelphia, 1995), 18-41

Bosanquet, G. (ed. and trans.), *Eadmer's History of Recent Events in England – Historia Novorum in Anglia* (London, 1964)

Bouet, P. and Dosdat, M. (eds), *Manuscripts et enluminures dans le monde normand (Xe-XVe siècles)* (Caen, 1999)

Bouet, P., Levy, B. and Neveux, F. (eds), *The Bayeux Tapestry: Embroidering the Facts of History* (Caen, 2004)

Bradbury, J., *The Medieval Archer* (Woodbridge, 1997)

Bradley, S. A.J. (ed. and trans.), *Anglo-Saxon Poetry* (London, 1995)

Bridgeford, A., *1066 The Hidden History of the Bayeux Tapestry* (London, 2004)

Brilliant, R., 'The Bayeux Tapestry: A Stripped Narrative for their Eyes and Ears', *Word and Image* 7/2 (1991), 98-126

Brooks, N.P., 'Arms, Status and Warfare in Late-Saxon England', in D. Hill (ed.), *Ethelred the Unready*, British Archaeological Reports (British Series) 59 (1978), 81-103

Brooks, N.P. and Walker, H.E., 'The Authority and Interpretation of the Bayeux Tapestry', *Anglo-Norman Studies* 1 (1978), 1-34

Brown, R.A., *English Castles* (London, 1976)

Brown, R.A., *The Norman Conquest* (London, 1984)

Brown, R.A., 'Castles of the Conquest', in R.A. Brown, *Castles, Conquest and Charters – Collected Papers* (Woodbridge, 1989a), 65-74

Brown, R.A., 'The Architecture of the Bayeux Tapestry', in R.A. Brown, *Castles, Conquest and Charters – Collected Papers* (Woodbridge, 1989b), 214-26

Brown, S.A., *The Bayeux Tapestry: Its Purpose and Dating* (unpublished PhD thesis, Cornell University, 1977)

Brown, S.A., *The Bayeux Tapestry, History and Bibliography* (Woodbridge, 1988)

Brown, S.A., 'The Bayeux Tapestry: Why Eustace, Odo and William?', *Anglo-Norman Studies* 12 (1990) 7-28

Brown, S.A., 'The Bayeux Tapestry: A Critical Analysis of Publications 1988-1999', in P. Bouet, B. Levy and F. Neveux (eds), *The Bayeux Tapestry: Embroidering the Facts of History* (Caen, 2004), 27-47

Brown, S.A. and Herren, M.W., 'The Adelae Comitissae of Baudri of Bourgeuil and the Bayeux Tapestry', *Anglo-Norman Studies* 16 (1994), 55-74

Bruce-Mitford, R.L.S., *The Sutton Hoo Ship Burial*, 3 vols (London, 1975-1983)

Budny, M., 'The Byrhtnoth Tapestry or Embroidery', in D. Scragg (ed.), *The Battle of Maldon* (Oxford, 1991), 263-78

Burgess, G. (trans.), *The Song of Roland* (London, 1990)

Butler, D., *1066 – The Story of a Year* (New York, 1966)

Cahn, W., *Romanesque Manuscripts, the Twelfth Century*, 2 vols (London, 1996)

Campbell, A. (ed. and trans.), *Encomium Emmae Reginae* (London, 1949)

Carver, M.O.H., 'Contemporary Artefacts Illustrated in Late Saxon Manuscripts', *Archaeologia* 108 (1986), 117-145

Chefneux, H., 'Les Fables dans la Tapisserie de Bayeux', *Romania* 60, 237-8 (1934), 1-35, 153-94

Chibnall, M. (ed.), *The Ecclesiastical History of Orderic Vitalis*, 6 vols (Oxford, 1968-1978)

Cholakian, R.C., *The Bayeux Tapestry and the Ethos of War* (Demar, 1998)

Christensen, A.E., *Guide for the Viking Ships* (Oslo, 1970)

Christensen, A.E., *Centenary of a Norwegian Viking Find: The Gokstad Excavations* (Sandefjord, 1979)

Christie, A.G., *English Medieval Embroidery* (London, 1938)

Church, S.D., 'Aspects of the English Succession, 1066-1199: the Death of the King', *Anglo-Norman Studies* 29 (2007), 17-34

Clapham, A.W., *English Romanesque Architecture Before the Conquest* (Oxford, 1964)

Clutton-Brock, J., 'The Animal Resources' in D.M. Wilson (ed.), *The Archaeology of Anglo-Saxon England* (London, 1976), 373-92

Collins, M., *Medieval Herbals, the Illustrated Traditions* (London, 2000)

Combes, P. and Lyne, M., 'Hastings, Haestingaceaster and Haestingaport', *Sussex Archaeological Collections* 133 (1995), 213-24

Corney, B., *Researches and Conjectures on the Bayeux Tapestry* (Greenwich, 1836)

Corney, B., *Researches and Conjectures on the Bayeux Tapestry* (Greenwich, 1838)

Coulson, C., *Castles in Medieval Society: Fortresses in England, France and Ireland in the Central Middle Ages* (Oxford, 2003)

Coward, D., *A History of French Literature from Chanson de geste to Cinema* (Oxford, 2002)

Cowdrey, H.E.J., 'Towards an Interpretation of the Bayeux Tapestry', *Anglo-Norman Studies* 10 (1988), 49-66

Croome, A., 'The Viking Ship Museum at Roskilde: Expansion Uncovers Nine More Early Ships; and Advances Experimental Ocean-sailing Plans', *The International Journal of Nautical Archaeology* 28.4 (1999), 382-93

Crossley-Holland, K. (trans.), *The Anglo-Saxon World, An Anthology (Including the Complete Beowulf)* (Oxford, 1999)

Crowfoot, E., Pritchard, F. and Staniland, K., *Textiles and Clothing c.1150 – c.1450* (London, 1992)

Crumlin-Pedersen, O. and Olsen, O. (eds), *The Skuldelev Ships* 1 (Roskilde, 2002)

Darcel, A., 'La Légende de Saint-Martin', *Annales archéologiques* 24 (1864), 73-84

Darlington, R.R. and McGurk, P. (eds), *The Chronicle of John of Worcester*, vol. II (Oxford, 1995)

Davis, R.H.C., 'The Carmen de Hastingae Proelio', *English Historical Review* 367 (1978), 241-61

Davis, R.H.C., Engels, L.J. et al, 'The Carmen de Hastingae Proelio: a discussion', *Anglo-Norman Studies* 2 (1980), 1-20

Davis, R.H.C. and Chibnall, M. (ed. and trans.), *The Gesta Guillelmi of William of Poitiers* (Oxford, 1998)

Dawson, C., 'The Bayeux Tapestry in the Hands of 'Restorers' and how it has fared', *Antiquary* 43 (1907), 253-8, 288-92

de La Rue, G., 'Sur la tapisserie de Bayeux', *Rapport général sur travaux*, Académie des sciences, arts et belles-lettres de Caen 2 (1811), 184

Delauney, H.F., *Origine de la Tapisserie de Bayeux prouvée par elle-même* (Caen, 1824)

Dickinson, T. and Härke, H., 'Early Anglo-Saxon Shields', *Archaeologia* 110 (1992), 1-94

Dodwell, C.R., *The Canterbury School of Illumination 1066-1200* (Cambridge, 1954)

Dodwell, C.R., 'The Bayeux Tapestry and the French Secular Epic', *Burlington Magazine* 108, No. 764 (November 1966), 549-60

Dodwell, C.R., *Anglo-Saxon Art, a new perspective*, (Oxford, 1985)

Dodwell, C.R., *The Pictorial Arts of the West 800-1200* (New Haven and London, 1993)

Dodwell, C.R. and Clemoes, P., *The Old English Illustrated Hexateuch*, Early English Manuscripts in Facsimile XVIII (Copenhagen, 1974)

Douce, F., 'Translation of a Memoir on the Celebrated Tapestry of Bayeux, by the Abbé de la Rue', *Archaeologia* 17 (1814), 85-109

Douglas, D.C., *William the Conqueror* (London, 1997)

Douglas, D.C. and Greenaway, G.W. (eds), *English Historical Documents II, 1042-1189* (London, 1981)

Dubosq, R., *La Tapisserie de Bayeux. Dix années tragiques de sa longue histoire. 1939-1948* (Caen, 1951)

du Méril, É., 'De la tapisserie de Bayeux et de son importance historique', *Etudes sur quelques points d'archélogie et d'histoire littéraire* (1862), 384-426

Edge, D. and Paddock, J.M., *Arms and Armour of the Medieval Knight* (London, 1988)

Farrell, A.W., 'The Use of Iconographic Material in Medieval Ship Archaeology, in S. McGrail (ed.), *Medieval Ships and Harbours* (Greenwich, 1979), 227-46

Fenwick, V. (ed.), *The Graveney Boat* (Greenwich, 1978)

Fernie, E., *The Architecture of the Anglo-Saxons* (London, 1983)

Fernie, E., 'Saxons, Normans and their Buildings', *Anglo-Norman Studies* 21 (1999), 1-10

Fowke, F.R., *The Bayeux Tapestry, A History and Description* (London, 1913)

Foys, M.K., *The Bayeux Tapestry Digital Edition* (CD 2003)

Freeman, E., 'The Authority of the Bayeux Tapestry', in R. Gameson (ed.), *The Study of the Bayeux Tapestry* (Woodbridge, 1997), 7-15

Freeman, E., 'The Ælfgyva of the Bayeux Tapestry', in R. Gameson (ed.), *The Study of the Bayeux Tapestry* (Woodbridge, 1997), 15-18

French, G., 'On the Banners of the Bayeux Tapestry and the earliest heraldic charges', *Journal of the British Archaeological Association* 13 (1857), 113-30

Fuglesang, S.H., *Some Aspects of the Ringerike Style* (Odense, 1980)

Gameson, R., 'The Romanesque Crypt Capitals of Canterbury Cathedral', *Archaeologia Cantiana* 110 (1992), 17-48

Gameson, R., 'The Romanesque Artist of the 603 Harley Psalter', *English Manuscript Studies 1100-1700* 4 (1993), 24-61

Gameson, R., *The Role of Art in the late Anglo-Saxon Church* (Oxford, 1995)

Gameson, R. (ed.), *The Study of the Bayeux Tapestry* (Woodbridge, 1997)

Garmonsway, G.N. (trans.), *The Anglo-Saxon Chronicle* (London, 1965)

Gem, R., 'The Romanesque Rebuilding of Westminster Abbey', *Anglo-Norman Studies* 3 (1981), 33-60

Gem, R., 'Towards an Iconography of Anglo-Saxon Art', *Journal of the Warburg and Courtauld Institutes* 46 (1983), 1-18

Gem, R., 'English Romanesque Architecture', in G. Zarnecki et al (ed.), *English Romanesque Art 1066-1200* (London, 1984), 27-40

Gem, R. (ed.), *St Augustine's Abbey Canterbury* (London, 1997)

Gibbs-Smith, C.H., 'Notes on the Plates', in F. Stenton (ed.), *The Bayeux Tapestry* (1957), 162-176

Gibbs-Smith, C.H., *The Bayeux Tapestry* (London, 1973)

Gosling, J., 'The Identity of the Lady Aelfgyva in the Bayeux Tapestry and some Speculations regarding the Hagiographer Goscelin', *Analecta-Bollandiana* 108.1 (1990), 71-9

Grape, W., *The Bayeux Tapestry* (Munich, 1994)

Gravett, C., *Norman Knight 950-1204 AD* (London, 1993)

Gravett, C., *Hastings 1066, the Fall of Saxon England* (London, 1996)

Gravestock, P., 'Did Imaginary Animals Exist?', in D. Hassig (ed.), *The Mark of the Beast* (London, 1999), 119-35

Grew, F. and de Neergaard, M., *Shoes and Pattens* (London, 1988)

Gullick, M., 'Professional Scribes in Eleventh- and Twelfth-Century England', *English Manuscript Studies 1100–1700* 7 (1998), 1-24

Gurney, H., 'Observations on the Bayeux Tapestry', *Archaeologia* 18 (1817), 359-70

Harrison, M., *Anglo-Saxon Thegn AD 449-1066* (Oxford, 1993)

Hart, C., 'The Canterbury contribution to the Bayeux Tapestry', in G. de Boe and F. Verhaeghe (eds), *Art and Symbolism in Medieval Europe* - papers of the 'Medieval Europe Brugge 1997' Conference (Zellik, 1997), 7-15

Hart, C., 'The Bayeux Tapestry and Schools of Illumination at Canterbury', *Anglo-Norman Studies* 22 (2000), 117-68

Hart, C., 'The Cicero-Aratea and the Bayeux Tapestry', in G.R. Owen-Crocker (ed.), *Harold II Godwinesson and the Bayeux Tapestry* (Woodbridge, 2005), 161-78

Haskins, C.H., 'King Harold's Books', *English Historical Review* 37 (1922), 398-400

Hawkes, S.C. (ed.), *Weapons and Warfare in Anglo-Saxon England* (Oxford, 1989)

Haywood, J., *Dark Age Naval Power, A Reassessment of Frankish and Anglo-Saxon Seafaring Activity* (Hockwold-cum-Wilton, 1999)

Heitz, C., 'The Iconography of Architectural Form', in L.A.S. Butler and R.K. Morris (eds), *The Anglo-Saxon Church*, CBA Research Report 60 (1986), 90-100

Henige, C., 'Putting the Bayeux Tapestry in its Place', in G.R. Owen-Crocker (ed.), *Harold II Godwinesson and the Bayeux Tapestry* (Woodbridge, 2005), 125-38

Henson, D., *A Guide to Late Anglo-Saxon England from Ælfred to Eadgar II* (Hockwold-cum-Wilton, 1998)

Herren, M.W. (trans.), 'Baudri de Bourgueil, Adelae Comitissae', in S.A. Brown (ed.), *The Bayeux Tapestry, History and Bibliography* (Woodbridge, 1988), 167-77

Herrmann, L., 'Apologues et anecdotes dans la tapisserie de Bayeux', *Romania* 65 (1939), 376-82

Heslop, T.A., 'A Dated Late Anglo-Saxon Illuminated Psalter', *Antiquaries Journal* 72 (1992), 171-4

Hicks, C., 'The Borders of the Bayeux Tapestry', in C. Hicks (ed.), *England in the Eleventh Century* (Stamford, 1992), 251-65

Hicks, C., *Animals in Early Medieval Art* (Edinburgh, 1993)

Hicks, C., *The Bayeux Tapestry, the Life Story of a Masterpiece* (London, 2006)

Higham, R. and Barker, P., *Hen Domen Montgomery, A Timber Castle on the English-Welsh Border*, 2 vols (Leeds, 1982)

Higham, R. and Barker, P., *Timber Castles* (London, 1992)

Hill, D., 'The Bayeux Tapestry: The Case of the Phantom Fleet', *Bulletin of the John Rylands University Library* 80, 1 (1998), 23-31

Hill, D. and McSween, J., *The Bayeux Tapestry: The Establishment of a Text* (forthcoming Oxford, 2008)

Hinz, H., 'Zu zwei Darstellungen auf dem Teppich von Bayeux', *Château Gaillard* 6 (1973), 107-120

Holden, A.J. (ed. and trans.), *Le Roman de Rou de Wace*, 3 vols (Paris, 1970-3)

Hollander, L.M. (trans.), *Heimskringla, History of the Kings of Norway* (Austin, 1964)

Holmes, U.T., 'The Houses of the Bayeux Tapestry', *Speculum* 34 (1959), 179-183

Hooper, N., 'Anglo-Saxon Warfare on the Eve of the Conquest: A Brief Survey', *Anglo-Norman Studies* 1 (1979), 84-93

Kahn, D., *Canterbury Cathedral and its Romanesque Sculpture* (London, 1991)

Kahn, D., 'Anglo-Saxon and Early Romanesque Frieze Sculpture in England', in D. Kahn (ed.), *The Romanesque Frieze and its Spectator* (London, 1992), 61-74

Kauffmann, C.M., *Romanesque Manuscripts, 1066-1190* (London, 1975)

Keefer, S., 'Body Language: a Graphic Commentary by the Horses of the Bayeux Tapestry', in G.R. Owen-Crocker (ed.), *Harold II Godwinesson and the Bayeux Tapestry* (Woodbridge, 2005), 93-108

Kerr, M. and Kerr, N., *Anglo-Saxon Architecture* (Aylesbury, 1983)

Kidd, P., 'A Re-examination of the Date of an Eleventh Century Psalter from Winchester', in B. Cassidy and R.M. Wright (eds), *Studies in the Illustration of the Psalter* (Stamford, 2001), 42-54

Kiff, J., 'Images of War, Illustrations of Warfare in Early Eleventh-Century England', *Anglo-Norman Studies*, 7 (1984), 177-94

Klingender, F., *Animals in Art and Thought to the end of the Middle Ages* (London, 1971)

Koslin, D., 'Turning Time in the Bayeux Tapestry', *Textile and Text* 13 (1990), 28-45

Krautheimer, R., 'Introduction to an Iconography of Mediaeval Architecture', *Journal of the Warburg and Courtauld Institute* 5 (1942), 1-33

Kuhn, A., 'Der Teppich von Bayeux in seinen Gebärden: Versuch einer Deutung', *Studi medievali* 33/1 (1992), 1-71

L., S. (otherwise anonymous), 'Letter concerning Queen Matilda's Tapestry', *Gentleman's Magazine*, 1, vol. 73 (1803), 1225-6

Laffetay, J.D., 'Notice historique et descriptive sur la Tapisserie dite de la Reine Mathilde, Exposée à la Bibliothèque Bayeux' (Bayeux, 1885)

Lancelot, A., 'Explication d'un monument de Guillaume la Conquérant', *Mémoires de litérature tirés des registres de l'Académie royale des Inscriptions et Belles-Lettres depuis l'année MDCCXVII jusques et compris l'année MDCCXXV* 6 (1729), 739-55

Lancelot, A., 'Suite de l'explication d'un monument de Guillaume la Conquérant', *Mémoires de litérature tirés des registres de l'Académie royale des Inscriptions et Belles-Lettres depuis l'année MDCCXXVI jusques et compris l'année MDCCXXX* 7 (1732), 602-68

Lampl, P., 'Schemes of Architectural Representation in Early Medieval Art', *Marsyas: Studies in the History of Art* 9 (1961), 6-13

Lang, J., *Corpus of Anglo-Saxon Stone Sculpture*, Volume III, York and Eastern Yorkshire (Oxford, 1991)

Lang, J., *Corpus of Anglo-Saxon Stone Sculpture*, Volume VI, Northern Yorkshire (Oxford, 2001)

Lemagnen, S., 'The Bayeux Tapestry under German Occupation, new light on the mission led by Herbert Jankuhn during the Second World War', in P. Bouet, B. Levy and F. Neveux (eds), *The Bayeux Tapestry: Embroidering the Facts of History* (Caen, 2004), 83-109

Lepelley, R., 'A Contribution to the Study of the Inscriptions in the Bayeux Tapestry: Bagias and Wilgelm', in R. Gameson (ed.), *The Study of the Bayeux Tapestry* (1997), 39-45

Lethaby, W.R., 'The Perjury at Bayeux', *Archaeological Journal* 74 (1917), 136-8

Levé, A., *La Tapisserie de la Reine Mathilde, dite la Tapisserie de Bayeux* (Paris, 1919)

Lewis, M.J., *The Archaeological Authority of the Bayeux Tapestry* (Oxford, 2005)

Lewis, M.J., 'The Bayeux Tapestry and Eleventh-century Material Culture', in G.R. Owen-Crocker (ed.), *Harold II Godwinesson and the Bayeux Tapestry* (Woodbridge, 2005), 179-94

Lewis, M.J., 'Identity and Status in the Bayeux Tapestry: the Iconographic and Artefactual Evidence', *Anglo-Norman Studies* 29 (2007), 100-120

Lewis, M.J., 'A New Date for Class A, Type IIA Stirrup-strap Mounts, and some Observations on their Distribution', *Medieval Archaeology* 51 (2007), 178-84

Lewis, M.J., 'The Mystery of Charles Stothard, FSA, and the Bayeux Tapestry Fragment', *Antiquaries Journal* 87 (2007), 400-6

Lewis, S., *The Rhetoric of Power in the Bayeux Tapestry* (Cambridge, 1999)

Lockett, L., 'An Integrated Re-examination of the Dating of Oxford, Bodleian Library, Junius 11', *Anglo-Saxon England* 31 (2002), 141-74

Lyttleton, G., *The History of the Life of King Henry the Second, and the Age in which he lived* (in five books, to which is prefixed *A History of the Revolutions of England from the Death of Edward the Confessor to the Birth of Henry the Second*) 1 (London, 1769)

Maclagen, E., *The Bayeux Tapestry* (London, 1945)

Mann, J., 'Arms and Armour', in F. Stenton (ed.), *The Bayeux Tapestry* (London 1957), 56-69

Mann, J., *Arms and Armour in England from the Early Middle Ages to the Civil War* (London, 1969)

Mann, V.B., 'Architectural Conventions on the Bayeux Tapestry', *Marsyas: Studies in the History of Art* 17 (1975), 59-66

Marignan, A., *La Tapisserie de Bayeux. Etude archéologique et critique* (Paris, 1902a)

McGurk, P. and Rosenthal, J., 'The Anglo-Saxon Gospel Books of Judith, Countess of Flanders: their Text, Make-up and Function', *Anglo-Saxon England* 24 (1995) 251-308

McNulty, J.B., 'The Lady Aelfgyva in the Bayeux Tapestry', *Speculum* IV (1980), 659-68

McNulty, J.B., *The Narrative Art of the Bayeux Tapestry Master* (New York, 1989)

Messent, J., *The Bayeux Tapestry Embroiderers' Story* (Thirsk, 1999)

Montfaucon, B. de., 'Monument d'Harold', *Les Monumens de la Monarchie françoise* 1 (Paris, 1729), 1-31, plates 1-9

Montfaucon, B. de., 'La Conquête de l'Angleterre par Guillaume le Bâtard, Duc de Normandie, dit le Conquérant', *Les Monumens de la Monarchie françoise* 2 (Paris, 1730), 1-31, plates 1-9

Montier, E. and Chirol, P., *L' Abbaye de Jumièges* (Rouen, 1923)

Morton, C. and Muntz, H. (eds), *The Carmen de Hastingae Prolio of Guy Bishop of Amiens* (Oxford, 1972)

Musset, L., *Normandie romane, La Haute-Normandie*, 2nd ed. (Saint-Léger-Vauban, 1985)

Musset, L., 'Récentes contributions scandinaves à l'exégèse de la Tapisserie de Bayeux', *Bulletin de la Société des Antiquaries de Normandie* 51 (1948-51), 275-9

Musset, L., *La Tapisserie de Bayeux: oeuvre d'art et document historique* (La Pierre-qui-Vire, 1989)

Musset, L., *La Tapisserie de Bayeux* (Paris, 2002)

Mynors, R.A.B, Thomson, R.M. and Winterbottom, M. (ed. and trans.), *William of Malmesbury, Gesta Regum Anglorum, The History of the English Kings*, Vol. 1 (Oxford, 1998)

Myrhøj, H.M. and Gøthche, M., *The Roskilde Ships* (Roskilde, 1997, www.natmus.dk)

Nevinson, J.L., 'The Costumes', in F. Stenton (ed.), *The Bayeux Tapestry* (London, 1957) 70-5

Nicolaysen, N., *The Viking Ship Discovered at Gokstad in Norway* (Christiania, 1992)

Noel, W., *The Harley Psalter* (Cambridge, 1995)

Ohlgren, T.H. (ed.), *Anglo-Saxon Textual Illustration* (Kalamazoo, 1992)

Okasha, E., *Hand-List of Anglo-Saxon Non-Runic Inscriptions* (Cambridge, 1971)

Olsen, O. and Crumlin-Pedersen, O., 'The Skuldelev Ships', *Acta Archaeologia* 38 (1967), 74-153

Olsen, O. and Crumlin-Pedersen, O., *Five Viking Ships from Roskilde Fjord* (Copenhagen, 1978)

Owen-Crocker, G.R., *Dress in Anglo-Saxon England* (Manchester, 1986)

Owen-Crocker, G.R., 'Hawks and Horse Trappings: the Insignia of Rank', in D. Scragg (ed.), *The Battle of Maldon* (Oxford, 1991), 220-37

Owen-Crocker, G.R., 'The Bayeux Tapestry: Culottes, Tunics and Garters, and the Making of the Bayeux Tapestry', *Costume* 28 (1994), 1-9

Owen-Crocker, G.R., 'Telling a Tale: Narrative Techniques in the Bayeux Tapestry and the Old English Epic *Beowulf*', in G.R. Owen-Crocker and T. Graham (eds), *Medieval Art, Recent Perspectives, A Memorial Tribute to C.R. Dodwell* (Manchester, 1998), 40-59

Owen-Crocker, G.R., 'The Bayeux 'Tapestry': Invisible Seams and Visible Boundaries', *Anglo-Saxon England* 31 (2002) 257-74

Owen-Crocker, G.R., 'Brothers, Rivals and the Geometry of the Bayeux Tapestry', in G.R. Owen-Crocker (ed.), *Harold II Godwinesson and the Bayeux Tapestry* (Woodbridge, 2005), 109-24

Owen-Crocker, G.R., 'The Interpretation of Gesture in the Bayeux Tapestry', *Anglo-Norman Studies* 29 (2007), 145-178

Paris, G., 'La Tapisserie de Bayeux', *Romania* 31 (1902), 404-19

Payne, A., *Medieval Beasts* (London, 1990)

Pétard, M., 'L'Homme de 1066, le combattant d'Hastings', *Galette des Uniformes* 32 (1976), 19-29

Pierce, I., 'Arms, Armour and Warfare in the Eleventh Century', *Anglo-Norman Studies* 10 (1988), 237-58

Pollock, J., *Bosham: Ecclesia as shown in the Bayeux Tapestry* (Selsey, 1995)

Prentout, C., 'An Attempt to Identify Some Unknown Characters in the Bayeux Tapestry', in R. Gameson (ed.), *The Study of the Bayeux Tapestry* (1997), 21-30

Prentout, H., 'La Conquête de l'Angleterre par les Normands - Le Sources - La Tapisserie de Bayeux', *Revue bimensuelle des cours et conferences* 23.2 (1921-22), 16-29, 193-200, 302-12

Pritchard, F., 'Footwear', in A. Vince (ed.), *Aspects of Saxo Norman London: II Finds and Environmental Evidence* (London, 1991) 213-40

Ralegh Radford, C.A., Jope, E.M. and Tonkin, J.W., 'The Great Hall of the Bishop's Palace at Hereford', *Medieval Archaeology* 17 (1973), 78-86

Reid, P., 'Knowing People Though their Feet: The Shoes of Lundenburg', *London Archaeologist* 9/10 (2001) 267-74

Renn, D.F., *Norman Castles in Britain* (London, 1973)

Renn, D.F., 'Burhgeat and Gonfanon: Two Sidelights from the Bayeux Tapestry', *Anglo-Norman Studies* 16 (1993), 177-198

Roberts, O.T.P., 'The Bayeux Tapestry Sails', *Mariner's Mirror* 67 (1981), 287-8

Rock, D., *Textile Fabrics; A Descriptive Catalogue* (London, 1870)

Ronay, G., 'Edward Aetheling, Anglo-Saxon England's Last Hope', *History Today* 34 (1984), 43-51

Ronay, G., *The Lost King of England, the East European Adventures of Edward the Exile* (Woodbridge, 1989)

Rowley, T., *Norman England* (London, 1997)

Rowley, T., *The Normans* (Stroud, 1999)

Rud, M., *La Tapisserie de Bayeux et la bataille du Pommier Gris* (Bayeux, 1976)

Searle, E. (ed. and trans.), *The Chronicle of Battle Abbey* (Oxford, 1980)

Scheller, R.W., *Exemplum: Model-Book Drawings and the Practice of Artistic Transmission in the Middle Ages (ca. 900-ca. 1450)* (Amsterdam, 1995)

Schwartz, M., 'The Buildings in the Bayeux Tapestry: Their Context and Relationship to Contemporary Manuscript Art' (unpublished MA thesis, University of York, 1994)

Sharpe, J. (trans.) and Stevenson, J. (ed.), *William of Malmesbury, A History of the Norman Kings (1066-1125) with the Historia Novella of History of His Own Times (1126-1142)* (Felinfach, 2000)

Short, I., 'The Language of the Bayeux Tapestry Inscription', *Anglo-Norman Studies* 23 (2001), 267-280

Sjøvold, T., *The Oseberg Find and Other Viking Ship Finds* (Oslo, 1957)

Sleewyk, A. W., 'The Ship of Harold Godwinson', *Mariner's Mirror* 67 (1981), 87-91

Smith, J.T., Faulkner, P.A. and Emery, A., *Studies in Medieval Domestic Architecture* (Leeds, 1975)

Sørensen, A.C., *Ladby, A Danish Ship-Grave from the Viking Age* (Roskilde, 2001)

Spear, D., 'Recent Publications on the Bayeux Tapestry', *Annales de Normandie* 57 (2007), 172-8

Staniland, K., *Embroiderers* (London, 1991)

Stenton, F. M., *The Bayeux Tapestry* (London, 1957)

Stenton, F., *Anglo-Saxon England* (Oxford, 1985)

Stevenson, J. (trans.), *Florence of Worcester, A History of the Kings of England* (Felinfach, 1996)

Stothard, C., 'Some Observations on the Bayeux Tapestry', *Archaeologia* 19 (1819), 184-91

Strickland, M., *Anglo-Norman Warfare, Studies in Late Anglo-Saxon and Anglo-Norman Military Organisation and Warfare* (Woodbridge, 1992)

Stukeley, W., *Palaographia Britannica, or Discourses on Antiquities in Britain* 2 (London, 1743), 1, 86, 90-1

Tanner, L.E. and Clapham, A.W., 'Recent Discoveries in the Nave of the Westminster Abbey', *Archaeologia* 83 (1933), 227-36

Tatton-Brown, T., 'Westminster Abbey: Archaeological Recording at the West End of the Church', *The Antiquaries Journal* 75 (1995), 171-88

Taylor, A., 'Belrem', *Anglo-Norman Studies* 14 (1992), 1-23

Taylor, H.M. and Taylor, J., *Anglo-Saxon Architecture*, 3 vols (Cambridge, 1965-78)

Temple, E., *Anglo-Saxon Manuscripts 900-1066* (London, 1976)

Temple, O. and Temple, R. (trans.), *Aesop the Complete Fables* (London, 1998)

Terkla, D., 'Cut on the Norman Bias: fabulous borders and visual glosses on the Bayeux Tapestry', *Word and Image* 11/3 (1995), 264-90

Thomson, R.M. and Winterbottom, M., *William of Malmesbury, Gesta Regum Anglorum, The History of the English Kings*, Vol II (Oxford, 1999)

Thorvildsen, K., *The Viking Ship of Ladby* (Copenhagen, 1975)

Thurlby, M., *The Hereford School of Romanesque Sculpture* (Logaston, 2000)

Tsurushima, H., 'Three Knights Depicted on the Bayeux Tapestry', *Rekishi Tohoku Historical Journal* 64 (1985), 38-74

Tweddle, D. Biddle, M. and Kjølbye-Biddle, B., *Corpus of Anglo-Saxon Stone Sculpture*, Volume IV, South-East England (Oxford, 1995)

Underwood, R., *Anglo-Saxon Weapons and Warfare* (Stroud, 1999)

Valentine, L.N., *Ornament in Medieval Manuscripts* (London, 1965) van der Horst, K., Noel, W. and Wüstefeld, C.M. (eds), *The Utrecht Psalter in Medieval Art* (Utrecht, 1996)

van Houts, E.M.C., 'The Gesta Normannorum Ducum: a History Without an End', *Anglo-Norman Studies* 3 (1980), 106-18

van Houts, E.M.C., 'The Ship List of William the Conqueror', *Anglo-Norman Studies* 10 (1988), 159-84

van Houts, E.M.C. (ed. and trans.), *The* Gesta Normannorum Ducum *of William of Jumieges, Orderic Vitalis, and Robert of Torigni*, 2 vols (Oxford, 1992-1995)

van Moé, E. A., *Illuminated Initials in Medieval Manuscripts* (London, 1950)

Walker, I.W., *Harold: The Last Anglo-Saxon King* (Stroud, 1997)

Walton, P., *Textiles, Cordage and Raw Fibre from 16-22 Coppergate, The Archaeology of York* 17/5 (York, 1989)

Webster, L. and Backhouse, J. (ed.), *The Making of England: Anglo-Saxon Art and Culture AD 600-900* (London, 1991)

Wekmeister, O.K., 'The Political Ideology of the Bayeux Tapestry', *Studi Medievali* 17. 2 (1976), 535-95

White, T.H. (trans.), *The Book of Beasts* (New York, 1984)

Whitelock, D. (ed.), *English Historical Documents I, 500-1042* (London, 1955)

Williams, A., 'Some Notes and Considerations on Problems Connected with the English Royal Succession, 860-1066', *Anglo-Norman Studies* 1 (1979), 144-67

Williams, A., 'Land and Power in the Eleventh Century: the Estates of Harold Godwinson', *Anglo-Norman Studies* 3 (1981), 171-87

Williams, A. and Martin, G.H., *Domesday Book* (London, 1992)

Wilson, D.M., *Anglo-Saxon Ornamental Metalwork 700-1100 in the British Museum* (London, 1964)

Wilson, D.M. (ed.), *The Archaeology of Anglo-Saxon England* (London, 1976)

Wilson, D.M., *Anglo-Saxon Art, from the Seventh Century to the Norman Conquest* (London, 1984)

Wilson, D. M., *The Bayeux Tapestry* (London, 1985)

Wingfield Digby, G., 'Technique and Production', in F. Stenton (ed.), *The Bayeux Tapestry* (1957), 37-55

Wood, M., *Norman Domestic Architecture* (Leeds, 1974)

Woodman, F., 'The Waterworks Drawings in the *Eadwine Psalter*', in M. Gibson, T.A. Heslop. and R.W. Pfaff (eds), *The Eadwine Psalter* (London, 1992), 168-77

Wormald, F., 'Decorated Initials in English Manuscripts from AD 900 to 1100', *Archaeologia* 91 (1945), 107-35

Wormald, F., *English Drawings of the Tenth and Eleventh Centuries* (London, 1952)

Wormald, F., *The Miniatures in the Gospels of St Augustine*, Corpus Christi College MS 286 (Cambridge, 1954)

Wormald, F., 'Style and Design', in F. Stenton (ed.), *The Bayeux Tapestry* (1957), 25-36

Wormald, F., 'The Inscriptions', in F. Stenton (ed.), *The Bayeux Tapestry* (1957), 177-80

Yapp, W.B., 'Animals in Medieval Art: the Bayeux Tapestry as an Example', *Journal of Medieval History* 13/1 (1987), 15-74

Zarnecki, G., 'Romanesque Sculpture in Normandy and England in the Eleventh Century', *Anglo-Norman Studies* 1 (1979), 168-190

Zarnecki, G. et al (ed.), *English Romanesque Art, 1066-1200* (London, 1984)

INDEX

Places